The Mountain Biker's Guide
to COLORADO

Linda Gong
Gregg Bromka

FALCON®

Helena, Montana

ᴀFALCONGUIDE®

Falcon® Publishing is continually expanding its list of recreational guidebooks. All books include detailed dexcriptions, accurate maps, and all the information necessary for enjoyable trips. You can order copies of this book and get information and prices for other Falcon® guidebooks by writing Falcon, P.O. Box 1718, Helena, MT 59624 or calling toll-free 1-800-582-2665. Also, please ask for a free copy of our current catalog. Visit our website at www.falconguide.com.

Printed in the United States of America
Published by Falcon® Publishing, Inc.
Helena, Montana

10 9 8 7 6 5 4

Library of Congress Cataloging-in-Publication Data

Gong, Linda
    The mountain bikier's guide to Colorado/ Linda Gong, Gregg
Bromka; foreword, introduction, and afterword by
Dennis Coello; [maps by Tim Krasnansky].—1st ed.
    p.   cm.
    —(Dennis Coello's America by mountain bike series)
    ISBN   1-56044-258-1
    1. All terrain cycling—Colorado—Guidebooks.
2. Colorado—Guidebooks.   I. Bromka. Gregg.   II. Title.
III. Series: America by mountain bike series.
GV1045.5C6G66   1994
796.6'4'09788—dc20

                                                94-27135
                                                CIP

Photos by the author unless otherwise credited
Maps by Tim Krasnansky
Cover photo by Brian Bailey

Falcon® Publishing, Inc.
P.O. Box 1718
Helena, Montana 59624

CAUTION

Outdoor recreational activities are by their very nature potentially hazardous. All participants in such activities must assume the responsibility for their own actions and safety. The information contained in this guidebook cannot replace sound judgment and good decision–making skills, which help reduce risk exposure, nor does the scope of this book allow for disclosure of all the potential hazards and risks involved in such activities.

Learn as much as possible about the outdoor recreational activities you participate in, prepare for the unexpected, and be safe and cautious. The reward will be a safer and more enjoyable experience.

 Text pages printed on recycled paper

Table of Contents

SUMMIT COUNTY

FAIRPLAY

VAIL

ASPEN/GLENWOOD SPRINGS

CRESTED BUTTE

GUNNISON

GRAND JUNCTION

MONTROSE

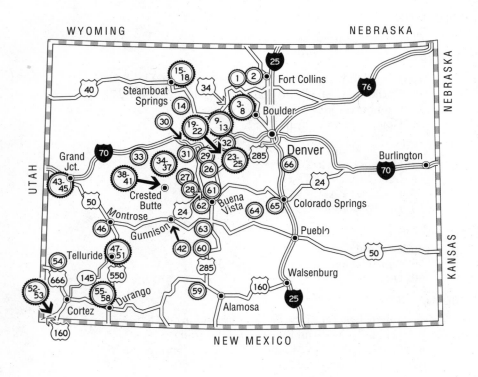

List of Maps

AMERICA BY MOUNTAIN BIKE *MAP LEGEND*

Ride trailhead   **Steep grade**

Primary bike trail	Direction of travel	(arrows point downhill)	Optional bike trail and trailhead	Other trail	Hiking trail

Interstate highways (with exit no.)	U.S. routes	State routes	Beartown Rd. Other roads	Unpaved, gravel or dirt roads (may be 4WD only)

U.S. Forest Service roads	Denver ◉ Boulder Cities	Crested Butte ◉ Gothic Towns or settlements	Dam Lake	River, stream or canal

0 ½ 1 MILES Approximate scale in miles	**N** True North	MAROON BELLS-SNOWMASS WILDERNESS Parklands	State Border

✈ Airport

♥ Archeological or historical site

▲ Campground (CG)

≡ Cattle guard

♦ Cemetery or gravesite

♠ Church

Cliff, escarpment or outcropping

Drinking water

Fire tower or lookout

Food

Gate

House or cabin

Lodging

Military test site

Mine or quarry

Mountain or butte

Mountain pass

△ Mountain summit
3312 (elevation in feet)

Museum

Observatory

Park office or ranger station

Picnic area

Power line, pipeline, fence or ski lift

Restrooms

Ranch or horse farm

Ski Area

Swimming Area

Transmission towers

Tunnel or bridge

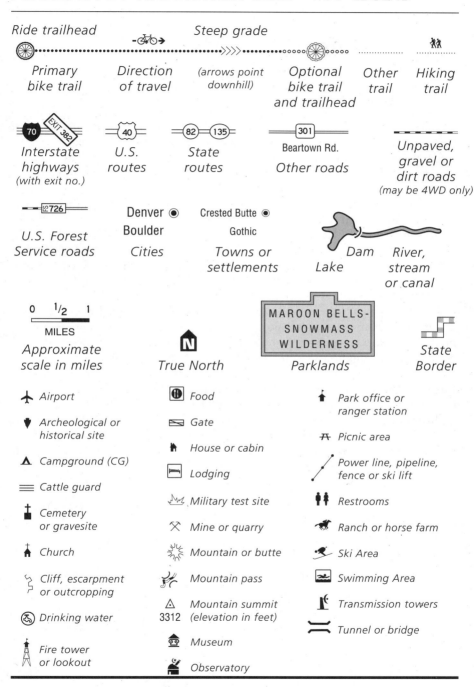

Acknowledgments

If you've ever written a book of this kind, you can appreciate the amount of work that went into it. If you've never had the pleasure of such a task, consider yourself lucky, for this particular book required lots of time and energy—more than either one of us anticipated—to complete. Countless hours were spent on research by phone and mail, in the saddle on the trails, and in front of the word processor. A great number of folks contributed their time, energy, and enthusiasm.

A deep heartfelt thank you to Eric and Steve of Kristi Mountain Sports in Alamosa, Steve and the Saguache U.S. Forest Service office, Eric of Telluride Sports in Telluride, Keith of the Sports Stalker in Winter Park, Julie of the Winter Park Resort, Greg of Cycle Logic in Boulder, Mary of Sore Saddle Cyclery in Steamboat Springs, Mike of the Breckenridge Fat Tire Society, Sandy of the Banana Belt Fat Tracks in Salida, Dick of The Trailhead in Buena Vista, and Steve of Life Cycles in Carbondale.

Thanks also go out to wonderful friends who accompanied me on the trail and gave their unwavering support, putting up with my notetaking, with being my photo subjects, and my requests for "one more photo." They were really good sports throughout the process. Thank you Nancy, Joëlle, Ken, Yolanda, Zack, OPB, Stacie and Tim, Marty, John, Terry, Janine, Mary, James and Carolyn, Mark, Susie and Raimond, Greg and Lisa, Lara, and Peter. Thank you, Gregg, for your help and encouragement. Thank you, Tim, for the great effort and time spent on creating the maps. Thank you, Menasha Ridge Press and Falcon Press, for the opportunity, and an even bigger thanks to Dennis, for having faith in me and giving me unending words of support. And, finally, thank you, Bruce, for your understanding, endurance, and patience; I couldn't have done it without you.

Linda Gong

This compilation of Colorado's best mountain bike rides would not have been possible without the assistance of the following people, who generously provided information on their favorite local rides. To each I express my sincere gratitude. If only we could rendezvous, just for a day, for a "group ride." Oh, the bike stories that would fill the air!

Thanks to Stewart Culp of Cycle Transport, Fort Collins; William L. Stoehr of Trails Illustrated, Evergreen; Jim Robb of ZIA Design Group and Mary Morrison of Latitude 40°, Inc., Boulder; Michael LaPorte of Winter Park FATS and Kip Hubbard of AdventureWorks, Winter Park; Laura Rossetter of Sage Creek Press, Silverthorne; Stuart Black of Denver Bicycle Touring Club, Denver; John Wilkinson of the Aspen Velo Cycling Club, Aspen; Steve Cook of Paradise Bikes and Skis, Crested Butte; Gregg Morin of the Tuneup Shop, Gunnison; Rick Corbin and Timms Fowler of COPMOBA, Grand Junction; Peggy Utesch of *Kokopelli's Trail* guidebook, Glenwood Springs; Bill Harris of *Bicycling the Uncompahgre Plateau,* Montrose; Joe Ryan and Mike Turrin of San Juan Huts, Telluride; Don Hoffheins of the Arapaho National Forest, Kremmling; Carol Boody of Mountain Bike Tour Guides, Cañon City; and countless others with whom I have conversed and from whom I have gained valuable information.

Additional thanks to Linda Gong for eagerly accepting coauthorship of the Colorado guide, and to series editor Dennis Coello for the opportunity to write both the Colorado and Utah guidebooks. And to Tricia for support, love, and understanding.

Gregg Bromka

Foreword

Welcome to *America by Mountain Bike,* a 20-book series designed to provide all-terrain bikers with the information they need to find and ride the very best trails everywhere in the mainland United States. Whether you're new to the sport and don't know where to pedal, or an experienced mountain biker who wants to learn the classic trails in another region, this series is for you. Drop a few bucks for the book, spend an hour with the detailed maps and route descriptions, and you're prepared for the finest in off-road cycling.

My role as editor of this series was simple: First, find a mountain biker who knows the area and loves to ride. Second, ask that person to spend a year researching the most popular and very best rides around. And third, have that rider describe each trail in terms of difficulty, scenery, condition, elevation change, and all other categories of information that are important to trail riders. "Pretend you've just completed a ride and met up with fellow mountain bikers at the trailhead," I told each author. "Imagine their questions, be clear in your answers."

As I said, the *editorial* process—that of sending out riders and reading the submitted chapters—is a snap. But the work involved in finding, riding, and writing about each trail is enormous. In some instances our authors' tasks are made easier by the information contributed by local bike shops or cycling clubs, or even by the writers of local "where-to" guides. Credit for these contributions is provided, when appropriate, in each chapter, and our sincere thanks goes to all who have helped.

But the overwhelming majority of trails are discovered and pedaled by our authors themselves, then compared with dozens of other routes to determine if they qualify as "classic"—that area's best in scenery and cycling fun. If you've ever had the experience of pioneering a route from outdated topographic maps, or entering a bike shop to request information from local riders who would much prefer to keep their favorite trails secret, or know how it is to double- and triple-check data to be positive your trail info is correct, then you have an idea of how each of our authors has labored to bring about these books. You and I, and all the mountain bikers of America, are the richer for their efforts.

You'll get more out of this book if you take a moment to read the Introduction explaining how to read the trail listings. The "Topographic Maps" section will help you understand how useful topos will be on a ride, and will also tell you where to get them. And though this is a "where-to," not a "how-to" guide, those of you who have not traveled the backcountry might find "Hitting the Trail" of particular value.

In addition to the material above, newcomers to mountain biking might want to spend a minute with the Glossary, page 361, so that terms like *hardpack, single- track,* and *water bars* won't throw you when you come across them in the text.

Finally, the tips in the Afterword on mountain biking etiquette and the land-use controversy might help us all enjoy the trails a little more.

All the best.

Dennis Coello
St. Louis

Preface

Who says you need to be an expert rider in order to enjoy mountain biking? Browse through these chapters and you'll realize that this is one book of trails that will appeal to cyclists of all abilities and skills, from backcountry explorers to hard-core-cyclists-in-training. Expert "gonzo" riders can test their mettle with the *Rabbit Ears Pass to Fish Creek Falls* or *Snake River–Sts. John Loop* routes, while novice cyclists who want to simply enjoy the outdoors on two wheels can pedal *Vasquez Creek,* parts of the *Kenosha and Georgia Passes* trails, or even the paved bikeways connecting Breckenridge to Vail. In fact, almost all trails can be enjoyed by all riders, so long as riders include "dismount-and-walk" in their repertoire of technical skills, they have reasonable stamina, and they can sustain the right frame of mind.

And who says you need an expensive mountain bike with all the technical gadgets before you can partake of the sport? We say to heck with that idea. Spending hoardes of money on equipment is unnecessary when a basic all-terrain bike that is correctly fitted to the cyclist will do just fine. After all, the mountain biking craze that has swept the country began, arguably, in Crested Butte, Colorado, with "clunker" bikes, long before feather-weight alloy frames, high-tech shock-absorbing forks, computerized cyclometers, sophisticated clipless pedals and shoes, or cool bar ends were ever invented. Novices, however, be forewarned that once you start riding and experiencing the trails, you just might get bitten by the bug and be compelled to choose between putting food on the table or buying that nifty bike accessory or titanium frame. Yes, these adult toys can be expensive.

One thing you *should* buy, however, if you're planning on a Colorado bike adventure, whether you're a novice or an expert, is this book. Why? Because it includes more than 60 rides in the state and offers leads to other little-known routes and resource guides. Let's face it, there are hundreds of rides in Colorado, with new ones being created and old unknown ones that could fill several more volumes. But what we have provided here are the "classics"—some of the *very* best rides in Colorado.

Anyone familiar with Colorado will agree that it's a state with a split personality. The terrain of the eastern half, east of the capital, Denver, is so flat that you'd swear you could see all the way into Kansas and Nebraska. On the other hand, the western half is home to the Continental Divide and the Rocky Mountain range, with 54 peaks towering over 14,000 feet. By geological standards, these are "young" mountains. And it is in this half of the state that we found the most dramatic, diverse, and interesting biking trails, along the Continental Divide Trail and the Colorado Trail, on plateaus in the west, over the desert terrain of the southwest, and through snowfields around mountain passes. This region is the prime focus of our book.

That is not to say the eastern half is unrideable. On the contrary, the Pawnee National Grasslands and the Comanche National Grasslands in the northeastern and southeastern quadrants of the state, respectively, offer uniquely flat terrain suitable for mountain biking. Though lacking in dramatic scenery, the eastern half is rich in history tied directly to the land. Long before trading posts were established on this side of the state, numerous Indian tribes inhabited the region. The Santa Fe Trail blazed through La Junta on its way to New Mexico. Today, when the high country is still thawing from the winter snow, bikers can hit the roads here in early spring, if not late winter.

Check our editor's "Hitting the Trail" section of the Introduction for some important tips. Here, we'll review several important aspects of trail riding that are unique to Colorado. For starters, let's talk briefly about Colorado's famed summer weather tendencies. Snow showers and blizzards have been known to occur in the higher elevations throughout the year—yes, even in midsummer. If you're traveling from the lower elevations, where the weather is sunny and warm, you can't always tell what's happening in the high country. It's a good idea to bring a variety of clothing for layering and protection, including hats and gloves, so that upon arrival at the trailhead, you can decide what's needed and leave the rest in the car. Be prepared for quick, unpredictable changes in weather.

Another Colorado weather phenomenon: afternoon thundershowers and lightning storms are typical in the summer. It's surprising—and frightening—how many people are uninformed or incorrectly informed about the potentially life-threatening hazards during these storms. Since the storms don't last for very long, you can wait them out, but you need to be prepared and know what precautions to take. Because this book provides only general information, you should refer to more authoritative books or consult experts on the subject of wilderness survival.

Avoid getting caught in a lightning storm. Generally and conservatively speaking, a five-second time lapse between a flash of lightning and the following thunderclap means the storm is about one mile away from you. By timing several flashes, you can determine quickly if a storm is approaching. For example, if you see lightning in the distance and count 20 seconds to its thunderclap, you can guesstimate that the storm is about 4 miles away. If the next thunderclap clocks in at less than 20 seconds, that means the storm is approaching and you should take precautions.

Should you get caught on exposed terrain during a lightning storm, get rid of that two-wheeled metal contraption between your legs, for heaven's sake. Look for dry shelter—if you can, flag down a motorist and ask if you may wait out the storm with him or her in the vehicle. Inside a hardtop car may be the only safe place available on the exposed higher elevations. Otherwise, look for a low spot or depression in the ground and crouch down in it as compactly as possible without lying down. Protect yourself from electrical ground currents by crouching on nonconducting material such as foam pads, extra clothing, and nonmetallic-framed bags and panniers. Move away from trickling water and metal objects, including cameras, camping gear, and bikes. They may not attract a direct strike but they can conduct ground currents. Stay away from lakes and ridges. Caves and rocky overhangs may be safe, but *only* if they are *much* deeper than their opening; otherwise, stay out. If you're below timberline, find shelter in a thick forest of trees as far down a slope as possible, but stay away from single trees, particularly trees that have already been struck. The chances of lightning strucking twice in the same place is good if the struck item is still the tallest thing around.

Hypothermia is another life-threatening hazard in the high country. The condition is characterized by subnormal body temperature leading to mental and physical collapse. Prolonged exposure to cold and exhaustion, aggravated by wetness and wind, is a prelude to hypothermia. If your body heat continues to drop despite exercising, you are draining your energy reserves, and this will speed exhaustion. Prevention is the key, and that means staying dry and warm. Replace wet clothing next to your skin with dry garments. Once again, this is basic information, and if you'd like to know more, consult any U.S. Forest Service ranger or authoritative wilderness survival guide.

Altitude sickness is another hazard, though not usually life-threatening unless it is ignored, in which case it can develop into something more serious. Mountain sickness, as it is often called, is caused by lack of oxygen due to higher elevation. Symptoms include nausea, dizziness, headache, and loss of appetite. It is possible to prevent by acclimating to Colorado's high altitudes, forgoing strenuous activity for three days to a week at elevation. If you experience the symptoms of mountain sickness on the trail, stop and rest more often, go slower, drink plenty of water, and eat high-energy foods. If these practices don't help, descend to a lower elevation where there is more oxygen.

Overall, Colorado is a mountain biker's heaven on earth. The sport is widely accepted here, and even heavily promoted in some regions. It's unfortunate that areas throughout the country, including Colorado, have been closed to mountain biking. Oftentimes, it's a result of opposition from other trail users, such as hikers and equestrians, who have run into a handful of disrepectful, inconsiderate, frequently downright rude bikers, who have given all of us a bad reputation. In fact, as bikers, we have met riders who were even rude to us. So, to preserve the state of peace and our privilege to ride these gorgeous regions, we can't overemphasize the importance of trail etiquette. Yield right-of-way to hikers and horseback riders. When other trail users yield to you, at least say "thank you" when you cruise by. After all, other trail users have right-of-way, not bikers.

The most important item you need to bring with you on the trail is a good head on your shoulders. That means *know the limits of your ability*, especially if you strive to improve your skills. Remember, dismounting and walking is a great option and, depending on your experience, might be the best way out of a tough spot. With all that said, go out and enjoy one of the most beautiful mountain biking states in the country.

Linda Gong
Gregg Bromka

P.S. *The Mountain Biker's Guide to Colorado* takes an interesting approach to presenting the state's best rides. Not only have we waded through volumes of material, surveyed hundreds of maps, pedaled countless miles, and finally selected from an endless list of potential classics what seems only a handful, we have provided an opportunity for locals to boast about their favorite routes as well.

Throughout the guide you will be introduced to numerous individuals, by means of biographical sketches, who generously have contributed route information for this guidebook. These people, whether guidebook authors themselves, bike shop owners or personnel, Forest Service employees, bike club members, or simply folks who get around on knobby tires, were deemed authorities, if not gurus, in their area. How better to learn about Colorado's best off-road rides than to hear them described by those who have written about them previously, have pioneered the routes, or have simply ridden them time and again? Thus, *The Mountain Biker's Guide to Colorado* is a compilation of our favorite off-road experiences augmented with the "locals' choice." Hats off, or rather, "helmets off" to those folks who have eagerly submitted descriptions for their favorite local mountain bike rides.

Introduction

TRAIL DESCRIPTION OUTLINE

Information on each trail in this book begins with a general description that includes length, configuration, scenery, highlights, trail conditions, and difficulty. Additional description is contained in eleven individual categories. The following will help you to understand all of the information provided.

Trail name: Trail names are as designated on United States Geological Survey (USGS) or Forest Service or other maps, and/or by local custom.

Length: The overall length of a trail is described in miles, unless stated otherwise.

Configuration: This is a description of the shape of each trail—whether the trail is a loop, out-and-back (that is, along the same route), figure eight, trapezoid, isosceles triangle, or if it connects with another trail described in the book.

Difficulty: This provides at a glance a description of the degree of physical exertion required to complete the ride, and the technical skill required to pedal it. Authors were asked to keep in mind the fact that all riders are not equal, and thus to gauge the trail in terms of how the middle-of-the-road rider—someone between the newcomer and Ned Overend—could handle the route. Comments about the trail's length, condition, and elevation change will also assist you in determining the difficulty of any trail relative to your own abilities.

Condition: Trails are described in terms of being paved, unpaved, sandy, hard-packed, washboarded, two- or four-wheel-drive, single-track or double-track. All terms that might be unfamiliar to the first-time mountain biker are defined in the Glossary.

Scenery: Here you will find a general description of the natural surroundings during the seasons most riders pedal the trail, and a suggestion of what is to be found at special times (like great fall foliage or cactus in bloom).

Highlights: Towns, major water crossings, historical sites, etc., are listed.

General location: This category describes where the trail is located in reference to a nearby town or other landmark.

Elevation change: Unless stated otherwise, the figure provided is the total gain and loss of elevation along the trail. In regions where the elevation variation is not extreme, the route is simply described as flat, rolling, or possessing short steep climbs or descents.

Season: This is the best time of year to pedal the route, taking into account trail condition (for example, when it will not be muddy), riding comfort (when the weather is too hot, cold, or wet), and local hunting seasons.

Note: Because the exact opening and closing dates of deer, elk, moose, and antelope seasons often change from year to year, riders should check with the local Fish and Game Department or call a sporting goods store (or any place that sells hunting licenses) in a nearby town before heading out. Wear bright clothes in fall, and don't wear suede jackets while in the saddle. Hunter's-orange tape on the helmet is also a good idea.

Services: This category is of primary importance in guides for paved-road tourers, but is far less crucial to most mountian bike trail descriptions because there are usually no services whatsoever to be found. Authors have noted when water is available on desert or long mountain routes, and have listed the availability of food, lodging, campgrounds, and bike shops. If all these services are present, you will find only the words "All services available in . . ."

Hazards: Special hazards like steep cliffs, great amounts of deadfall, or barbed-wire fences very close to the trail are noted here.

Rescue index: Determining how far one is from help on any particular trail can be difficult due to the backcountry nature of most mountain bike rides. Authors therefore state the proximity of homes or Forest Service outposts, nearby roads where one might hitch a ride, or the likelihood of other bikers being encountered on the trail. Phone numbers of local sheriff departments or hospitals have not been provided because phones are almost never available. If you are able to reach a phone, the local operator will connect you with emergency services.

Land status: This category provides information regarding whether the trail crosses land operated by the Forest Service, Bureau of Land Management, a city, state, or national park, whether it crosses private land whose owner (at the time the author did the research) has allowed mountain bikers right of passage, and so on.

Note: Authors have been extremely careful to offer only those routes that are open to bikers and are legal to ride. However, because land ownership changes over time, and because the land-use controversy created by mountain bikes still has not completely subsided, it is the duty of each cyclist to look for and to heed signs warning against trail use. Don't expect this book to get you off the hook when you're facing some small-town judge for pedaling past a "Biking Prohibited" sign erected the day before. Look for these signs, read them, and heed the advice. And remember there's always another trail.

Maps: The maps in this book have been produced with great care, and, in conjunction with the trail-following suggestions, will help you stay on course. But as every experienced mountain biker knows, things can get tricky in the backcountry. It is therefore strongly suggested that you avail yourself of the detailed information found in the 7.5 minute series USGS (United States Geological Survey) topographic maps. In some cases, authors have found that specific Forest Service or other maps may be more useful than the USGS quads, and tell how to obtain them.

Finding the trail: Detailed information on how to reach the trailhead and where to park your car is provided here.

Sources of additional information: Here you will find the address and/or phone number of a bike shop, governmental agency, or other source from which trail information can be obtained.

Notes on the trail: This is where you are guided carefully through any portions of the trail that are particularly difficult to follow. The author also may add information about the route that does not fit easily in the other categories. This category will not be present for those rides where the route is easy to follow.

ABBREVIATIONS

The following road-designation abbreviations are used in the *America by Mountain Bike* series:

CR	County Road
FR	Farm Route
FS	Forest Service road
I-	Interstate
IR	Indian Route
US	United States highway

State highways are designated with the appropriate two-letter state abbreviation, followed by the road number. *Example:* CO 6 = Colorado State Highway 6.

Postal Service two-letter state codes:

AL	Alabama	KY	Kentucky
AK	Alaska	LA	Louisiana
AZ	Arizona	ME	Maine
AR	Arkansas	MD	Maryland
CA	California	MA	Massachusetts
CO	Colorado	MI	Michigan
CT	Connecticut	MN	Minnesota
DE	Delaware	MS	Mississippi
DC	District of Columbia	MO	Missouri
FL	Florida	MT	Montana
GA	Georgia	NE	Nebraska
HI	Hawaii	NV	Nevada
ID	Idaho	NH	New Hampshire
IL	Illinois	NJ	New Jersey
IN	Indiana	NM	New Mexico
IA	Iowa	NY	New York
KS	Kansas	NC	North Carolina

ND	North Dakota	TX	Texas
OH	Ohio	UT	Utah
OK	Oklahoma	VT	Vermont
OR	Oregon	VA	Virginia
PA	Pennsylvania	WA	Washington
RI	Rhode Island	WV	West Virginia
SC	South Carolina	WI	Wisconsin
SD	South Dakota	WY	Wyoming
TN	Tennessee		

TOPOGRAPHIC MAPS

The maps in this book, when used in conjunction with the route directions present in each chapter, will in most instances be sufficient to get you to the trail and keep you on it. However, you will find superior detail and valuable information in the 7.5 minute series United States Geological Survey (USGS) topographic maps. Recognizing how indispensable these are to bikers and hikers alike, many bike shops and sporting goods stores now carry topos of the local area.

But if you're brand new to mountain biking you might be wondering "What's a topographic map?" In short, these differ from standard "flat" maps in that they indicate not only linear distance, but elevation as well. One glance at a "topo" will show you the difference, for "contour lines" are spread across the map like dozens of intricate spider webs. Each contour line represents a particular elevation, and at the base of each topo a particular "contour interval" designation is given. Yes, it sounds confusing if you're new to the lingo, but it truly is a simple and wonderfully helpful system. Keep reading.

Let's assume that the 7.5 minute series topo before us says "Contour Interval 40 feet," that the short trail we'll be pedaling is two inches in length on the map, and that it crosses five contour lines from its beginning to end. What do we know? Well, because the linear scale of this series is 2,000 feet to the inch (roughly 2 ¾ inches representing 1 mile), we know our trail is approximately ⅘ of a mile long (2 inches x 2,000 feet). But we also know we'll be climbing or descending 200 vertical feet (5 contour lines x 40 feet each) over that distance. And the elevation designations written on occasional contour lines will tell us if we're heading up or down.

The authors of this series warn their readers of upcoming terrain, but only a detailed topo gives you the information you need to pinpoint your position exactly on a map, steer yourself toward optional trails and roads nearby, plus let you know at a glance if you'll be pedaling hard to take them. It's a lot of information for a very low cost. In fact, the only drawback with topos is their size—several feet square. I've tried rolling them into tubes, folding them carefully, even cutting them into blocks and photocopying the pieces. Any of these systems is a pain, but no matter how you pack the maps you'll be happy they're along. And you'll be even happier if you pack a compass as well.

In addition to local bike shops and sporting goods stores, you'll find topos at major universities and some public libraries where you might try photocopying the ones you need to avoid the cost of buying them. But if you want your own and can't find them locally, write to:

USGS Map Sales
Box 25286
Denver, CO 80225

Ask for an index while you're at it, plus a price list and a copy of the booklet *Topographic Maps*. In minutes you'll be reading them like a pro.

A second excellent series of maps available to mountain bikers is that put out by the United States Forest Service. If your trail runs through an area designated as a national forest, look in the phone book (white pages) under the United States Government listings, find the Department of Agriculture heading, and then run your finger down that section until you find the Forest Service. Give them a call and they'll provide the address of the regional Forest Service office, from which you can obtain the appropriate map.

TRAIL ETIQUETTE

Pick up almost any mountain bike magazine these days and you'll find articles and letters to the editor about trail conflict. For example, you'll find hikers' tales of being blindsided by speeding mountain bikers, complaints from mountain bikers about being blamed for trail damage that was really caused by horse or cattle traffic, and cries from bikers about those "kamikaze" riders who through their antics threaten to close even more trails to all of us.

The authors of this series have been very careful to guide you to only those trails that are open to mountain biking (or at least were open at the time of their research), and without exception have warned of the damage done to our sport through injudicious riding. My personal views on this matter appear in the Afterword, but all of us can benefit from glancing over the following International Mountain Bicycling Association (IMBA) Rules of the Trail before saddling up.

1. *Ride on open trails only.* Respect trail and road closures (ask if not sure), avoid possible trespass on private land, obtain permits and authorization as may be required. Federal and State wilderness areas are closed to cycling.

2. *Leave no trace.* Be sensitive to the dirt beneath you. Even on open trails, you should not ride under conditions where you will leave evidence of your passing, such as on certain soils shortly after rain. Observe the different types of soils and trail construction; practice low-impact cycling. This also means staying on the trail and not creating any new ones. Be sure to pack out at least as much as you pack in.

3. *Control your bicycle!* Inattention for even a second can cause disaster. Excessive speed can maim and threaten people; there is no excuse for it!

4. *Always yield the trail.* Make known your approach well in advance. A friendly greeting (or a bell) is considerate and works well; startling someone may cause loss of trail access. Show your respect when passing others by slowing to a walk or even stopping. Anticipate that other trail users may be around corners or in blind spots.

5. *Never spook animals.* All animals are startled by an unannounced approach, a sudden movement, or a loud noise. This can be dangerous for you, for others, and for the animals. Give animals extra room and time to adjust to you. In passing, use special care and follow the directions of horseback riders (ask if uncertain). Running cattle and disturbing wild animals is a serious offense. Leave gates as you found them, or as marked.

6. *Plan ahead.* Know your equipment, your ability, and the area in which you are riding—and prepare accordingly. Be self-sufficient at all times. Wear a helmet, keep your machine in good condition, and carry necessary supplies for changes in weather or other conditions. A well-executed trip is a satisfaction to you and not a burden or offense to others.

HITTING THE TRAIL

Once again, because this is a "where-to," not a "how-to" guide, the following will be brief. If you're a veteran trail rider these suggestions might serve to remind you of something you've forgotten to pack. If you're a newcomer, they might convince you to think twice before hitting the backcountry unprepared. **Water:** I've heard the questions dozens of times. "How much is enough? One bottle? Two? Three?! But think of all that extra weight!" Well, one simple physiological fact should convince you to err on the side of excess when it comes to deciding how much water to pack: a human working hard in 90-degree weather needs approximately ten quarts of fluids every day. Ten quarts. That's two and a half gallons—12 large water bottles or 16 small ones. And, with water weighing in at approximately 8 pounds per gallon, a one-day supply comes to a whopping 20 pounds.

In other words, pack along two or three bottles even for short rides. And make sure you can purify the water found along the trail on longer routes. When writing of those routes where this could be of critical importance, each author has provided information on where water can be found near the trail—if it can be found at all. But drink it untreated and you run the risk of disease. (See *Giardia* in the Glossary.)

One sure way to kill both the bacteria and viruses in water is to boil it for ten minutes, plus one minute more for each 1,000 feet of elevation above sea level. Right. That's just how you want to spend your time on a bike ride. Besides, who wants to carry a stove, or denude the countryside stoking bonfires to boil water?

Luckily, there is a better way. Many riders pack along the effective, inexpensive, and only slightly distasteful tetraglycine hydroperiodide tablets (sold under the names Potable Aqua, Globaline, and Coughlan's, among others). Some invest in portable, lightweight purifiers that filter out the crud. Yes, purifying water with tablets or filters is a bother. But catch a case of Giardia sometime and you'll understand why it's worth the trouble.

Tools: Ever since my first cross-country tour in 1965 I've been kidded about the number of tools I pack on the trail. And so I will exit entirely from this discussion by providing a list compiled by two mechanic (and mountain biker) friends of mine. After all, since they make their livings fixing bikes, and get their kicks by riding them, who could be a better source?

These two suggest the following as an absolute minimum:

tire levers
spare tube and patch kit
air pump
allen wrenches (3, 4, 5, and 6 mm)
six-inch crescent (adjustable-end) wrench
small flat-blade screwdriver
chain rivet tool
spoke wrench

But, while they're on the trail, their personal tool pouches contain these additional items:

channel locks (small)
air gauge
tire valve cap (the metal kind, with a valve-stem remover)
baling wire (ten or so inches, for temporary repairs)
duct tape (small roll for temporary repairs or tire boot)
boot material (small piece of old tire or a large tube patch)
spare chain link
rear derailleur pulley
spare nuts and bolts
paper towel and tube of waterless hand cleaner

First-aid kit: My personal kit contains the following, sealed inside double Ziploc bags:

    sunscreen
    aspirin
    butterfly-closure bandages
    Band-Aids
    gauze compress pads (a half-dozen 4″ × 4″)
    gauze (one roll)
    ace bandages or Spenco joint wraps
    Benadryl (an antihistamine, in case of allergic reactions)
    water purification tablets
    Moleskin / Spenco "Second Skin"
    hydrogen peroxide, iodine, or Mercurochrome (some kind of antiseptic)
    snakebite kit

Final considerations: The authors of this series have done a good job in suggesting that specific items be packed for certain trails—raingear in particular seasons, a hat and gloves for mountain passes, or shades for desert jaunts. Heed their warnings, and think ahead. Good luck.

Dennis Coello
St. Louis

COLORADO RIDES

Fort Collins

RIDE 1 OLD FALL RIVER ROAD

This ride traverses the east face of the Rockies, a dynamic world comprised of knobs and domes of eroded igneous granite, metamorphic schist, and banded gneiss. From lofty vantage points along the route you will be treated to powerful views of Rocky Mountain National Park's tallest 14,000′ peaks, combined with impressive overviews of the Rockies' foothills as they slip into the sprawling expanse of the Great Plains 7,000′ below.

The loop's 30-mile length alone might make a substantial ride, even if located on the plains below. Now, toss in 3,000′ of climbing in 9.5 miles (up inclines that approach 10 to 20%) and elevations approaching 12,000′. Even well-seasoned riders with good lungs and strong legs will not scoff at Old Fall River Road. Keep in mind, though, that this is not an eye-on-the-front-tire training ride. You will stop occasionally to rest, then more often as your senses overflow with magnificent sights, curious sounds trickling down from the outstretched mountains above, and fresh scents wafting on cool breezes.

The loop's first 9.5 miles follow Old Fall River Road, a maintained dirt road suitable for passenger cars. Conditions are normally good with minimal washboards even on the steepest sections or around corners, but dust from passing motorists during dry seasons may be a problem. The 20-mile return descent is along the paved Trail Ridge Road. The entire route requires almost no technical skill, but tight, twisting curves upon descending warrant attentiveness. Old Fall River Road is one-way, making the loop travel counterclockwise. Those cyclists who think "one-way" applies only to motor vehicles will be rudely awakened by patrolling rangers.

General location: This ride is equidistant between Boulder and Fort Collins and immediately west of Estes Park. Begin this ride at the Endovalley Picnic Area, located 4 miles west of the Fall River Entrance Station for Rocky Mountain National Park, located about 50 miles northwest of Boulder, Colorado.
Elevation change: The Endovalley Picnic Area rests at 8,590′. Over the next 9.5 miles, Old Fall River Road climbs to a lofty 11,800′ at the Alpine Visitor Center located atop Fall River Pass. Here, the route connects with pavement but climbs an additional 400′ to its highest point (12,180′) at the Gore Range Overlook along Trail Ridge Road. Trail Ridge Road then drops nearly 4,000′ to the loop's lowest point (8,520′) near Sheep Lakes.

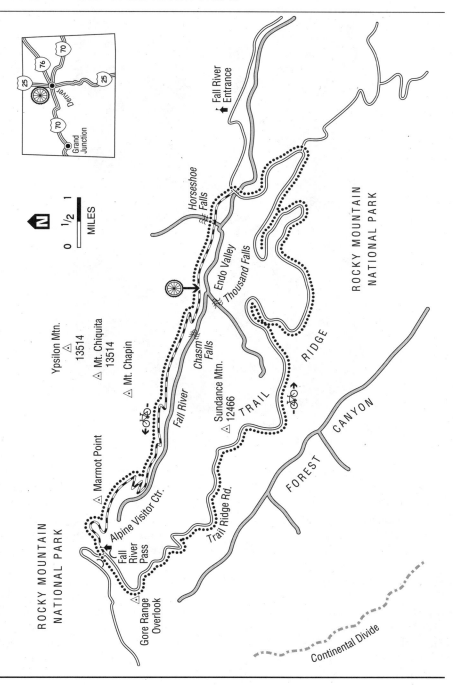

Riding through Rocky Mountain National Park. Photo: Dennis Coello.

Season: The Old Fall River Road typically opens the Fourth of July and closes again by mid-October; Trail Ridge Road will open by mid-May. Weather and temperatures are variable and can be severe due to changes in altitude, slope, and exposure. Be prepared! Carry raingear and warm clothing even if early morning skies are clear. Afternoon showers are common and may be accompanied by sharp drops in temperature. Weekend and holiday traffic can be heavy, so plan an early start.

Services: You will find water at the Endovalley Picnic Area, and hot food, beverages, and shelter at the Alpine Visitor Center (conveniently located at the top of the dirt-road climb). Camping is available throughout the park, and all visitor services are available in the nearby town of Estes Park.

Hazards: Aside from the possibility of rapidly changing weather (accompanied by lightning and strong winds if you ride the Trail Ridge Road during a squall), vehicular traffic will be your greatest concern. Expect little or no shoulder throughout the loop, and remember that motorists are busy driving *and* looking at the scenery. Roadside gravel and "chip" can make cornering on steep descents tricky. If at all possible, avoid weekends and holidays, when traffic is heavy.

Rescue index: Assistance is seldom far away at any point along the roads. Rangers patrol the area periodically, and flagging down a passing motorist is usually easy.

Land status: Rocky Mountain National Park.

Maps: USGS 7.5 minute quadrangles: Estes Park, Fall River Pass, and Trail Ridge, Colorado. USGS Rocky Mountain National Park. Obtain the general park map at the entrance station along with the informative Old Fall River Road brochure (available at Endovalley for a quarter), which offers explanations of the 24 numbered stops along the road.

Finding the trail: The route begins on the Old Fall River Road at the Endovalley Picnic Area, located about 4 miles west of Rocky Mountain National Park's Fall River Entrance Station. According to park regulations, vehicles may be parked at the picnic area, but they may not be left overnight.

Sources of additional information:

> Superintendent
> Rocky Mountain National Park
> Estes Park, CO 80517-8397
> (303) 586-1399

Notes on the trail: A quick glance at the words above concerning narrow roads, heavy traffic, sudden temperature changes, strong winds, and lightning might make any biker choose another route. But do not forgo this alpine wonderland. Just plan accordingly—call ahead for weather reports, ride in the early hours on weekdays—and ride carefully. And remember that while the Old Fall River Road is narrow and has some very steep switchbacks, the traffic is all one-way, and the speed limit is only 15 mph. You will find drivers to be extremely courteous, and although you may eat a bit of their dust, their yells of encouragement make the meal almost palatable.

Rising through Rocky Mountain National Park, the Old Fall River Road passes through three distinct life zones. The montane zone marks the lower elevations where aspens line the road and fernlike groundcover blankets the hillsides. Soon, in the subalpine zone, aspens are replaced with spruce, lodgepole pine, and fir higher up. Along the final climb, the timberline marks the alpine zone—a land of snow, rock, ice-blue skies, and tundra. Deep, cuspate valleys, or cirques, hang overhead, and narrow chutes stripped of foliage attest to ravaging avalanches.

For most riders the amazing mountain scenery is the greatest attraction. But naturalists will also appreciate the abundant wildlife: nutcrackers, kinglets, gray jays, chickadees, bluebirds, horned larks and other birds, tassel-eared squirrels and marmots, marten, deer, elk, and more.

The route is also one of history. The Fall River Road, completed in 1920, was the original transmountain highway through Rocky Mountain National Park, used long before the paved Trail Ridge Road. Thirty-eight convicts worked for 8 long years to build it, and their cabins lie as ruins visible shortly before the Endovalley Picnic Area. The Trail Ridge Road follows the paths of the Ute and Arapaho, forged across the mountains centuries ago.

RIDE 2 *LORY STATE PARK*

Lory State Park and nearby Horsetooth Mountain Park offer endless recreational opportunities. Besides being playgrounds for mountain biking, with more than 50 miles of trails, these parks offer backcountry hiking and camping, picnic facilities, and all forms of water recreation. This loop is one of the easier routes and serves as a good introduction to the Fort Collins area. It offers fantastic views of Horsetooth Reservoir, Fort Collins, and the bordering Great Plains on the distant horizon.

Most of this six-mile loop follows a rolling single-track through both Lory State Park and neighboring Horsetooth Mountain Park. High user traffic from hikers, equestrians, and other bikers packs the surface to a smooth tread. Along the route are short, demanding climbs offset by gradual descents. The one-mile climb on the dirt service road in Horsetooth Mountain Park is perhaps the most arduous. The final descent through Lory State Park and back to the parking area is loose and technical, but short. This ride should be within the grasp of most novice cyclists, provided they are in modest condition and ride sensibly.

[This trail description was submitted by Stuart Culp,* Fort Collins, Colorado.—G. B.]

General location: Lory State Park is located 8 miles west of Fort Collins.
Elevation change: The parking area in Lory State Park is at about 5,400'. The first leg of the loop heads south and is relatively flat. The service road in Horsetooth Mountain Park climbs, steeply at times, to 6,300' at Loggers Trail (the route's highest point). Loggers Trail declines to meet Mill Canyon Trail. Mill Canyon descends rapidly back through Lory State Park and to the parking area. Total climbing is just over 900'.
Season: Mid-April through October.
Services: Water is available in Lory State Park, but only at the entrance station.

---

*Stuart Culp is the former manager of Cycle Transport, the leading bicycle shop specializing in mountain bikes in Northern Colorado. For more information about Cycle Transport, see "Sources of additional information."

Stuart Culp, former manager of Cycle Transport, and still a nice guy.

Full visitor services are available in LaPorte, 4 miles to the north, and in Fort Collins, 8 miles to the east.

Hazards: Three barbed-wire gates must be opened and closed. The final descent through Lory State Park on the Mill Canyon Trail can be technically difficult.

Lory State Park is a premier equestrian center, so horse traffic is common on trails. When encountering horses, make your presence known well in advance and allow them the right of way by dismounting and pulling off to the side of the trail.

Rescue index: Since the park's trail system is quite popular, other recreationists are commonly encountered. First aid can be obtained from any park ranger at the park entrance, at the horse stables, or at the park office, where there is also a telephone. A hospital is located in Fort Collins.

Land status: Lory State Park is part of the Colorado State Parks system;

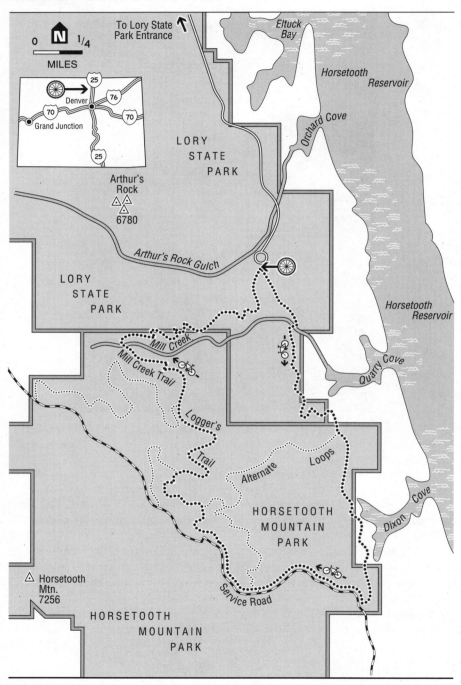

Horsetooth Mountain Park is operated by Larimer County Parks Department. Trail use is regulated in each park and entrance fees apply.

Maps: USGS 7.5 minute quadrangle: Horsetooth Mountain, Colorado. Individual maps for Lory State and Horsetooth Mountain parks are available at their respective entrances. A new mountain bike trail map to Lory State and Horsetooth Mountain parks and other nearby areas is available at Cycle Transport in Fort Collins.

Finding the trail: From US 287 north of Fort Collins, follow signs to Lory State Park. Park at the end of the dirt road about 2 miles south of the park's entrance station.

Sources of additional information:

Lory State Park
708 Lodgepole Drive
Bellevue, CO 80512
(303) 493-1623

Larimer County Parks Department
1800 South County Road 31
Loveland, CO 80537
(303) 679-4570

Cycle Transport
650 South College Avenue
Fort Collins, CO 80524
(303) 221-2869
Cycle Transport is a full-service bicycle shop specializing in mountain bikes in Northern Colorado. They were first to carry and help design the early Ritchey, Fisher, and Specialized mountain bikes. Cycle Transport is active in promoting responsible mountain biking in the Fort Collins area and strives to maintain the positive relationships that mountain bikers have with state and county parks.

Notes on the trail: From the end of Lory State Park's service road (2 miles south of the park entrance) ride on the horse trails to the south for 2 miles. Do not worry about which trail to take, as they will all end up in the same area. You will be riding fairly level terrain in the meadows parallel to the red stone ridge on your left. After crossing through three barbed wire gates (please be sure to close each behind you), turn right and climb the service road (now in Horsetooth Mountain Park) for 1.3 miles. Pass the junction for Stout Trail and continue to Loggers Trail (a marked right turn, after a particularly steep section on the service road). Loggers Trail rolls along back to the north for 1.3 miles until it joins up with the Mill Creek Trail. Continue following Mill Creek for 1.7 miles (through a red gate marking your return to Lory State Park from Horsetooth Park). The last section into the meadow and within sight of the parking lot is pretty technical, so be ready for it!

If 6 miles is not enough and you want to combine more climbing with the most exciting descent in the parks, do not turn off on Loggers Trail at mile 3.3. Instead, continue up the service road for 1.3 more miles (and 700´ more climbing!) until you see a water trough and the sign for the top of the Mill Creek Trail on your right. Turn right and descend 1.8 miles to the Mill Creek–Loggers junction, then turn left and descend back to the parking lot. This extended loop is about 8 miles.

Lory State Park, residing in the transition ecology of the Rocky Mountain foothills, is noted for its varied terrain and vegetation. Low-lying portions of the park rest in grassy plains with views of the red sandstone hogbacks bordering Horsetooth Reservoir. Many of these inclined ridges dip into and disappear beneath the reservoir. At higher elevations, grasses are replaced by shrubs and flowering plants, and ultimately, Ponderosa pine forests. Tilted sandstone layers around the reservoir abut the granite core of Horsetooth Mountain to the southwest and Arthur's Rock to the northwest.

Lory and Horsetooth parks are as diverse in wildlife as they are in vegetation. Mule deer, wild turkey, black bear, mountain lion, bobcat, coyote, Abert squirrel, cottontail rabbit, blue grouse, mourning dove, various songbirds and, occasionally, prairie rattlesnake inhabit the parks.

Estes Park

RIDE 3 *HOUSE ROCK*

Estes Park, like Aspen, Crested Butte, and Telluride, is in the right place—only for different reasons. There is no gold, silver, or coal here; Estes Park has been a tourist town almost from the start. Joel Estes plunked himself down in the valley in 1859; Colorado's first dude ranch followed in the 1870s. Estes Park is the gateway to Rocky Mountain National Park. Estes Park is breathtaking—period.

The combined views of Longs Peak (14,256´) and Mount Meeker (13,911´) will knock your socks off. These two mountains were once known as The Two Guides to the Arapaho Indians, The Two Ears to the French, and served as landmarks—lighthouses for the prairie schooners—for these mountains simply jut out of the plains.

The route to House Rock is neither flat nor all downhill—just up and back, then up and back, again. This 11-mile out-and-back ride is moderate to strenuous in difficulty and requires intermediate bike handling skills. It follows a minimally maintained, four-wheel-drive road that harbors the typical assortment of ruts, rocks, and stones; the higher up you go the worse it gets. But anything for a view, right?

[This trail information was submitted by William L. Stoehr,* Evergreen, Colorado.—G. B.]

General location: House Rock is 36 miles northwest of Boulder and 8 miles south of Estes Park on CO 7.
Elevation change: The starting elevation at Meeker Park is 8,600´. House Rock rises to 9,300´. Near the ride's midpoint, the road dips just below 8,300´.

---

*A Wisconsin native, William L. Stoehr moved with his family to Evergreen, Colorado, in 1982. He and his wife, Mary, own Trails Illustrated, a recreational-map company that has published more than 70 topographical maps of Colorado, Utah, and western national parks. In addition, Trails Illustrated produced the *Moab Area Mountain Bike Routes* trail map.

Stoehr's writing has appeared in regional and national publications, and he has written two best-selling mountain bike books (see "Sources").

RIDE 3 *HOUSE ROCK*

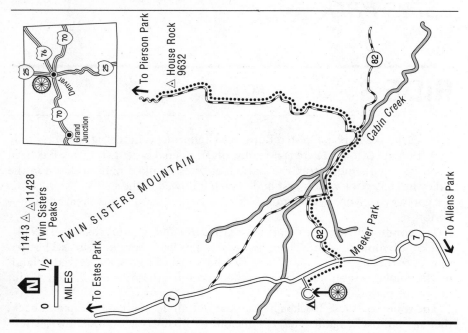

Afterwards, you face a trying, 1,000-foot climb over the next 3 miles, but the visual rewards greatly offset the expended effort.

Season: Late spring through early fall. Be prepared for sudden weather changes; expect rain in the early afternoon.

Services: Complete visitor services are available in Estes Park.

Hazards: No unusual hazards exist. Keep an eye on changing mountain weather.

Rescue index: You can expect occasionally to see other riders and four-wheel-drive vehicles in the area. This is a moderate-use area.

Land status: Roosevelt National Forest.

Maps: USGS 7.5 minute quadrangles: Allens Park, Raymond, and Panorama Peak, Colorado. USGS 1:50,000 scale county maps: Boulder County, Larimer County #4. Trails Illustrated® map: #200, Rocky Mountain National Park.

Finding the trail: Park and unload in the Meeker Park picnic ground 8 miles south of Estes Park on CO 7.

Longs Peak as viewed from House Rock. Photo: William Stoehr.

Sources of additional information:

Roosevelt National Forest
Estes-Poudre Ranger District
148 Remington Street
Fort Collins, CO 80524-2834

Mountain Bike Rides in the Colorado Front Range, by William L. Stoehr. Boulder, Colorado: Pruett Publishing, 1988.

Bicycling the Backcountry, a Mountain Bike Guide to Colorado, by William L. Stoehr. Boulder, Colorado: Pruett Publishing, 1987.
Available throughout the intermountain West.

Notes on the trail: From the Meeker Park picnic ground, pedal less than a mile south on CO 7 to Cabin Creek Road (County Road 82), then turn left (east). Wind through a residential section, then up to an unmarked intersection; turn right and continue east on CR 82 along Cabin Creek. A mile or so farther follow signs for House Rock, Pierson Park, and Estes Park, left and to the north. Midway through the climb, follow the left fork on Pierson Park Road to the base of House Rock. If you are game, pass through the gate and continue 3 more miles to Pierson Park or 7 miles to Estes Park.

Longs Peak (14,256´), discovered by Major Stephen D. Long during his 1820 Colorado expedition, is the northernmost "fourteener" in the Rocky

William L. Stoehr.

Mountains. The Diamond, the sheer east face of Longs Peak, is a classic rock climb. This and the San Juan's Lizard Head are considered *the* Colorado climbs.

Mt. Meeker, Meeker Park, Meeker Ridge, and the town of Meeker are all named after Nathan C. Meeker, one of the founders of Greeley. In 1879, while an agent at the White River Ute Indian Agency, Meeker and the other agency employees were massacred by Indians.

Boulder

RIDE 4 SWITZERLAND TRAIL

This route follows the old railroad grade of the Switzerland Trail of America, a late-nineteenth-century rail project that connected the mountain towns of Eldora and Ward. The railway provided an overland route for prospectors seeking fortune in the numerous gold and silver mines that lined the track. And in its heyday during the summer of 1917, the route attracted ten thousand tourists. Although construction began in 1883, progress was stalled many times by arduous conditions, including the torrential flood of 1894.

The Switzerland Trail winds from ridge to valley and back again. Panoramic views of the Continental Divide, foothills, and plains are interspersed throughout the ride. Prominent topographic features in the first 5.5 miles are Sugarloaf Mountain and Bald Mountain. Each contains challenging routes for the hardcore off-road cyclist. This mountain environment, collectively known as the montane, is forested with ponderosa pine and alpine fir. Sections traversing into Left Hand Canyon pass through numerous aspen groves that are brilliant in color during autumn.

The entire Switzerland Trail route is an 18-mile point-to-point trip. Set up a car shuttle to avoid the long return miles via paved roads. The trail can also be ridden in shorter out-and-back segments (less than five miles each), beginning at one of the prominent trailheads.

The Switzerland Trail of America has been converted to a nonmaintained county road with generally hard-packed dirt conditions. And because the grade of the old railroad never rose more than 4 to 5%, it is a great ride for beginners or for those visiting the mile-high metro area. A short section along Sawmill Road at the Left Hand Canyon trailhead requires portaging 100 yards across a steep talus slope.

[Trail information was submitted by Mary Morrison and Jim Robb,* Boulder, Colorado.—G. B.]

---

*Mary Morrison of Latitude Design and her husband, Grant, make their home in Nederland; Jim Robb of ZIA Maps and his wife, Gigi, live in Sugarloaf. Graduates of the University of Colorado with degrees in geography, Mary and Jim produced ZIA's *Boulder County Mountain Bike Map*.

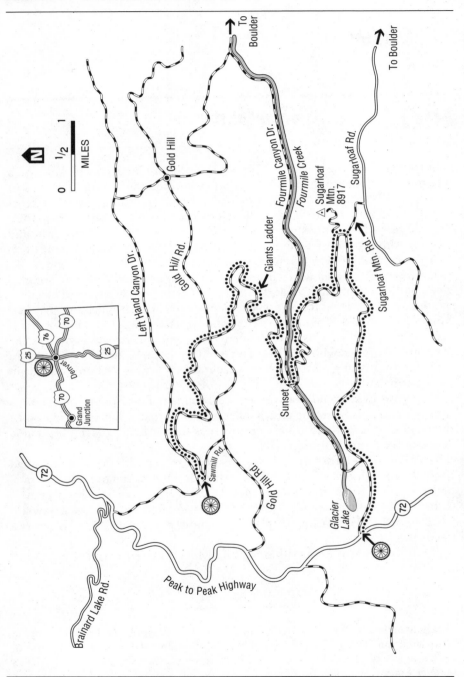

General location: The Switzerland Trail has 5 trailhead locations: Sugarloaf Mountain, Glacier Lake, Sunset, Gold Hill Road, and Left Hand Canyon Drive. All are west of Boulder.

Elevation change: From the Glacier Lake trailhead (9,050′), the road descends pleasantly to the base of Sugarloaf Mountain (8,440′), then continues downhill to Sunset, at 7,760′. Continuing north from Sunset, the route rises out of the valley to Gold Hill Road (8,560′), levels off, then climbs only 100′ more to Sawmill Road. Overall, total elevation loss is 1,400′. Elevation gains in between total less than 800′.

Season: Midspring to late fall, depending on snow fall. Some portions may be ridden during midwinter. The trail is extremely popular with four-wheel-drive traffic, most notably on holidays.

Services: There are no services along the route. Limited services, including food and minor repairs, may be found in Nederland, Gold Hill, and Ward. Of course, Boulder has it all—and then some. Campground information can be obtained from the Forest Service District Ranger Office in Boulder.

Hazards: The road is suitable, on the whole, for passenger cars, though it's a rough ride. But motorists are often discouraged by the hard-packed, sometimes washboarded conditions. Keep an eye out for vehicles when rounding blind curves. Motor traffic is heaviest on weekends and holidays. Always be prepared for rapid weather changes; thunderstorms frequent the mountains during the summer.

Rescue index: Passing motorists and other cyclists are common. Emergency assistance is from 30 minutes to 2 hours away. Aside from scattered houses near the main access points, Gold Hill is the closest sizeable community near the trail.

Land status: Roosevelt National Forest.

Maps: USGS 7.5 minute quadrangles: Gold Hill and Ward, Colorado. *Boulder County Mountain Bike Map,* by ZIA Maps. Based on USGS topographic maps, this 2-sided map shows an enhanced topographic map on one side and a computerized 3-D terrain map on the other, to visualize the area's relief.

Finding the trail: *Sugarloaf Mountain trailhead:* Drive west on CO 119 (Boulder Canyon Drive), then turn right onto Sugarloaf Road. After 5 miles turn onto Sugarloaf Mountain Road. The trail begins at the base of Sugarloaf Mountain. *Glacier Lake trailhead:* Five miles north of Nederland on CO 72, look for a dirt road branching to the right one-quarter mile past mile marker 38. *Sunset trailhead:* Travel west on Boulder Canyon Drive (CO 119); turn right onto Fourmile Canyon Drive and travel 10 miles. Do not plan on parking in Sunset, for the entire town is posted with No Parking signs (nothing is worse than returning to find your vehicle missing). Park near the 9-mile marker to be safe. *Gold Hill Road trailhead:* The Gold Hill Road access is located 12 miles up Sunshine Canyon Drive from the Boulder city limits (in Boulder this road is called Mapleton Avenue). Just past the 12-mile marker, look for the Forest

Service sign. Gold Hill has 2 restaurants and a natural food store. *Left Hand Canyon trailhead:* The northern trailhead is located at Sawmill Road in Left Hand Canyon, approximately 18 miles west of Foothills Highway (US 36).

Sources of additional information:

Roosevelt National Forest
Boulder Ranger District
2995 Baseline Road
Boulder, CO 80303
(303) 444-6600

Boulder County Mountain Bike Map, by ZIA Maps (Boulder, Colorado).

Notes on the trail: For the extended ride, begin at the route's ends at either Glacier Lake or Left Hand Canyon Drive/Sawmill Road. From each location, the road descends to Sunset in Fourmile Canyon, roughly midroute, then climbs gradually to the opposite trailhead. Sunset and Gold Hill Road (located near the trail's midsection) are good starting locations for shorter segmental trips.

Pedaling downhill to Sunset, you pass remains of numerous gold and silver mines that once lined the track. The ensuing climb up to Gold Hill was dubbed "The Giant's Ladder" by old railroad engineers. Just before reaching Gold Hill Road, you pass the remains of Mount Alto Park. Opened in July 1898, this retreat was complete with a spacious dancing pavilion, picnic grounds, and a lavish fountain of white quartz. Its large stone chimney and fireplace are all that remain.

RIDE 5   *SOURDOUGH TRAIL*

The pure joy of riding an exhilarating single-track that is still open to mountain bikes makes this one of the most popular rides in the Boulder County Front Range.

The Sourdough Trail remains in the mixed forest of aspen, lodgepole pine, and Douglas fir the entire way; however, at certain points, the trees open up to offer outstanding views of the Continental Divide above, the foothills below, and the Great Plains to the east. Near the Peace Memorial Bridge, the dense forest canopy mimics that of the lush Pacific Northwest.

Riding the Sourdough Trail as a 10.5-mile point-to-point trail necessitates a car shuttle. Closing the loop requires pedaling about 15 additional miles on the paved Peak-to-Peak Highway.

The majority of the trail is a maintained Forest Service single-track. Still, technical sections and challenging conditions make "finesse" the word of the

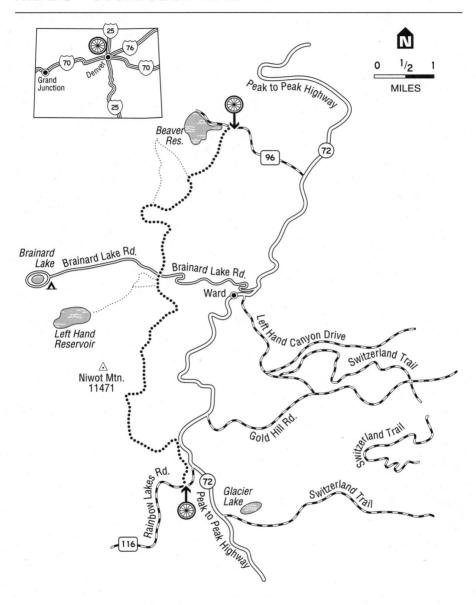

day. Intermediate to advanced mountain bikers with good bike handling skills will find total enjoyment on the Sourdough Trail.

[This route information was submitted by Mary Morrison and Jim Robb, Boulder, Colorado.—G. B.]

General location: The trail is located about 15 miles west of Boulder. Although this route can be started from numerous points, the best place to start is at County Road 116, one-half mile west of the Peak-to-Peak Highway (CO 72). A Forest Service sign marks the trailhead. Other trailheads are on the Brainard Lake Road and off of CR 96 near Beaver Creek Reservoir.

Elevation change: From the southern trailhead off of CR 116, the Sourdough Trail begins at 9,250′ and climbs to its highest point of 10,200′ in the first 4.5 miles. The remaining 6 miles descend to a final elevation of 9,100′ near Beaver Reservoir.

Season: End of May through October, depending on snowfall. Be prepared for rapidly changing temperatures and sudden thunderstorms during the summer months. Even though early morning weather is clear and sunny, pack along an extra layer of clothing and raingear to be safe. Since this is a popular multi-use trail, expect moderate to heavy user traffic on weekends.

Services: A number of fine restaurants and stores, including the Millsite Inn, Neapolitans Restaurant, and the Mountain Peoples Co-Op, can be found in the town of Ward (at the bottom of the Brainard Lake Road) and farther south at Nederland on CO 72. There are a number of developed campgrounds near the Sourdough Trail; contact the Boulder Ranger District Office for detailed information. Boulder provides all visitor services, including many fine bike shops.

Hazards: The trail itself contains the usual mountain bike hazards, or "challenges," as some say. The higher your skill level, the lower the hazard index and the greater the rewards of the Sourdough Trail. Be prepared for rapidly changing alpine weather.

Rescue index: Although the trail is popular and on-trail assistance is common, emergency help is usually 30 minutes to 2 hours away in Boulder.

Land status: Roosevelt National Forest.

Maps: USGS 7.5 minute quadrangle: Ward, Colorado. *Boulder County Mountain Bike Map,* by Mary Morrison and Jim Robb. Boulder, Colorado: ZIA Maps.

Finding the trail: The Peak-to-Peak Highway (CO 72) provides access to the Sourdough Trail's 3 main trailheads. *Southern trailhead:* Travel on Boulder Canyon Drive (CO 119) to Nederland. Turn north on CO 72, then travel about 8 miles to CR 116. The trailhead is about one-half mile to the west. *Brainard Lake Road middle trailhead:* Travel north of Nederland on CO 72 about 15 miles to Ward. Head west on the Brainard Lake Road about 3 miles to the trailhead. *Beaver Reservoir northern trailhead:* Continue north of Ward on CO 72, about 3 miles, and turn west on CR 96. The trailhead is near the end of the road by the reservoir.

Sources of additional information:

> Roosevelt National Forest
> Boulder Ranger District
> 2995 Baseline Road
> Boulder, CO 80303
> (303) 444-6600

Boulder County Mountain Bike Map, by ZIA Maps (Boulder, Colorado).

Notes on the trail: From the southern trailhead, the first 4.5 miles climb gently to the trail's highest point. This is followed by a 1.5-mile, gradual descent to Brainard Lake Road, the route's middle trailhead and the endpoint for a pleasant 2- to 3-hour, out-and-back trip. Continuing toward Beaver Reservoir, the trail first descends steeply to Saint Vrain Creek and is technically challenging. Riding this section uphill from the other direction is difficult. Finally, the remainder of the route descends a moderately technical trail to Beaver Reservoir, the route's northern trailhead. From here your choices are three: 1) retrace your tracks (of course, you are packing along extra water, food, and plenty of stamina); 2) pedal back along the paved Peak-to-Peak Highway; or 3) dig out a frosty beverage from the cooler in your shuttle vehicle and recap the day's adventure.

RIDE 6 · *CONEY FLATS LOOP*

Spectacular mountain views of the Indian Peaks Wilderness, lush foliage, and an exhilarating variety of riding terrain are the rewards of this moderately challenging 14.25-mile loop. Seasoned novice and expert riders love this ride because the mostly four-wheel-drive trail has all kinds of conditions: hardpack, fine gravel, stretches of large and small boulders that force you to "pick your line" as you make your rugged descents, primitive log bridges across rushing streams, and a short stretch on the Peak-to-Peak Highway. Hard-core riders with strong climbing legs can opt to take a 1-mile shortcut on the Sourdough Trail, which trims almost 6 miles off the 14.25-mile loop, making an 8.25-mile loop. In mid-June, Bruce, my biking partner, and I found the trail interrupted with ponds, most of which were small and shallow enough to make cruising through them a child's delight. Though steep portions are generally short and rideable, a few areas were strewn with boulders that forced us to hoof it.

Located north of Boulder, this rides takes you to an entry point of the heavily used Indian Peaks Wilderness. Backcountry camping is allowed within the Wilderness, but biking is not. Nevertheless, hiking and camping in this inspiring mountain area are worth leaving your bike locked at the entry. Consider car-camping, too, since this area contains many mountain bike trails.

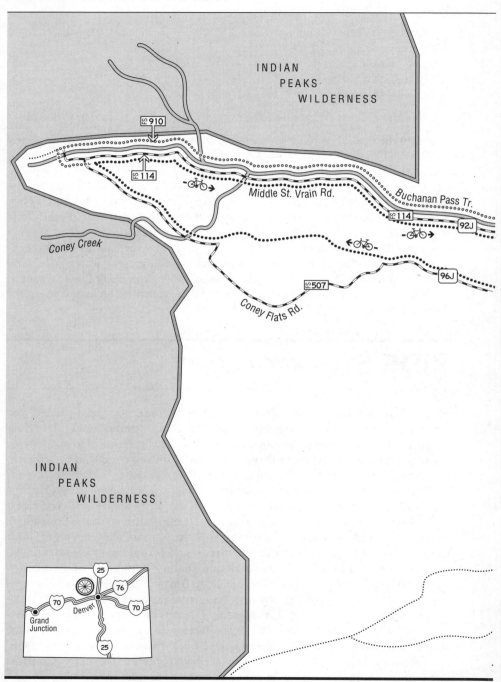

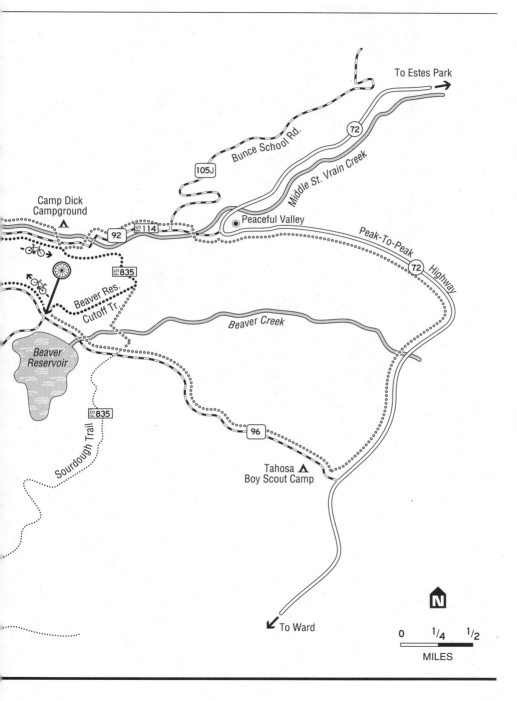

To Estes Park

Bunce School Rd.

105J

72

Middle St. Vrain Creek

Camp Dick
Campground

Peaceful Valley

92 FS 114

Peak-To-Peak

72 Highway

FS 835

Beaver Res.
Cutoff Tr.

Beaver Creek

Beaver
Reservoir

Sourdough Trail

FS 835

96

Tahosa
Boy Scout Camp

N

To Ward

0   1/4   1/2

MILES

Linda does a short balancing act across Coney Creek.

General location: You can find this ride about 31 miles northwest of Boulder, just off CO 72 (the Peak-to-Peak Highway). The little town of Ward is approximately 3 miles away.

Elevation change: Going clockwise, the Coney Flats Road trailhead starts at 9,160′ and climbs to 9,800′ within the first 3.5 miles, for a gain of 640′. Thereafter, the next 5 miles are a gradual descent to the lowest point, 8,520′, at the Peak-to-Peak Highway, for a loss of 1,280′. Once on the pavement, the remaining 5.75 miles climb 640′ back to the trailhead. Overall elevation gain is about 1,280′.

Season: The best time to ride this trail is late spring through midfall. Prior to that, late snowfall and spring rains may result in larger ponds and muddier spots. Throughout the summer months, be prepared for afternoon thunderstorms and lightning. In the fall, snow in early September is rare, but has been known to happen, so check the weather forecast and bring appropriate clothing. Those of you gifted with the chemistry of attraction may want to bring insect repellant.

Services: No services are available at the Coney Flats trailhead. Water and rest rooms are available at Camp Dick and Peaceful Valley Campgrounds. Camping at both areas requires a fee and reservations between June 1 and September 15. Backcountry camping is allowed. Rooms and meals are frequently available at the privately owned Peaceful Valley Lodge, but call first. There are few eateries in Ward—the Millsite Inn on CO 72 is a favorite stop for both locals and mountain bikers.

Hazards: Long stretches of loose rocks and boulders, especially on the descents, force you to be quite alert and pick your line of travel quickly. Some of the ponds on the trail can be quite deep and throw you into the water. If you choose to finish the loop via the highway, watch out for traffic, as this is a well-traveled road. Fortunately, there is ample shoulder for single-file riding.

Rescue index: This is a popular spot for campers, so help is generally available at the campgrounds. Four miles of the Middle Saint Vrain Creek Road allow off-road vehicles. An emergency phone is located a few yards from the Camp Dick entrance on CO 72, at the Peaceful Valley Lodge entrance.

Land status: Roosevelt National Forest.

Maps: Trails Illustrated® maps: #102 Indian Peaks–Gold Hill. This map labels the Coney Flats Road as both Forest Service Road 507 and County Road 96J. The Middle Saint Vrain Road is marked as both FS 114 and CR 92J. Unlike the other maps listed below, this map shows the Buchanan Pass Trail 910. It's a rideable single-track trail paralleling the Middle Saint Vrain Road, just on the other side of Middle Saint Vrain Creek, and it eventually rejoins the Middle Saint Vrain Road.

USGS 7.5 minute quads: Allens Park and Ward, Colorado.

Colorado Rocky Mountain Front Range Travel & Recreation Map.

A map of trails and route descriptions, published by Latitude 40°, Inc., Box 4086, Boulder, CO 80306. Phone: (303) 258-7909. This map identifies the Coney Flats Road as CR 96J and the Middle Saint Vrain Road as CR 92J. Buchanan Pass Trail is not shown.

Finding the trail: From downtown Boulder, heading northwest on CO 36, drive 8 miles to Left Hand Canyon Drive (CO 106) and turn left. Follow the sign to the town of Ward and continue through it to CO 72 (the Peak-to-Peak Highway), turn right, and head north. Make a left onto a wide dirt road, CO 96, leading to the Tahosa Boy Scout Camp. Follow this road for about 3 miles to the west side of Beaver Reservoir, where you find the Coney Flats Road trailhead. Parking is permitted on the side of the road.

Sources of additional information:

Roosevelt National Forest
Boulder Ranger District
2995 Baseline Road
Boulder, CO 80303
(303) 444-6600
Indian Peaks Wilderness camping permits: (303) 444-6003

Cycle Logic
2525 Arapahoe Avenue
Boulder, CO 80302
(303) 443-0061
Ask Greg Thayer or any staff member for other ride suggestions. A bike mechanic is usually on duty here, or check other store locations in Denver, Littleton, and Greeley.

Notes on the trail: Before starting, you need to decide which direction to take. You can tackle this trail clockwise or counterclockwise; either way is moderately challenging.

Counterclockwise: This route keeps you off CO 72 and allows you to descend a short, narrow, steep, and tree-trunk-laden portion of the Sourdough Trail. This single-track spur on the eastern end of the loop shortens the ride by almost 6 miles for a total of nearly 9 miles, round-trip. Admittedly, this portion may be a bit intimidating to the novice rider; hoofing it is always an option. Following the Sourdough segment is the climb up the Middle Saint Vrain Road, a gradual but extremely rough all-terrain-vehicle road.

If you opt for the clockwise direction, the Sourdough portion is a steep uphill ride. You'll need great stamina and advanced technical skills to hop huge tree roots. Fortunately, this stretch is less than a mile long.

Clockwise: For the first half-mile, the Coney Flats Road (FS 507 and CR 96J on some maps) is a moderately challenging, uphill, rocky jeep road. After almost 1.5 miles, the road splits. You can either stay on the wider jeep road to the left or follow FS 507, a wide single-track. We opted for the single-track which, after a mile, reconnects with the jeep road. (The difference in length between the single-track and jeep road is negligible.) At about 3 miles, cross Coney Creek on the footbridge. Follow the trail mileage sign, and stay to the right on the jeep trail.

At this creek crossing, majestic, mountainous views of the Indian Peaks Wilderness are offered straight ahead, looking westward. Continue on the jeep road for about a mile to the junction of Middle Saint Vrain Road (FS 114), another rugged jeep road. This junction gives you two options: you can either go left for a few yards, cross the creek, and pick up the Buchanan Pass Trail (a single-track trail simply marked as 910) or turn right, due east, on the jeep road, FS 114.

We opted for the jeep road and enjoyed a bumpy but fun gradual descent along the Middle Saint Vrain Creek. After 3.5 miles on this jeep road, the eastern end of the Buchanan Pass Trail rejoins the Middle Saint Vrain Creek Road. Pedal through tall pine and aspen trees, and pass Camp Dick Campground. Look to your right for the Sourdough Trail. As mentioned earlier, you can enter the Sourdough Trail shortcut at this point and return to the start in less than a mile. Or, continue on FS 114 for about a mile to CO 72. Turn right onto the paved shoulder and cruise on almost 3 miles of rolling hills back to the Tahosa Boy Scout Camp dirt road, CO 96. Make a right turn again onto the dirt road and pedal for almost 3 more miles back to your car.

RIDE 7 *CERAN SAINT VRAIN TO MILLER ROCK*

Here's a short and sweet ride that has a little of everything: narrow dirt single-tracks teased by 50′-plus drop-offs; brief stretches of loose, rocky, steep ascents and descents; boulders waiting to grab your pedals; tree roots and trail bars for your bunny-hopping pleasure; and gravel to challenge your traction and braking skills. Combine all that with the soothing melody of South Saint Vrain Creek and the peaceful groves of lodgepole pine and aspen. Once you reach the top, take a break and make your way up to Miller Rock or just picnic on its outcroppings—either way, the views into Peaceful Valley and the Indian Peaks Wilderness are magnificent.

This outing can be ridden as a six-mile loop by following the trail through a private Seventh Day Adventist camp (permitted if you stay on the trail) and then connecting with a two-wheel-drive dirt road back to the trailhead. Or, you can do an out-and-back ride to the back gate of the camp, about three-and-a-half miles one-way, almost seven miles total. Personally, I prefer to do this ride as an out-and-back for several reasons: first, my contact lenses protest violently to dirt roads that are frequently traveled by cars and trucks. Second, the scenery remains beautifully primitive throughout the entire ride.

Unless the rider has nerves of steel, I don't recommend this trail for a novice's first single-track experience. Those sheer, deep drop-offs that skirt the trail by inches in some areas can be intimidating. Intermediate skill and moderate stamina levels are needed to enjoy this outing. Of course, willingness to walk the bike happily will do just fine—the scenery is just as splendid whether viewed on foot or from the saddle.

General location: The Ceran Saint Vrain trailhead is situated about 4 miles east of Jamestown, which is approximately 24 miles northwest of Boulder.
Elevation change: The trailhead begins at about 8,330′ and reaches a height of almost 8,600′, for a total elevation change of 270′.

RIDE 7 *CERAN SAINT VRAIN TO MILLER ROCK*

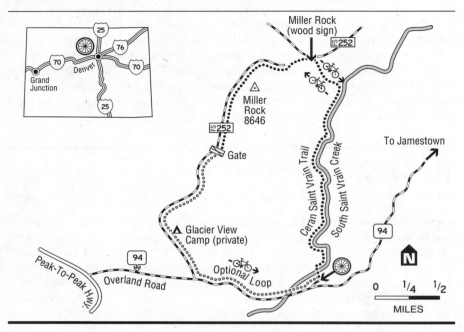

Season: Early spring through late fall are the ideal times to tackle this out-and-back. Although late November can be unseasonably dry, you're likely to encounter some slushy snow patches.

Services: There are no services available at the trailhead. Creek water flows year-round, but should be treated before consumed. About 10 unmarked campsites are available at the trailhead, and camping virtually any place off the trail is permitted. There is no fee for camping.

Hazards: Boulders and tight turns on the sections that skirt deep drop-offs require great caution. A couple of erosion bars are in place to protect the trail. As with all such bars, go over and not around them. Gravel, loose dirt, and skree—classic wipeout conditions—call for controlled speed on the descents. During summer months, this is a popular hiking trail, so be prepared to dismount frequently to let approaching hikers pass, especially in the narrow sections. Honor trail etiquette and give all us bikers a positive image by yielding to others on the trail.

Rescue index: Due to the trail's popularity in the summer months, you are likely to find someone who may be of assistance in case of emergency. Pay phones are located just over 4 miles away in Jamestown. Complete medical facilities are available in Boulder, 24 miles away.

Land status: Roosevelt National Forest and private property.

High rock walls and steep dropoffs add to the drama of this single-track.

Maps: Trails Illustrated® map: #102 Indian Peaks–Gold Hill. USGS 7.5 minute quads: Allens Park and Ward, Colorado. *Colorado Rocky Mountain Front Range Travel & Recreation Map.* A map of trails and route descriptions, published by Latitude 40°, Inc., Box 4086, Boulder, CO 80306. Phone: (303) 258-7909.

Finding the trail: The trailhead is located on the north side of County Road 94, a west-east road connecting CO 72 (the gloriously scenic Peak-to-Peak Highway), Jamestown, and US 36. If you're traveling from CO 72, turn eastward onto CR 94, also known as the Overland Road, here a two-wheel-drive dirt road. The trailhead is approximately 2 miles from the turnoff. If you're coming west from Jamestown, follow the paved Overland Road (CR 94) for about 2 miles until it becomes a dirt road. Continue on for approximately 2.25 miles to the signed trailhead on the north side (your right) of CR 94.

Proof that fresh mountain air makes Bruce just happy to be here.

Sources of additional information:

Roosevelt National Forest
Boulder Ranger District
2995 Baseline Road
Boulder, CO 80303
(303) 444-6600

Cycle Logic
2525 Arapahoe Avenue
Boulder, CO 80302
(303) 443-0061
Ask Greg Thayer or any staff member for other ride suggestions. A bike mechanic is usually on duty, or check other store locations in Denver, Littleton, and Greeley.

Notes on the trail: At the trailhead, there's only one way to start and that's to cross the wooden bridge over South Saint Vrain Creek. For the next 2 miles, follow the narrow, single-track trail—barely one bike's width—as it weaves between boulders, aspen, and lodgepole pines and skirts steep drop-offs in a few sections. Trail conditions range from hardpack to loose dirt to gravel. In these 2 miles, the trail cruises up and down alongside the creek, taking you as high as 90′ above the water, back down to water level, and then up again. It's a bit scary, but still fun.

At about 2 miles, the trail crosses a tiny spur of the creek. For the next several yards, the trail turns away from the creek and begins a steep climb on loose dirt, a great test of your traction and weighting skills. After a few yards, the trail becomes punctuated with boulders, big enough to snag a pedal, but still rideable. Shortly after that, you arrive at a trough strewn with loose rocks. Never a dull moment on this ride!

Once you've grunted and groaned to the top of the trough, continue on for a very short distance until you come to another trail. Though unmarked, this is Miller Rock Road (Forest Service Road 252), an obvious four-wheel-drive road. Turn left (west) onto this road. After pedaling a few yards, look to the left of the trail for a primitive wooden sign carved with the words "Miller Rock." Follow the pointer to the left (southwest), onto a wide, single-track trail.

At this point, the ground becomes quite steep, full of gravel and soft dirt, and laced with tree roots. Eventually, after about a mile, the trail levels out and, once again, takes you through lovely groves of pine and aspen. On your right are large outcrops of boulders. This isn't Miller Rock, but it makes a great lunch or rest stop. Look down the trail and through the trees, due southwest, and you can see Miller Rock rising above the treetops. Local folklore claims that a thief named Miller escaped the authorities by taking refuge here long ago. There isn't an actual trail leading up to Miller Rock, but if you feel like exploring, leave your bike at the trail and find your way through the forest. Look for an interesting boulder area called the "Devil's Bath," shaped like hollowed-out, huge "bowls" and created by water erosion many years ago.

Back at the trail, travel past these boulders for almost a mile and you reach the back gate of Glacier View Camp, a Seventh Day Adventist retreat. At this point, you can turn around and return the way you came or, as mentioned earlier, you can make a loop on the dirt road.

Making the loop: Though a "No Trespassing" sign is posted, another sign slightly farther down the path grants access, provided you stay on the trail. And remember to leave that gate the way you found it, open or closed. Follow the trail and it soon takes you past horse stables. All of a sudden, you're in the middle of an encampment of small houses. Follow the trail as it turns into a wide, two-wheel-drive dirt road that takes you through the camp and eventually leads you out the main entrance. You'll have to follow your nose and instincts for a few yards in order to find your way out. The two-wheel-drive dirt road you want, CR 94, is off to your left, due south. Once you reach CR 94, turn left and watch out for traffic. Pedal just over a mile back to the trailhead and your car.

RIDE 8   ROLLINS PASS

Surmounting the Continental Divide is as tall an order for bikers as it was for the trains that chugged and wheezed their massive steel bodies up the slopes in the early 1900s. Today, we can ride the abandoned railroad path as it gradually climbs 2,500′ in about 15 miles to Rollins Pass. Total mileage of this out-and-back route is about 29 miles. All cyclists, from novices to experts, can enjoy this ride because, other than the sustained but gentle climbing, little technical skill is needed. For more of a challenge, experienced riders can test their bike handling mastery by taking a detour that parallels the main route and rejoins it after 3.5 miles. So, riders of all abilities in your group can be easily accommodated. With a little determination and enduring stamina, virtually everyone can enjoy the expansive vistas of snow-edged ridges, ride past the dramatic beauty of rugged mountains and valleys all the way to the top, and be able to say, "I rode up to the Continental Divide!"

Laid in the early 1900s, the Rollins Pass tracks were the the primary line over the Continental Divide for the Denver, Northwestern, and Pacific Railway Company. In 1927, at the expense of $18 million and 19 lives, the 6.2-mile-long Moffat Tunnel was completed, replacing the Rollins Pass route.

Today, Moffat Tunnel is still used by Amtrak, offering service from Denver to Winter Park and points beyond on both sides of the Divide. The Pass road itself has been graded to accommodate passenger vehicles, though conditions have become more rugged over the years due to rock slides. Still, vehicles can drive to within several miles of the Pass, ending at Needle Eye Tunnel. Though this tunnel is blocked to vehicles, bikers and hikers can walk their way through and still reach Rollins Pass. In fact, for a challenging and creative loop, consider biking up to Rollins Pass, and down into Winter Park, spending the night at a hotel or campground, and on the next day, biking back over the Pass and down to your car.

General location: The east portal of Moffat Tunnel is located about 60 miles west of Denver. The starting point of this ride is about a mile from the east portal, located 9 miles west of Rollinsville.

Elevation change: The ride begins at 9,187′ and climbs to Rollins Pass at 11,660′, for a total elevation gain of 2,473′.

Season: The time for virtually snow-free riding is between mid-May and late October. When I rode this trail in mid-August, it became extremely cold as I approached the Pass. Because of the altitude, be prepared with warm clothing, including well-insulated gloves, no matter when you ride.

Services: There are no services offered at the beginning of the route. Though Rollinsville is located about 9 miles from the trailhead, don't count on finding services available as it is a tiny town. Your best bets for finding water, food, toilet, phone, and lodging, are in the larger towns of Nederland, Central City, Boulder, Arvada, and Golden. Several creeks cross the trail at 5.5 and 9.5 miles, but water must be treated before consuming.

Hazards: During the summer, this road is popular with sightseeing motorists, so watch out for vehicular traffic, at least up to Needle Eye Tunnel. On the return, the descent is fast and fun. Keep your speed under control and stay tight on curves, particularly ones that are obscured by dense groves of trees. I was having so much fun blasting downhill that I almost flattened myself on a car just as I was rounding such a curve. Regarding weather, the last several miles before the Pass are above timberline and, hence, completely exposed. Keep an eye on the weather to avoid being caught on these exposed parts during a thunder and lightning storm. Lastly, I strongly suggest you carry insect repellant, just in case the man- and woman-eating flies are hungry.

Rescue index: Since this is a popular sightseeing road, you're certain to find motorists who may be of help should you require emergency attention. Except for the nearly 2 miles between Needle Eye Tunnel and Rollins Pass, the entire route is accessible by two-wheel-drive vehicles. If you need a phone, you should plan on driving back into Rollinsville or try several homes near the trailhead. No phones are available at Rollins Pass or at the trailhead.

Land status: Roosevelt National Forest and Arapaho National Forest.

Maps: Trails Illustrated® map: #103 Winter Park, Central City, Rollins Pass. USGS 7.5 minute quads: Nederland and East Portal, Colorado.

Finding the trail: *From Interstate 70:* Just east of Idaho Springs, take US 6 for several miles and then turn left (north) onto CO 119. Travel almost 22 miles to Rollinsville. *From Boulder:* Follow CO 119, Canyon Boulevard, due west; then curve south toward Nederland and Rollinsville. Follow CO 119 for about 17 miles to Rollinsville. *From Denver:* Take US 6 west, through Golden and Clear Creek Canyon for over 12 miles to CO 119. Turn right (north) onto CO 119 and drive almost 22 miles to Rollinsville. In the tiny town of Rollinsville, turn west onto CO 16 (Forest Service Road 149, a dirt road), and drive for 9 miles, at which point CO 16 is joined by CO 117 on the right, leading off to the east. At this point, CO 117 and FS 149 are the same road, leading you all the way to Rollins Pass. You can see the east portal of Moffat Tunnel from this viewpoint. Park your car off to the side of the road and start your ride here.

RIDE 8 ROLLINS PASS

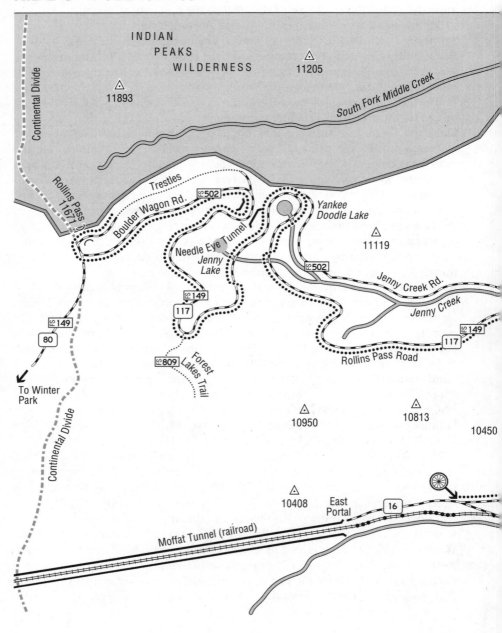

INDIAN
PEAKS
WILDERNESS

△ 11205

South Fork Middle Creek

△ 11893

Continental Divide

Rollins Pass
11671

Trestles

Boulder Wagon Rd.

FS 502

Needle Eye Tunnel

Yankee
Doodle Lake

Jenny
Lake

△ 11119

FS 149

117

FS 502

Jenny Creek Rd.

Jenny Creek

FS 149

117

FS 149

80

Rollins Pass Road

FS 809

Forest Lakes Trail

To Winter
Park

Continental Divide

△ 10950

△ 10813

10450

△ 10408

East
Portal

16

Moffat Tunnel (railroad)

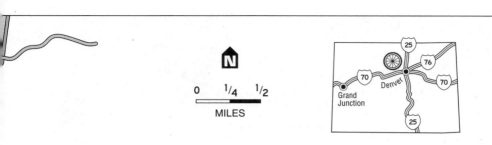

N

0   1/4   1/2

MILES

△ Bryan Mtn.
10810

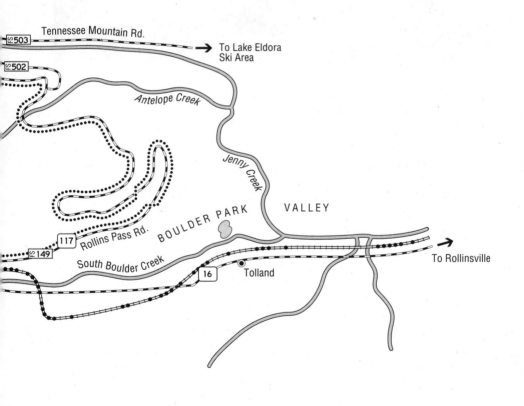

Tennessee Mountain Rd.

FS 503

FS 502

To Lake Eldora
Ski Area

Antelope Creek

Jenny Creek

BOULDER PARK   VALLEY

117   Rollins Pass Rd.

FS 149

South Boulder Creek

16   Tolland

To Rollinsville

Going head-to-head with the Continental Divide.

Sources of additional information:

Roosevelt National Forest and Arapaho National Forest
Boulder Ranger District
2995 Baseline Road
Boulder, CO 80303
(303) 444-6600

Colorado State Parks
1313 Sherman Street, Room 618
Denver, CO 80203
(303) 866-3437
For more information about the rail trail program in Colorado.

Notes on the trail: CO 117 (FS 149) is a fairly easy road to follow, so you won't need to look at your map too often. Whenever you come to a fork in the road, just stay on the main two-wheel-drive road. The path is wide enough to accommodate two cars. For the first 5.5 miles, the road heads east, turns to the west, back east again, and gradually back to the west. Through this portion your view of the Boulder Park Valley widens as you gain elevation. Each turn of the road offers magnificent, expansive views of the snow-rimmed mountaintops of both the Indian Peaks Wilderness and the majestic Continental Divide. It's glorious!

A rider zooms down the alternate Jenny Creek Road, to reconnect with Rollins Pass Road further down.

After almost 6 miles on the trail, Jenny Creek Road (FS 502) leads off on the right. As mentioned earlier, this is the beginning of the detour route for riders wanting a slightly more technical challenge. It is a rugged jeep trail that follows Jenny Creek, climbing about 3.5 miles before rejoining the main route. This alternate trail is not really a shortcut for it trims only about a half-mile off the main route. What's great about this option, though, is that a group of novice and experienced bikers can go separate ways and rejoin about 3.5 miles farther up on the main road. (A rider I met atop Rollins Pass rode up Jenny Creek Road from the Eldora Ski Area. He assured me that this road is more challenging, is fun, and has no cars. So, if you're into exploring new trails, check the maps and vow to return with additional directions from local riders.)

If you skip the detour, continue on and in approximately 10 miles Jenny Creek Road comes in on the right. If riders in your group opted for this challenging trail 3 miles earlier, this is where you will regroup. From here, follow the main road around the north side of Yankee Lake, skirting the timberline. About a half mile from Yankee Lake is the trailhead to Jenny Lake, which offers a good spot for lunch or rest.

Within 2 miles from Jenny Lake, the main road passes the trailhead to Forest Lakes and rises above timberline. Look across the mountainside and you see the road continuing up for less than 1 mile to Needle Eye Tunnel. Though this is the end of the road for motor vehicles, bicyclists and hikers can continue through this short tunnel. Dismount and walk over and around the boulders that block the tunnel. At this point, you've pedaled 13.5 miles and are about 2 miles from Rollins Pass.

As you emerge from Needle Eye Tunnel, follow the main road as it curves northward. Get ready for a gorgeous view of the snow-peaked mountains in the Indian Peaks Wilderness. It's a terrific sensation to realize that, at approximately 11,300´, you're riding at almost the same height as those peaks. Continue on for a few yards, where you reach a fork in the road. To the left and up is Boulder Wagon Road (FS 502). To the right is the trail, leading through boulders that were deliberately placed across the path. These boulders signal that the road ends, just around the curve, at the edge of an abandoned trestle. Danger signs are posted, warning us to keep off. After you've checked out this interesting piece of Colorado railroad history, backtrack a few yards to Boulder Wagon Road and follow it for the final 2 miles to Rollins Pass.

When you reach the Pass, you'll understand why railroad workers in the early 1890s nicknamed this Corona Pass—the crown of the "Top of the World." If you continue on the main road due west, you'll wind up in Winter Park. Otherwise, return the way you came, relishing the fact that it's downhill all the way! Remember to keep an eye out for cars.

Winter Park

Unlike a growing number of communities in other states, mountain biking is intensely encouraged in the Fraser Valley. The towns of Winter Park and Fraser, as well as the Winter Park Ski Resort, recognize mountain biking's popularity and see the advantages—and disadvantages—of embracing the sport. Their foresight has transformed the region into a mountain biking mecca, rivaled only by nearby Summit County.

Winter Park is a planned and managed-growth community, and therefore avoids the unbridled and disjointed development, aggravated by fierce opposition from groups of hikers and equestrians, and mountain bikers, in other towns. A West Coast newspaper recently reported that in California, the war on bikers had escalated to violent levels. It seems that an illegal single-track had been constructed and enjoyed by local mountain bikers who knew of its existence. When discovered by the opposition, the path was booby-trapped with logs, rigged to tumble down the trail. Whether the intention was to cause physical harm or be a mere warning is unknown. Ultimately, a group of 40 hikers and environmentalists gathered to destroy the illegal trail once and for all, a sad loss for bikers in California.

In Colorado, however, through the collective efforts of Winter Park, Fraser, the resort, the Winter Park Fats (the local mountain biking club), and a group of district forest rangers, virtually the entire Fraser Valley, including the ski resort, have been linked with over 600 miles of mountain bike trails. There are plans to create new paths, as well as to improve existing ones to accommodate riders with a wide range of skills and experience, from safer routes for the youngest of families to world-class race courses for professional bikers. Paved bike paths and dirt trails are fairly well marked. Maps and printed trail descriptions are free and easily found in boxes attached to bike path signs throughout the communities. Thanks to mountain biking, what used to be a one-season community centered on winter skiing has now become almost a year-round boomtown.

RIDE 9

UPPER ROOF OF THE ROCKIES TO WINTER PARK BASE

I must confess that the thought of paying hard-earned money for a lift to the top of a mountain and then riding through a ski resort, dodging chairlift towers, and zipping over trimmed and barren terrain, did not appeal to me whatsoever. Give me good old Mother Nature and all her raw beauty anytime. On the other hand, I couldn't ignore the praises from biker friends who had ridden the trails at the Winter Park Ski Resort. And I couldn't ignore the fact that the folks at the resort and communities in the Fraser Valley were doing an outstanding job of integrating and promoting mountain biking in and around this world-class ski center. Reluctantly, I decided to check it out.

So hush my mouth. Julie Klein, a longtime resident of Winter Park, offered to show me what it was like to bike at the resort. It was not as I expected. We started by hopping the chairlift at the Winter Park Base to "Upper Roof of the Rockies," a single-track trail with a "more difficult" rating. After we pedaled farther up the mountain, Julie led me on several different trails back down to the Base for a total of about 10 miles. Most of the trails were single-track and weaved through hillsides so densely forested that chairlift cables and towers were hidden from view. The trails seemed to be thoughtfully planned—I could easily have been "out in the woods," away from civilization. Trail difficulty was varied and challenging enough to make me completely forget that I was riding through a ski resort. On a particularly steep downhill section, Julie warned me of a set of incredibly tight hairpin turns that she always found tough to ride without putting a foot down. They were indeed tight turns but, this time, Julie managed to manuever triumphantly through them with both feet in the pedals at all times. I bit the dust a couple of times and wound up walking.

Winter Park Resort has indeed successfully—and beautifully—incorporated their three ski mountains (Vasquez, Mary Jane, and Winter Park) into one of the state's most enjoyable and friendly mountain bike regions. I informed Julie that I was a changed person. She just chuckled—she knew I would be!

General location: Winter Park Resort, Winter Park, and Fraser are located about 65 miles northwest of Denver. The resort, where you'll find the Upper Roof of the Rockies, is located several miles south of Winter Park on US 40.

Elevation change: The Winter Park Base sits at 9,120′. From here, for a fee, you and your bike can hitch a ride on the Zephyr Express chairlift up to the trailhead of Upper Roof of the Rockies. (Of course, you're welcome to forego the chairlift and pedal up on your own power.) The elevation at the top of the chairlift where you unload and begin pedaling is 10,700′. The highest point on the trail is approximately 10,840′, and you reach it within several miles after you start pedaling. Total elevation gain is 140′, followed by a loss of 1,740′ from the high point back to the Base.

RIDE 9 *UPPER ROOF OF THE ROCKIES TO WINTER PARK BASE*

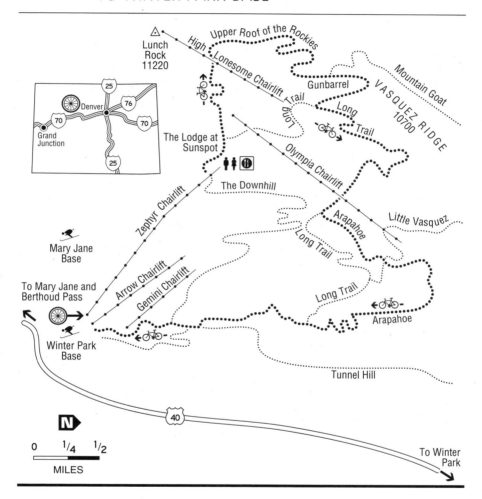

Season: Winter Park Resort is open daily for mountain biking, generally from mid-June through the first weekend in September, and usually for several weekends thereafter. Call for updated information on conditions if you want to ride before or after these dates. Snow tends to linger into early June on Upper Roof of the Rockies, so it may not be open to bikers until mid- to late June. A gorgeous time to ride this trail is in September, when the autumn leaves are turning gold and red amidst forests of evergreen trees.

Services: Drinking water and toilet facilities are available at both the Winter

Julie remembers to stop and smell the forest instead of just zipping down a run at the Winter Park Resort.

Park Base and up at The Lodge at Sunspot, adjacent to the top of the Zephyr Express chairlift. Food and restaurants can be found at the resort, with a greater variety of eating establishments in town. Being a world-class ski resort, Winter Park also has lodging, ranging from modest to extravagant, from bed-and-breakfast inns and guest ranches to elegant hotels and condominiums, both near the resort or in town. Several central reservation services are available and can be reached by phone: From outside Colorado, call Winter Park Central Reservations at (800) 453-2525. Within the state, call (303) 726-5587. From Denver, call (303) 447-0588. To reach Winter Park Vacations Reservation Service from outside Colorado, call (800) 228-1025; from within the state, call (303) 726-9421; and from Denver, call (303) 825-0705.

For the rugged, John Muir–type folks, there are four campgrounds nearby, though it seems that all sites are taken early in the day during the summer months. The Fraser Valley Lions Club, in cooperation with the Arapaho

National Forest, maintains and operates these four sites and charges a small fee. There are two campgrounds between Berthoud Pass and the town of Winter Park: Robbers Roost and Idlewild. West of Fraser, on Saint Louis Creek Road, there are two sites: Saint Louis Creek and Byers Peak.

Hazards: Mountain biking is allowed in almost all parts of the mountains within the Winter Park Resort boundaries. Some trails allow only hiking and are so marked. In preparing for the ski season, construction crews maintain and improve facilities during the summer. That means trails that are normally open to cyclists may be closed for safety reasons. Dirt roads used by resort service crews are not recommended as bicycling paths due to frequent use by maintenance vehicles.

Rescue index: No matter where you are within the resort, you're never far from an emergency phone. Resort maps show where the phones are located. Safety and responsive medical attention is a big concern at Winter Park Resort, if you haven't already guessed.

Land status: Arapaho National Forest. Winter Park Resort operates under a special use permit from the U.S. Forest Service.

Maps: *Trail Map and Activity Guide.* Published and distributed by Winter Park Resort, it's updated annually and free of charge. Trails Illustrated® BikeMap: #503, Winter Park/Grand Lake. Trails Illustrated® map: #103, Winter Park, Central City, Rollins Pass.

Though #103 shows trails, the routes are not always drawn in their entirety. Map #503 was designed expressly for mountain biking but here, too, the routes are not completely depicted. The incompleteness of both maps is no fault of the mapmaker. There simply is such an abundance of trails in the Fraser Valley, with new routes being established and existing ones interconnected, that it's difficult to stay current. Nevertheless, these are extremely useful maps. USGS 7.5 minute quads: Fraser and Berthoud Pass, Colorado. These maps will undoubtedly suffer from the same problem as the Trails Illustrated® maps discussed above.

Winter Park/Fraser Valley Mountain Bike Trail Guide. Published by Winter Park Resort and the Winter Park/Fraser Valley Chamber of Commerce. This is a useful little pamphlet that contains ride descriptions and maps. You can pick one up free in boxes attached to bike path signs throughout Winter Park, as well as from numerous merchants.

Finding the trail: To reach Winter Park Resort from Denver, drive west on Interstate 70, take Exit 232, and go due north on US 40. Drive over Berthoud Pass and continue on US 40 as it winds down into the Fraser Valley. Once you reach the valley floor, the Winter Park Resort will be on your left, after the Mary Jane turnoff. Park your car in any of the free lots provided. Gather your bike gear and pedal to the chairlift ticket window to purchase an activity ticket for yourself and a bicycle transport ticket for your bike. Or, if you had Wheaties for breakfast, you can begin pedaling up any trail. Otherwise, hop aboard the Zephyr Express while the lift attendant loads your bike. Once at the top, another attendant unloads your bike and off you go. Look for the Upper Roof of the Rockies Trail straight ahead, bearing left. Look for trail markers. Incidentally, the activity ticket is good for one lift on Zephyr Express, but the bike ticket is good all day.

Sources of additional information:

Winter Park Resort
Winter Park Recreational Association
Box 36
Winter Park, CO 80482
(303) 726-5587
Or dial direct from Denver: 447-0588

The Winter Park/Fraser Valley Chamber of Commerce and Visitor Center
US 40 and Vasquez Road
P.O. Box 3236
Winter Park, CO 80482
(303) 726-4118
(800) 722-4118

Sport Stalker/Sore Saddle Cyclery
Cooper Creek Square at US 40
Winter Park, CO 80482
(303) 726-8873
These folks operate a bike rental shop at the Winter Park Base too. If you're lucky enough to find Keith Sanders on duty at either location, ask him for other biking suggestions to fit your skill and stamina levels.

Winter Park Fat Tire Society (FATS)
P.O. Box 1337
Winter Park, CO 80482
(303) 726-8044 or (800) 521-BIKE
"Life's too short to ride paved roads," boasts the Winter Park Fat Tire Society (FATS)—a nonprofit, volunteer organization of Winter Park/Fraser bicycling enthusiasts and local businesses united to promote mountain biking. FATS's main objectives are the development, maintenance, signage, and expansion of the Winter Park mountain bike trail system. Through the efforts of cornerstone members Keith Sanders, Michael LaPorte, Greg Foley, and Kip Hubbard, FATS has joined forces with the Forest Service to produce what is claimed to be the world's largest trail network designated for mountain bikes. With 600 miles of routes plus several centralized "orientation" maps, the Winter Park/Fraser area has emerged as a premier mountain bike destination.

FATS, a key promoter of the Winter Park Mountain Bike Festival and King of the Rockies mountain bike race series also holds weekly events, including slalom races, mountain bike polo, and group rides.

Other ski resorts that offer mountain biking:

Copper Mountain: (800) 458-8386
Steamboat Springs: (303) 879-6111
Keystone: (800) 451-5930 or (303) 468-4275
Breckenridge: (800) 789-7669 or (303) 453-5000
Durango/Purgatory: (home of the 1990 World Mountain Bike
    Championships) (800) 525-0892
Mount Crested Butte: (800) 545-4505
Vail: (800) 525-2257
Beaver Creek: (303) 949-5750
Breckenridge Nordic Centers: (303) 453-6855
Frisco Nordic Center: (303) 668-0866
These ski resorts are in different phases of integrating mountain bike trails
and chairlift operations. If riding in a resort is your cup of tea, you have
plenty of choices.

Notes on the trail: Assuming you saved your Wheaties for another morning
and you hopped aboard the Zephyr Express to the top, pick up the Upper Roof
of the Rockies by pedaling straight ahead, then bearing left onto a single-track
trail. Follow the trail as it climbs through a forest of sweet-smelling pine trees
to a fork in the path. Take the left fork and continue a gradual half-mile climb
to the intersection with the Mary Jane ski trail. The Continental Divide looks
powerfully majestic from here, doesn't it?

Continue your climb, crossing a service road on your way to the highest point
of this ride. Follow the single-track as it cruises under a chairlift line, crosses
another road, and eventually goes over a small bridge. You've reached the top
and, from here, it's all downhill.

Let the descent begin! If you consult your Winter Park Resort *Trail Map and
Activity Guide,* you'll see that there are many optional routes down the mountain. Unfortunately, you can only be one place at a time, so you just have to
come back up and try the other routes. Continuing on, follow directional signs
to the Gunbarrel Trail, another single-track that's slightly easier than Upper
Roof of the Rockies. Cruise down Gunbarrel for about a mile until you come
to the junction of Long Trail. Switch over to this easy single-track trail and
continue your downhill run to the junction of Upper Arapaho Trail.

Let's add a little spice to this downhill run. Go left onto Arapaho Trail,
following the signs. Here, the single-track trail becomes slightly steeper and the
hairpin turns tighter. The trail is narrow, with stubs of trees and exposed roots
for your bunny-hopping pleasure. You soon come to the intersection with Little
Vasquez Trail. (If you want an easy way to the Winter Park Base, turn right onto
Little Vasquez and almost immediately reconnect to Long Trail, following it all
the way down the mountain.) Cross Little Vasquez trail and pick up Lower
Arapaho Trail.

On Lower Arapaho, the single-track trail becomes slightly more difficult, with tighter hairpin turns. Follow it down through a sparsely forested, steep, challenging, but fun section. After almost 2 miles, the trail rejoins Long Trail. From there, follow Long Trail for almost 2 miles to reach the Winter Park Base. At this point, you can decide whether or not to buy another ride on the Zephyr Express and do it all again.

RIDE 10 *HIGH LONESOME TRAIL*

Judging from the landscape and location of this quietly beautiful ride, lonesome could be another word for remote. In fact, you have a greater chance of seeing wildlife, including moose, on this trail than on most of the other Winter Park trails. Not too many bikers visiting Winter Park will take the time to find it, much less set up shuttle vehicles, especially since there are so many great rides closer to town. Still, anyone who makes the effort will find this 14.5-mile, technically challenging, and totally enjoyable point-to-point ride well worth the effort.

And yes, I did say "moose." In fact, according to my local riding companion, Keith Sanders of the Sport Stalker/Sore Saddle Cyclery bike shop in Winter Park, these 1,000-pound Bullwinkles have been spotted strolling down the street in Fraser and Winter Park. "Yeah, right, Keith," I thought. But it's true. It all started back in late 1978, when the Colorado Division of Wildlife released 24 moose at a location approximately 80 miles from here. Since then, the moose population has grown to over 600 in the valley. On occasion, Keith has seen moose on this route, quietly grazing in the meadows. I kept my eyes peeled for a sighting, but wasn't so lucky. So, for now, I'm inclined to believe Keith. After all, anyone who is as significant a voice and catalyst in the Winter Park FATS as Keith is must know what he's talking about.

The High Lonesome Trail is part of the Continental Divide Trail, basically a single-track hiking trail that runs north to south, threading through some of Colorado's most spectacular terrain and wilderness areas. The bikeable portion of High Lonesome, also signed as the Continental Divide Trail, begins near Meadow Creek Reservoir, skirting the southwestern edge of the Indian Peaks Wilderness. Eventually, as this majestic path enters the wilderness area, we say goodbye to the single-track trail and pedal several jeep roads back to US 40 and to where we left a shuttle vehicle.

One last note about this fabulous trail. As you cruise through the forest, notice how the trail itself has been reinforced and maintained. At first glance, you may not notice the efforts of Amy Bauer and her dedicated U.S. Forest Service volunteer crew. That's because they went to great pains to restore the terrain to its natural appearance after reinforcing soft and waterlogged spots on

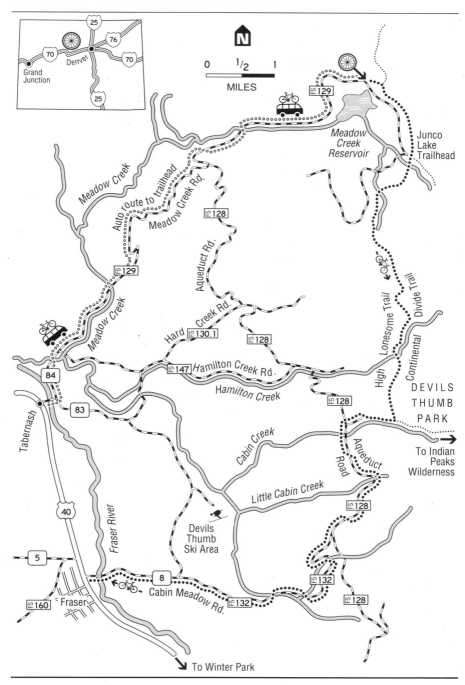

0   1/2   1
MILES

Grand
Junction

Denver

Meadow Creek

Auto route to trailhead

Meadow Creek Rd.

FS 128

Aqueduct Rd.

FS 129

Meadow Creek

Hard Creek Rd.

FS 130.1

FS 128

FS 147 Hamilton Creek Rd.

Hamilton Creek

FS 128

84

83

Tabernash

High Lonesome Trail

Continental Divide Trail

DEVILS
THUMB
PARK

Cabin Creek

Aqueduct Road

To Indian
Peaks
Wilderness

Meadow
Creek
Reservoir

Junco
Lake
Trailhead

FS 129

40

Little Cabin Creek

FS 128

Fraser River

Devils
Thumb
Ski Area

5

8

Cabin Meadow Rd.

FS 132

FS 132

FS 128

FS 160   Fraser

To Winter Park

A lot of muscle and sweat go into building and maintaining the trail. Just ask Amy Bauer of the U.S. Forest Service, and her crewmates Cindy and Cathy. Keith Sanders appreciates the work.

High Lonesome Trail. After implanting steel rivets and soil-stabilizing concrete blocks on top of plastic tarps, they returned the soil, moved humongous boulders back into place, reseeded the area, and replanted trees. So, when you enjoy this trail and others throughout the state, celebrate the generous heart and soul that preserved the trail—and do your part to maintain it.

General location: The beginning of this route is approximately 15.5 miles north of Winter Park, which is 67 miles northwest of Denver.

Elevation change: The trail begins at approximately 10,170′ adjacent to Meadow Creek Reservoir and climbs 230′ in 4 miles to the highest point, at 10,500′. After that, it's a downhill cruise to the lowest point of 8,850′, where the end shuttle vehicle is placed at the intersection of US 40 and County Road 8. Total elevation loss is 1,650′.

Keith cruises the single-track through tall pines and quiet mountain air. There's a reason why it's named High Lonesome.

Season: You can enjoy this ride generally between mid-May and late September. A midsummer ride is likely to reward you with meadows of brilliant wildflowers. In mid- to late September, you're sure to find the landscape showing off its autumn colors.

Services: Potable water and toilet facilities are not available at the trailhead or on the route. Though water is found at several spots—Meadow Creek Reservoir and several creeks—it must be treated before drinking. Camping is permitted in the national forest areas. All services are available in Fraser and Winter Park.

Hazards: The single-track portions of this ride are fairly level, with some short ascents and descents. The trail is rated as highly technical due to large boulders, tree roots, and water bars in the trail. Less experienced riders may frequently catch a pedal. Still, as both Keith and I agreed, an experienced novice with the right attitude and basic skills—including knowing when to dismount and walk—can enjoy this entire ride. A more experienced rider who endeavors to pedal the entire route without stopping will find this to be expert-rated terrain.

As there are a few wet, marshy areas along the High Lonesome Trail, you can expect man- and woman-eating vampires, also known as nasty mosquitoes. (I'm sure they would devour a child without hesitation, so I don't recommend this route for a young family ride.)

Lastly, be aware that on rare occasions, mountain lions and black bears and, more frequently, porcupines, have been spotted on the High Lonesome Trail.

Rescue index: Only 6 miles of this 14.5-mile ride is on single-track trails. The rest of the route uses two- and four-wheel-drive dirt roads. So, in an extreme situation where evacuation is required, you may be able to get out fairly quickly. Emergency medical attention can be found in Winter Park, with limited services in Fraser. Phones can be found in Fraser, and people living in the houses on the dirt roads near the end of the ride may be able to offer assistance.

Land status: Arapaho National Forest, Colorado state land, and private property.

Maps: Trails Illustrated® map: #102, Indian Peaks–Gold Hill. USGS 7.5 minute quads: Monarch Lake, Strawberry Lake, East Portal, and Fraser, Colorado.

Finding the trail: From the town of Winter Park, drive north on US 40 for 6 miles through Fraser, to the intersection of CR 83 on the east side of US 40. Turn right onto CR 83 and immediately make a left onto CR 84, a two-wheel-drive dirt road, following the sign to Devil's Thumb Ranch, Strawberry Road, and Meadow Creek Reservoir. The dirt road curves toward the northeast and begins its uphill journey to the reservoir. Stay on this road as it becomes Meadow Creek Road, Forest Service Road 129 and, after 7 miles, the reservoir will come into view. Follow the dirt road around the northwest side of the reservoir to a parking area that's marked with a High Lonesome and Continental Divide Trail sign. Park here and begin your ride by pedaling southward on the trail.

Sources of additional information:

Winter Park Resort
Winter Park Recreational Association
Box 36
Winter Park, CO 80482
(303) 726-5587
Or dial direct from Denver: 447-0588

The Winter Park / Fraser Valley Chamber of Commerce and Visitor Center
US 40 and Vasquez Road
P.O. Box 3236
Winter Park, CO 80482
(303) 726-4118
(800) 722-4118
Or dial direct from Denver: 442-0666

Sport Stalker/Sore Saddle Cyclery
Cooper Creek Square at US 40
Winter Park, CO 80482
(303) 726-8873
If you're lucky enough to find Keith Sanders on duty, ask him for other
biking suggestions to fit your skill and stamina levels.

Winter Park Fat Tire Society (FATS)
P.O. Box 1337
Winter Park, CO 80482
(303) 726-8044 or (800) 521-BIKE

Notes on the trail: The High Lonesome Trail and the Continental Divide Trail
(indicated by a black and blue triangular symbol) are one and the same
throughout most of the single-track portion. Hop onto this trail and follow it
around the eastern side of the reservoir, heading due south, and you immediately enter a dense forest of lodgepole pine and aspen. The view to the northeast is the Indian Peaks Wilderness. After a half-mile, cross an old logging road
and pick up the single-track trail again. Several yards farther is another
Continental Divide Trail marker, pointing left. Follow the sign and continue a
gentle climb over large tree roots, boulders, and water bars.

Emerge from the forest and pedal through wide open meadows. Note that the
trail through the meadows is not as well-defined, so look for cairns formed by
piles of stone or deliberately placed dead tree branches. Fluorescent orange
ribbons hanging from tree limbs are snowmobile trail markers, not necessarily
the bike trail. Keep your eyes peeled and cycle quietly and you be may rewarded
with elk, deer, and porcupine sightings and, if you're really lucky, a moose or
two. As you pedal farther, you begin to see blue spruce trees and, depending on
the time of the year, a profusion of wildflowers, including fuchsia-colored
Indian paintbrushes and blue lupine.

After pedaling almost 3 miles from the starting point, you reach 10,500'—
the high point of the route. From this spot, the terrain gradually descends.
When you cross Hamilton Creek, you've ridden just over 4 miles. Continuing
farther, you soon come to a huge wooden fence barrier. The sign on it declares:
"Open only to hikers, bikers, snowmobilers, and equestrians. No motor

bikes." Cross the creek again, bear left, and look for the trusty Continental Divide Trail marker posted on the narrow single-track. Stay on the narrow path, not the wider trail.

Cross another creek and about 1.5 miles from the fence barrier, say good-bye to the Continental Divide Trail as it forks to the left (east), toward Devil's Thumb Pass in the Indian Peaks Wilderness. At this point, bear right (west) and, after a short distance, you reach yet another creek, this one with a small dam across it. The single-track ends here, turning into a four-wheel-drive jeep road. As you pedal slightly farther down the road, you come to a T intersection where your road runs into Aqueduct Road (WB 128), another wide dirt road. (Incidentally, WB is the abbreviation for Water Board, as designated by the Denver Water Department.) Turn left onto WB 128 and follow it over roller-coaster terrain for several miles.

From here on out, your sense of direction and distance will be tested. Unmarked roads will begin to connect to your road more frequently and your maps may not show the new roads for the residential developments taking place here. Persevere and continue an easy cruise down to the valley, interrupted by a few short, steep climbs.

As you continue descending, the dirt road becomes wider and you begin to see evidence of logging activity. Follow the main road, bearing right at junctions and eventually catching glimpses of the Fraser Valley below. Farther down the road, the view of the valley becomes more expansive and you can identify Devil's Thumb Ranch and the tiny town of Tabernash. Looking across the valley, you can see Sheep Mountain (10,671') in the northwest and Byers Mountain (12,804') slightly southwest. Eventually, about 2.5 miles from the creek dam, turn onto CR 8, also known as FS 132 on the Trails Illustrated® map. Remember, other than a few small roller-coaster hills, you should be descending, basically due west, into the valley. You're on the correct road if you pass the dirt roads marked FS 807, FS 808, and Spruce Way. The closer you get to US 40, the more homes you see. Follow CR 8, still a dirt road, also known as Cabin Meadow Road. When you come to a Y intersection, don't take the left fork that leads to an area called Ptarmigan. Take the right fork that crosses the river and ends at US 40, where you left a shuttle vehicle. If you feel totally lost, you can always knock on any resident's door and ask for directions. Total point-to-point mileage is 14.5 miles.

RIDE 11 *CREEKSIDE, FLUME, AND CHAINSAW*

Wouldn't these make great names for dogs? That's what Nancy, my riding pal, and I thought. I can see it now—Creekside is a bloodhound, Flume is an Afghan, and Chainsaw is a little Chihuahua. Actually, Creekside is a level,

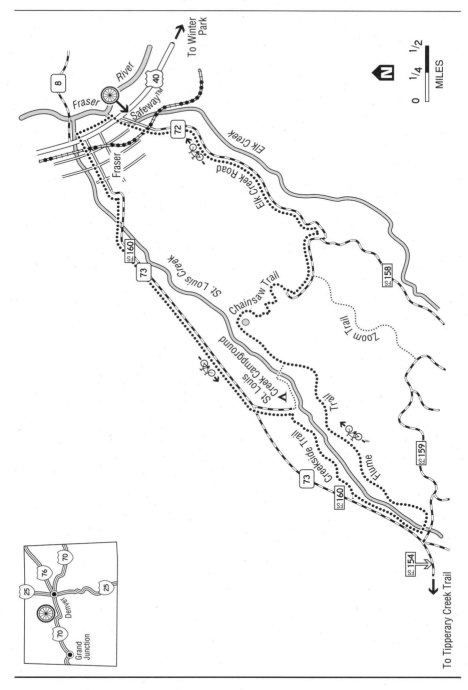

After soaking in the view of a peaceful meadow, Nancy
continues down the gorgeous single-track.

double-track trail running through a forest of aspen and pine, while Flume and
Chainsaw are fun narrow single-track trails weaving down and through a
dense, green forest. We intended to ride this route as a point-to-point by using
two vehicle shuttles. Though it was just as easy to leave our car in town and ride
this as a loop, we didn't feel like eating dust and dirt on a two-and-a-half-mile
stretch of a heavily traveled road. We're smart girls, or so we thought. I guess
we were so excited about the idea of riding here and savoring the fragrant
smells of the forest that we inadvertently left the keys to the end shuttle locked
in the top car! So, we wound up turning the ride into an 11-mile loop, completing it in under two hours.

This fun ride is rated moderately difficult, using single- and double-track
trails, old logging roads, two-wheel-drive gravel roads, and a short stretch on
pavement. Most of the ride is through densely forested terrain skirting the edge
of the Fraser Experimental Forest. If you're a quiet rider, with a bit of luck you

may see lots of wildlife, including moose, particularly near the beaver pond and in the open meadows. Portions of Flume and Chainsaw are thick with undergrowth, surrounding aspen and pine trees. It's so thick that visibility is limited, requiring you to be alert to avoid colliding with oncoming riders and hikers.

If you want to make your visit to the Fraser Valley a biking weekend and still keep costs low, consider camping at Saint Louis Creek Campground. You'll find basic conveniences here: drinking water, picnic tables, campfire rings, toilets, and trash dumpsters. Many other rides of the Winter Park–Fraser network are accessible from this camp, including the Tipperary Creek Classic route (see Ride 12, next chapter, for a description of this challenging ride). One last word of advice: if you plan to camp here, be forewarned that Fraser is known as the "Icebox of the Nation" because frigid air has a tendency to sit in this spot of the valley. Take my word for it, even in mid-August, camping here can be chillier than at other locations. And mornings greet you with an ice-cold smack in the face.

General location: This loop begins in the town of Fraser, which is about 3 miles north of Winter Park on US 40. From Denver, Fraser is approximately 69 miles due northwest.

Elevation change: Beginning at approximately 8,520′, the route climbs to the highest point at 9,080′ before gently cruising back to the starting point. Total elevation gain is 560′.

Season: You can enjoy this ride between late spring and midautumn, depending on prevailing snow conditions. Wildflowers in the meadows are quite showy typically in June, while from mid- to late September the Fraser Valley is painted with golds, reds, and greens. If you're interested in camping, note that the Saint Louis Creek Campground is open between Memorial Day and Labor Day.

Services: At the Saint Louis Creek Campground, near the Creekside trailhead, drinking water and toilets are available. Other services are available in Fraser and Winter Park, including food, restaurants, lodging, phone, gas, bike shops, and other retail stores. In fact, the starting point of this loop is the Safeway shopping center parking lot in Fraser. This is the ideal place to buy food (a picnic, perhaps?), fill your water bottles, and use the rest rooms. You can also grab a great cup of coffee—or cappuccino—at The Coffee & Tea Market, also at this location.

Hazards: As mentioned earlier, limited visibility while on Flume and Chainsaw can be hazardous. Because Mother Nature has abundantly covered the terrain with thick and tall, green undergrowth, it's possible not to see oncoming riders and hikers on the trail until it's too late. So, keep your speed under control and dismount to let hikers pass.

Another hazard to note here is vehicular traffic. The beginning and ending parts of the loop involve pedaling on pavement on busy US 40 and going through a well-traveled intersection (fortunately, it's controlled by signal lights). Elsewhere, CO 72 and CO 73 are frequently used two-wheel-drive gravel roads, and though they are wide roads, motorists tend to kick up a lot of dust and aggravate bikers—especially those of us who wear contact lenses. Some drivers realize it's no fun eating dust and will slow down as they pass you.

Rescue index: Other than the single-track trails of Flume and Chainsaw, all portions of the loop are two-wheel-drive accessible. So, if you need to be driven to get help, your chances are good for getting a ride. Chances are also good that you'll find people who can call for help or take you to the nearest medical facility in Fraser or Winter Park. Though there is no phone at St. Louis Creek Campground, phones can be found at many locations in Fraser, and you can try the nearby residents along Elk Creek Road, toward the end of the loop.

Land status: Arapaho National Forest and Fraser Experimental Forest.

Maps: Trails Illustrated® BikeMap: #503, Winter Park–Grand Lake. Trails Illustrated® map: #103, Winter Park, Central City, Rollins Pass. Even though the entire route is difficult to distinguish on it, #503 is the more complete and clearer of the two maps. It's not the map's fault that this trail is unclear, it's just that there are so many trails, it's hard to pinpoint this one. USGS 7.5 minute quads: Fraser and Bottle Pass, Colorado. Chances are these maps will not be current, and updates in the near future are unlikely.

Winter Park/Fraser Valley Mountain Bike Trail Guide. Published by Winter Park Resort and the Winter Park/Fraser Valley Chamber of Commerce. This is a useful little pamphlet that contains ride descriptions and maps. You can pick one up free in boxes attached to signs on the bike path throughout Winter Park, as well as from numerous merchants.

Finding the trail: From Winter Park, drive north on US 40 for about 3 miles to the Safeway shopping center. Leave your car here, parked along the outer edges of the lot.

Sources of additional information:

Winter Park Resort
Winter Park Recreational Association
Box 36
Winter Park, CO 80482
(303) 726-5587
Or dial direct from Denver: 447-0588

The Winter Park/Fraser Valley Chamber of Commerce and Visitor Center
US 40 and Vasquez Road
P.O. Box 3236
Winter Park, CO 80482
(303) 726-4118
(800) 722-4118
Or dial direct from Denver: 442-0666

Sport Stalker/Sore Saddle Cyclery
Cooper Creek Square at US 40
Winter Park, CO 80482
(303) 726-8873
Ask Keith Sanders or anyone on his staff for ride suggestions. A bike mechanic, if not several, is generally on duty.

Notes on the trail: Begin your ride from the Safeway shopping center by pedaling north on US 40 for a short distance to the intersection with a Quik-Stop gas and food store. Turn left here—watch out for the fast traffic—and follow the paved road over the railroad tracks. Make a left turn at any of the next several intersections, and pedal through a small residential section until the road runs into CO 73. Turn right here onto CO 73, which is also known as Forest Service Road 160. After a short distance, the pavement becomes gravel.

Pedal a very gentle 2.5 miles uphill on CO 73 to the left-hand turnoff to the Saint Louis Creek Campground, also marked as FS 160. Take this turnoff and travel about a half mile to a small clearing located just before the actual campground entrance. At this point, look for the Creekside Trail marker on your right.

Follow Creekside Trail as it meanders through a pine forest, following the route of Saint Louis Creek far off on your left. Stay on this level, mildly rugged, double-track trail for just over a mile. Watch for the trail to split, with one fork leading to the left through a more densely populated grove of trees, and the other connecting to a two-wheel-drive dirt road, FS 160. Follow the single-track as it threads through the trees alongside the creek. If you miss the fork and end up on the dirt road, turn left—you're basically still on the right track. The two paths parallel each other, separated by about 50 yards of trees and shrubs and, after nearly a mile, the two paths reconnect at a seemingly major intersection. (Incidentally, if you are pedaling on the dirt road, FS 160, you'll see that Tipperary Creek Road, FS 154, connects just before the major intersection.) The jeep roads of FS 160 and FS 159 make up this major intersection. (Note: Trails Illustrated® map #103 seems to have incorrectly labeled FS 159 as FS 163. However, Trails Illustrated map #503 and the *Winter Park/Fraser Valley Mountain Bike Trail Guide* have these two roads correctly listed.)

When you reach this unsigned junction, turn left onto FS 159, ride over East Saint Louis Creek, and immediately look to your left for the marked trailhead to Flume, a single-track trail. For all you eagle-eyed cyclists who found and followed the Creekside Trail single-track fork back there, the trail ends at this intersection.

Ready for some more single-track fun? Turn off onto Flume and enjoy a moderate descent through lush aspen and lodgepole pine forests. The trail is mostly dirt, with tree roots and lots of twists and turns. There's thick undergrowth along here and, in some areas, oncoming riders or hikers are difficult to see, so be alert. Follow this lovely, peaceful trail as it weaves through the forest and meadows. After nearly 2.5 miles, you reach the junction of a shortcut trail back to the Saint Louis Creek Campground. This is a good bail-out route if the weather's rotten or you want to shorten the loop.

Assuming you want to continue with the downhill fun, bear right onto the Chainsaw Trail. The single-track now becomes an old, double-track logging road, edged with lush undergrowth. Keep quiet, because after a half mile through the dense forest, you'll reach a small opening with a beaver pond and meadow and, if you're lucky, you might see a moose or other wildlife. Follow the trail as it leads you around the pond. Get ready to put your bike into a lower gear, because as the pond disappears behind you, the trail begins a steep but short quarter-mile climb.

When you reach the top of the climb, the forest is not quite as dense, and you'll see evidence of current logging activity. Fortunately, selective logging is practiced here, which means a number of trees are left uncut, leaving the forest an enjoyable area in which to ride. Stay on the main double-track logging road and, 1.25 miles from the beaver pond, find the signed Zoom Trail connecting with Chainsaw. (Vow to come back and partake of Zoom, another fun, challenging, single-track trail. At this junction, Zoom would be an uphill climb. To reach the top of Zoom, continue on FS 159 instead of turning left onto Flume. After about a mile, you'll find the top of Zoom leading off on your left.)

Continue your descent on Chainsaw and, after almost 3 miles, emerge from the forest into a large meadow. At this point, Chainsaw ends at Elk Creek Road (County Road 72), a wide, two-wheel-drive dirt and gravel road. Turn left onto Elk Creek Road, and follow it past ranch homes for a fast, easy, 2.5-mile descent to the starting point at the Safeway shopping center where you left your car.

RIDE 12 *TIPPERARY CREEK CLASSIC*

The Tipperary Creek Classic is the main event at the Winter Park Mountain Bike Festival hosted by the Winter Park Fat Tire Society, attracting hundreds of racers and spectators alike. The route also plays a starring role in the festival's "King of the Rockies" stage race (a bike competition—road or mountain—composed of multiple events, i.e. hill climb, cross country, and downhill, with individual-event and overall champions). This legendary ride was also named "Best Ride in Colorado" in 1988 by *Rocky Mountain Sports and Fitness* magazine (which also named Winter Park's trail system "Best Trail System in Colorado" in 1989).

Located only a few miles west of the Continental Divide, this route will engulf you with central Colorado's breathtaking terrain. Rugged 12,000′ peaks that overhang the pristine Fraser/Winter Park Valley dart into view through

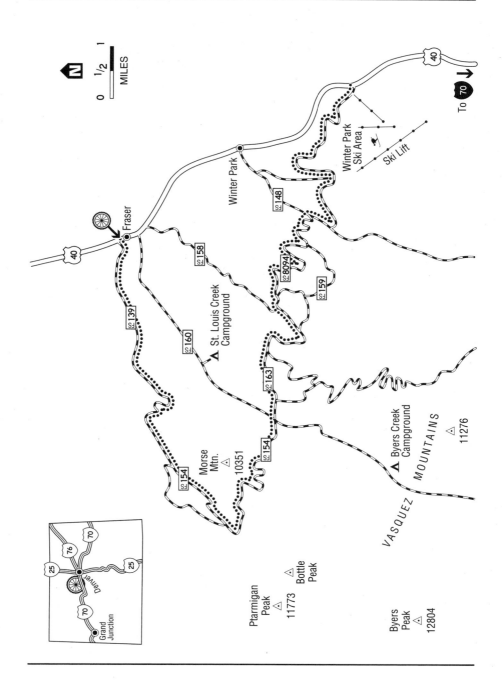

Plan on getting your toes wet along Tipperary Creek.
Photo: Winter Park FATS.

sporadic openings in the densely timbered canopy. And, from higher ground, frigid, crystal streams cut lush meadows or create ponds amidst fields of wild-flowers.

This 30-mile point-to-point ride covers a range of backcountry cycling terrain, with 80 percent of the route following single-track. Riders will experience the whole gamut of off-road alpine cycling conditions over the course of the riding season. Riders are advised to consider the strenuous nature of the Tipperary Creek tour and plan accordingly. Fortunately, a number of dirt roads and trails intersect the trail, allowing for a vast array of shortened versions of varying difficulty.

[Information on the Tipperary Creek Classic was provided by Kip Hubbard of the Winter Park Fat Tire Society.—G. B.]

General location: The Tipperary Creek Classic begins just west of Fraser, which is about 5 miles northwest of Winter Park, and ends at the Winter Park Ski Area.

Elevation change: The town of Fraser marks the route's lowest point, at about 8,600′. A few leisurely miles west of town the route begins its most arduous ascent, a 1,300′ rise up the Tipperary Creek drainage and across the top of Morse Mountain, the route's highest point at just over 10,000′. Countering this ascent is a brisk 1,000′ drop to Saint Louis Creek. The rest of the route is a giant roller coaster zipping between 9,000′ and 9,500′, marked by shorter but aggressive climbs over hills that divide the mountain's prominent drainages. Overall vertical gain approaches 3,000′.

Season: Seasonal snowfall will dictate the opening and closing of the summer mountain bike season, but trails are usually clear from late May or early June through October. Much of the Tipperary Creek Classic contours northeast-facing slopes, and these protected hillsides may harbor lingering snowdrifts and muddy conditions well into June.

Services: Winter Park and Fraser provide all visitor services. Along this trail, though, you will find no services. Fraser will be your last outpost to stock up on supplies. Streams are plentiful along the route, but their water should be purified before drinking. Potable water can be found at the Saint Louis Creek Campground.

Hazards: Riding Tipperary can be a major undertaking whether you are a novice or an advanced rider. Because of this trail's length and varied terrain, riders are cautioned to prepare thoughtfully before embarking. Of course, keep an eye on the changing and often unpredictable alpine weather, for afternoon storms are not uncommon.

Rescue index: Since Winter Park boasts more than 600 miles of mountain bike trails, it is common to find complete solitude on any given trail. Along this route, people tend to use the areas near Vasquez Creek and the Winter Park Ski Area. Other sections of the trail may be considered remote.

Both Fraser and Winter Park have medical clinics, and a fire station is located between the 2 towns. A volunteer mountain bike patrol, formed in cooperation with the Forest Service, polices Winter Park's trail system, but it cannot cover every trail each day.

Land status: Arapaho National Forest.

Maps: USGS 7.5 minute quadrangles: Bottle Pass and Fraser, Colorado. *Winter Park Fat Tire Trails Map,* by KRD Enterprises, Inc.

Finding the trail: From downtown Winter Park, pedal or car-top your bikes to Fraser, located about 5 miles northwest on US 40. On the north end of Fraser, turn left onto County Road 5, then left on CR 50, and park at the softball fields. Begin by pedaling west on CR 50. Soon it will become Forest Service Road 139, then FS 154 as the road parallels Tipperary Creek.

Sources of additional information:

Arapaho National Forest
Sulphur Ranger District
62429 US 40
P.O. Box 10
Granby, CO 80446
(303) 887-3331

Winter Park Fat Tire Society (FATS)
P.O. Box 1337
Winter Park, CO 80482
(303) 726-8044 or (800) 521-BIKE

AdventureWorks Mountain Bike Guide Service
P.O. Box 37
Winter Park, CO 80482
(303) 726-9192

Notes on the trail: From the softball fields in Fraser, head west on CR 5 and CR 50 (soon it becomes FS 139). Connect with the Tipperary Creek Road (FS 154, a double-track) and ascend the drainage. FS 154 turns south, rises through a saddle west of Morse Mountain, then drops to Saint Louis Creek. Zigzag on FS 160 and then FS 163, which cross the creek and pass the campground.

Continue on the logging road (the Flume) to its intersection with FS 158 (Elk Creek Road). Turn right and head southwest about .5 mile, then turn left onto a four-wheel-drive road that connects with FS 8094. An established single-track branches from FS 8094 to FS 8095, then to FS 148, a difficult single-track section (novice riders should just continue on 8094).

Follow FS 148 southwest (uphill) less than a mile, turn left on FS 8097 (cross Vasquez Creek), bear left at the next fork, and go left on Blue Sky Trail, heading into the forest and through the Winter Park Ski Area. Turn left on FS 156, then immediately right on Ice Hill Trail. Where the trail splits, go right up Procrastination and then right on Tracks Trail. A number of trails will bring you to the resort's base, but the easiest way is to branch left from Tracks Trail to Serenity and then back to Tracks Trail again in less than .5 mile. Now, follow Serenity to the base facilities. Yikes, where is my compass!

Granted, this twisting, angling course may rekindle unsettling memories of high school geometry, but all routes (whether Forest Service roads and trails or not) are marked with 4´ tall brown posts, most with a bicycle symbol.

Here are a few shortcuts to consider if your endurance and sense of direction begin to fail: Saint Louis Creek Road (FS 160) and Elk Creek Road (FS 158) each drop to US 40; Vasquez Creek Road (FS 148) will return you to the town of Winter Park.

RIDE 13 *VASQUEZ CREEK*

Looking for a route that's close to town, virtually traffic-free for youngsters, yet still interesting and satisfying for adults? Then round up the family and check out this easy eight-mile loop. Traveling on mostly two-wheel-drive dirt roads, the elevation gain is painless—approximately 613′ in almost 4.5 miles. Think of all the wonderful picnic sites your family can find as the trail cruises alongside lovely Vasquez Creek for most of the route.

Several options are available if you want to add more miles or test your bike handling skills. Option One is a 4-mile out-and-back spur, adding 8 miles to the original 4.5-mile loop. Option Two is a shortcut detour on a narrow, slightly technical, single-track trail. Neither option is recommended for children.

General location: Winter Park is about 67 miles northwest of Denver and 25 miles north of Interstate 70 on US 40.

Elevation change: Starting at 8,800′, the route climbs to a high of 9,413′, for a total elevation gain of 613′ in approximately 4.5 miles. The optional out-and-back spur climbs to about 10,160′, for an additional gain of 747′ in almost 4 miles.

Season: Enjoy this loop midspring through late autumn. The optional out-and-back spur is open between May 15 and November 1.

Services: All services are available in Winter Park, near the ride's starting point, including a public parking garage. Next to the garage is the Visitor Center, which, during business hours, provides water and toilet facilities. On the north side of the parking structure is Cooper Creek Square, a small shopping complex housing cafes, retail shops, and the Sports Stalker bicycle store. The folks at the Sports Stalker are friendly, and a bike mechanic is usually on duty.

Hazards: Watch out for vehicular traffic, especially on the 1 mile of paved road starting from the garage. Once you reach the dirt road and proceed farther from town, traffic thins out.

Rescue index: During the summer months, this is a popular road for hikers, campers, and bikers. Chances are good that someone may be of assistance. The nearest public phone is back in town, though there are a few homes within a mile or 2 from the start.

Land status: Arapaho National Forest.

Maps: Trails Illustrated® BikeMap: #503, Winter Park–Grand Lake. USGS 7.5 minute quads: Fraser and Berthoud Pass, Colorado. *Winter Park/Fraser Valley Mountain Bike Trail Guide.* Produced and published by the Winter Park Resort and the Winter Park/Fraser Valley Chamber of Commerce. Available from the Visitor Center and in boxes attached to signs along the bike path.

RIDE 13 *VASQUEZ CREEK*

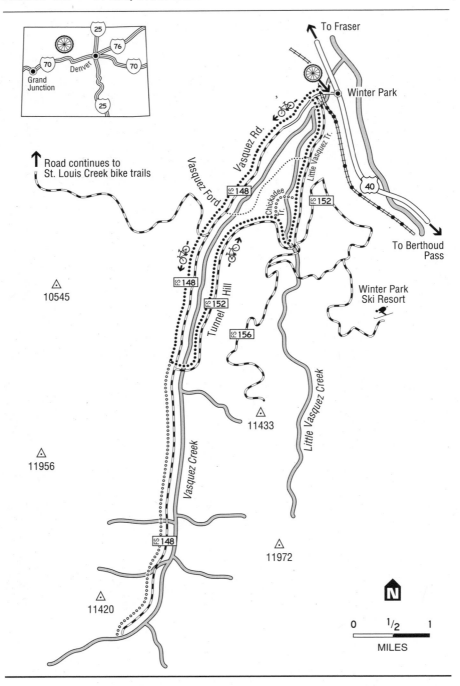

To Fraser

Winter Park

Road continues to
St. Louis Creek bike trails

Vasquez Ford

Vasquez Rd.

Little Vasquez Tr.

FS 148

Chickadee Tr.

FS 152

40

To Berthoud
Pass

⚠ 10545

Winter Park
Ski Resort

Tunnel Hill

FS 148

FS 152

FS 156

⚠ 11433

Little Vasquez Creek

⚠ 11956

Vasquez Creek

FS 148

⚠ 11972

⚠ 11420

N

0   ¹/₂   1
MILES

25

76

70

70

Denver

Grand
Junction

25

This smooth, wide trail is ideal for family outings with options that will please skilled riders.

Finding the trail: From the town of Winter Park, you can either drive or pedal to the start of this ride. This route begins at the public parking garage, next to the Visitor Center, at the intersection of US 40 and Vasquez Road on the west side of US 40.

Sources of additional information:

Winter Park Fat Tire Society (FATS)
P.O. Box 1337
Winter Park, CO 80482
(303) 726-8044 or (800) 521-BIKE

Sport Stalker/Sore Saddle Cyclery
Cooper Creek Square at US 40
Winter Park, CO 80482
(303) 726-8873

Winter Park/Fraser Valley Chamber of Commerce and Visitor Center
US 40 and Vasquez Road
P.O. Box 3236
Winter Park, CO 80482
(303) 726-4118
(800) 722-4118
Or dial direct from Denver: 442-0666

Notes on the trail: From the intersection of US 40 and Vasquez Road, start pedaling on paved Vasquez Road, due west. After a short distance, cross a set of railroad tracks. Continue on the road for almost a mile until it is replaced by a smooth, two-wheel-drive dirt road. Stay on the dirt road marked Forest Service Route 148 as it enters Arapaho National Forest. Listen—you can hear Vasquez Creek singing through the groves of lodgepole pine trees on your left.

Pedal up several short, gentle hills, bypassing a turnoff marked Vasquez Ford on your left. Continue on the main dirt road for a short distance to the fork marked FS 159. This is a major intersection with Elk Creek and Saint Louis Creek roads toward the right and "Vasquez Roadless" to the left. Why it's labeled "Roadless" is beyond me—as far as this ride is concerned, there are enough dirt roads and trails to make our intended loop. Continue left on FS 148 and vow to return to explore FS 159. (If you refer to any local mountain biking maps, you'll see that FS 159, Elk Creek, and Saint Louis Creek roads connect to the valley's vast network of bike trails.) At this point, you have ridden about 3 miles.

In the next couple of miles, the road climbs gently and remains fairly smooth and wide. Vasquez Creek continues to sing off to your left. Very soon thereafter, you reach a diversion dam in the creek and the intersection of FS 152 in an open space. Turn left onto FS 152, named "Tunnel Hill," cross over the creek, and climb a short distance as it curves back around almost 180 degrees. (Note that FS 148 continues straight, due south, toward a gate. This is the beginning of Option One, the out-and-back spur that was mentioned earlier. A more detailed description is presented at the end of this chapter.)

From this point on, you're in for an easy ride back down to Winter Park. As you rise above Vasquez Creek and treetops on your left, the Continental Divide spreads majestically in front of you. On your right are aspen, blue spruce, and fir trees, and you can still hear the creek singing below. Continue your downhill cruise and stay on the main road, FS 152, as there are a few trails taking off from this road. Say good-bye to Vasquez Creek as the road begins to curve to the right and your view expands to include the Winter Park Ski Resort.

After a short distance, a single-track trail sweetly named "Chickadee" connects to the road you're on. (This shortcut is Option Two, and it rejoins the main route after almost a mile of single-track. See description at end of chapter.) If you'd rather take the easier route, bypass this turn-off and stay on FS 152 as it continues to curve to the right and downhill.

If you continue following FS 152, at the bottom of the hill, cross over Little Vasquez Creek and take a left onto Little Vasquez Trail, a double-track path. After about a half-mile descent with Little Vasquez Creek on your left, the Chickadee Trail crosses the creek and rejoins your road. Continue on the double-track as it widens and cruises down through residential neighborhoods and terminates at paved Arapaho Road. Watch out for traffic as you follow Arapaho Road to Vasquez Road. Turn right on Vasquez and head back into town to your starting point.

Option One: The Out-and-Back Spur. This 4-mile segment, a continuation of FS 148, begins back at the diversion dam. The road is a very wide single-track and slightly more demanding on technical skills and stamina than the main trail. It's steeper, rockier, and strewn with loose gravel in spots. There are several creek crossings on primitive log bridges, and the trail may be riddled with ponds, depending on the last occurance of rain or snow. You may have to carry your bike, at least over the primitive log bridges. This is fun stuff for the experienced rider. A beginner would find it challenging. Eventually, the single-track becomes less obvious and somewhat overgrown. The trail ends in the gushing creek, within a tree-lined, lush, wide open area. From here, you can see the ridge of the Continental Divide (from right to left): Mount Nystrom (12,652´), Vasquez Peak (12,947´), Vasquez Pass, and Stanley Mountain (12,521´). What a lovely place to take a break before returning to civilization.

Option Two: Chickadee Trail. I don't recommend the Chickadee Trail to beginners because it's a bit steep with tight switchbacks, loose rocks, soft dirt, and an occasional low branch. Still, if you're up for the challenge, have at it. It's short and you can always dismount.

Steamboat Springs

RIDE 14 *GORE PASS LOOP*

For Stacie, Tim, and me, getting out of town took intensive planning and effort. We vowed that we would not let the spectacle of Colorado's autumn colors come and go without us paying tribute to them, even if it killed us. So, on our way to a relaxing weekend in Steamboat Springs, we decided to check out this loop ride, which we had heard was long, tame, but totally enjoyable. It sounded like the sort of ride we needed to decompress from the stresses of our jobs. The Gore Pass Loop was just what the doctor ordered: a 27.5-mile loop on jeep roads, threading in and out of serene forests of aspen, spruce, and pine, with lots of gradual climbs and exhilarating downhills. The hills were never severe and, actually, it felt good to be huffing and puffing and getting physical after weeks of demanding workdays. The trail required no technical skills, which was great because it allowed us to switch our brain cells to automatic pilot. If 27.5 miles sounds too long, an alternate road cuts the loop to only 18 miles.

When we rode this loop in early September, our timing was off—we were slightly too early to witness colorful fall foliage. But, what the heck. There was still the rest of the weekend to fulfill our goal. In any case, we came away from this loop feeling rejuvenated and just plain happy to be out of town.

General location: The loop is located approximately 108 miles northwest of Denver and nearly 55 miles south of Steamboat Springs. The trailhead itself is on CO 134, at Gore Pass, halfway between Interstate 70 and Steamboat Springs.

Elevation change: The ride starts at Gore Pass, 9,527´. Throughout the entire loop, the roads cruise up and down, eventually reaching the highest point of about 10,000´ and a low of 8,900´. Total elevation gain is approximately 1,100´ in 27 miles.

Season: A good time to ride this loop is between early May and mid-September. Though the autumn colors are gorgeous in the latter part of September and early October, take note that this is a popular area for hunting, which generally commences in September. For exact dates of the various hunting seasons, call the Colorado Division of Wildlife at (303) 297-1192.

Services: Drinkable water and primitive toilet facilities are available at 2 nearby campgrounds. The closest campground is Gore Pass, with 14 campsites, on CO 134 at FS 185, near the trailhead. Blacktail Creek Campground, also on

RIDE 14 *GORE PASS LOOP*

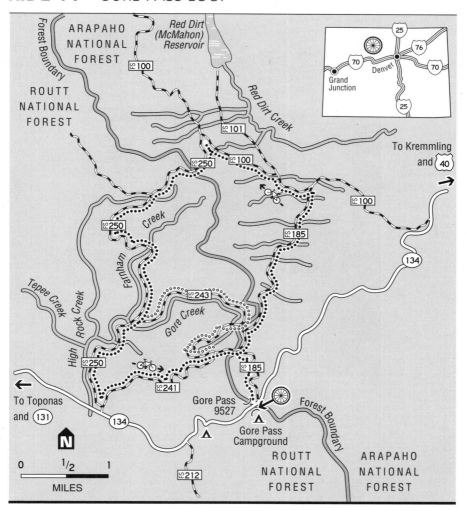

CO 134, is about 1 mile west of Gore Pass, with 8 campsites. Other camp-grounds—Lynx Pass and Toponas Creek—are several miles west of Blacktail Creek. Food and phones can be found in the nearby towns of Kremmling, 17 miles southeast on CO 134 and US 40, and Yampa, nearly 26 miles west of Gore Pass on CO 134 and CO 131. Steamboat Springs, located approximately 60 miles north of this trailhead on US 40, offers a variety of lodging and dining facilities, ranging from basic to world-class. All services can also be found in Granby, 37 miles east on US 40.

Tim and Stacie enjoy a leisurely downhill cruise through golden stands of aspen with the Continental Divide off in the distance.

Hazards: Sections of this loop have vehicular traffic. The short 2 to 3 mile segment on FS 100 is a popular access road to Red Dirt Reservoir. Some logging activity is allowed here, so be aware of humongous tree-hauling trucks. Avoid riding here during hunting season, between mid-September and mid-November.

Rescue index: Chances are good that you will not meet many people on this ride. So, if emergency attention is required, you'll have to ride back to your car or send someone to bring a vehicle to the injured person (the loop is comprised entirely of four-wheel-drive dirt roads). Note that if you need to call for assistance, the nearest phone is in Kremmling, 17 miles southeast of the trailhead, on CO 134 and US 40. You may get assistance from campers at the nearby campgrounds.

Land status: Routt National Forest. Arapaho National Forest.

Maps: Trails Illustrated® map: #119, Gore Pass. USGS 7.5 minute quads: Gore Pass and Tyler Mountain, Colorado.

Finding the trail: From Kremmling, travel north on US 40 to the junction of CO 134. Turn left, (west) onto CO 134 and drive 10 miles up to Gore Pass, at which point you'll come to a small clearing and find FS 185 leading off the north side of the road. Park your car in the clearing and begin cycling north on the dirt road, FS 185. Gore Pass Campground is on the south side of the road, less than a half-mile west of FS 185.

From Steamboat Springs, the loop is accessible from several directions. You can drive 49 miles south on US 40 to the junction of CO 134, and follow the directions as described above. An alternate route from Steamboat Springs is to drive south on US 40 for several miles, turn onto CO 131 and proceed south toward Yampa. From this turnoff point, travel approximately 38 miles to the junction of CO 134. Make a left (east) onto CO 134 and continue driving nearly 14 miles to Gore Pass and FS 185, as described above. Neither route from Steamboat is noticeably shorter or longer, but CO 131 is a quiet road that takes you through pleasant countryside.

Sources of additional information:

Routt National Forest
29587 West US 40, Suite 20
Steamboat Springs, CO 80487
(303) 879-1722

Arapaho National Forest
Middle Park Ranger District
210 South Sixth Street
P.O. Box 1210
Kremmling, CO 80459
(303) 724-9004

Sore Saddle Cyclery
1136 Yampa Street
Steamboat Springs, CO 80477
(303) 879-1675

Notes on the trail: You can ride this loop in either direction, as neither way is more strenuous. This description is counterclockwise. Begin this loop by pedaling north on FS 185, a four-wheel-drive jeep road, through sparse groves of aspen and pine. Throughout the first 5 miles, the road condition is mostly smooth dirt, accented with spots of loose rocks and erosion caused by rainstorms. At nearly 5.5 miles, FS 185 intersects FS 100, a two-wheel-drive, wide dirt road. Turn left (due northwest) onto FS 100.

Shortly thereafter, you reach the junction of FS 101, a smooth dirt road signed for Red Dirt Reservoir. FS 100 and FS 101 are popular access roads to the reservoir, so watch out for motor vehicles. Bypass FS 101, staying on FS 100 for almost 2 miles more, at which point the road intersects FS 250 indicated by a brown road sign. Hang a left onto FS 250, a jeep road, following it for the first half-mile as it climbs steeply and then levels out on top of a plateau, amidst a wide open clearing. Though FS 250 is not named here, it is known as Farnham Creek Road. Pedal on FS 250 for nearly 7 miles. Stay on the main jeep road, bypassing other roads that may connect to it. Cross over Farnham Creek and continue on FS 250. After several miles more, Farnham Creek Road is joined by FS 243, also identified at this junction as Gore Creek Road by another brown sign. Here is that alternate route that shortens the loop to about 18 miles: At this intersection, turn left onto FS 243 and follow it for nearly 6.5 miles back to FS 185. FS 243 is a lovely ride on an easy, smooth, dirt road that climbs ever so slightly and parallels Gore Creek. Once you reach FS 185, turn right and retrace the path back to your car.

If you choose to continue on the longer loop, go through the intersection of FS 250 and FS 243, staying on FS 250 due south along High Rock Creek and toward CO 134. After 3 miles, just before you reach CO 134, turn left (north) onto FS 241 and begin your last, gradual uphill climb of 4.5 miles to FS 185. When you reach FS 185, turn right (south) and return to your car, for a complete loop of approximately 27.5 miles.

RIDE 15 *RABBIT EARS PASS TO FISH CREEK FALLS*

Think you're a hot gonzo rider with exceptional mastery of technical skills? Then this ride's for you. Actually, almost everyone ranging from experienced novices to expert riders can enjoy most of this ride. It's the Fish Creek section of this route that's the monster—the acid test to see what you're made of. When Stacie and I rode the gonzo segment on a late September afternoon, it was so difficult that we began to think, "Maybe we're on the wrong trail. How could anyone possibly ride this stuff? Anyone who does has got to be quite the expert. Or suicidal." We were neither, but had a good attitude, strong stamina, and knew the limits of our abilities—that means we carried our bikes.

But, all you mere mortals, don't write this one off. As I mentioned before, the upper portion near Rabbit Ears Pass is a fabulous ride in itself, traveling on fairly level terrain through forests and meadows of wildflowers, and around subalpine lakes. In fact, most folks will enjoy this trail by riding it as an out-and-back, 9 to 10 miles one-way, for a total riding distance of almost 20 miles, depending on when and where you turn back. On the other hand, if you're unlike most folks, and want to ride the Fish Creek gonzo section, then you'll need to arrange a vehicle shuttle, one car at the beginning at Dumont Lake

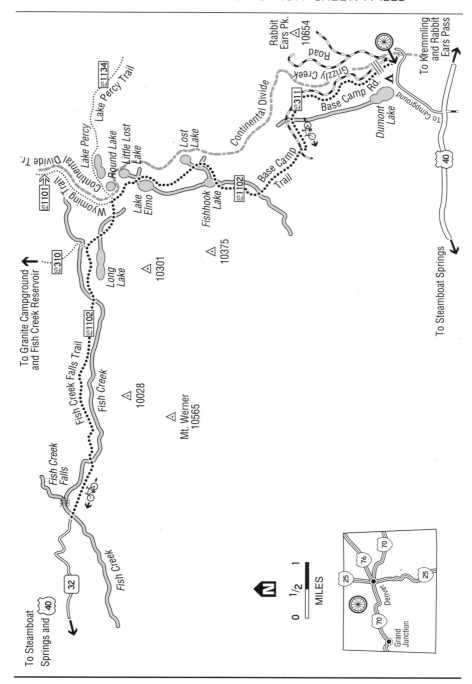

Campground, near Rabbit Ears Pass, and the other at the ride terminus in the town of Steamboat Springs. Total pedaling distance of this shuttle ride is about 16 miles.

To give you an idea of how tough the Fish Creek Trail was, let's just say we carried our bikes down a narrow, winding, single-track trail for nearly three miles, over humongous boulders and steep slopes. The mountainsides were covered with rich autumn colors, as if someone had spilled buckets of brilliant red, gold, and green paint on the landscape. Roaring Fish Creek sang to us as the Yampa Valley stretched ahead of us in the distance, twinkling its lights at us like homing beacons. It was downright stunning, and the terrain tested our moxie—and our night vision. When we drew near the end of the route, the trail led us under lush canopies of aspen and pine trees. Darkness fell quickly and we finished with barely enough light to walk, much less ride safely. Afterwards, I spoke with a couple of local mountain bikers who confirmed that we were indeed on the right trail and that some bikers actually *do* ride it. I thought, "Holy cow! You gotta be kidding me!"

General location: Steamboat Springs is about 157 miles northwest of Denver. The trailhead is at Dumont Lake Campground, just on the west side of Rabbit Ears Pass on US 40 and 24.5 miles southeast of Steamboat Springs. If you choose to ride the Fish Creek Falls gonzo section, the ride terminus is just on the eastern edge of town.

Elevation change: The trailhead starts at 9,573′ and gently climbs to 10,320′ within the first 4 miles, for a gain of 747′. After that, the next 7 miles to Long Lake are mostly level, with a few short, steep hills. If you ride the gnarly Fish Creek segment all the way back into town, the ending elevation is about 7,500′, for a total loss from start to finish of 2,820′.

Season: Try this ride between late May and mid-October. Because of the elevation, snow may linger on the trail well into spring, and light snow may fall as early as mid-September. During the summer, expect the area around lakes and meadows to be home to annoying mosquitoes. So, consider bringing your favorite insect repellant.

Services: Water and pit toilets are available at Dumont Lake Campground, where the trailhead begins. No phone is available. This lovely, well-maintained, popular campground has 22 sites, is accessible to the handicapped, and is open between mid-June and early October. A camping fee is charged. For day-users, there is a large picnic area adjacent to the lake, offering over 10 tables with fireplace grates. Other services, such as lodging, restaurants, phone, gas, and grocery stores are available in the resort town of Steamboat Springs, nearly 25 miles northwest on US 40.

Hazards: Other than the gnarly, 2- to 3-mile section along Fish Creek, the trail contains typical mountain biking hazards scattered throughout the route. Expect to encounter tiny, rock-filled water crossings, some footbridges that require dismounting, shallow potholes, fallen trees, exposed tree roots, and annoying, blood-sucking mosquitoes. Be aware of possible thunder and lightning storms, especially during the first 4 to 5 miles over exposed terrain. If you tackle the Fish Creek section, bionic physical and mental endurance is required. You need to be able to assess the limits of your technical skills, realistically and constantly. Three to four miles of this kind of terrain can be a long, draining challenge.

Rescue index: Except for a few miles at the start of the ride, this route is mostly single-track and is inaccessible to most vehicles. So, if you get in an emergency situation, you'll have to bike or hike back out to Dumont Lake Campground and find help there, or drive to Steamboat Springs, nearly 25 miles northwest on US 40. Another possibility, if you're near Long and Round lakes, is to locate FS 310 and hike or bike it for several miles to Granite Campground, near Fish Creek Reservoir, where you may find assistance from campers and other folks enjoying the lake. If you're near the gnarly Fish Creek section, my suggestion is to *hike* down (due west) 2 to 3 miles, toward the Falls, where you're likely to find hikers or tourists who may be of assistance. I don't recommend biking this treacherous section on your way to get help, as your chances of additional injury will be greatly enhanced by the stress of the existing emergency situation.

Land status: Routt National Forest.

Maps: Trails Illustrated® map: #118, Steamboat Springs South. USGS 7.5 minute quads: Rabbit Ears Peak, Mount Werner, and Steamboat Springs, Colorado.

Finding the trail: The trailhead is found at Dumont Lake Campground, which is located on the north side of US 40, almost 2 miles west of Rabbit Ears Pass. The campground is marked with a U.S. Forest Service sign for Routt National Forest, and the paved road leading into the site is Forest Service Road 315. Follow the road for almost 2 miles as it curves eastward, passing meadows of brilliant wildflowers and offering you a splendid view of Rabbit Ears Peaks. Eventually, on the north side of the road, you see a boulder monument commemorating Rabbit Ears Pass. Turn here, drive past this stone marker, and park near the wooden gate. Begin your ride here by cycling through the large gate (not the trail to the right of it) and onto FS 311, Base Camp Road.

Sources of additional information:

Routt National Forest
29587 West US 40, Suite 20
Steamboat Springs, CO 80487
(303) 879-1722

Notes on the trail: Once you park your car and pass through the wooden gate, you're on Base Camp Road, FS 311, a four-wheel-drive jeep road. For the first several miles, as you ride towards the northwest, the dirt road gradually climbs to just over 700′, threading through open meadows, marshy patches, and groves of evergreen trees. This is easy terrain with simply exhilarating wide open spaces. After 4.5 miles, look for a single-track trail that leads into the woods, off on your right. That's FS 1102, the Base Camp Trail. (You may find parked cars at this trailhead.)

Take Base Camp Trail, continuing due north for about 1 mile to Fish Hook Lake. Go about half a mile farther on the single-track and reach Lost Lake. Pedal just over 1 mile more and you come to Lake Elmo, with Little Lost Lake several yards beyond it. Keep pedaling, and in another half mile you reach Round Lake.

At Round Lake, amidst a pine forest, you arrive at the 4-way intersection of Lake Percy Trail (FS 1134), the Wyoming Trail (FS 1101, the Continental Divide Trail, continuing straight ahead from the trail you're on), and the beginning of Fish Creek Trail (FS 1102). Hang a left onto Fish Creek Trail, a single-track, and follow it westward about half a mile to Long Lake. Continue on the trail as it skirts the north side of the lake. Bypass an unmarked trail leading off to the left, near a tall post with some sort of solar panel on it. Several yards later, you reach the junction of another trail with a directional sign indicating that Fish Creek Falls is off to the left. On your right is another trail that takes you to Fish Creek Reservoir and Granite Campground, via the Divide Road (FS 310). This is where we separate the expert rider and suicidal gonzo from the average mountain bike enthusiast. You can follow FS 1102 toward the Falls for about 3.5 miles, at which point you'll reach the gnarly section I spoke of earlier, and eventually descend back into town where you have placed a shuttle vehicle. Or, you and your sane friends can turn around and return the way you came. Or, if you have the time, consider exploring the route to Fish Creek Reservoir (and Granite Campground) and the Wyoming Trail, which you passed earlier. (See the next chapter on Ride 16, the Wyoming Trail, for additional routing possibilities.) Whichever route you choose, you're sure to agree that this outing was worth your efforts.

RIDE 16 *WYOMING TRAIL*

The Wyoming Trail is part of the Continental Divide National Scenic Trail. Unlike other portions of the Continental Divide, which are defined by towering rock pyramids and formidable terrain, this section is marked by subdued peaks and lush fields surrounding sparkling alpine ponds. On the northern skyline, however, you will catch a few retreating glimpses of the Mount Zirkel Wilderness Area—a postcard-perfect representation of the rugged Central Rocky Mountains.

Besides good vistas of the surrounding mountains, this trail offers a few outstanding canyon views—down Fish Creek near Long Lake and the steep-walled North Fork of Fish Creek.

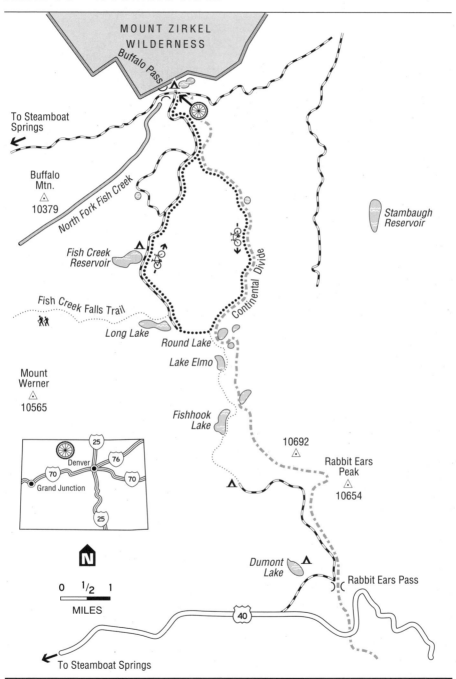

MOUNT ZIRKEL
WILDERNESS

Buffalo Pass

To Steamboat
Springs

Buffalo
Mtn.
△
10379

North Fork Fish Creek

Stambaugh
Reservoir

Fish Creek
Reservoir

Continental Divide

Fish Creek Falls Trail

Long Lake

Round Lake

Lake Elmo

Mount
Werner
△
10565

Fishhook
Lake

10692
△

Rabbit Ears
Peak
△
10654

Denver

25

76

70

70

Grand Junction

25

10

Dumont
Lake

Rabbit Ears Pass

N

0   1/2   1

MILES

40

To Steamboat Springs

Nearby, Mount Zirkel Wilderness Area rises above the tree tops. Photo: Gregg Bromka.

The Wyoming Trail is considered intermediate in cardiovascular difficulty, due mainly to its 10,000′ elevation. Visitors from the lowlands may find even gentle inclines unusually difficult. This 15-mile clockwise loop is a combination of well-traveled single-track, four-wheel-drive roads, and improved dirt roads suitable for passenger cars. Overall, the route is low in technical difficulty except for a mile-long stretch of rocky single-track between Grizzly and Round lakes.

General location: The trailhead is located about 14 miles northeast of Steamboat Springs on the Continental Divide.

Elevation change: This portion of the Wyoming Trail begins at Buffalo Pass near Summit Lake and Campground (10,300′). Within the first mile, the route rises to its highest point of 10,520′. Then it continues for several miles over rolling terrain. Past Granite Campground on the shore of Fish Creek Reservoir, the path dips to its lowest point of 9,870′. A 2-mile, moderate but consistent climb leads back to the trailhead.

Season: Typical of high elevation trails in Colorado, this route has a relatively short riding season, opening in late June to early July and closing by early October. Wildflowers reach their peak as late as mid-July. As can be expected, afternoon storms are common and are usually accompanied by cold temperatures and possibly lightning. Since the area is fairly moist, bugs are prevalent during midsummer.

Services: No services or potable water are available along the route. Purify surface and lake waters before drinking them. Developed camping (but no water) is available at Summit Lake and Fish Creek Lake. Steamboat Springs has all visitor services and a hospital.

Hazards: Downed timber may block the single-track, especially early in the season. Portions along the Continental Divide may be wet and swampy early in the season when snow is melting. A short stretch of rocky terrain along the Divide may make bike handling difficult, and expect a bit of dust to be kicked up by passing motorists along the dirt road between Fish Creek Reservoir and Buffalo Pass. Do not forget insect repellant during early to midsummer!

Rescue index: The number of trail users is variable along the Continental Divide single-track segment. Campers, hikers, and fishermen are common near Fish Creek Lake and Granite Campground as well near the route's beginning at Buffalo Pass and Summit Lake and Campground.

Land status: Routt National Forest.

Maps: USGS 7.5 minute quadrangles: Buffalo Pass, Rabbit Ears Peak, and Mount Werner, Colorado. (These quadrangles may not show the trail system accurately since they are out of date.)

Finding the trail: From downtown Steamboat Springs, turn north on Third Street (signed for Fish Creek Falls), turn right on Oak, then left on Amethyst Drive. Amethyst weaves through the foothills, then past the middle school. Follow signs for Strawberry Park/Hot Springs, then turn right on County Road 38, signed for Buffalo Pass. Follow about 10 miles of combined smooth, washboard, and rough dirt roads, suitable for passenger cars if driven cautiously. A parking area is provided at Buffalo Pass.

Sources of additional information:

Routt National Forest
29587 West Highway 40, Suite 20
Steamboat Springs, CO 80487
(303) 879-1722

Hahns Peak Ranger District
P.O. Box 771212
57 10th Street
Steamboat Springs, CO 80477
(303) 879-1870

Notes on the trail: Begin this ride at Buffalo Pass and pedal south and uphill on Forest Service Road 310 about 1.5 miles to a junction with the Wyoming Trail (Forest Service Trail 1101), which forks to the left. Turn left and ride the single-track 5.5 miles south through rolling terrain, meadows, and occasionally challenging rocky conditions to the junction with Trail 1102. Turn right (west) and descend moderately 1 mile to Long Lake. A four-wheel-drive road heads northwest away from the lake to a junction a mile ahead. Follow either the single-track or the jeep road; they both arrive at Fish Creek Reservoir near Granite Campground. From here, simply return to the parking area 5 miles away, by heading uphill on FS 310.

The route hovers right at timberline, where pockets of fir and spruce forests line succulent sedge meadows. (Sedge is not to be confused with sage—a stout bush denoting dry regions. Sedge is a thick grass restricted to moist, cool, highland areas.) The predominance of rich greenery is interrupted by pastel wildflowers, including paintbrush, columbine, lupine, bluebell, and snow lily.

Below, the town of Steamboat Springs rests quietly amidst the tranquil Yampa River Valley, a picturesque valley rich in natural mineral springs. In the mid-1800s, according to legend, 3 French trappers first heard one of the gurgling hot-water spouts and declared, "There's a steamboat, by gar!" Today, many of the springs may be visited, and several have been developed into soaking pools.

A visit to Steamboat Springs would not be complete without a trip to Fish Creek Falls, a thundering cascade crashing through a narrow canyon. A short footpath leads to 2 misty viewpoints, and a moderately strenuous hike leads above the falls and farther upstream.

RIDE 17 *MAD CREEK LOOP*

If there was ever a quintessential Colorado woman, it would be my friend Mary Yamamoto. After seeing many parts of the world by bike, she calls Steamboat Springs her home. And with good reason. What every mountain bike enthusiast dreams of is in her backyard. She showed me her secret fishing hole in a newly designated wilderness area and took me on a lovely mountain bike ride along Mad Creek. Had it not been for our work schedules, we might still be out there exploring and enjoying other rides in her backyard.

Mary's Mad Creek Loop is a delightful six-mile ride, starting along Mad Creek and ending on a paved stretch of CO 129. Comprised of mostly single-track, well-defined trails, the route requires moderate technical skills and some climbing endurance. It isn't an intense, mentally demanding route—we were able to catch up on conversations while riding. The path skirts tame drop-offs for about a mile, threads through pleasant, serene forests, and finishes with a one-mile ride on tree-lined pavement—just the sort of terrain that keeps experienced novices and intermediate riders happy.

While you're in Steamboat Springs and in need of bicycle repairs or accessories, check out Sore Saddle Cyclery. With any luck, you may find Mary working there instead of playing in her backyard. Don't hesitate to ask her or any of the other good folks at Sore Saddle for other trail suggestions.

General location: The trailhead is about 8.5 miles north of Steamboat Springs, on CO 129, towards the tiny town of Clark.

Elevation change: From the parking lot, the trailhead begins at 6,763´ and climbs 877´ to a high point of 7,640´ in just over 3 miles. After the first 2 miles, there is a short section that climbs 420´ in less than a half mile. Other than that, the elevation gain is painlessly gradual.

Season: The best time to ride this is between late April and mid-October, depending on the snow conditions. Autumn here is a painter's dream, as the hillsides display a thousand shades of golds, reds, and greens.

Services: Except for ample car parking, no services are available at the trailhead. Your nearest source for water, food, toilet, and phone is in Steamboat Springs, about 8.5 miles south. Because it's a world-class ski resort, you'll find lots of lodging and restaurants too. The little town of Clark, about 15 miles north of the trailhead on CO 129, has limited service.

Hazards: The trails comprising this loop are basically single-track, varying from narrow to wide throughout the route, and are popular with hikers and horseback riders. That means you'll need to control your speed around curves and dismount to let others pass. Rattlesnakes have been spotted, particularly around the rocky portions near the trailhead. Watch out for motor vehicles on the last 1.5 miles of the loop, which is paved road. Fortunately, this section is not heavily traveled, and there is a small shoulder on which you can ride comfortably in single file.

Rescue index: Should you need emergency first-aid assistance, you may be able to find someone at the ranger house, near the junction of the Mad Creek Trail (officially called Swamp Park Trail, Forest Service Road 1100) and the Saddle Trail (FS 1140). This trail sees only moderate use, so don't count on other trail users being around to help. Depending on where you are on the loop and the severity of the situation, you should either make your way back to the trailhead and drive back into Steamboat Springs, or attract the help of a passing motorist.

Land status: Routt National Forest.

Maps: Trails Illustrated® map: #117, Clark, Buffalo Pass. USGS 7.5 minute quad: Mad Creek, Colorado.

Finding the trail: From Steamboat Springs, drive north through town on US 40. After several miles, CO 129 connects to US 40 at a T intersection. Turn right here (north) onto CO 129 and drive about 6.5 miles, at which point, on your right, you'll see the Swamp Park Trailhead parking lot alongside Mad Creek. Park here and begin the ride going up the rocky, single-track trail.

Sources of additional information:

Routt National Forest
29587 West US 40, Suite 20
Steamboat Springs, CO 80487
(303) 879-1722

RIDE 17 *MAD CREEK LOOP*

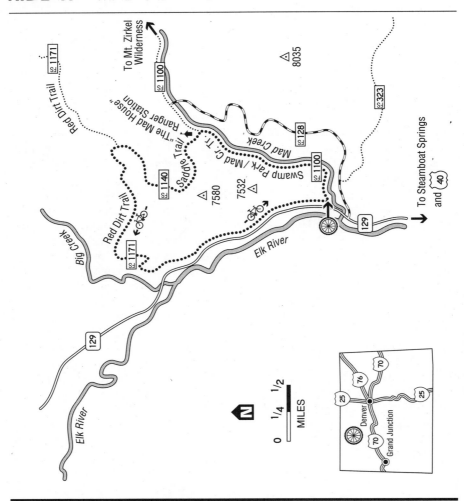

Sore Saddle Cyclery
1136 Yampa Street
Steamboat Springs, CO 80477
(303) 879-1675

Notes on the trail: The ride begins from the Mad Creek parking lot by climbing over a rocky segment along the creek. This is the Mad Creek Trail, also
called the Swamp Park Trail (FS 1100), and it starts off as a wide single-track,

Between Mary and the dark evergreen trees on the mountainside, about 100´ below, is roaring Mad Creek.

becoming narrow in some sections. It's not a long or steep climb, and experienced novices may find the loose gravel a test of their traction skills. The surrounding terrain is a mixture of boulders with dense evergreen trees and shrubs all around. As Mad Creek rushes by and the trail gradually leads you higher, views of the creek below and the valley beyond become more stunning. You'll find yourself just happy to be here.

After riding the trail for about 1.5 miles, Saddle Trail (FS 1140) joins Swamp Park Trail on the left. The intersection is marked by a wooden sign. Continuing straight on Swamp Park Trail takes you past the Mad House—the forest ranger station—and, after 2 miles, to the Mount Zirkel Wilderness boundary. If you want more mileage, ride this portion to the boundary as an out-and-back.

Meanwhile, back at the intersection: take Saddle Trail to your left as the sign directs. Now begins the moderate climb. Your granny gear might be needed, but rest assured that it's for only a half mile. Before you know it, you've reached a saddle and the trail levels out. Cruise on for another half mile and then begin the last, short climb to Red Dirt Trail (FS 1171). (Here's another opportunity to add mileage to your outing. If you hang a right onto Red Dirt Trail and follow it for almost 3 miles, you'll reach the Mount Zirkel Wilderness boundary. Take note, though, this is one heck of a climb, gaining 1,000´ in nearly 1.5 miles.) Otherwise, turn left (west) onto Red Dirt Trail and coast 2 miles down to CO 129. At CO 129, a paved road, go left (south) and continue for just over a mile back to the Mad Creek trailhead. The loop, without the optional out-and-back to the wilderness boundary, is 6 miles.

RIDE 18 *GREENVILLE–REED CREEK LOOP*

Here's a loop that can be enjoyed by riders who have moderate stamina and basic bike handling skills. For the most part, Stacie, Tim, and I considered this 11-mile route to be fairly easy and generally level. Sound boring? Not in the least. A couple of ingredients added spice to this route.

First, there's the elevation gain of about 600´. But, since this loop is 95% flat, that can have only one meaning: the climbs are extremely steep and mercifully short. This endurance challenge should keep you awake.

Second, it's likely that roads will be deeply tire-rutted, guaranteed to test the alertness and the bike handling skills of all riders, especially on fast descents. And the likelihood of ruts also means that the roads are tire-devouring mud traps during wet weather—just the thing to stop you dead in your tracks, throwing you off balance and landing one foot in the mud. For experienced riders, these are the sorts of obstacles that make mountain biking so much fun.

Third, there is a slight inaccuracy in the maps and the corresponding mileage. We rode with the Trails Illustrated® map and two cyclometers (for automatic mileage counts). A section of the map simply threw us for a loop, so to speak, because it didn't jive with our mileage readings and the road signs we found at various intersections. We encountered roads that were not identified on the map or by signs, and that added to our map-reading confusion. (Don't get me wrong, though. I love the Trails Illustrated® maps. They are, by far, the most accurate and most up-to-date maps available, and this one is still the best map to have on this outing.) Other maps were no help in solving this mystery. Nevertheless, the road signs were well placed, and we were able to find our place on the map again, after following our noses for a mile or two. Though we may have taken an alternate spur, we never had to backtrack and never actually got lost. In fact, it was kind of fun, testing our directional and mileage instincts, and map-reading skills.

So, go out and enjoy this ride—it's still an adventure. Maybe you'll discover an interesting detour.

General location: The start of this loop is just over 3 miles east of the tiny town of Clark, which is approximately 16 miles north of Steamboat Springs, on CO 129. Steamboat Springs is 166 miles northwest of Denver.

Elevation change: This loop begins at 8,269′ and immediately climbs to the highest point, 8,600′, within the first mile, for a gain of 331′. After that, the route travels up and down, gradually dropping to the lowest point, 8,000′, after 7 miles. Other than the initial climb, there are no steep ascents or descents—a pleasant, generally level ride. Total elevation change is 600′.

Season: Steamboat Springs's legendary snow conditions make this loop accessible from mid-June to late October—a short season, to be sure. Take note that this is a popular area during hunting season, which begins in mid-September.

Services: Water, food, and toilet facilities are available at the country store in Clark, and your patronage is appreciated by the owners. Be forewarned, though, business hours may vary. The Home Ranch, a guest ranch, offers luxurious lodging in cabins (reservations recommended). You'll find all services, including food stores, restaurants, lodging, and shops, in Steamboat Springs, about 16 miles south of Clark, on US 40. The Steamboat Springs Chamber Resort Association operates a general reservation board that includes virtually all lodging in the valley, covering all price ranges. They can be reached at (800) 922-2722. For camping, you can choose from many public and private campgrounds. Though not required, reservations can be made for many campgrounds in Routt National Forest by calling (800) 283-CAMP. For privately operated campgrounds, contact the Steamboat Springs Chamber of Commerce, (303) 879-0880.

Hazards: The loop is comprised of mostly four-wheel-drive jeep roads and old logging roads. These roads have occasional traffic, particularly from cattle ranchers, so expect the trails to be deeply rutted in spots. Hunting season is generally mid-September through November. Personally, I wouldn't be caught dead here at that time, but if you really want to add a thrill to this otherwise tame ride, be my guest. If you do, dress appropriately—that is, wear bright, neon, blaze-orange clothing.

Rescue index: Though this is an easy 9.75-mile loop, remember that it's still a long ways back to civilization. Since the entire route is accessible by four-wheel-drive vehicle, emergencies are generally less threatening. The nearest phone is in Clark.

Land status: Routt National Forest and private land.

Maps: Trails Illustrated® map: #117, Clark, Buffalo Pass. USGS 7.5 minute quads: Floyd Peak and Clark, Colorado.

Finding the trail: From Steamboat Springs, drive north through town on US 40. After several miles, Colorado 129 connects to US 40 at a T intersection. Turn right (north) onto CO 129 and travel about 15 miles to the little town of Clark. Leading off on the right (east) side of CO 129 is a two-wheel-drive dirt road, Forest Service Road 440, also known as Greenville Road. Turn here and travel on Greenville Road for approximately 3 miles, where you eventually

RIDE 18 *GREENVILLE–REED CREEK LOOP*

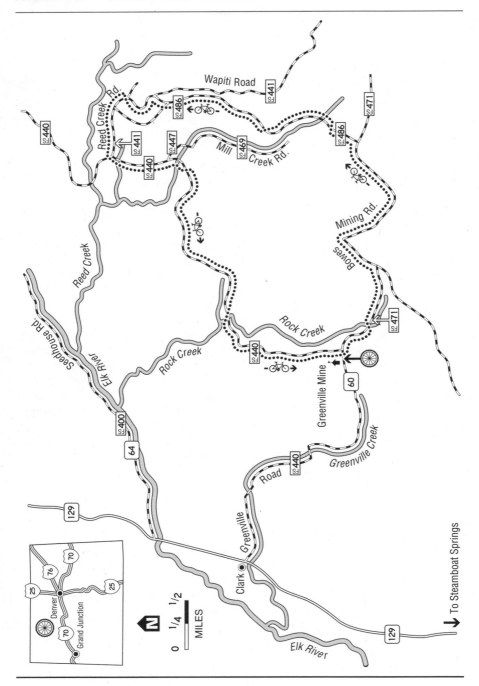

Imagine cruising through towering groves of golden aspen set against a deep blue sky, with the crisp, sunny chill of autumn in the air.

reach a gate at the junction of FS 440 and FS 471. Park here and start riding the loop from this point.

Sources of additional information:

Routt National Forest
29587 West US 40, Suite 20
Steamboat Springs, CO 80487
(303) 879-1722

Sore Saddle Cyclery
1136 Yampa Street
Steamboat Springs, CO 80477
(303) 879-1675

Notes on the trail: You can ride this loop in either direction. By riding it counterclockwise, you tackle the toughest climb in the first half mile. If you pedal the loop clockwise, you save this steep section as a fast, short, downhill run back to your car. Still, what goes up must come down. Though the clockwise direction works your climbing muscles more than the counterclockwise way, the change in terrain is so gentle that it's not a significant difference overall.

Here's the ride presented in the counterclockwise direction: Begin the loop by pedaling southeast on FS 471, through the cattle gate. The road immediately starts a steep climb. Don't despair—it's only a half mile long. At the top of the climb, among aspen, pine, and conifer trees, the road levels out considerably, just enough to let you catch your breath. Continue on for another half mile, being aware that there are several dead-end logging roads leading off from FS 471. Stay on the main road, FS 471. Within a half mile from the top, you reach the marked intersection of FS 468. Watch out for a primitive wire gate across the road! We didn't see the gate until we were practically snared by it. At this point, you have pedaled just over a mile. You're now at approximately 8,400′, traversing a gently sloping mountainside, and the clearing gives you an open view toward the Big Creek valley on the southwest horizon.

Turn left (north) onto FS 468. It's another four-wheel-drive road, probably with jeep tire ruts that are just deep enough to keep you alert and challenged. The road now takes you over the ridge, beginning a 3-mile downhill run through both dense and sparse forests of aspen and evergreen. The urge to fly down this stretch is strong, but watch out for the tire ruts, especially as you ride through alternating sunny and shadowy portions of the road.

At 3 miles from where you turned onto FS 468, you reach the junction of FS 441. I must confess, however, that when we rode this route, we were somewhat lost in that the maps didn't seem to jive with what we encountered. We weren't too concerned, however, because it was the unexpected road signs we found at the intersection that first made us suspect the accuracy of the maps. Instead of consulting the map through this confusing section of the route, we just followed the direction of several road signs marked FS 441. So, what you need to do is go left at the first signed FS 441 junction, a fairly smooth, two-wheel-drive road.

After almost a half mile, you reach another junction, (which we suspected was Reed Creek Road). By now, you will have ridden about 7 miles from where you parked your car. Go left (west) for another half mile and you come to a clearing with the signed intersection of FS 441 and FS 440. Make a left turn onto FS 440 and follow it for almost 2 miles, to the marked junction of FS 447. Bypass this road, as well as other unmarked roads, staying on FS 440. By now, the route has become a four-wheel-drive, tire-rutted road again, taking you through a small, open valley.

Almost 10 miles into the ride, the road takes you up a gut-wrenching, steep climb. Maybe when you ride this portion there won't be deep tire ruts to tax your uphill battle, like there were for us. Fortunately, this heart-throbbing stretch is short—less than a quarter mile. After you make it to the top, continue on for the next half mile back to your car, cruising up and down through aspen groves and serene, small meadows. Total mileage of this loop, at least according to my cyclometer, is about 11 miles. So what if the maps were slightly off? It was still a fun ride, spiced with a pinch of exploring and map-reading challenges.

Summit County

RIDE 19 *SNAKE RIVER–STS. JOHN LOOP*

If you enjoy that "top of the world" sensation, this is your ride. Rugged peaks highlight the entire route, and the view from Teller Mountain is filled with mountains, mountains, and more mountains. From the ride's high point, surrounding ridges open up to wide and rolling expanses. Hardy tundra plants cover the landscape, and ice-carved valleys drop in all directions.

The old townsite of Sts. John (originally designed to duplicate the founder's hometown of Boston) was the site of Colorado's first silver strike in 1863. During the area's heyday in the 1880s, the surrounding valleys and mountains were some of the most heavily mined areas of Summit County. Rubble from these mining endeavors dots the mountainside, especially in the Sts. John drainage, which hosted many successful operations. Although hopeful fortune-seekers continue to stake their claims, it is the United States Backcountry Association that occupies one of the townsite's last remaining structures.

This 14-mile, advanced-level loop has many lengthy ascents and fast-paced descents, all at elevations between 10,000′ and 13,000′. The four-wheel-drive roads that comprise the route are frequently covered with loose and imbedded rocks and may be gouged with deep ruts. These conditions demand a solid grasp of technical skills. Some climbs are steep enough to require walking, while a few descents call for intense concentration.

[This trail description was submitted by Laura Rossetter,* Silverthorne, Colorado.—G. B.]

General location: This route originates near the small town of Montezuma, located about 6 miles east of Keystone, Colorado, which is 75 miles west of Denver.

*Laura Rossetter, a Summit County local, has spent many summers exploring every bikeable nook and cranny of Summit County. During this time, she rode over 1,500 miles of the area's backcountry to gather information for her guidebook, *The Mountain Bike Guide to Summit County, Colorado.*

In addition to being an avid mountain biker, Laura is a skilled backcountry skier, tele-mark racer, kayaker, and windsurfer. When not out exploring the nearby mountains, Laura divides her time between freelance writing and teaching for the Summit County schools.

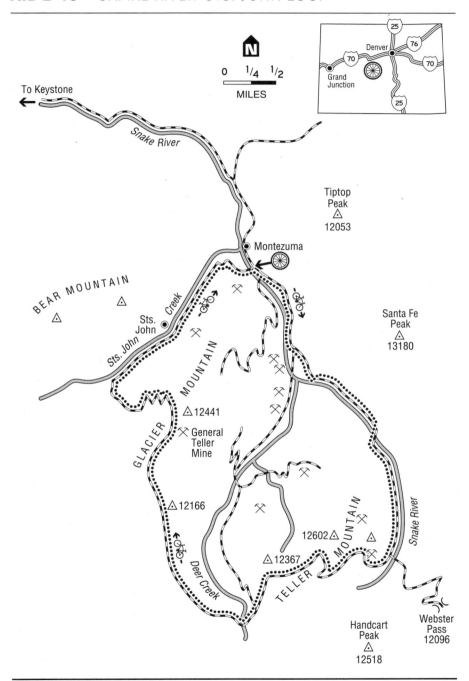

To Keystone

Snake River

N

0   1/4   1/2

MILES

Denver

Grand
Junction

25
76
70
70
25

Tiptop
Peak
△
12053

Montezuma

BEAR MOUNTAIN
△
△

Sts.
John
⊙

Sts. John Creek

MOUNTAIN

Santa Fe
Peak
△
13180

GLACIER

△12441

✗ General
Teller
Mine

△12166

Deer Creek

△12367

TELLER MOUNTAIN

12602△
△

Snake River

Handcart
Peak
△
12518

Webster
Pass
12096

Laura Rossetter. Photo: Todd Powell.

Elevation change: The ride begins in Montezuma at 10,300′. The road climbs 2,315′ to the high point on Teller Mountain, at 12,615′. A series of sharp descents and ascents punctuates the next few miles of riding and adds quickly to the total elevation gain. The final 500′ climb to 12,360′ on Glacier Mountain is followed by a 2,060′ descent to Montezuma.

Season: The majority of this route is rideable in June, but wet conditions and snowdrifts clinging to the highest ridges may exist well into July. High elevations mean snow can occur at any time throughout the summer, yet this route is generally dry through mid-October.

Services: Telephones and water are available in Montezuma; otherwise, all services (including bike rentals, restaurants, lodging, and shopping) can be found in Keystone. The United States Backcountry Association (a backcountry adventure organization offering helicopter mountain bike excursions) has snacks and drinks for sale—sometimes.

Hazards: Four-wheel-drive traffic may be encountered, and since the roads are often narrow, be prepared to pull to the side to let them pass. Most of this ride is above timberline, with no cover available to wait out storms. Get an early start and be prepared for changing weather. The ruins and mining debris scattered throughout the area are fascinating to explore, but please be respectful of any "No Trespassing" signs.

Rescue index: Help can be obtained in Montezuma. Six miles of riding down any valley dirt trail will bring you quickly to town.

Land status: Arapaho National Forest.

Maps: USGS 7.5 minute quadrangles: Montezuma and Keystone, Colorado. USGS 1:50,000 scale county map: Summit County #2, Colorado. Trails Illustrated® map: #104, Loveland Pass.

Finding the trail: Once you are in Summit County, drive east on US 6 and pass through Keystone. Turn right onto Montezuma Road then take the first left, following the sign to Montezuma. Drive 5.5 miles into Montezuma and park off the road by a spur forking right to Sts. John.

Sources of additional information:

Arapaho National Forest
Dillon Ranger District
P.O. Box 620
Silverthorne, CO 80498
(303) 468-5400

The Mountain Bike Guide to Summit County, Colorado, by Laura Rossetter. Silverthorne, Colorado: Sage Creek Press, 1989.
This guide describes 30 rides that explore the areas around Breckenridge, Keystone, Dillon, Montezuma, Frisco, Copper Mountain, Vail Pass, and Lower Blue River Valley. Summit County, an ideal playground for mountain bikes, boasts an unbeatable combination of unique terrain, spectacular scenery, and fascinating mining heritage with a vast network of backcountry roads and trails. Laura's other guidebook, *Mountain Biking Colorado's Historic Mining Districts*, directs riders along backroad byways that pass old mines and settlements remaining from Colorado's mining era. For information on *The Mountain Bike Guide to Summit County, Colorado,* and *Mountain Biking Colorado's Historic Mining Districts,* contact Sage Creek Press, P.O. Box 1373, Silverthorne, CO 80498.

Bicycling the Backcountry, A Mountain Bike Guide to Colorado, by William L. Stoehr. Boulder, Colorado: Pruett Publishing, 1987.

Notes on the trail: The large number of old mining roads branching from the main route necessitates a turn-by-turn description to prevent confusion. At first, pedal south up the well-maintained Montezuma Road for about a mile. Turn left onto a rocky, four-wheel-drive road signed for Webster Pass. It passes through a beautiful, high alpine meadow enhanced by dilapidated mining structures and beaver ponds. Cross the Snake River and continue up the right side of the valley. Later, fork right at a signed junction toward Deer Creek to a steep climb past the remains of Cashier Mine (the left fork rises to Webster Pass). The road seems to disappear before reaching the top of Teller Mountain but actually veers to the far right for a final gut-busting ascent (walking required).

Descend from Teller Mountain through a rolling expanse of high alpine tundra and connect with a road *ascending* from Deer Creek. Turn right and follow this road down a short distance to the next junction signed for Montezuma. (If threatening weather looms or your endurance has waned, take this road back down to Montezuma.)

To continue the loop, turn left at the Montezuma sign and ride along a ridge crossing the upper edge of the Deer Creek drainage. Now, heading north through rolling terrain, stay to the right at the next two major junctions, always following signs for Sts. John. Two steep climbs ("walkers") mark the approach to Glacier Mountain. Afterward, the road swings past (above) General Teller Mine and then caps Glacier Mountain just to the west of its true summit. A tricky descent follows, with lots of loose rocks and deep ruts. Near treeline, the remains of the Wild Irishman Mine are a welcomed distraction from the intense concentration this downhill demands. The road winds down into the valley and through the old mining community of Sts. John and then switchbacks down to Montezuma.

Don't be put off by the idea of exposed, formidable terrain or navigational difficulty. Although much of the route rises above treeline, the first and final sections follow icy, crystal streams that cut through beautiful alpine meadows. Beaver ponds are set amidst grassy fields of columbine and paintbrush mixed with Engelmann spruce and subalpine fir. And once you are riding it, the route unfolds before you and becomes quite evident.

RIDE 20 *BOREAS PASS*

The fascinating combination of cruising along an old railroad route and being surrounded by the grandeur of the Rocky Mountains makes Boreas Pass an extremely appealing mountain bike excursion. Riding toward Boreas Pass, you will climb through thick stands of blue spruce and aspen; once you are above timberline, the landscape changes to high alpine tundra dotted with clumps of willows and a few hardy stands of pine. The long flank of Bald Mountain falls behind as Boreas Mountain looms to the east. To the west, the Tenmile Range pierces the horizon, and once on top of Boreas Pass, you will see the flat expanse of South Park opens below.

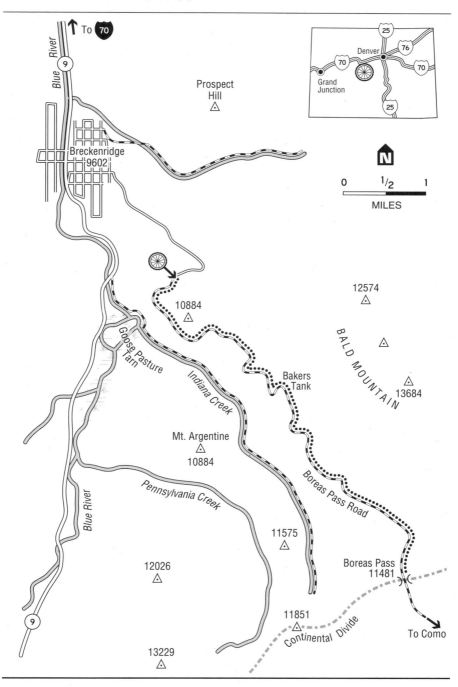

Century-old cabin along Boreas Pass Road. Photo: Laura Rossetter.

Named for the god of wind, Boreas Pass proved a tough challenge for the railroad industry. Intense winters, strong winds, and avalanche dangers threatened to block efforts to bring the nation's highest narrow-gauge railroad to Breckenridge before its completion in 1882. Several log cabins, a stone engine house, and a post office (at one time the nation's highest) weathered the severe winters on the Continental Divide, but when the railroad discontinued service in 1937 most of the buildings fell into disrepair or burned. Only a two-story log cabin remains standing.

This is a good 12.5-mile out-and-back ride for those just acquiring their "mountain bike legs." But keep in mind that this ride begins at 10,360′, where air is very thin. Following the old Denver–South Park–Pacific railroad grade, the Boreas Pass Road climbs gradually to the Continental Divide. The hard-packed, consistently smooth surface makes the road great for mountain bikes, although slightly rocky conditions are encountered just before the top of Boreas Pass.

[The Boreas Pass route description was submitted by Laura Rossetter, Silverthorne, Colorado.—G. B.]

General location: This ride begins at the winter trailhead parking area on the Boreas Pass Road, 3.5 miles southeast of Breckenridge. Breckenridge lies 85 miles west of Denver.

Elevation change: Over its 6-mile course, the road rises just over 1,000′, beginning at 10,360′ and climbing to 11,481′ at Boreas Pass.

Season: Late May through October. The road is usually muddy for a couple of weeks after snow melts. The best times to pedal Boreas Pass are in late September and early October when large groves of aspen lining the road explode into shimmering shades of gold.

Services: All services, including food, lodging, shopping, bike rentals, and repairs, are available in Breckenridge.

Hazards: Vehicle traffic can be heavy, especially on weekends, although the road easily accommodates both cars and bicycles. If the summer has been dry, passing motorists may kick up some dust. Be prepared for quick changes in weather because summer thunderstorms can roll in unexpectedly.

Rescue index: Help can often be obtained from passing motorists, and you are never more than 10 miles from Breckenridge.

Land status: Arapaho National Forest.

Maps: USGS 7.5 minute quadrangles: Breckenridge and Boreas Pass, Colorado. USGS 1:50,000 scale county map: Summit County #2, Colorado. Trails Illustrated® map: #109, Breckenridge South.

Finding the trail: Drive south through Breckenridge on CO 9. Turn left onto Boreas Pass Road shortly after the stoplight on the south end of town. Drive up the winding road 3.5 miles to the pavement's end; park in the pulloff near the trailhead sign.

Sources of additional information:

Arapaho National Forest
Dillon Ranger District
P.O. Box 620
Silverthorne, CO 80498
(303) 468-5400

The Mountain Bike Guide to Summit County, Colorado, by Laura Rossetter. Silverthorne, Colorado: Sage Creek Press, 1989. Contact the press at P.O. Box 1373, Silverthorne, CO 80498.

Bicycling the Backcountry, A Mountain Bike Guide to Colorado, by William L. Stoehr. Boulder, Colorado: Pruett Publishing, 1987. Contact the press at 2928 Pearl Street, Boulder, CO 80301.

Notes on the trail: The Boreas Pass Road is a main artery from which branch many interesting bike routes that pass relics of yesteryear's mining activity. In addition, the main road continues down the south side of the pass, still following the railroad grade for another 10 miles to the small town of Como and eventually connecting with CO 285. But, it takes a strong rider to complete the entire circuit in one day. First-time mountain bikers tackling Boreas Pass may want to use a car shuttle and ride only the descent from the pass back toward Breckenridge.

What better way to experience the heart of Colorado than along a trail system that bears its name? The 470-mile-long Colorado Trail offers the adventurist an opportunity to assimilate the scenic mountain grandeur, pristine backcountry, varied communities, and colorful history that comprise Colorado. The route links the metropolitan plains of Denver with the southwestern flair of Durango while crossing eight mountain ranges, seven national forests, six wilderness areas, and five major river systems along the way. The Colorado Trail incorporates existing paths, roads, and routes as much as possible, and supplements them with volunteer-built trails. The result is a people's trail system created primarily by private and public support.

Mountain-goers may come to the Colorado Trail with different intentions: perhaps to find temporary solace from the confines of urban life, to seek divine isolation among majestic mountains, or simply to exercise in nature's gymnasium. Undoubtedly all will leave inspired by the varied terrain, the ever-changing flora and fauna, and indelible impressions these mountains make upon the psyche.

Naturally, tackling the Colorado Trail in its entirety, whether on foot or bike, is a monumental feat and one that takes considerable planning as well as physical and mental conditioning. But much of the trail's appeal is that it is easy to get to from multiple trailheads. For the mountain biker, this is particularly inviting since the prospect of an overnight bike-packing endeavor (and locally primitive trail sections) might prove overly daunting. With little logistical planning, though, the Colorado Trail can be pedaled as incremental point-to-point segments, as short loops incorporating side routes, or simply as out-and-back explorations. Since the trail passes through designated Wilderness Areas, where mountain bikes are prohibited, you will have to follow alternate routes in places in order to enjoy an uninterrupted riding experience.

Initially proposed by the Forest Service nearly two decades ago, the Colorado Trail eventually came to its fruition at the hand of volunteers—volunteers like Gudy Gaskill. A devoted proponent of the Colorado Trail from its infancy, Gaskill carried the burden of recruiting volunteer trail builders even while the trail system's original managing organization, the Colorado Mountain Trails Foundation, faltered. At one point, a pessimistic newspaper article called it "Trail to Nowhere," reflecting the diminishing hope of the trail's completion. But when former Governor Richard Lamm lent his ardent support and a new organization was formed (Colorado Trail Foundation), headed by an ever more energetic Gaskill, the subsequent outpouring of volunteers from around the nation led to the trail's completion in 1987. "Gudy's Rest," an unobtrusive

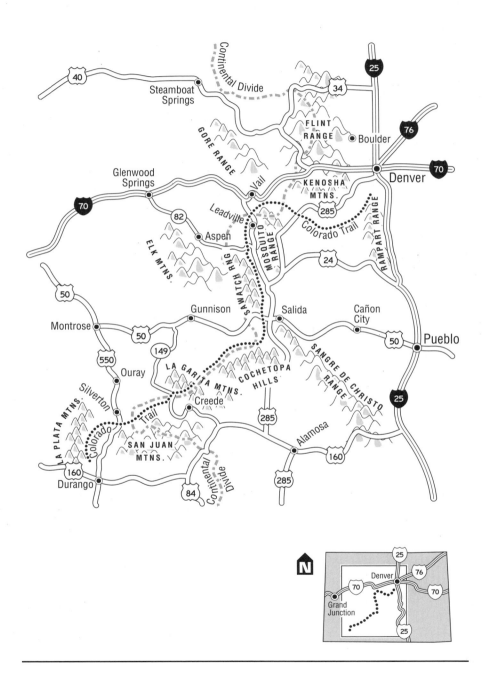

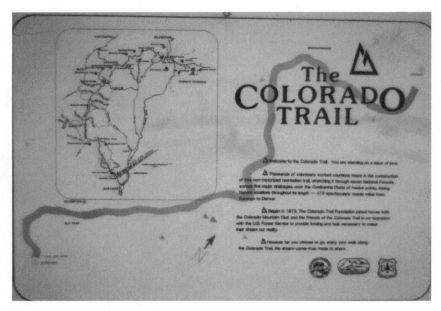

Trailhead plaque.

bench overlooking the forested foothills of the La Plata Mountains near the route's Durango trailhead, is a tribute to her efforts.

To obtain additional information on the Colorado Trail, contact The Colorado Trail Foundation, 548 Pine Song Trail, Golden, CO 80401, (303) 526-0809. Detailed route information is provided in *The Colorado Trail: The Official Guide Book,* by Randy Jacobs, also available through the Colorado Trail Foundation.

RIDE 21 *SEARLE PASS*

The Searle Pass section of the Colorado Trail follows Guller Creek as it tumbles through a willow-filled valley dotted with placid beaver ponds. The surrounding ridges are blanketed with dense forests of blue spruce, and with a little luck you may spy the elk herd that frequents this area. The valley has remained fairly unmarked by man, except for a few dilapidated cabins and collapsed structures—remnants of an old sawmill.

One of the many rewards for completing the steep climb to Searle Pass is the 360-degree panorama of the mountains. On the southeastern skyline are the pointed peaks of the Tenmile Range; in all other directions the jagged Gore and Holy Cross ranges fill the view. These peaks include Jacque Peak, Jacque Ridge, and Elk Mountain.

Directly below and south of Searle Pass, the settling ponds of the Climax Molybdenum mining operation cover the remains of the towns of Kokomo and Robinson. These two silver-mining communities thrived during the 1880s, well before the discovery of molybdenum.

Mountain bikers of intermediate to advanced ability will enjoy this challenging, 14-mile (total) out-and-back single-track. The first mile follows the paved bike path toward Vail Pass. Shortly thereafter, you will be on a well-used trail that begins climbing steadily toward Searle Pass. Several extremely rocky sections, stream crossings (many spanned by footbridges), and steep climbs through a series of switchbacks will be encountered.

[The Searle Pass trail description was provided by Laura Rossetter, Silverthorne, Colorado.—G. B.]

General location: This trail begins near the Union Creek base lodge of Copper Mountain Ski Resort, located 75 miles west of Denver.

Elevation change: The ride begins at 9,880'. The trail climbs 2,120' over 6 miles to 12,000' at the trail's end on Searle Pass.

Season: Late June through October. Snow lingers on the north side of the gulch and on Searle Pass well into July. Stream crossings are numerous and footbridges may be flooded during peak runoff.

Services: Bike rentals, repairs, food, lodging, and shopping are available at Copper Mountain.

Hazards: Riders need to keep their eyes on the trail and watch their speed in anticipation of loose rocks, boggy areas, water bars that lie across the path, and occasional horse and foot traffic. The final section above timberline provides little shelter, so watch for fast-moving thunderstorms.

RIDE 21 *SEARLE PASS*

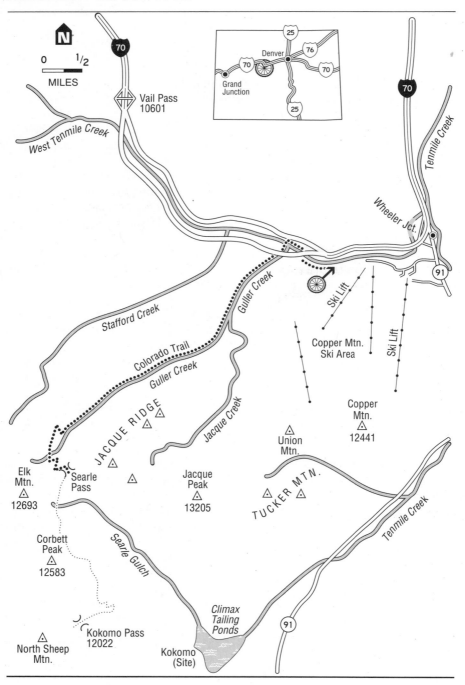

N

0   1/2
MILES

70

Vail Pass
10601

West Tenmile Creek

Tenmile Creek

70

25

Denver

76

70

Grand
Junction

70

25

Wheeler Jct.

91

Stafford Creek

Guller Creek

Ski Lift

Copper Mtn.
Ski Area

Ski Lift

Colorado Trail

Guller Creek

Jacque Creek

Copper
Mtn.

12441

JACQUE RIDGE

Union
Mtn.

Elk
Mtn.

12693

Searle
Pass

Jacque
Peak

13205

TUCKER MTN.

Tenmile Creek

Corbett
Peak

12583

Searle Gulch

Climax
Tailing
Ponds

91

Kokomo Pass
12022

North Sheep
Mtn.

Kokomo
(Site)

Rescue index: You are never more than 7 miles from assistance at Copper Mountain, but since the route is single-track, getting help on the trail itself could prove time consuming and arduous.

Land status: Arapaho National Forest.

Maps: USGS 7.5 minute quadrangles: Vail Pass and Copper Mountain, Colorado. USGS 1:50,000 scale county maps: Summit County #2, Colorado. Trails Illustrated® maps: #108, Vail Pass and #109, Breckenridge South.

Finding the trail: Traveling on Interstate 70, take Exit 195 south at Copper Mountain. Turn right onto Copper Road and follow it through Copper Mountain Ski Resort to its end near the Union Creek base lodge. Park at the nearby parking lot.

Sources of additional information:

Arapaho National Forest
Dillon Ranger District
P.O. Box 620
Silverthorne, CO 80498
(303) 468-5400

Summit Huts and Trails Association
P.O. Box 2830
Breckenridge, CO 80424
(303) 453-8583

The Mountain Bike Guide to Summit County, Colorado, by Laura Rossetter. Silverthorne, Colorado: Sage Creek Press, 1989. Contact the press at P.O. Box 1317, Silverthorne, CO 80498.

Notes on the trail: This route follows a portion of the 470-mile Colorado Trail that originates in Denver and spans the state, ending in Durango. Largely the product of volunteer trail crews, construction began in 1976 to commemorate Colorado's Centennial celebration. Except for sections passing through 6 designated Wilderness Areas, the entire trail is currently open to mountain bikes.

Once you are on the Colorado Trail the route is evident. But, a few words are needed to guide you along the route's initial portion. The first mile follows the paved bike path toward Vail Pass; then the route turns left toward Guller Gulch. After crossing the bridges over West Ten Mile and Guller creeks, the dirt single-track skirts the edge of Copper Mountain Ski Area, passes under I-70, crosses over Guller Creek again, and then begins climbing steadily toward Searle Pass. Stay on the single-track (Colorado Trail) all the way to timberline. Above timberline the trail becomes faint but is marked by cairns (rock piles). The final climb veers to the south over a rough section of trail before reaching the wide saddle of Searle Pass. Strong riders interested in extending their trip can continue on the Colorado Trail as it winds southwest from Searle Pass.

Single-track highlights the Searle Pass trail. Photo: Laura
Rossetter.

After 3 miles of strenuous climbing along tundra-like Elk Ridge, you will reach
Kokomo Pass—a good turnaround point.

   Near timberline and adjacent to the trail, the Summit Huts and Trails
Association has constructed a series of backcountry cabins.

RIDE 22 *PEAKS TRAIL LOOP*

All bikers started off as novices. While it's true that some riders like Julie Furtado and Ned Overend were novices for maybe a couple of yards or miles, they were, nevertheless, novices at the beginning of their careers. Of course, most of us don't aspire to be lean, mean, biking machines, but if you're just getting into the sport, the ever popular Peaks Trail Loop is a great introduction to single-track riding. This is not to say that more experienced riders will find this loop boring. Not in the least. It's as challenging as you want to make it: ride its entirety without stopping, or tackle it as an out-and-back, or take the optional Gold Hill trail, which is rated more difficult.

There are the typical obstacles: tree roots, water crossings, mud and runoff, pedal-catching boulders, short but steep ups and downs, hikers and bikers to heed—all the features that are exhilarating challenges to some riders, yet heart-stopping hazards to others, depending on one's ability. Perhaps the most important lesson a mountain biker needs to learn is this: Don't ride around wet spots or around obstacles in the trail. Instead, dismount and walk or carry your bike around or over it. Practicing low-impact riding helps preserve the environment and vegetation alongside the trail, and reduces trail erosion.

When I rode this loop with Michael Zobbe, one of the driving forces behind the Breckenridge Fat Tire Society, he lamented how much wider the Peaks Trail—meant to be a single-track trail—had become because of riders' carelessness. Severe damage has been inflicted by bikers who ride around obstacles such as mud, boulders, water bars, and other potential hazards in the trail. The vegetation along the trail has been trounced and, in some spots, short side trails have been created around mud or difficult spots. What used to be a truly single-track trail has now become a well-worn path. Don't get me wrong; the forest is still beautiful, lush, and serene, despite this man-made scar called the Peaks Trail. While it's true that appropriate attention was not given to redirecting and avoiding snow and water runoff at the time the trail was built, the Forest Service is slowly improving problem areas of the trail. In the meantime, Michael and the Fat Tire Society and other bike enthusiasts, such as the folks at Mountain Cyclery bike shop in Breckenridge, try to educate riders in hopes of preservation.

Described here is a 17.5-mile round-trip loop, rated moderate in both skill and endurance. It starts in Breckenridge, in a clockwise direction, and combines single- and double-tracks, paved bike path, and a short section of paved street roads. The Peaks Trail is a lovely, gradually climbing 7-mile stretch of single-track that threads through lush, dense forests of aspen and pine. A little-known 2-mile stretch of double-track is incorporated as a shortcut to the Blue River bike path, effectively bypassing a heavily used section of the path in Frisco.

RIDE 22 *PEAKS TRAIL LOOP*

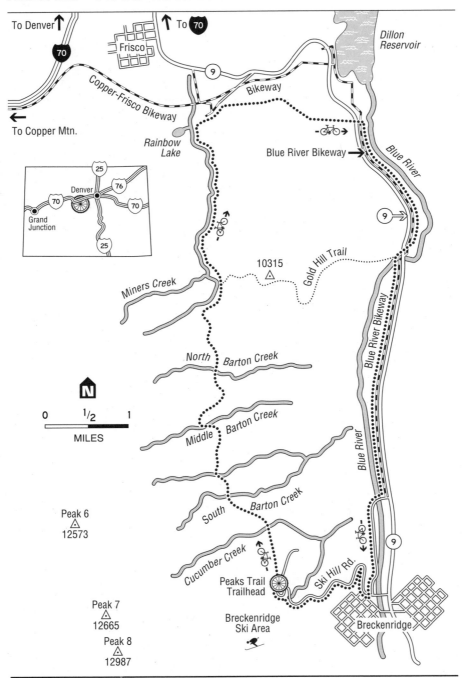

To Denver ↑

↑ To 70

Frisco

70

To Copper Mtn.

Copper-Frisco Bikeway

9

Bikeway

Dillon Reservoir

Rainbow Lake

-⊙🚲→

Blue River Bikeway →

Blue River

Denver
25
76
70
70
Grand Junction
25

9

Miners Creek

10315
△

Gold Hill Trail

Blue River Bikeway

North Barton Creek

N

0   ½   1
MILES

Middle Barton Creek

Blue River

South Barton Creek

Peak 6
△
12573

Cucumber Creek

-⊙🚲→

9

Peaks Trail Trailhead

Ski Hill Rd.

Peak 7
△
12665

Breckenridge Ski Area

🎿

Breckenridge

Peak 8
△
12987

Mike pedals the results of hardworking trail maintenance crews. If not for them, we wouldn't be able to enjoy this route.

Include 5.5 miles on the Blue River bike path and nearly 3 miles on paved streets through Breckenridge and the result is a fine loop ride.

The Peaks Trail, with all its glory and spots of misery, shows bikers of all levels the results of insensitive riding practices. Contrast the condition of this single-track to, say, the nearby Kenosha and Georgia Passes Trail (Ride 24), or the Mill Creek to Jud Wiebe Loop (Ride 50) in Telluride. Whether you're a novice or an expert, you'll realize the importance of low-impact riding more than ever.

General location: The loop encompasses a narrow stretch of land between Frisco and Breckenridge. The starting point is in Breckenridge, which is approximately 76 miles west of Denver.

Elevation change: Though you can start this loop at several points, we started at the Peaks trailhead in Breckenridge, next to the Peak 8 ski area and alpine slide. The trail starts at 10,000′ and weaves up and down for 4 miles before reaching the highest point at 10,280′, for a total gain of 280′. It then descends through roller-coaster terrain to the lowest point at 9,050′, for an elevation loss of 1,230′. The loss is gradually regained in the last 8.5 miles over paved routes, back to the starting point.

Season: The recommended time to enjoy this loop is between late June and late September, depending on wet weather conditions. The Peaks Trail has a great tendency to be wet well into the spring, particularly since it lies on east-facing slopes. These slopes are protected by a dense forest covering that encourages snow to linger longer than in other parts of the loop. Meadows are usually dotted with wildflowers from late June to late July, while mid-September will generally be blessed with autumn colors of golds and reds among the evergreen trees—and drier trail conditions.

Services: The Peaks Trailhead is adjacent to the Peak 8 base ski area and alpine slide. The slide is open daily from mid-June to early September. Water, food, and toilet facilities are available here during hours of operation. Though you will encounter creeks and streams along the loop, their waters must be purified before consumed. All services are found in both Breckenridge and Frisco, including restaurants, food stores, gas stations, public phones, bike and other retail stores, and lodging. Breckenridge Central Reservations can be reached by calling (800) 221-1091 from out of state, and (800) 822-5381 in state. Numerous Forest Service campgrounds exist in the Dillon Reservoir vicinity and reservations are highly recommended; call (800) 283-CAMP. Private campgrounds are also available in Breckenridge.

Another welcomed service is the "Summit Stage," a bus providing free transportation between Breckenridge, Frisco, Copper Mountain, Silverthorne, and Keystone. Most buses are equipped with 4 exterior bike racks, and the transporting of bikes is free of charge on a first-come, first-served basis. For more information on bus stops and times, call (303) 453-1241 or (303) 453-1339.

Hazards: Depending on your skill level, obstacles in the trail can be either fun challenges or scary hazards. Tree roots and pedal-snagging boulders inhabit this trail, as do mudholes, water bars, and water crossings. Be alert for other trail users on all portions of the loop, especially on the bike path along CO 9. Users of the path include adults and children on bikes and in-line skates, as well as walkers and runners. Use extreme caution when following the bike path across CO 9; it's extremely busy and the traffic seems to whizz by unforgivingly. And, if you dislike vampires as much as I do, bring insect repellant as the Peaks Trail segment is home to millions of vicious, voracious, blood-sucking mosquitoes.

Rescue index: If a medical emergency arises, rest assured that except for the 7-mile, single-track stretch on the Peaks Trail, the loop is easily reached by passenger vehicles. You're never too far from help since Breckenridge and Frisco are on the loop and each town has medical facilities. On the single-track portion, chances are good that you will meet other trail users who may render assistance.

Land status: Arapaho National Forest.

Maps: Trails Illustrated® maps: #108, Vail Pass and #109, Breckenridge South. USGS 7.5 minute quads: Frisco and Breckenridge, Colorado. *Summit County Bike Path and Mountain Bike Map,* produced by the Summit County Community Development Department and distributed throughout the county (address listed below).

Finding the trail: Start the loop in Breckenridge by driving or riding to the Peaks trailhead. To reach the trail from town, find the intersection of Main Street and Ski Hill Road (known as Lincoln Avenue on the east side of Main Street). Travel north on Ski Hill Road for about 2 miles, following it up and around to the Peak 8 base. Continue by the base and look for the brown Forest Service sign marking the Peaks Trail, on your left, adjacent to a small parking area. Start your clockwise loop here.

Sources of additional information:

Arapaho National Forest
Dillon Ranger District
P.O. Box 620
Silverthorne, CO 80498
(303) 468-5400

Mountain Cyclery
112 South Ridge Street
Breckenridge, CO 80424
(303) 453-2201

Breckenridge Fat Tire Society
P.O. Box 2845
Breckenridge, CO 80424
(303) 453-5548

Summit County Government
Community Development Department
P.O. Box 68
Breckenridge, CO 80424
(303) 453-2561

Summit County Chamber of Commerce Information Centers
Mailing address:
P.O. Box 214
Frisco, CO 80442
(303) 668-5800 or (303) 668-0376

Two Visitors Centers:
In Dillon, at 220 US Highway 6
In Frisco, at 110 South Summit Boulevard

Notes on the trail: As you begin your ride, you'll notice that the Peaks Trail is well marked with mileage signs and blue diamond symbols tacked onto trees along the route. Basically, this part of the loop heads toward Frisco, approximately 7.5 miles north. Almost a mile from the start, cross Cucumber Creek over a wooden bridge.

Follow the trail as it meanders through lodgepole and aspen forests, heading gradually downhill with occasional short and steep climbs. The trail is enjoyably rugged, with exposed tree roots, boulders, and some wet and muddy spots. Remember to do your part to preserve the trail by dismounting and walking over or through the muddy areas instead of around them. Fortunately, the hardworking Forest Service crew has constructed several wooden bridges across creeks as well as over perpetually wet and marshy areas.

At nearly 2 miles from the starting point, follow the trail across South Barton Creek. At almost 3.5 miles, cross Middle Barton Creek and pedal along the banks of a diversion ditch (at least in the summer of 1993, water was being diverted). Continue on and, just before reaching 4 miles, cross North Barton Creek and stay on the trail (which may or may not be paralleled by another diversion ditch).

A short distance from the last creek crossing, the trail emerges from the dense forest into an expansive clearing. The entire hillside has been logged clean, leaving a meadow dotted with wildflowers in between leftover piles of dead trees and brush. Without the trees to obscure your sight, the view of the Bald Mountain range towards the southeast is spectacular. Continue on and in about a half mile, you reach the junction of Miners Creek Trail, a hiking path. You can't miss it as there are several brown Forest Service signs at this intersection. Stay on the Peaks Trail, going toward Gold Hill Trail, Rainbow Lake, and Frisco.

In a half mile from the well-signed intersection, you reach the junction of Gold Hill Trail. (This is a good bail-out route if you need to shorten the loop due to threatening weather. After an initial 1-mile climb on Gold Hill Trail, it's a 2.5 mile descent to the paved bike path. Novices with little single-track experience may feel uneasy on this trail, particularly on the moderately steep sections, and may prefer to walk. And, as mentioned earlier, more experienced riders may delight in this alternate single-track route. A description for this alternate route is offered at the end of this chapter.)

Bypass Gold Hill Trail and continue on the Peaks Trail as it skirts Miners Creek on your left. After nearly 2 miles of gradual downhill, the trail becomes steeper and your adrenalin kicks in because the wide, single-track trail has become an exhilarating, fast, downhill flight. The trail conditions become slightly more challenging, with dips, boulders, loose rock, and tree roots to add to the fun. If you can interrupt your fun, stop and enjoy the scenery. Check out the beaver ponds alongside the creek and you might spot a furry head swimming at water line.

Sadly, the fun Peaks Trail terminates at a four-wheel-drive dirt road, almost 7.5 miles from the starting point. Also at this point is a sign designating Rainbow Lake towards the left. If you're looking for a picnic spot, check out this tiny lake, a quarter of a mile away by bike. Continuing on, follow the dirt road due north for about a half mile to a small clearing where double-track trails and dirt roads converge. Look for a wide double-track trail on your right, which is not identified but is marked by a general Forest Service trail users sign.

At this point, you can stay on the dirt road and, after a few yards, reach the paved bike path. To reach the town of Frisco, go left on the bike path. After checking out Frisco, return to Breckenridge by hopping back on the bike path and riding south along CO 9. If you don't wish to visit Frisco and want to bypass a heavily used portion of the bike path, you can turn right onto the double-track trail marked by the trail users sign and follow it into the woods, up and down several short hills. Stay to the right at junctions, passing a weathered United Church of Christ sign on your left. A short distance farther, the dirt road ends at CO 9. Watch for an opening in the traffic and go to the paved bike path on the other side of the highway.

On the bike path, you can enjoy the scenery while you cruise the next 5.5 miles back to Breckenridge. The terrain climbs ever so gently, crossing busy CO 9 several more times. Watch out for oncoming cyclists and other trail users on the path. If you're running out of water, rest assured that there is a bicyclist's rest stop along this stretch to Breckenridge.

Follow the the bike path to its terminus at a gravel parking lot in Breckenridge, near the intersection of Main Street and Watson Avenue, behind the Information Center. Go across the parking lot, bearing right towards North Park Avenue. Follow North Park Avenue due south to the intersection of Ski Hill Road. Turn right onto Ski Hill Road and climb the last 2 miles back to your car at the Peaks trailhead. Total distance for the loop is approximately 17.5 miles.

Alternate route: The Gold Hill Trail is a single-track and, in this direction, is rated moderate in terms of skill and stamina. Turn off the Peaks Trail onto Gold Hill Trail, due east, and climb almost a mile to the top of the hill. After that, the route cruises downhill through meadows for nearly 2.5 miles and eventually ends at the paved bike path. Turn left onto the path and follow it into Frisco to the Miners Creek Road (County Road 1000), a dirt road. Go left onto Miners Creek Road towards Rainbow Lake and follow the previous description in the reverse direction, pedaling south on the Peaks Trail all the way back to the Peak 8 base and your car. Total distance on this alternate loop is approximately 21 miles.

Fairplay

RIDE 23 KENOSHA CREEK

This ride heads east up Kenosha Creek and toward the Kenosha Mountains. Kenosha means pike (as in fish), although this creek is not considered a fishing hot spot. The Pass, Gulch, Creek, and Range were named by a stage coach driver from Kenosha, Wisconsin. Now, I don't know if you have ever been to Wisconsin, but I can tell you from experience that Kenosha, Wisconsin, does not look like Kenosha Creek, Colorado.

Rising along Kenosha Creek, trees change from aspen and lodgepole pine to Engelmann spruce as you pass from the montane to subalpine life zone. Snowcaps dot the highlands and, along the route's upper portion, South Park comes into view. Large mountain valleys, meadows, and grasslands here are called "parks," as in wild game parks or preserves. The Colorado Rocky Mountains are separated by four large, high altitude valleys: North Park, South Park, Middle Park, and the San Luis Valley. South Park covers roughly 900 square miles. It is a grand view.

Kenosha Creek is a 12.5-mile out-and-back trip that starts out easy but becomes moderately strenuous after 3 miles. The entire route travels a minimally maintained four-wheel-drive road. An intermediate skill level is required in some areas; otherwise, technical difficulty is low. If the road is wet after spring thaw or an afternoon rain, a few portions become muddy—real muddy, like grease.

[Trail information was submitted by William L. Stoehr of Evergreen, Colorado.—G. B.]

General location: Approximately 60 miles southwest of Denver between Bailey and Fairplay, near Kenosha Pass.
Elevation change: Kenosha Pass campground rests at 10,000′. The route climbs to 11,400′, then returns to the campground.
Season: Late spring through early fall. Be prepared for sudden weather changes and afternoon storms. Snowstorms are not uncommon, even in late spring.
Services: Complete visitor services are available at Fairplay. Limited services are available in Bailey.

RIDE 23   *KENOSHA CREEK*

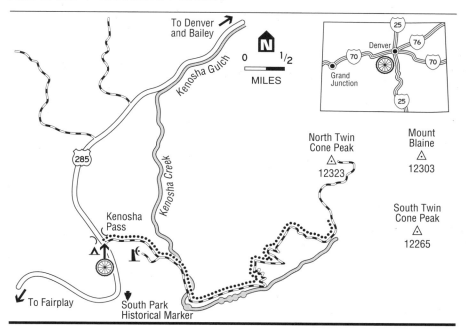

Hazards: This route contains no unusual hazards. Just be aware that if you follow the route as an up-and-back ride, the descent can be very fast, so check your speed.

Rescue index: You can expect to see other bikers and four-wheel-drive vehicles occasionally on this route, for it is a relatively high-use area.

Land status: Pike National Forest.

Maps: USGS 7.5 minute quadrangles: Mt. Logan and Jefferson, Colorado. USGS 1:50,000 county maps: Park County #1 and #2.

Finding the trail: Follow US 285 south and west out of Denver. Kenosha Pass is midway between Bailey and Fairplay. Start at the large parking area near the campground along US 285.

Sources of additional information:

Pike National Forest
South Park Ranger District
P.O. Box 219
Fairplay, CO 80440
(719) 836-2031
The office is located at the Northwest junction of US 285 and CO 9.

Mountain Bike Rides in the Colorado Front Range, by William L. Stoehr. Boulder, Colorado: Pruett Publishing, 1988.

Notes on the trail: A good place to park and begin this ride is at the campground at Kenosha Pass off US 285 (to the left when coming from Denver). Pedal through the campground on a good dirt road, staying to the right. Stay on the main road as it parallels Kenosha Creek about a mile later for a series of ups and downs, then go through a Forest Service gate (close it behind you).

Two miles from the campground there is a road to the left. Stay on the main road and continue through the aspens; watch for the beaver lodge. All along Kenosha Creek you will find beaver dams and the truncated aspens that serve as both construction material and food for these big rodents. You may see "evidence" (a euphemism) of elk, but no elk. You may also discover heavily browsed and rubbed aspens. Elk are naturally attracted to aspen, eating the leaves, twigs, and bark and using the trunk as a scratching post to rub the dry velvet from their antlers in late summer.

Pass through another gate and continue the prolonged climb. Just when you begin to tire, a rewarding flat stretch greets you. But, one more ascent at about 4.5 miles brings you into the upper drainage, then down and through a pretty meadow. Six miles from the trailhead is a good place to turn around, although jeep roads continue to climb the hillsides and are worthy of exploration.

RIDE 24 *KENOSHA AND GEORGIA PASSES*

If you want to see knock-your-socks-off autumn colors, this is the ride for you. Well, okay, there are lots of other rides in Colorado that show off its fall glory, but this is one of the best, hands down. My riding buddies, Stacie, Tim, and Marty, agreed with me, along with lots of other mountain bikers and hikers we met on the day we rode this stretch of the Colorado Trail.

The route is a smooth, single-track trail. This long out-and-back is about 24 miles, punctuated by short, heart-throbbing ascents and restful descents. Though little technical skill is required, great stamina is a must due to the distance and elevation. Of course, you need not go the distance. (The ride can be shortened; read on.) In fact, this is an ideal trail to introduce novices to single-track riding.

We started the ride by picking up the Colorado Trail at the top of Kenosha Pass, at 9,994′, and eventually reached Georgia Pass, at 11,585′. As we pedaled through groves of aspen and lodgepole pine, the sun was dancing in and out of the trees and the aspen were showering their golden leaves on us. We felt like the grand marshalls in an old-fashioned confetti-and-ticker-tape parade. Once out of the trees, we were shocked by incredibly awe-inspiring views of color-

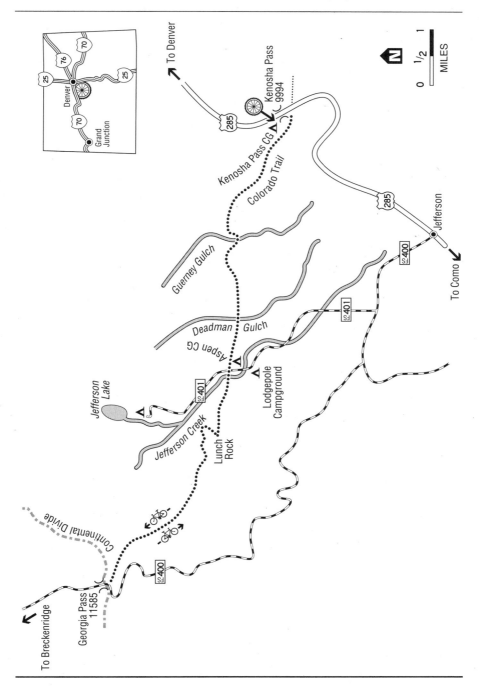

What better way to spend an autumn day than riding a
single-track trail through forests of golds and reds?

drenched mountain ranges, near and far. On that mid-September afternoon, the
four of us agreed that there was no better place to be than here.

General location: This ride is approximately 60 miles southwest of Denver and
about 20 miles north of Fairplay, off US 285.
Elevation change: Pick up the trailhead at 9,994′ and climb to 11,585′, for a
total elevation gain of 1,591′. Though the trail cruises up and down, climbs are
neither severely steep or long.
Season: Early summer to early fall is the best time to ride this out-and-back.
Due to elevation, expect snow from November to May.
Services: Drinking water is available at Kenosha Pass and Aspen campgrounds, as well as at the Beaver Ponds Picnic Ground. There are toilet facilities at the Kenosha Pass Campground trailhead. All campgrounds require a fee,
and because camping is limited to designated areas, reservations may be

required. For current information, call the Pike National Forest, South Park Ranger District, at (719) 836-2031. Food and limited lodging are available in Bailey, Como, and Fairplay.

Hazards: Two hazards demand special attention. First is the typical afternoon thunder and lightning. If you're planning to ride the entire 24 miles, start early enough to avoid the usual storms. The terrain becomes increasingly more exposed as you approach the Pass. If you want an electrifying afternoon, literally, this is the place to be during a lightning storm. It's best to start your ride early. Depending on your group's stamina, this ride requires 5 to 8 hours to complete.

The second hazard is that deer and elk hunting is permitted for blackpowder, bow, and rifle hunters. Hunting season typically is mid-September through mid-November. It's best to call the Colorado Division of Wildlife at (303) 297-1192 for current information.

Rescue index: Since this is a popular ride during the summer and early fall, you're sure to meet other riders and hikers on the trail who might be of help. Jefferson Creek and Aspen campgrounds, about 6 and 5 miles from the Kenosha Pass trailhead respectively, are accessible by four-wheel-drive vehicles. The nearest phone is in the tiny town of Jefferson, about 4 miles south of the trailhead on US 285.

Land status: Pike National Forest.

Maps: The Colorado Trail maps: #5 and #6. USGS 7.5 minute quads: Jefferson, Boreas Pass, Colorado.

Finding the trail: When you reach Kenosha Pass, park on the west side of US 285 in the dirt area just outside the campground entrance. Day users are asked not to park in the campground.

Sources of additional information:

> Pike National Forest
> South Park Ranger District
> 320 Highway 285
> P.O. Box 219
> Fairplay, CO 80440
> (719) 836-2031

Notes on the trail: Hats off to the volunteers of the Colorado Trail system for doing an excellent job of marking this route. You'll find frequent markers on trees and cairns in the open meadows.

From where you park, pedal a few yards into the campground. Drinking water and toilet facilities are available here. Ready? Find the Colorado Trail just to the left of these facilities.

For the first mile, gradually ascend through a lovely grove of aspen. While pedaling through the grove, you won't notice the trail leveling out because you'll be teased by majestic glimpses of the Continental Divide and the South Park valley peeking through the trees. Continuing for almost 1.5 miles, still within the grove, the trail gently begins its descent into the valley. Then, all of a sudden, boom! Mother Nature delivers a shock to your system with a wide, gloriously colored, unobstructed view of the valley. We got hit with this view on a semi-sunny, autumn-colored morning. Note this, you photography buffs, because from our approach on the trail, the morning light cast a radiant glow on the aspen. On this portion of the ride, you can see the little town of Jefferson to the south, and the Continental Divide and Mount Guyot (13,370′) to the northwest. Georgia Pass (11,585′) is just east of Mount Guyot.

Continue descending amidst this incredible scene for just over 2 miles, where you'll cross Guernsey Creek. After about a half mile more of fairly level terrain, begin a gradual ascent of just over a mile, at which point you will cross Deadman Gulch and probably see campers at Aspen Campground. (If you have a four-wheel-drive vehicle, you could shorten this ride to Georgia Pass by 9 miles if you start here. You can reach this spot by traveling a dirt road from the town of Jefferson.)

After about a mile of gently rolling terrain through groves of aspen and pine, the trail begins a rather steep climb. Not to worry, though, for it's a short section—less than a quarter mile. The trail eventually meets a gate. At this point you are almost 5.5 miles from the trailhead. After you pass through, remember to leave the gate the way you found it: open or closed.

Descend through a lovely canopy of pine and aspen for a half mile, and you'll meet a two-wheel-drive road. Turn right and pedal on this road for a few yards until you pick up the trail again on the left; watch for the Colorado Trail sign. Once you reach this spot, you're halfway: mileage signs here indicate 6 miles to Kenosha Pass and 6 miles to Georgia Pass. We know which way we're going, don't we?

Onward-ho! After pedaling a short distance, cross Jefferson Creek and get ready to put your bike in a lower gear; the gradual steady climb to Georgia Pass begins here. On these next 3 to 4 miles, the aspen are fewer and the lodgepole pines more abundant. The trail becomes slightly more challenging, with rocks buried and tree roots unburied in spots of soft dirt, accented by a couple of hairpin turns. Eventually, you reach an area of huge rock outcroppings amid the pines. It's not marked, but you know that this is Lunch Rock, a popular stop for a break with a great view from north to south. You're almost 8 miles into the ride when you reach this spot.

From Lunch Rock, the trail turns sharply west. The grade is not overly steep, but combine that with the elevation gain and you have one heck of an aerobic workout. Persevere! After 2.5 miles, you'll be at 10,600′, the highest elevation on this ride. At this point, the timberline gives way to wide open spaces with Mount Guyot and Bald Mountain staring at you from the left. During the spring, this area is dazzling with wildflowers.

Push on! You're almost there. The last 1.5 miles is marked by cairns. The trail gradually climbs through alpine tundra, making the trail extremely bumpy. When you reach the two-wheel-drive jeep road, hang a left and pedal for a few yards to Georgia Pass, at 11,585´. You made it! Enjoy the spectacular views of Pike and Arapaho national forests before making your way back to Kenosha Pass.

RIDE 25 *WELLINGTON LAKE LOOP*

This region of the eastern Rockies lies amidst the junction of several front-range mountain systems: the Rampart Range to the south (home to 14,110´ Pikes Peak); the Kenosha Mountains to the west (where the Lost Creek Wilderness Area is found); and the greater Denver Front Range to the north (capped by Mount Evans). Wonderfully rounded peaks, craggy exposures, and stiletto spires in this area are composed of the porphyritic Pikes Peak granite. Enjoy outstanding views of the surrounding mountains from the Wellington Lake Overlook, including "the Castle," a small peak perched above the lake.

The encompassing mountain scenery is the most significant highlight of this ride. But, testing your mountain bike skills on the intersecting Colorado Trail adds an enticing twist to this otherwise nontechnical route. The grandiose multi-use trail, linking Denver with Durango, crosses the Wellington Lake Loop twice. Try short, out-and-back segments on the rolling single-track or be creative and construct loops connecting with the main dirt roads throughout the area.

Essentially no technical skills are required for the 20-mile Wellington Lake Loop, for it follows maintained Forest Service dirt roads. Usually these roads are smooth, packed dirt, but rocky and washboard sections may occur, most notably at corners. Several lengthy, moderately difficult climbs will be encountered. The "Wellington Wall," a steep rise up to the lake, will challenge all but elite riders. Exploring portions of the Colorado Trail requires advanced riding skills and good physical conditioning.

[This trail description was submitted by Stuart Black,* Denver, Colorado.— G. B.]

---

*Stuart Black has been characterized as having more bikes than brains. An avid cyclist for the past 15 years, he owns three ATBs (one of which is broken due to overuse), a road bike, and a tandem, which he rides with his four-year-old daughter. Since 1983 Stuart has devoted much of his leisure time to mountain biking and has learned to appreciate both single-track and dirt-road tours in the Denver/Front Range area.

Stuart has served as the ATB Tour Director of the Denver Bicycle Touring Club (DBTC) for two years, and as Head Tour Director for an additional year. He has lead dozens of mountain bike rides, including the annual 50-mile Georgia Pass tour and an ATB Century.

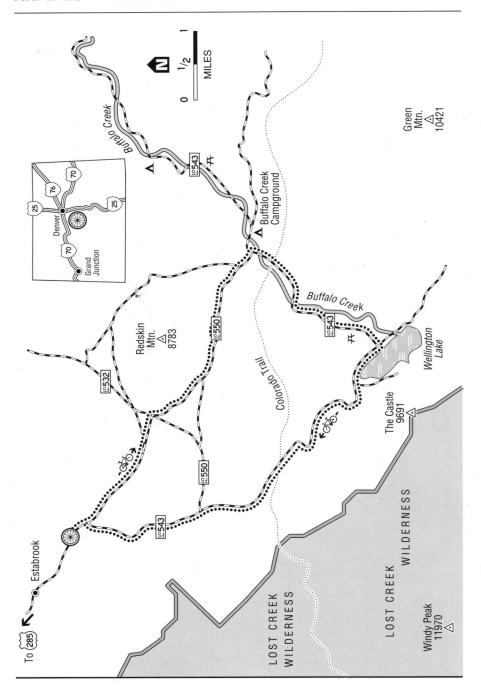

General location: This route begins near Estabrook, less than 45 miles southwest of Denver.

Elevation change: The ride starts at about 7,600′ near Estabrook and drops to 7,300′ at Buffalo Creek. From Buffalo Creek, the route climbs to 8,400′ northwest of Wellington Lake before returning to the starting location near Estabrook.

Season: May through October. Some winter riding may be possible, but this is highly unpredictable and depends on snowfall.

Since this part of the Rockies is usually quite dry, abundant Douglas fir and ponderosa pine cover the hillsides. Dispersed among these mighty conifers are stands of aspen and spruce intertwined with scrub oak and hardwoods. Naturally, during the latter part of September and early October, forested slopes become a patchwork of golden quakies, multi-colored hardwoods, and luxuriant pines.

Services: The small grocery store at Wellington Lake is open seasonally and offers the standard cuisine of trail munchies and cold drinks, but there are no other services along the route. Water can be found at Buffalo Creek Campground. Estabrook has no services, but Bailey (just 4 miles to the west) has a small store, a restaurant, and other services.

Hazards: Hazards along this route are minimal. Watch for occasionally rocky and washboarded road conditions. As always, be prepared for unpredictable and changing alpine weather throughout the summer.

Rescue index: Do not rely on others for help for traffic is typically light. Campers are common at Buffalo Creek and around Wellington Lake. The general store at the lake has a phone.

Land status: Pike National Forest. Wellington Lake and adjacent lands are privately owned.

Maps: USGS 7.5 minute quadrangles: Green Mountain and Windy Peak, Colorado. USGS 1:50,000 scale county maps: Park County #1, Jefferson County #1, and Jefferson County #2, Colorado. The *Pike National Forest Travel Map* clearly shows this route and portions of the intersecting Colorado Trail.

Finding the trail: From the southwest Denver area, follow US 285 for 41 miles to Bailey, then turn left (east) at the bottom of the hill. Estabrook is about 4 miles east on Forest Service Road 543. The ride starts at the top of the hill about a half mile east of Estabrook, where parking is also available.

Sources of additional information:

Pike and San Isabel National Forest
South Platte Ranger District
19316 Goddard Ranch Court
Morrison, CO 80465
(303) 697-0414

Denver Bicycle Touring Club
P.O. Box 8973
Denver, CO 80201
The Denver Bicycle Touring Club, established in the late 1960s, is a noncompetitive, touring-oriented, volunteer organization with approximately 1,500 members. DBTC offers a full schedule of both ATB and road rides throughout the year with up to 12 Front Range rides per week during the summer, catering to all abilities. In addition, the club offers multi-day tours throughout the intermountain West. Highlighting the summer's events is the DBTC's Front Range Century held on the second Sunday of September.

Notes on the trail: From the parking area just east of Estabrook, FS 550/FS 532 undulates a few miles and gently declines to Redskin Creek and then to Buffalo Creek. Turn right (south) near Buffalo Creek Campground and begin climbing on FS 543 to Wellington Lake. After 1.5 miles, the gently rising road steepens, then ascends the "Wellington Wall"—about a half mile of 20% grades. Follow FS 543 northwest of the lake to return to the parking area at the junction with FS 550/FS 532 near Estabrook.

The Colorado Trail intersects the Wellington Lake Loop in several locations, making it possible to construct numerous shorter side trips. Trail crossings are clearly marked south of Buffalo Creek Campground on FS 543 and again about 4 miles northwest of Wellington Lake.

Vail

THE TENTH MOUNTAIN DIVISION AND HUT SYSTEM

What makes history so fascinating, at least to me, is how the past manages to touch our lives today. Take the role of the railroads of the 1800s in Colorado. Brought by the promise of prosperity in mining, the rails spurred the settlement of previously isolated territory, connecting small communities, some of which still thrive today as reminders of Colorado's historical roots. From a different era and of equally great importance to the history of the state is the Tenth Mountain Division of the U.S. Army and the veterans who returned to Colorado after World War II. These former GIs ultimately became the driving force behind the state's multi-million-dollar ski tourism industry.

In 1942, a year after the bombing of Pearl Harbor and the entry of the United States into World War II, a winter training base for an elite ski corps was established at Camp Hale. Located north of Leadville, south of Vail Pass, the site became home to a group known as the Tenth Mountain Division. Over 14,000 soliders were stationed here from all over the country and trained to do battle with the Nazis in the snow-covered regions of Europe. Throughout the nearby Gore and Sawatch ranges, these troops camouflaged themselves in white uniforms and practiced under extreme winter conditions at elevations well over 13,000 feet. Known as "phantoms of the snow," they honed their snow combat techniques by engaging in war exercises. And they did all that while carrying 90-pound packs and wearing seven-foot skis, in subzero temperatures and waist-deep snow. Fortunately, the war ended and many of them never tested their specially developed skills against the Nazis.

Having developed a great love and respect for the snowy high country of Colorado, a number of the veterans returned and settled here. Pete Seibert, a veteran of the Tenth Mountain Division, has been arguably the most important catalyst in the development of Vail Valley's ski industry. He, along with Earl Eaton, established Colorado's first ski resort at Loveland Pass. Soon after, skiing became popular throughout the state and, eventually, the nation. Colorado's snow skiing industry was born.

The Tenth Mountain Trail Association Hut System was established in 1980 by backcountry enthusiasts, some of whom were veterans. In 1982, with donations from friends and families, five huts were built to commemorate members of the Division who died in World War II. Today, within this roughly 34-square-mile region of the White River and San Isabel national forests, there are 14 huts, 12 of which are accessible by mountain bikes.

Though little physical evidence of Camp Hale remains, the spirit of the Tenth Mountain Division lives on. An outstanding display of text and photographs has been constructed at the site of Camp Hale to commemorate the troops. Located between Tennessee Pass and Red Cliff on US 24, the site is a worthwhile visit. As you bike through this region, let your imagination conjure up scenes of the "phantoms of the snow," setting out on their military manuevers, with the snow muffling their sounds as if to subtly remind them—and you—of the beauty and power of Mother Nature.

Sources of additional information:

Tenth Mountain Trail Association
1280 Ute Avenue
Aspen, CO 81611
(303) 925-5775
Reservations for use of huts required. This is a nonprofit organization and membership is encouraged.

Colorado Ski Museum
15 Vail Road
P.O. Box 1976
Vail, CO 81658
(303) 476-1876
Visit here for a photographic display of Camp Hale and life of the soliders stationed there. Several books penned by veterans are offered in the bookshop. The Colorado ski industry is also featured, from past to present.

Colorado Hut to Hut: A Guide to Skiing and Biking Colorado's Backcountry, by Brian Litz. Englewood, Colorado: Westcliffe Publishers, Inc., 1992. To order, write Westcliffe Publishers, Inc., 2650 South Zuni, Englewood, CO 80110.

Ski the High Trail: World War II Ski Troopers in the Colorado Rockies. A historical personal account by Private Harris Dusenbery. Portland, Oregon: Binford & Mort Publishing, 1991. To order, write Binford & Mort Publishing, P.O. Box 10404, Portland, OR 97210.

RIDE 26 *CAMP HALE TO FOWLER–HILLARD HUT*

Before you start off on this 8-mile out-and-back ride—16 miles total—to the Fowler-Hilliard Hut, take time to appreciate what the Tenth Mountain Division ski corps did here in the early 1940s. To reach the trailhead, you must

RIDE 26   *CAMP HALE TO FOWLER-HILLIARD HUT*

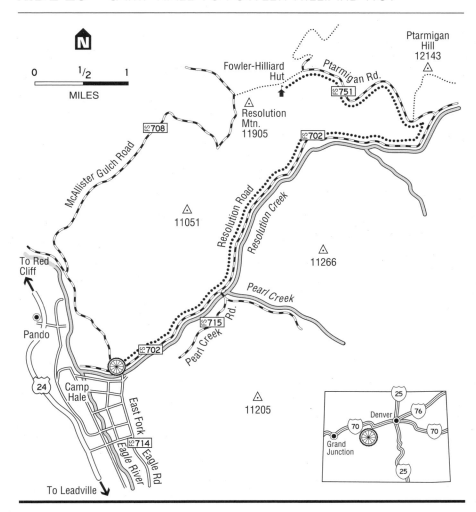

first drive through Camp Hale. There, you'll find informational displays describing a chapter of American military history that took place in this area. Complete with reproductions of archival photos, the display tells about the elite ski troopers who trained here, in the winters between 1942 and 1945, for anticipated combat against the Nazis in the snow-covered regions of Europe. In what was considered the ideal terrain in which to perfect their snow survival skills, the soliders endured waist-deep snow throughout the day, often spending the night in the field inside their igloos. Hard to imagine in the summertime,

The majestic panorama and the meadows of dazzling wildflowers make this ride worth every breath.

I suppose, as you look east toward the majestic and serene Elk Ridge. The conditions they endured were truly awesome. Use that thought as inspiration when you huff and puff up this trail to the Fowler-Hilliard Hut.

This is an easy route that doesn't require much technical skill. In fact, the trail follows a wide dirt road. The only real challenge is that the first seven miles are a moderately steep, relentless climb. But don't despair, for once you reach the Fowler-Hilliard Hut, sitting atop a ridge at 11,500′, you'll realize that it was well worth the effort. The views of the Holy Cross Wilderness and the Sawatch Range are stunning, especially in the early morning or late afternoon, when the clouds are moving in from the west. Consider staying overnight at the hut so that you can experience a magnificent sunrise or sunset, and relax in the peace and quiet of a ridgetop, the golden afternoon light illuminating the surrounding meadows of wildflowers.

Janine and I rode this route in mid-August. Upon reaching the site of the hut, we were rewarded with a dazzling, thick carpet of flowers—deep purple lupines, huge patches of blue columbines, and fiery red Indian paintbrushes, to name a few. We thought this must be the Land of Oz. But the best reward was being greeted at the hut by an outrageously delightful bunch of employees from the local REI stores in Denver (part of the national cooperative of outdoor equipment stores). Turns out they were having a planning meeting to discuss their continued sponsorship of outdoor events for the public. They feasted us with wine and a gourmet pasta dinner in exchange for our opinions about their terrific, highly educational wilderness programs. Following dinner, we hopped back on our bikes and raced the setting sun and threatening clouds back to our car at Camp Hale. Fortunately, it was downhill the entire way. What a wonderful trip, we thought. Great food, great company, great scenery. The steep climb was worth it, every inch.

General location: Camp Hale is located about 148 miles due west of Denver. From Leadville, it's 18 miles north on US 24. If you're traveling on Interstate 70, take Exit 171 towards Minturn, heading south on US 24 for 18.5 miles.

Elevation change: The Resolution Creek Road trailhead sits at 9,250', while the Fowler-Hilliard Hut is at 11,500'. Total gain in elevation is 2,250' in 8 miles.

Season: The best time to bike this route is between May and October, though snowstorms have been known to occur as early as mid-September and as late as June. If you're wacky enough to enjoy riding in the snow and mud, and don't want the winter to stop you from mountain biking, consider persuading a friend to steer a four-wheel-drive vehicle to the hut while you and other buddies bike the tire tracks. The climbing will surely keep you warm and toasty. Spend the night at the hut and on the next day, ski the powdery backcountry, then bike back down to Camp Hale. Who says you can't have it all?

Services: Water and pit toilets are available at Camp Hale, about a mile before the ride's starting point, as well as at the Fowler-Hilliard Hut. For an overnight stay at the hut, please call the Tenth Mountain Trail Association, listed below. At Camp Hale, 21 campsites are available, generally from June to Labor Day. Several ponds and creeks near the campgrounds reportedly offer good fishing. Reservations are recommended and can be made by calling Mistex at (800) 283-CAMP. All services, including lodging, gas, phone, food, and restaurants, are available almost 15 miles south on US 24 in Leadville, and in Red Cliff and Minturn, about 5 miles and 12 miles north on US 24, respectively.

Hazards: The altitude and exposed ridges are the only real hazards. Take plenty of water with you as you'll be huffing and puffing above 10,000'. After the first 6 miles, the trail traverses the wide open saddle of Ptarmigan Hill. Though the view is expansive and exhilerating, don't get caught in a thunder and lightning storm here, for there is no real safe shelter nearby.

Rescue index: The entire route is on moderately rugged jeep roads. Though you may meet other outdoor enthusiasts here, this is not a tremendously popular road. So, if you get caught in a serious emergency, plan on biking back down to your car and, perhaps, driving to the nearest phone in Red Cliff, about 5 miles north on US 24, or flagging down a motorist for help. Otherwise, in dry conditions, a two-wheel-drive passenger vehicle, even with low clearance, can make it up the dirt roads.

Land status: White River National Forest.

Maps: Trails Illustrated® map: #109, Breckenridge South. USGS 7.5 minute quad: Pando, Colorado.

Finding the trail: Camp Hale is located on the east side of US 24, between Tennessee Pass and Red Cliff. Turn into Camp Hale and, before proceeding past the memorial area, take a moment to appreciate the history featured by the informational signs and photos here. Note, there are several highway turnoffs to the camp. The one you want is *not* the one signed Camp Hale *South,* though there are more historical signs and ruins there to inspect. Three trailheads originate in this wide, open area. Find the road leading east into the hills, near the northern end of Camp Hale, at the junction of paved East Forest Eagle Road (Forest Service Road 714) and Resolution Creek Road (FS 702, a dirt road). Park and begin your ride from this point.

Sources of additional information:

White River National Forest
Holy Cross Ranger District
24747 US 24
Minturn, CO 81645
(303) 827-5715

Tenth Mountain Trail Association
1280 Ute Avenue
Aspen, CO 81611
(303) 925-5775
Reservations are required for hut stays.

Notes on the trail: This is a fairly straightforward, easy-to-follow route. Still, since there are several junctions and turnoffs, it's best to have a map with you. Begin your ride by pedaling up Resolution Creek Road, FS 702, with the creek on your right. After several miles, FS 715 intersects FS 702. Stay left on FS 702 and continue traversing the hillside with the creek below, a few yards on your right.

As you slowly but steadily grind your way up the gradual hill, the road travels through groves of aspen and pine, alternating between dense, lush growth and wide open meadows. If you're lucky, you might spot elk or deer near the creek.

Almost 5 miles into the ride, after climbing nearly 2,110′, you reach a wide, open area. You're at approximately 11,360′. Farther up, at the junction of Ptarmigan Road (FS 751, a jeep road), turn left. You're now heading northwest and rising above timberline. Ahead of you, looking across the Eagle River valley, is a magnificent, expansive view of the Sawatch Range and the Holy Cross Wilderness. Keep your eyes peeled for wildlife off in the distance.

The steepness of the road levels out slightly. In less than a quarter mile, you come to a narrow hiking trail leading off to your right and uphill. This path takes you to the top of Ptarmigan Hill, at 12,143′. If you're aching for more steep climbing, tackle this little spur—it gains 703′ in about a half mile.

Otherwise, stay on the main jeep road and continue the gradual climb. Follow the road as it curves to the right and mostly flattens out. As you round the curve, you'll see the Fowler-Hilliard Hut straight ahead and across the valley. The road gently takes you up and down a hill for about 1 more mile. Eventually, you reach a turnoff leading down and then up to the left. Take this turnoff and follow it through a wide gate and open area signed "10th Mountain Hut Parking Area." Pedal past the gate and to the hut.

To return, go back the way you came, enjoying a fast descent to Camp Hale. Watch out for an occasional car and for off-road vehicles.

RIDE 27 *TENNESSEE PASS TO HOLY CROSS WILDERNESS*

Here's a 6.5-mile stretch of single-track trail that takes you from Tennessee Pass to the Holy Cross Wilderness boundary, via the lovely Colorado Trail. Total distance of this out-and-back route is about 13 miles. Because there are few technically difficult, rocky spots, experienced novices can still enjoy this ride as much as intermediate-skilled riders. Several portions of the trail contain a single obstacle and are so narrow that all riders are likely to dismount, take a couple of steps over it, and then hop back on their bikes. If you possess great bunny-hopping skills, here's where they come in handy. Easy. That shouldn't discourage anyone from trying this route. Just being on the trail, as it weaves through peaceful aspen and pine groves, and wide open meadows of brilliantly colored wildflowers, with views of the snow-rimmed Continental Divide set against a deep blue sky, makes the tricky parts worthwhile.

If you're ambitious, consider these two possibilities: One, pedal a detour stretch to a hut named the Tenth Mountain Division Hut and use that as your base camp from which to explore other biking and hiking routes. Two, gather up your camping gear, pedal to the Holy Cross Wilderness boundary, park your bike there, and then hike into the Holy Cross Wilderness for an overnighter. (Bikes are prohibited in all designated Wilderness Areas.)

General location: This trail is about 142 miles southwest of Denver. The trailhead at Tennessee Pass is located on US 24, about 9 miles northwest of Leadville and 24.5 miles south of Interstate 70.

Elevation change: The trailhead begins at Tennessee Pass (10,424′) and reaches 10,900′ at the Holy Cross Wilderness boundary, for a gain of about 476′. From the trailhead to the Tenth Mountain Division Hut, at 11,520′, the gain is 1,096′.

Season: The best biking time is from midspring to early autumn. By late spring, you may find lingering patches of snow leaving puddles on the trail. As with other high altitude rides in Colorado during this time of year, be prepared for

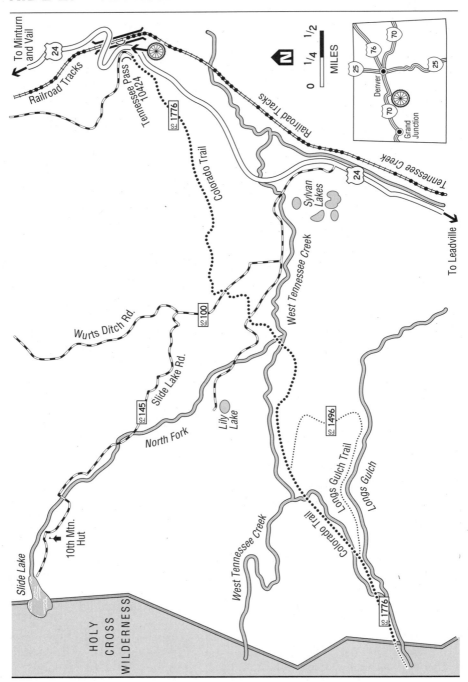

The trail is spiced with some challenging and exciting sections.

thunder and lightning storms as well as occasional freak snow showers.

Services: Water is not available at the Tennessee Pass trailhead, though pit toilets are. Your nearest, most reliable source for water is in Leadville in the Safeway shopping center, located at the junction of US 24 and CO 91, about 9 miles away. Several segments on the trail to Holy Cross Wilderness, as well as the detour to the Tenth Mountain Division Hut, run alongside creeks, but this water must be treated before consuming. All other services, such as food, lodging, restaurants, and phone, can be found in Leadville. For camping information, call the San Isabel National Forest Leadville Ranger District, listed below.

Hazards: Several short sections of the trail are fairly rugged, and may require dismounting. Your greatest concern will most likely be thunder and lightning storms, since portions of the trail travel through wide open meadows. The trail is mostly single-track, and visibility is partially obscured by dense stands of trees. For that reason, be aware that hikers and other bikers may be on the trail.

Rescue index: This section of the Colorado Trail is more popular with hikers than bikers, and does not see heavy use. For emergency assistance, you should return to the trailhead, where your chances of finding help from passing motorists are greater. Located across US 24 from the trailhead is Ski Cooper, but because it is closed during the summer, you shouldn't anticipate finding aid or an accessible telephone. The nearest public phone is in Leadville. Should you need to expedite evacuation, take note that the Colorado Trail intersects a rugged, two-wheel-drive dirt road about 3 miles from the trailhead.

Land status: San Isabel National Forest. White River National Forest.

Maps: The Colorado Trail map: # 8. Trails Illustrated® maps: #109, Breckenridge South, and #126, Holy Cross Wilderness. USGS 7.5 minute quads: Homestake Reservoir and Leadville North, Colorado.

Finding the trail: The trailhead is reached from the parking lot at Tennessee Pass. From the junction of US 24 and CO 91 in Leadville, drive northwest on US 24 for almost 9 miles to the Pass, where you'll find a parking lot on the west side of US 24. From I-70, take the Minturn exit (Exit 171) onto US 24 and proceed south for almost 24.5 miles to the Pass. Across from the parking lot is the entrance to Ski Cooper as well as a large granite monument commemorating World War II soliders of the Tenth Mountain Division.

Sources of additional information:

San Isabel National Forest
Leadville Ranger District
2015 North Poplar
Leadville, CO 80461
(719) 486-0749

White River National Forest
Holy Cross Ranger District
P.O. Box 190
24747 US 24
Minturn, CO 81645
(303) 827-5715

Tenth Mountain Trail Association
1280 Ute Avenue
Aspen, CO 81611
(303) 925-5775
Reservations are required for hut stays.

The Colorado Guide, by Bruce Caughey and Dean Winstanley. Golden, Colorado: Fulcrum Publishing, 1991. To order, write Fulcrum Publishing, 350 Indiana Street, Suite 350, Golden, CO 80401.

Notes on the trail: From the parking lot, the Colorado Trail can be reached at two spots: the north and south ends of the lot. You want the south end trailhead. Like other portions of the Colorado Trail, this is a fairly well-marked, straightforward route. The first several miles roll gently up and down, weaving through dense groves of aspen and pine. Every so often, you can catch a glimpse of the Tennessee Park valley to the south. If you're quiet, you may be rewarded with the sight of grazing deer.

Trail condition is delightfully rideable, with a few narrow, gravel, and rocky sections. After about 2.5 miles and several water crossings on well-made wooden bridges, the Colorado Trail intersects Wurts Ditch Road, a rugged two-wheel-drive dirt road identified as Forest Service Road 100. Follow the arrow on the sign, pointing to the continuation of the Colorado Trail, bypassing FS 100. (To reach the Tenth Mountain Division Hut, you would make a right turn onto Wurts Ditch Road, heading north and, shortly thereafter, take a left turn onto Slide Lake Road, FS 145.)

Almost immediately you reach a short, steep downhill section that's riddled with loose rocks and boulders. Experienced gonzo riders might want to lower their seats for better control, while novices can consider dismounting. It's only a few yards long. About a half mile from this point, you reach another dirt road crossing, which is also marked with directional pointers to the Colorado Trail and Lily Lake. This short 1-mile detour to Lily Lake is worth exploring, either now or on the return trip.

Continuing on the Colorado Trail, cross Tennessee Creek at 2 points and follow signs and cairns. After the second creek crossing, the Colorado Trail travels a jeep road due south for a few yards. On the right side of the road, look for a small sign indicating the continuation of the Colorado Trail and follow it. There are several paths wandering off this road, one of which leads to a gravel pit site. If you reach this point, you just missed the Colorado Trail turnoff.

Back on the Colorado Trail, the path is generally a smooth, dirt, single-track with few gravel and rocky sections. It is basically level and leads you through serene groves of aspen trees. After several miles, you reach the junction of Long Gulch Trail. Bypass Long Gulch and proceed for almost a half mile to the Holy Cross Wilderness boundary. After enjoying lunch or a break by the creek or a short hike into the Wilderness area, return the way you came.

If you like to explore, consider taking the Long Gulch Trail on your return, as indicated on the Trails Illustrated® maps and the Colorado Trail map #8. I have not ridden this spur, which is actually a ski trail, but if you like an adventure, check it out. Note that ski trails are not always suitable for biking—you may wind up abandoning this spur. According to the maps, this route rejoins the Colorado Trail after 3 miles and a steep climb.

RIDE 28 *HAGERMAN TUNNEL*

Imagine being surrounded by three designated Wilderness Areas as you pedal through a bit of Colorado railroad history. To say that the surrounding landscape is absolutely, breathtakingly gorgeous is understating the rewards of this outing. Flanked by Holy Cross Wilderness on the north, Hunter-Fryingpan Wilderness and the Continental Divide on the west, and Mount Massive Wilderness on the south, every inch of this route is a feast for the eyes and spirit.

This route is a 16-mile out-and-back-with-a-loop ride, give or take a mile, depending on how much you want to explore. It combines Hagerman Pass Road (a two-wheel-drive dirt road) and the Midland Railroad Grade Trail, and is moderately demanding on endurance—other than the initial climb up, the terrain is mostly level. In fact, most of the ride is on abandoned railroad grades. As for technical requirements, there are several short segments that are quite difficult but, for the most part, the trail is intermediate with plenty of challenges to keep the pedaling fun. Novices with some single-track experience may feel more comfortable walking their bikes through the tough sections. Something else to consider is the fact that the Skinner Hut of the Tenth Mountain Division Hut System is nearby and can make a great base camp from which to explore other, slightly more challenging bike routes on both sides of Hagerman Pass. (For more information about the huts, refer to the introduction to this section.)

History and railroad buffs will find plenty to enjoy here. Construction of Hagerman Tunnel, at 11,530′, was completed in 1887. Crews bored a route through the Continental Divide, between Leadville and the Roaring Fork Valley. Several years later, the maintenance costs became too high, so crews constructed another tunnel, the Busk-Ivanhoe Tunnel, later known as the Carlton Tunnel, just 800′ lower. Hagerman Tunnel came back into use again in 1898, only to be finally abandoned the following year.

Though the railroad companies carved and rumbled through this region in the late 1800s, Mother Nature has reclaimed her scarred land and virtually healed it with awe-inspiring splendor. Today, there are many fascinating spots to explore, such as the old railroad town of Douglas and the now-collapsed Colorado Midland Railroad Bridge. You'll see remnants of history along the trail—wooden railroad ties, abandoned rail beds, collapsed trestles, and ghost cabins. Sound like a mess? Not really. All this ruin is dwarfed by the powerful aura of the surrounding mountains and valleys; it is profoundly humbling. When Janine, my biking friend, and I rode this route in early August, we were wonderfully surprised at Mother Nature's generous and dazzling display of late-blooming wildflowers, many of which grew alongside bits and pieces of the once-mighty railroad. We even encountered a huge patch of snow on the trail, hiding behind several boulders and burying wooden rail beams. It's incredible how Mother Nature can be so forgiving of the scars we inflict upon her. She heals herself, and we are all so lucky for it.

General location: This area is about 105 miles southwest of Denver. The start of the route is approximately 9 miles west of Leadville, due southwest from Turquoise Lake.

Elevation change: The ride begins at 10,220′, at the junction of South Turquoise Lake Road and Hagerman Pass Road. The highest point is 11,530′, at the east portal of Hagerman Tunnel. Total elevation gain is 1,310′.

Season: The trail is usually rideable from late spring through early fall, depending on weather conditions. Due to elevation, occasional snow showers in the late summer are possible.

Services: There are no services throughout the trail. Though several lakes and small creeks offer water, you must treat it before drinking. During the summer, potable water and toilets are available at May Queen Campground, about 2 miles past the Hagerman Pass Road junction on South Turquoise Lake Road. A convenient, one-stop source for drinkable water, food, toilets, and public phone is at the Safeway store in Leadville, located just over 9 miles from the trailhead at the intersection of US 24 and Mountain View Drive. Lodging and restaurants abound in Leadville. Eight campgrounds, totaling over 368 campsites, surround Turquoise Lake. For summer camping, reservations are highly recommended since this is a popular fishing and boating lake and sites fill quickly. Most of the campgrounds are open between Memorial Day and Labor Day, so call the San Isabel National Forest Ranger District Office for up-to-date information, (719) 486-0749.

Hazards: Watch for vehicular traffic while pedaling on Hagerman Pass Road, the well-traveled dirt road leading up to the Colorado Midland Railroad Centennial trailhead. Be especially alert on this section on the return to your parked car as it can be a fast descent around curves and potholes, and over washboard conditions. On the level, single-track portions, the trail weaves tightly around boulders of all sizes. Consequently, there are numerous opportunities to catch a pedal and be thrown off balance. If you're a novice, you may want to dismount.

Rescue index: Medical attention can be found in Leadville, about 9.5 miles away. During the summer, this is a popular hiking route and you might find other trail users who may be of help. Two-wheel-drive vehicles can survive the drive up Hagerman Pass Road all the way to the Colorado Midland Railroad Centennial trailhead. Since none of the campgrounds around Turquoise Lake have public phones, the nearest one is in Leadville at the Safeway shopping center.

Land status: San Isabel National Forest.

Maps: Trails Illustrated® maps: #126, Holy Cross Wilderness and #127, Independence Pass. USGS 7.5 minute quads: Homestake Reservoir and Mount Massive, Colorado. The Colorado Trail map: #9.

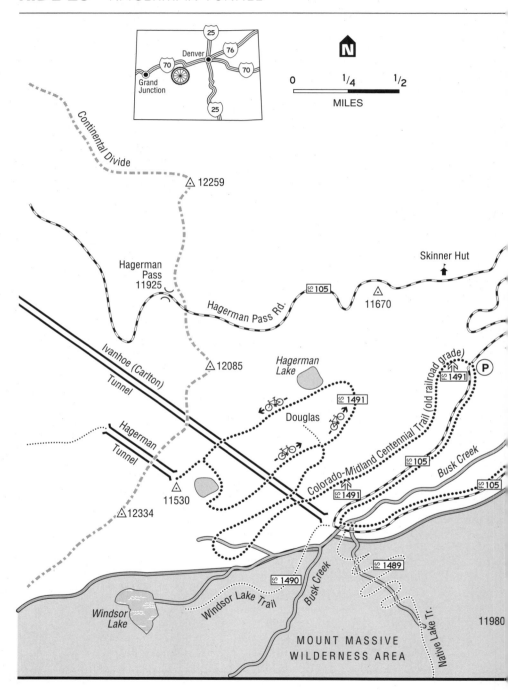

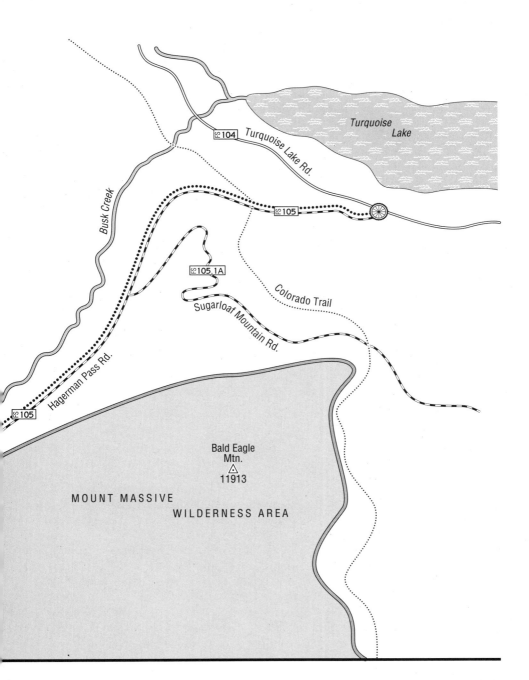

Trust us, Mother Nature really outdid herself when she created the landscape here. This black and white photo is merely a hint.

Finding the trail: These directions are from the Safeway on the northern edge of Leadville, located at the junction of US 24 and Mountain View Road. Drive west on Mountain View Road and follow the road as it curves to the north, then back towards the west again. When the road reaches a T intersection adjacent to a set of railroad tracks, turn right (north) and parallel the tracks for a short distance. At the first opportunity, turn left (west) and cross over the tracks, still on pavement. At 3.5 miles from Safeway, you enter the San Isabel National Forest. At the first stop sign, after you pass the U.S. Forest Service entrance sign, you should see markers showing that a right turn is toward the Baby Doe Campground, while a left turn goes to the Molly Brown campsite. Turn left (south). At the next intersection, with Turquoise Lake barely visible through lodgepole pine trees on your right, turn right (west) and immediately find yourself crossing the Sugarloaf Dam face. Continue driving along the lake and, after several miles, the Hagerman Pass Road intersects on your left, marked by a sign. Turn onto this dirt road and proceed a few yards up until you find a small pulloff area on the right for your car. Park and start your ride from here.

Sources of additional information:

San Isabel National Forest
Leadville Ranger District
2015 North Poplar
Leadville, CO 80461
(719) 486-0749

Colorado State Parks
1313 Sherman Street, Room 618
Denver, CO 80203
(303) 866-3437
For more information about the Rails-to-Trails program in Colorado.

Tenth Mountain Trail Association
1280 Ute Avenue
Aspen, CO 81611
(303) 925-5775
Reservations are required for hut stays.

The Colorado Guide, by Bruce Caughey and Dean Winstanley. Golden, Colorado: Fulcrum Publishing, 1991. To order, write Fulcrum Publishing, 350 Indiana Street, Suite 350, Golden, CO 80401.

Notes on the trail: Begin pedaling up Hagerman Pass Road at its junction with South Turquoise Lake Road. This is a two-wheel-drive dirt road, accented with washboard sections, frequent potholes, and vehicular traffic. After climbing almost 4 miles and gaining 576′, stay on the main road, bypassing the trailhead to Rock Creek and an abandoned mine, both on your left. Continue for another mile and keep an eye out for a sign marking the Colorado-Midland Centennial Trail, also on your left. There may be a "closed" sign at the trailhead—not to worry, it applies to motor vehicles, not bikers or hikers. Across from this trailhead is an open area for car parking.

By the way, Hagerman Pass Road continues much farther beyond this point as a four-wheel-drive road. After several miles, it leads you past the Skinner Hut, over and down Hagerman Pass to the other side of the Sawatch Range, towards Ruedi Reservoir and Basalt. The Skinner Hut is one of 14 in the Tenth Mountain Trail Association Hut System, and, like the others in the system, it is "luxuriously" rustic, equipped with the basic amenities. It makes an excellent base camp from which to explore other biking routes. Reservations are required. (If you'd like more information, contact the Tenth Mountain Trail Association at the address listed above.) You can have lots of riding and exploring adventures from here!

Now, let's turn our attention back to the Colorado-Midland Centennial Trail. Here is where the railroad grade, single-track path begins and it's pure fun. At first glance, Janine and I didn't think this was the trail because it looked more like a narrow, rocky creek bed. Upon closer inspection, we realized that this is a short, intermittently wet section, bounded on both sides by tall boulders. As you ride through this wet segment, you begin to realize that the path contains buried rail ties. Dodging the chunks of rocks in the creek is fun, but keeping your feet in the pedals instead of in the water can be tricky.

A couple of miles later the path becomes a dry, dirt single-track with scattered rocks throughout a gradual ascent. Pine and blue spruce trees abound and, as you pedal further, you can't help but notice the snow-covered, treeless peaks coming into view straight ahead. On your left, through the trees, you can see the valley and the Hagerman Pass Road on which you rode up. Eventually, the trail seems to end abruptly, facing west, at an extremely steep drop-off. At this point, look over your right shoulder and you'll discover that the trail continues to the northeast, up a steep, very technical, rocky section. Take heart, for this segment is very short and the trail quickly becomes an easy, wide single-track again as it heads northwest.

Your next landmark is a four-way intersection, marked by a wooden sign inscribed with an arrow pointing to your right. Before taking this right turn, consider staying straight past the intersection for a few yards. This detour leads you to several abandoned cabins, the weathered remains of the town of Douglas. The cabins were small, but the scenery and view of the Continental Divide definitely made up for it.

After the detour, backtrack to the intersection and follow the trail as directed by the arrow. The route is a gentle, uphill climb, alternating between wide and narrow single-track. Pedal over scattered rail ties and begin weaving through loose rocks, boulders, and blue spruce trees. The narrow single-track soon becomes a wider path, covered with charcoal-colored gravel. More rail ties are scattered about and the trail is edged with a profusion of brilliant wildflowers.

Follow the rail-bed trail and, eventually, it will end at a drop-off, with a narrow path leading down the left side. Look straight ahead about 200 yards, and you'll realize that the rail bed resumes on the other side of a deep ravine. Scattered in and among the shrubs are wooden ties, evidence that a trestle once connected the railroad across this trough. And, sitting majestically behind your left shoulder is the snow-rimmed Continental Divide. What a glorious place. Continue down the narrow path on the left and shortly thereafter rejoin the rail-bed path.

The trail winds to the left, toward the north, and then curves to the west. On your right is Hagerman Lake, an ice-cold, secluded lake sitting at timberline, about 11,360′. For all you fans of fishing, hooking small cutthroat trout is reportedly fair at this lake. Pedal about a half mile more to reach the east portal of Hagerman Tunnel. In 1887, at the time of completion, it was the highest railroad tunnel in the world, standing at 11,530′ above sea level. Face the now blocked tunnel entrance, and directly behind you, below the trail, is a tiny, serene lake.

After visiting the tunnel and enjoying the expansive view to the east, backtrack for several yards on the same trail. Look to your right, towards the tiny lake, for a lone, weathered telegraph pole, a few yards from the main path. Use this pole as your turnoff marker, and follow the narrow single-track trail as it leads away from the main rail route and down to the lake. This section is steep and twisting, shaped by boulders and loose rocks. It's technically challenging—dismounting is an option! This short stretch soon levels out, remaining quite rocky. Ride over more rail ties and continue around the lake.

Eventually, this trail takes you back to the dilapidated town of Douglas, where you pass a few more abandoned cabins. If you have time and good weather, this area is worth exploring, as the Busk-Ivanhoe Tunnel (later called the Carlton Tunnel) is nearby. The trail soon leads you to the 4-way intersection that you previously crossed. You've just pedaled a loop. From here, make a right turn and retrace the path back to the trailhead at Hagerman Pass Road, and, ultimately, to your car.

RIDE 29   *SHRINE PASS AND LIME CREEK ROADS TO RED CLIFF*

When my biking friends—Ken, Jolanda, and Zack—and I got together for this ride in mid-October, the day was sunny, cool, and refreshingly crisp—sort of like a welcome smack in the face. By now, the aspen had already turned golden and shed most of their leaves. The skies were clear and brilliantly blue. What a perfect day for an exhilarating, downhill ride from Shrine Pass Road to Red Cliff, via Shrine Pass and Lime Creek Road. Our hearts and lungs got a workout within the first three miles from the Vail Pass exit off Interstate 70 (10,601') up to Shrine Pass (11,089'). After that, it was all downhill—nine miles—to Red Cliff. Throughout the 12-mile ride, the only technically challenging section we encountered was on lower Lime Creek Road. Other than that, both of these two-wheel-drive roads were generally smooth, with a few washboard sections. Admittedly, rumors of tasty Mexican food and cold beer served in several of Red Cliff's restaurants provided additional incentive to ride that day. We confirmed the rumors upon our arrival.

How did we return to the start with a full belly, you ask? By car. We made this a point-to-point ride by arranging a vehicle shuttle with the top car at Vail Pass and the bottom car in Red Cliff. (Several other options are listed at the end of this chapter.)

The scenery was enticing too. Once named Holy Cross Trail, Shrine Pass Road offers outstanding views of the Mount of the Holy Cross (14,005') from Shrine Pass. In 1929, Herbert Hoover was so awed by the sight that he desig-

RIDE 29 *SHRINE PASS AND LIME CREEK ROADS TO RED CLIFF*

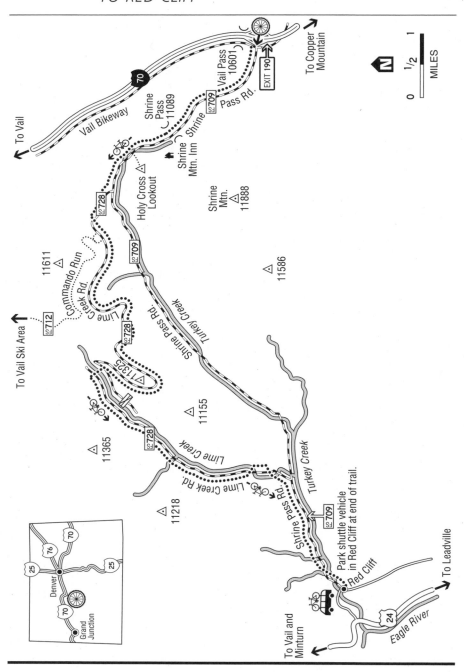

Splish, splash as Linda crosses tiny Lime Creek.

nated it and the adjacent area a national monument. Good call, Mr. President. From the very beginning of the ride, we couldn't ignore the 180-degree, majestic view of the mountain ranges behind us: the Gore Range in the northeast, and the Tenmile Range along the southeast horizon. Once over the pass, we began to catch glimpses of the Sawatch Range to the southwest and the Flat Tops in the far west. What more enticement do you need?

How about history? While you're storming down the west side of Vail Pass, try to imagine the world engaged in battle during World War II. Visualize snow-covered mountains, windswept white peaks, and subzero temperatures. In the winters between 1942 and 1945, the area just southwest of Shrine and Vail passes became home to the Tenth Mountain Divison, an elite ski corps of the U.S. Army. About 14,000 soliders trained here for later combat against the Nazis in the snow-covered regions of Europe. In 1980, veterans, families, and friends organized the Tenth Mountain Trail Association to commemorate the ski troopers. Historical sites were marked and preserved. Trails were expanded and 10 fully operational huts were built with at least 6 more planned.

All huts are well-equipped and available for year-round overnight stays. Reservations are required and should be placed months in advance. What can we say? Once you've been to one of the huts, you'll understand why they're so popular. Refer to the introduction to this section for more information about the Tenth Mountain Division and the Hut System. One of the most luxurious of these huts is the Shrine Mountain Inn near Shrine Pass, just three miles from your start at Vail Pass. This hut is unlike others in the system in that it is a privately owned and operated restaurant and lodge.

This is a great ride with great accommodations right on the trail.

General location: Exit 190 for Vail Pass, approximately 84 miles west of Denver on Interstate 70.

Elevation change: The ride begins at an elevation of 10,580´, virtually atop Vail Pass, and then climbs up and over Shrine Pass, at 11,089´, for a gain of 509´ in 2.5 miles. From there, via Lime Creek Road, the route gradually rises to 11,120´, a whopping gain of 31´ in 5 miles. After that, the route descends to the town of Red Cliff, at 8,680´, for a loss of 2,440´ in nearly 8 miles.

Season: Consider enjoying this route between late May and late October. Light snowfall in late spring and midautumn is not unusual, leaving some slushy, muddy segments throughout the route. In the summer, occasional afternoon thundershowers are a fact of life up here. Wildflowers have been known to carpet the rolling hillsides and meadows near Shrine Pass between late spring and midsummer.

Services: At the start of the ride at the Vail Pass rest area (Exit 190), water, flush toilets, a pay phone, and a heavily used parking lot are available. Red Cliff is a sleepy little town with limited services. Vail, being a world-famous resort town, has an abundance of lodging and eating establishments, as well as cultural events and festivals throughout the summer.

Hazards: On smooth, hardpack, rip-roaring fast descents, be alert for occasional potholes, which love to devour a front tire and send the rider flying off the bike for a perfect face-plant. Ouch! The last couple of miles of Lime Creek Road as you approach Red Cliff are somewhat technical, with loose rocks and boulders, becoming steep in some spots. Experienced riders will love this section, but beginners are sure to find it intimidating. Don't be discouraged if you're a beginner—there's nothing wrong with dismounting and walking or carrying your bike down the short, difficult segments. Be aware of approaching thunderclouds as you don't want to be around the open, exposed terrain of Shrine Pass during a lightning storm.

Rifle hunting season generally commences in September. For current information, call the Colorado Division of Wildlife at (303) 297-1192.

Rescue index: Shrine Pass Road is accessible by two-wheel-drive vehicles and is frequently traveled in the summer. Though not popular with sightseers, Lime

Creek Road is mostly accessible by four-wheel-drive and, occasionally, you may see a rancher tending stock. If you have an emergency while you're on Lime Creek Road, your chances of finding help from other trail users are better back on Shrine Pass Road. If you can't find help there, pedal back up to the Shrine Mountain Inn, to the Vail Pass rest area, or down into Red Cliff and call for help.

Land status: Arapaho National Forest. White River National Forest.

Maps: Trails Illustrated® map: #108, Vail Pass. USGS 7.5 minute quads: Vail Pass and Red Cliff, Colorado.

Vail & Eagle Valley Mountain Biking & Recreation. A map of trails and ride descriptions published by Latitude 40°, Inc., Box 4086, Boulder, CO 80306. Phone: (303) 258-7909. This useful map of trails contains route descriptions. It's sold in area bike shops and other retail outlets.

Finding the trail: Since this route requires a vehicle shuttle, place the return car in Red Cliff at the end of Shrine Pass Road. Then transport all riders and bikes to the starting point at Exit 190 off I-70, just on the east side of Vail Pass. Park on the south side of I-70 in the rest area. Reach Shrine Pass Road by pedaling on the road back toward I-70. Just before the overpass, make a hairpin left turn onto a paved road marked Forest Service Road 709. The road becomes a two-wheel-drive dirt road shortly thereafter. (Don't follow the bicycle sign that indicates the frontage road skirting I-70—that's the continuation of the Vail Bikeway. Look for a description of that trail in Ride 32.)

Sources of additional information:

White River National Forest
Holy Cross Ranger District
P.O. Box 190
24747 US 24
Minturn, CO 81645
(303) 827-5715

Tenth Mountain Trail Association
1280 Ute Avenue
Aspen, CO 81611
(303) 925-5775
Reservations for overnight stays in any of the huts are required. Dinner reservations at the Shrine Mountain Inn are recommended.

Rocky Mountain News Ride Guide, by David Nelson. Denver, Colorado: Denver Publishing Company, 1992. To order, write Denver Publishing Company, 721 Grape Street, Denver, CO 80220.

Bicycling the Backcountry, A Mountain Bike Guide to Colorado, by William L. Stoehr. Boulder, Colorado: Pruett Publishing, 1987. To order, write Pruett Publishing, 2928 Pearl Street, Boulder, CO 80301.

The Colorado Guide, by Bruce Caughey and Dean Winstanley. Golden, Colorado: Fulcrum Publishing, 1991. To order, write Fulcrum Publishing, 350 Indiana Street, Suite 350, Golden, CO 80401.

Notes on the trail: Following Shrine Pass Road (FS 709) is fairly easy since it is an obvious, well-traveled, two-wheel-drive dirt road. You could put your bike in automatic pilot as you cruise up and down the road for about 2.5 miles to Shrine Pass. The grade varies between 10 and 20% in sections while the expansive view of the snowcapped Gore Range mountains spurs you onward. The fragrance of spruce, lodgepole pine, and fir trees fills the senses. As you breathe a little harder, you'll find yourself thinking, "What fresh air! It's great to be here!"

Approaching the Pass, you can see Shrine Mountain Inn off in the near distance, peacefully sitting in the rolling, open meadows. If you picked the right time of year, you'll be greeted with a carpet of colorful wildflowers. The gated entrance to the Inn is almost 3 miles from the Vail Pass rest area.

Continue past the Inn, leaving Arapaho National Forest and entering White River National Forest, staying on the smooth dirt road. As you descend the Shrine Pass summit, listen closely and you'll hear Turkey Creek running down the valley on your left. After 4 miles, also on your left, is a turnoff leading a few yards down a single-track trail to a viewing platform of the Holy Cross Wilderness and the Mount of the Holy Cross. It's worth a look. The Cross is created by variations in the mountain terrain and is easy to see if there's lingering snow covering the mountainside.

Back on the main road, pedal a few yards and then hang a right onto FS 728, Lime Creek Road. (An option here is to stay on FS 709 (Shrine Pass Road) all the way into Red Cliff. It's a smooth, easy, downhill cruise that saves you about 4 miles and bypasses the short, somewhat technical section on Lime Creek Road.)

Pedal a short distance and arrive at another fork marked FS 712, leading off to your right. This is the top of Commando Run. Skip this spur, stay on FS 728, and bypass yet another spur marked Two Elk. (No one in our group had ever ridden the Commando Run and Two Elk trails, which are really premier cross-country ski trails. However, I am told that both trails can be ridden with bikes and, ultimately, lead you down to the Golden Peaks runs at the Vail ski resort, then into the town of Vail. If you want to explore these routes, I highly suggest taking a detailed topo map that shows Commando Run and Two Elk, as the trails are reportedly not well marked. Lastly, get directions from a local rider or bike shop.)

Keep pedaling on Lime Creek Road, FS 728, and pass another spur marked FS 728A. Stay on this two-wheel-drive road for about 2 miles and then begin a downhill cruise. Continue on the road for another mile as it descends more steeply, at which point the route begins to deteriorate into a narrow jeep trail. Keep your eyes peeled here, because after a sharp hairpin turn to the left, you need to turn off onto a tiny, single-track trail, obscured by trees, leading down and off to the right of the jeep trail. It's an easy turnoff to miss, especially on a fast downhill. We flew right past it the first time. If you reach a wide gate across the jeep road, you've gone too far by about one-quarter mile. Back to that sneaky little turnoff: follow this narrow single-track for a few yards as it takes you down through the woods and across a tiny creek (this is the very beginning of Lime Creek). On the other side of the creek, find another jeep road and head south (to your left). At this point, you have pedaled almost 12 miles. Lime Creek is now off in the distance to your left, and the road begins a gentle, downhill run through a narrow, open valley. It's easy to pick up speed and feel the exhilaration as you fly down this section, but be aware that there are a few potholes waiting to send you airborne.

After cruising for a couple of miles, the trail begins to narrow and become rocky and steep in spots. Intermediate technical skill is needed here, though dismounting and walking works too. At the end of this segment, the trail rejoins Shrine Pass Road, just several miles from Red Cliff. Turn right onto Shrine Pass Road and follow it alongside Turkey Creek. Pedal through a gate and over a bridge into Red Cliff and to where you have left your return vehicle.

RIDE 30 *LOST LAKE LOOP*

Lost Lake is a small alpine pond lined with plump lily pads and hidden among dense fir and spruce forests. Powerful reflections of the Gore Range's snow-draped peaks shimmer in its placid waters. Fishing is known to be respectable, and the pond is rimmed with numerous, secluded rest sites. Where the forest parts, noble Mount of the Holy Cross and Grouse Mountain can be seen hanging over the distant Beaver Creek Ski Area.

The Lost Lake Loop blends all aspects of alpine mountain biking, but the highlight is a playful single-track that is perfect for honing your riding skills. Weave through lanky lodgepole pine, bunny-hop and dodge neatly spaced boulders, then coast along a silky-smooth trail coated with crunchy pine needles. You just may want to do this ride twice!

This 12.5-mile, counterclockwise loop combines good dirt roads and rough, four-wheel-drive roads with both smooth and exacting single-track. Moderate climbing is mixed with a handful of lung-busting surges. Overall, the route is suited for intermediate bikers, although the single-track section stemming from Lost Lake may force even skilled riders to dismount and take to foot occasionally. Expect to lift or shoulder your bike over the deadfall that litters the trail around Lost Lake. If pedaling straight from Vail, the ride to and from the trailhead combined with the described loop is advanced level.

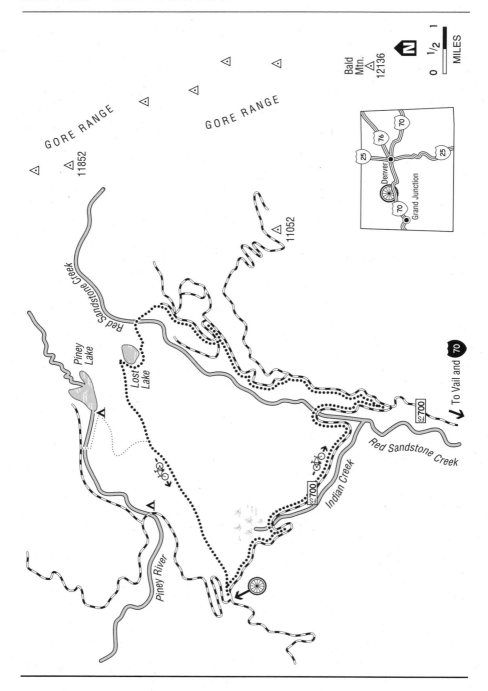

Dodging the pines along the Lost Lake trail. Photo: Gregg Bromka.

General location: Eight miles north of Vail.

Elevation change: From the upper Lost Lake hiking trail parking area (9,627'), the route begins with a gentle 400' descent on the Red Sandstone Road. The climb to Lost Lake is progressive, ending at 10,160'. The route's highest point of 10,248' follows before the trail descends gently back to the trailhead.

Season: Most of the route is free of snow by early June, but patches may linger around Lost Lake well through the month. Expect cold temperatures and flurries by mid-October.

Services: No services or water taps will be found along this route. All surface waters should be purified. Vail has all visitor services, from basic to extravagant.

Hazards: The Lost Lake hiking trail is a lesson in learning exactly how much clearance your pedals and chain rings will allow, for the trail is loaded with golf ball–to basketball–sized rocks. Plus, you will master the fine art of gauging tire pressure; too little will result in the inevitable snakebite flat, too much and your bike becomes a bucking bronco.

Be courteous to hikers, equestrians, and other bikers on the single-track by allowing them the right of way. Since the trail leading from the parking area is a relatively easy hike, families with children are common.

Rescue index: Red Sandstone Road is very popular with motorists. On weekends and holidays vehicles may pass every few minutes. Dirt roads leading to Lost Lake are more remote. Hikers and equestrians are common on the Lost Lake hiking trail.

Land status: White River National Forest.

Maps: USGS 7.5 minute quadrangles: East Vail and West Vail, Colorado. USGS 1:50,000 scale county map: Eagle County #2, Colorado.

Finding the trail: Adjacent to the West Vail shopping center, drive east on paved roads signed for Red Sandstone Road. (The shopping center is located on the north side of Interstate 70 near Exit 173/West Vail). Fork left on Forest Service Road 700. Red Sandstone Road, a maintained dirt road, winds up the side of the red cliff–lined canyon for about 4 miles to the signed junction with Lost Lake motorized trail (to the right) and Piney Lake (to the left). Continue left on the main dirt road for 4 more miles to a corralled parking area signed for Lost Lake hiking trail. Please register.

Sources of additional information:

White River National Forest
Holy Cross Ranger District
24747 US Highway 24
P.O. Box 190
Minturn, CO 81645
(303) 827-5715

The Mountain Biking Guide to Vail, Colorado, by Michael J. Murphy. Silverthorne, Colorado: Alpenrose Press, 1990.

Notes on the trail: On this loop you will have to pedal about 4 miles on the Red Sandstone Road, a well-maintained, sometimes washboarded, almost always very dusty dirt road. Get this out of the way first so the thrill of single-track riding will be your everlasting memory.

Pedal down the Red Sandstone Road through open meadows enclosed by mixed conifer and aspen. Cross Indian and Upper Red Sandstone creeks, then turn left on the Lost Lake motorized trail, a four-wheel-drive road. After 1.3 miles, fork left onto FS 786. Within a mile, cross over the South Fork of Red Sandstone Creek and ride parallel to it. Shortly thereafter, note a small clearing marked by several primitive campsites. Turn left on a narrower, more rocky, four-wheel-drive road marked by an ATV decal posted to a tree. Bear left at an upcoming junction (trees marked with blue paint confirm the route), then switchback to the right. Stay left at an upcoming fork and descend gradually to the Lost Lake trailhead.

The Lost Lake Trail starts just down the hill and immediately crosses a wooden footbridge. Farther ahead, cross a primitive log bridge spanning a mud hole, then go up the challenging trail clogged with rocks and root networks. Wrap around a marshy area; Lost Lake is just ahead. Skirt the lake in whichever direction seems to have the more developed path (usually clockwise) to its opposite side. The hiking trail branches northwest from the lake, but this junction can be *very* vague. Keep poking around, you will find it.

Once on route, a trail sign is within .3 mile; turn left and go up steep, rocky terrain. Now the trail is quite obvious. Pass straight through the first logged area, curve gradually left through the second clearing, staying next to the jeep road, and then go up a steep hill. After the third logged zone, it is a straight, 2-mile shot atop a subtle ridge back to the parking area.

If you have energy left over, extend the day with a 9-mile round-trip ride to Piney Lake. Just follow the Red Sandstone Road west down into the elongated Piney River Valley. Above the lake stands Mount Powell (13,534´), a stately peak named after pioneer surveyor John Wesley Powell.

RIDE 31 *MEADOW MOUNTAIN LOOP*

Meadow Mountain was once a ski area. Its slopes are now silent meadows dotted with columbine, daisies, and "mule ears" and wrapped in aspen glades. A glance over your shoulder near the ride's beginning reveals the tips of the Gore Range rising above inclined ridges to the northeast. Lionshead Rock, named for its shape, is to the southeast, along with limited views of the Sawatch and Ten Mile ranges. Views grow more majestic with each rising switchback, while the quiet hamlet of Minturn dwindles below.

Highlighting this route is a riveting single-track dropping feverishly through aspen forests and across open meadows. But, just like everywhere else, in the mountain biking world, there is no such thing as a free lunch. This ride begins with a hefty, five-mile, 2,000´ ascent. Those rolling their eyes at this prospect may find riding the gondola up Vail Mountain more inviting. But if you welcome a little sweat and burning quadriceps, the payoff is worth the effort.

Meadow Mountain Loop is a solid, intermediate-level, 12-mile clockwise loop that requires healthy lungs, conditioned legs, and good riding skills. The route begins with moderate to strenuous climbing on four-wheel-drive roads generally with low technical difficulty. The single-track descent ranges from a delightful, gently wavering path to a tight slalom course clogged with roots and rocks. Mostly, though, it is somewhere in-between. Half a dozen trickling

RIDE 31 *MEADOW MOUNTAIN LOOP*

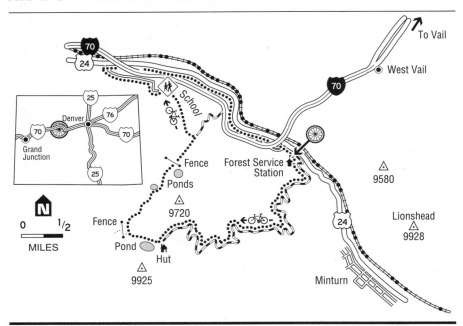

creeks and one larger mud hole are encountered; all are rideable and leave you with only light "backspackle." A few miles of flat paved roads close the loop.

General location: The Meadow Mountain Loop is about 2 miles west of West Vail and about a mile south of Interstate 70 toward Minturn.

Elevation change: The trail begins at 7,750′. Within 5 miles the route rises nearly 2,000′ to its highest point at 9,700′ at the old Forest Service cabin. Then it's back down 2,000′ along single-track dipping just below 7,700′ to the highway. The flat, paved road returning to the parking area is a good cool-down and a chance to reminisce about the preceding adventure.

Season: Meadow Mountain Loop is usually free of snow from late May or early June through October. Early summer, when wildflowers are in bloom and lingering snow drapes the surrounding peaks, and autumn, when aspens give off a golden glow, are enlightening times to pedal this route.

Services: Water is plentiful along the route in numerous streams and ponds but must be purified before drinking. There is no other way to get potable water. Full visitor services can be found in Vail, and in Minturn 1 mile south of the trailhead.

Hazards: The single-track portion of the loop contains the usual challenges,

Sweeping vistas of the Gore Range adorn the Meadow Mountain trail. Photo: Gregg Bromka.

including exposed roots, loose and protruding rocks, water crossings, and steep downhills. Watch for downed trees across the path, especially early in the season. Logging operations may be taking place at any time along the first half of the ride, and hikers are common on the narrow single-track; ride in control and with respect for other trail users.

Rescue index: Meadow Mountain Loop is a popular route for both bikers and hikers. A Forest Service work station is located at the trailhead and there are a high school and a residential area at the trail's end. You are never more than 5 miles from the paved highway. Emergency and medical services are located in Vail, less than 3 miles to the east.

Land status: White River National Forest.

Maps: USGS 7.5 minute quadrangle: Minturn, Colorado. USGS 1:50,000 scale county map: Eagle County #4, Colorado.

Finding the trail: From West Vail, travel 2 miles west on I-70 to Exit 171/Minturn. Head .7 mile southeast on US 24 to the Meadow Mountain parking area on the right side of the road, marked by a Forest Service work station and an assortment of government-green trucks. The trail begins at a green gate behind some houses.

Sources of additional information:

> White River National Forest
> Holy Cross Ranger District
> 24747 US Highway 24
> P.O. Box 190
> Minturn, CO 81645
> (303) 827-5715

The Mountain Biking Guide to Vail, Colorado, by Michael J. Murphy. Silverthorne, Colorado: Alpenrose Press, 1990.

Notes on the trail: From behind the Forest Service work station and the residential area, pass around the green gate and begin a gentle climb on the four-wheel-drive road paralleling the highway. Soon the dirt road turns west and steepens. Find your favorite climbing gear and enjoy the long, winding pull. Where the road enters a stand of aspens 2.7 miles from the start, fork right on Forest Service Road 748 and savor the shade. After a short level stretch, the road climbs a steep pitch to a logged area at 4.2 miles where views are inspiring. Keep chugging up the hill (south) to the 1-room Forest Service cabin in the meadow for a well-deserved break.

The single-track branches west on the north side of the hut and passes a small pond. Less than .3 mile ahead, turn right and go downhill just *before* a wooden fenceline. Do not continue straight on what may seem the more traveled path. Let the fun begin!

The ensuing single-track (a portion of the Whiskey Creek hiking trail) descends both steeply and gently on a smooth and moderately technical trail through fir and aspen forests and past a few beaver ponds. Cross an open meadow bounded by aspen and serviceberry at 7.2 miles, pass through a wire fence, then resume on a four-wheel-drive road. Within one-third mile, branch left from the dirt road and descend on a single-track. (Here, the four-wheel-drive road turns east and descends sharply.) This exciting path drops quickly for 1 mile before exiting at the Battle Mountain High School. Head west on the frontage road a short distance, then turn back east following US 6 and US 24 to the parking area.

RIDE 32 *THE VAIL-TO-BRECKENRIDGE BIKEWAYS*

If you've ever driven on Interstate 70 between Vail and Frisco, you may have noticed a tiny, narrow, paved path meandering through the lush green meadows and forests alongside the freeway. You may also have noticed cyclists, in-line skaters, and walkers—young and old—enjoying the path. Novice or expert, you owe it to yourself to pedal this 35-mile stretch of beautifully paved bikeways that connect Vail, Copper Mountain, Frisco, and Breckenridge, with excursions to Dillon and Keystone. Heading east from Vail, the Vail Bikeway climbs over Vail Pass. At that point, the path is renamed the Tenmile Canyon Recreation Trail, and travels through a steeply walled canyon on its way to Copper Mountain and Frisco. In Frisco, the path is called the Summit County Recreation Trail and skirts the southern edge of town. Finally, turning south towards Breckenridge, it becomes the Blue River Bikeway.

This ten-foot-wide, two-lane path is completely closed to motor vehicles. Though the routes occasionally intersect streets and even share portions of roads, the bikeways are virtually free of motor traffic. And that's comforting news to young families who want to partake of this healthy sport together.

But don't underestimate this route. Experienced cyclists, whether on mountain, hybrid, or road bikes, can still enjoy it. It all depends on how much of it you want to ride, which direction you want to take, and the time you have. Though little technical skill is required, great stamina is needed if you intend to surmount Vail Pass, sitting at 10,580'. Climbing from the town of Vail to the Pass is no piece of cake, either, for the elevation gain is 2,430' in 14.5 miles. Strong cyclists who don't mind riding with panniers filled and weighted with gear can consider camping at several campgrounds throughout the route. Spending the night in any of the towns' or resorts' charming lodges can be a fun alternative too.

And, if you want to add more miles on paved bike trails, consider exploring other parts of Summit County. The town of Dillon and the Keystone ski resort are also accessible on the county's extensive network of paved trails. All in all, you could cover lots of territory and never leave the pavement.

General location: The Vail-to-Breckenridge bike route is located basically between Breckenridge and Vail, ranging from 70 to 100 miles west of Denver. For the longest point-to-point distance, the paved path begins in Breckenridge, 85 miles from Denver, and travels through Frisco and Copper Mountain, terminating in Vail, 100 miles from Denver. The path generally follows I-70 over Vail Pass and can be entered from numerous rest areas along the route.

Elevation change: At one extreme end of the path is Breckenridge, sitting at 9,603'. The other end is Vail at 8,150', which is also the lowest point of the path. The highest point of the route is Vail Pass, 10,580', making 2,430' the total elevation gain from Vail in 14.5 miles. From Breckenridge to the Pass, the gain is 977' in 16 miles.

Season: The bike path is generally free from snow from mid-May to early September. The landscape is gorgeously green and spotted with brilliant wildflowers through the summer, particularly near Vail Pass. As you might suspect, the higher the elevation, the colder the temperatures and the greater the chances of lingering snow. And that applies throughout the summer—freak snowstorms have occurred around Vail Pass in July. Likewise, early snow may make riding

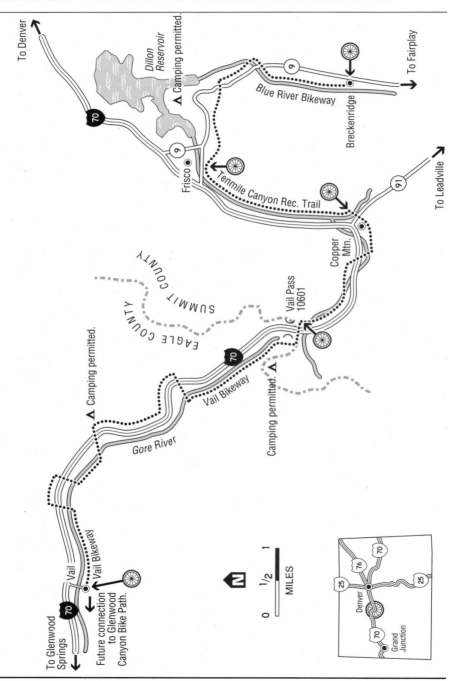

Accessible at numerous points, this easy, beautifully landscaped, paved bikeway stretches 35 miles over rolling hills and valleys.

in October and November a chilly proposition. One of the undisputedly best times to pedal the path is during the change of season in mid- to late September, sometimes even into October. Though the air may be chilly, it's worth bundling up to ride among color-drenched mountainsides painted with breathtaking autumn shades of golds, reds, and greens.

Services: All services can be found in the towns of Breckenridge, Frisco, Copper Mountain, and Vail. Being popular resort towns, they have a wide variety of food and eating establishments, lodging, retail stores (including bike shops), medical facilities, and visitor information centers. Maintained water and toilet facilities are available at several rest areas adjacent to I-70 exits. Any water found in creeks or ponds along the path must be treated before drinking.

Hazards: Generally speaking, the hazards you will encounter on this bike route involve other trail users and auto traffic. Basically, there are more trail users the closer you get to any of the towns. Trail etiquette and safety require bikers to ride on the right side of the bikeway. Though there is a yellow dashed line down the center, watch out for speedy oncoming cyclists and folks riding double-file. It's a good idea to let someone know you're about to pass, either by ringing a bell attached to your bike or by saying, "Passing on your left."

Auto traffic is another hazard. Most of the bike trail meanders alongside a motor route and is generously and safely separated from whizzing traffic. However, there are points along the path that cross highways and share the road with motorists. Watch out for traffic at highway rest areas, too. Traffic hazards are briefly highlighted here: Beginning in Breckenridge, the trail intersects a couple of streets and crosses heavily traveled CO 9 several times. Traffic is frighteningly fast on CO 9 and extreme caution is required, particularly when riding with children. In Frisco, a few streets intersect the path and you'll encounter more people using the trail. In Copper Mountain, a short stretch of the bike route shares the street with motorists before becoming a separated path again. As you descend into East Vail, the trail becomes Old US 6 for about 5 miles. After that, it becomes the paved bike route again as it cruises into East Vail and Vail Village. As you enter Vail Village, the bike path uses city streets. The bike route itself ends just before West Vail.

Rescue index: Since the route follows major highways, you can catch a ride or drive to get help throughout the ride. Medical facilities can be found in the towns. Rest areas include a public pay phone.

Land status: White River National Forest. Arapaho National Forest.

Maps: Trails Illustrated® maps: #108, Vail Pass and #109, Breckenridge South. USGS 7.5 minute quads: Vail Pass, Red Cliff, Vail East, Vail West, Frisco, and Breckenridge, Colorado.

Vail & Eagle Valley Mountain Biking & Recreation. A map of trails and descriptions, published by Latitude 40°, Inc., Box 4086, Boulder, CO 80306. Phone: (303) 258-7909.

Summit County Bike Path and Mountain Bike Map. Prepared in 1993 and subject to updates by the Summit County Chamber of Commerce, P.O. Box 214, Frisco, CO 80442.

Bicycling Colorado. A general state map that highlights 7 paved bike routes. Prepared in 1989 by the Colorado Department of Highways, 4201 East Arkansas Avenue, Denver, CO 80222. Sold at numerous area bike shops and bookstores.

Finding the trail: You can pick up the bike path at turn-outs and rest areas along CO 9 between Frisco and Breckenridge and on I-70 between Frisco and Vail.

In Breckenridge, the bike route is called Blue River Bikeway. It begins in the town block formed by Main, Watson, North Park, and French streets. You can park at any public spot alongside the path.

In Frisco, there are many marked bike paths but the one that connects with the Blue River Bikeway and leads to Vail Pass via the Ten Mile Canyon Bikeway is called the Summit County Recreation Trail. It is located on the south side of town, and can be entered from the end of Second or Seventh streets, or from the west end of Mount Royal Avenue.

In Copper Mountain, pick up the Ten Mile Canyon Recreation Trail, as it is called here, in the ski resort. To reach the access point, exit I-70 at CO 91, head south over the freeway and immediately turn right into the ski resort on Copper Road. Follow Copper Road for several miles through the resort, past the post office and medical center. Watch for bike route signs as the road curves to your left. The bike path is adjacent to the Club Med complex and a convenient parking lot.

In the Vail Valley, the path is known as the Vail Bikeway and can be entered at numerous locations along the path. Here are some general locations from I-70: anywhere along Bighorn Road or Sunburst Drive (take Exit 180); Vail Valley Drive, Willow Road, West Meadow Drive, and Matterhorn Drive (take exits 176 or 173). There's a parking structure at the Transportation Center in Vail Village (Exit 176, on Vail Road, near intersection of Vail Village Drive) that is usually free of charge, with no time limit. Other access points allow on- and off-street parking, but only in designated areas.

Sources of additional information:

Arapaho National Forest
Dillon Ranger District
P.O. Box 620
Silverthorne, CO 80498
(303) 468-5400

White River National Forest
Holy Cross Ranger District Office
P.O. Box 190
24747 US 24
Minturn, CO 81645
(303) 827-5715

Mountain Cyclery
112 South Ridge Street
Breckenridge, CO 80424
(303) 453-2201

Summit County Chamber of Commerce Information Centers
Mailing address:
P.O. Box 214
Frisco, CO 80442
(303) 668-5800 or (303) 668-0376

Two Visitors Centers:
In Dillon, 220 US 6
In Frisco, 110 South Summit Boulevard

Vail Resort Association/Chamber of Commerce
P.O. Box 7
Vail, CO 81658
(800) 525-2257

The Colorado Guide, by Bruce Caughey and Dean Winstanley. Golden, Colorado: Fulcrum Publishing, 1991. To order, write Fulcrum Publishing, 350 Indiana Street, Suite 350, Golden, CO 80401.

Notes on the trail: Getting lost is almost impossible here, since all bikeways from Vail to Breckenridge are well marked with bicycling symbols. Still, it's a good idea to carry a map, particularly if you're shy about asking directions or want to be totally independent.

An area of possible confusion is in Frisco, since several other trails connect to the Summit County Trail. If your desired direction is Vail Pass, follow the signs to the Tenmile Canyon Recreation Trail. Incidentally, you can ride other bikeways to Dillon from Frisco and to Keystone from Dillon.

In Copper Mountain, the bike route and Copper Road are one and the same—the bikeway is in the street rather than being a narrow, separated path. Watch for traffic on this short stretch. The separate paved path resumes on the western end of Copper Road, next to the Club Med complex.

If you're headed for Vail, you reach the rest area just before you conquer Vail Pass. The rest area interrupts the lovely bikeway but offers a chance to refill water bottles, make a phone call, and use the rest rooms. In any case, follow the trusty old brown bike signs as you ride through the rest area. The bike path is the auto road, curving north towards the interstate. Watch for more bicycle symbol markers pointing to the beginning of the paved Vail Bikeway, between Shrine Pass Road (a gravel road) and the south side of I-70. If you cross over I-70, you just missed the Vail Bikeway. Once on the path, climb for about a quarter of a mile to Vail Pass.

Riding into or out of Vail is a bit tricky in that the route travels for nearly 5 miles on Old US 6 before becoming a bike path again. Once again, follow the signs.

Aspen/Glenwood Springs

RIDE 33 *GLENWOOD CANYON BIKE PATH*

After much debate between environmentalists and developers, Interstate 70 now snakes through towering, majestic Glenwood Canyon. While it's true that the canyon's beauty has been pierced and diminished by this 12-mile stretch of steel and concrete, much of its awesome splendor still can be felt and appreciated. The Colorado River continues to roar through, from east to west, carrying thrill-seeking rafters and kayakers over white-water rapids. Spruce trees still cling to sheer rock walls and cliffs, while the Denver & Rio Grande Western Railroad line, here since 1883, still hugs and chugs along the south side of the river. On the north side is Interstate 70, an astonishing achievement of engineering design and construction because it complements the surrounding landscape remarkably well. Following alongside and beneath the interstate and skirting the Colorado River within a few feet is the Glenwood Canyon Bike Path.

As of September 1993, almost nine miles of this eight-foot-wide concrete path had been completed. Eventually, it will connect to the existing Vail, Copper Mountain, Frisco, and Breckenridge bike paths, totaling well over 100 miles. Newly constructed rest stops offer drinking water, picnic tables, and toilets. For now, what makes this scenic 18-mile out-and-back ride a classic is that it is accessible to all road and mountain bikers, young and old, beginner to expert. It is a smooth, fairly level, wide, easy path that is free from whizzing traffic, making it ideal for young families' outings. There are at least three trails extending northward from the bike path within these first nine miles alone. These trails lead deep into White River National Forest and offer some spectacular terrain that you can explore either on foot or by mountain bike (see "Notes on the trail" for details and location).

General location: The bike path starts at the eastern end of Glenwood Springs and follows I-70 eastward towards Dotsero.

Elevation change: When the path between Dotsero (6,120´) and Glenwood Springs (5,750´) is completed, elevation change will total 370´ over 19 miles. Currently, the completed section between Glenwood Springs and Hanging Lake has an elevation change of about 200´.

Season: Virtually year-round, depending on run-off.

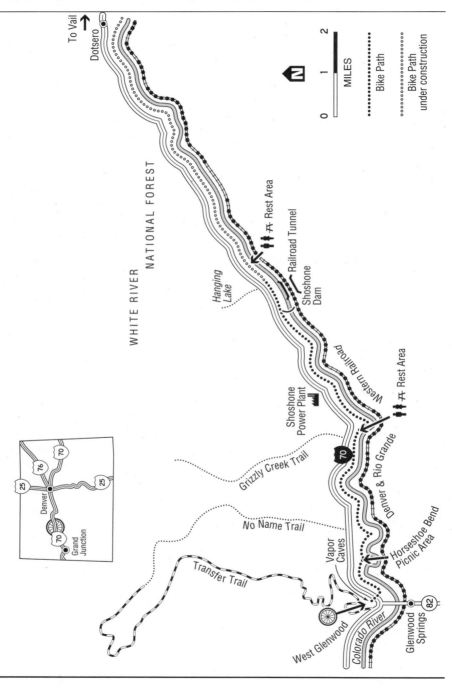

This super-easy paved bike path is worth riding just to experience the sights and sounds of spectacular Glenwood Canyon.

Services: All services available in Glenwood Springs. At the Grizzly Creek rest area (at Exit 121, about 5 miles east of Glenwood Springs), water, picnic tables, toilets, phone, and automobile parking are available. A private campground is available at No Name exit, Exit 119, between Grizzly Creek rest area and Glenwood Springs.

Hazards: During the summer months, expect to see lots of cyclists (children and adults), walkers, and in-line skaters. Heavy snowmelts in the spring have caused the Colorado River to flood portions of the path.

Rescue index: You're more than likely to meet people who can offer some emergency assistance since this is a fairly popular path, especially on weekends. A pay phone is available at Grizzly Creek rest area, about 5 miles from the start of the bike path.

Land status: State of Colorado, Department of Highways. White River National Forest.

Maps: USGS 7.5 minute quadrangles: Glenwood Springs, Shoshone, Dotsero, and Carbonate, Colorado. Note: These maps show the connecting trails but do not show the new bike path. *Hiking and Biking Trails in Glenwood Springs and the White River National Forest.* This is the most up-to-date map to be found that shows the bike path. It's available from Glenwood Springs Chamber Resort Association, or Alpine Bicycle (addresses and phone numbers below).

White River National Forest map. The new bike path will not be shown on versions of this map produced before 1993.

Finding the trail: You can enter the bike path at 2 points: from the Yampah Hot Springs Vapor Caves in Glenwood Springs or from Grizzly Creek rest area. From town, drive or pedal east on the frontage road north of I-70 until you reach the Vapor Caves spa. Park your car on the street (not in the spa parking lot) please! Cycle past the Vapor Caves and onto the paved bike path, which immediately takes you over to the south side of I-70. The other access point is Exit 121, Grizzly Creek rest area, about 5 miles east of town. This rest area can be reached from both the westbound and eastbound directions on I-70. Plenty of parking is available for all sizes of vehicles. The bike path is adjacent to the river.

Sources of additional information:

> White River National Forest
> 9th and Grand Avenue
> P.O. Box 948
> Glenwood Springs, CO 81601
> (303) 945-2521

> Glenwood Springs Chamber Resort Assocation
> 1102 Grand Avenue
> Glenwood Springs, CO 81601
> (800) 221-0098

> Alpine Bicycle
> Glenwood Springs Mall
> 51027 US 6 & US 24
> Glenwood Springs, CO 81601
> (303) 945-6434

Notes on the trail: Because this path is so easy to follow, you really don't need a map—unless, of course, you plan to do some exploring off the path. It is beautifully paved from Glenwood Springs to Hanging Lake, about 9 miles out. The path generally runs below the interstate, never on the same level as the whizzing cars and trucks. Segments of the path are directly underneath the interstate. Occasionally, you can hear—and feel—the vehicles rumbling past overhead; other times the roar of the Colorado River drowns out the traffic noise.

Starting at the Vapor Caves, pedal just over 2 miles to Horseshoe Bend, a lovely spot for a picnic. (Actually, there are many wonderful picnic spots all along the path.) At this point, the bike route follows the Colorado River, while I-70 disappears into a tunnel.

Still heading east, about one-half mile from Horseshoe Bend is No Name rest area. (As of this writing, the construction of this rest area was incomplete.) For you explorers, the No Name Trail can be reached here by taking the road leading over to the north side of I-70. (I personally have not ridden this trail, but I am told that a 20-mile loop can be made via the Transfer Trail—that's after an initial climb of 11 miles and 3,700′ on single-track! If you're up for tackling this option, talk to the folks at the local bike shop as well as the U.S. Forest Service for details.)

Continue on for almost 3 more miles before arriving at the Grizzly Creek rest area. Water, toilet, and a phone are available here. Look for rafters and kayakers having a screaming good time on the river, but watch out for folks on the path, especially near this rest area. To hike the Grizzly Creek Trail (bikers not permitted), follow the road leading underneath I-70 from the rest area.

Pedal 2 miles farther, underneath the highway, and find the Shoshone Powerplant. Caution! There are several blind, tight curves, and vehicles may be using the boat ramp.

Almost 3 miles later, following the river eastbound, you arrive at Hanging Lake rest area. Mileage from the Vapor Caves starting point to here is approximately 9 miles. If you're up to it, park your bike here (no bikes allowed on trail) and hike up 900′ for just over a mile to a peaceful emerald lake, magnificently laced with waterfalls.

At the time of this writing, the bike path stops here. By the time you read this, more of the path will have been finished. Happy exploring!

RIDE 34 *TALL PINES TRAIL*

In my search for memorable bike rides, I asked Steve Wolfe, the owner and operator of Life Cycles in Carbondale, to recommend several local trails. He enthusiastically replied that if I had time to enjoy only one route in his area, Tall Pines Trail should be it.

This ride leads you through mostly wooded terrain, though a few sections are open and involve pedaling on long hills. You can tackle this outing as a point-to-point ride, which would require a shuttle-vehicle arrangement. Or, if you have superior endurance and start early in the day, you could ride this as a complete loop by pedaling back to the start on CO 133, or even return by reversing direction. The length of the point-to-point ride is just shy of 17 miles, while the loop is almost 34 miles. Beginners to expert riders can still have lots of fun on this moderate trail because highly developed technical skills are not required, though a short but rugged section at the end may persuade some beginners to dismount and walk. Depending on your skill and endurance level, count on three to seven hours to complete the point-to-point ride.

Also consider allowing enough time to explore the tiny but historically interesting mining town of Redstone—be sure to check out the Redstone Inn and the

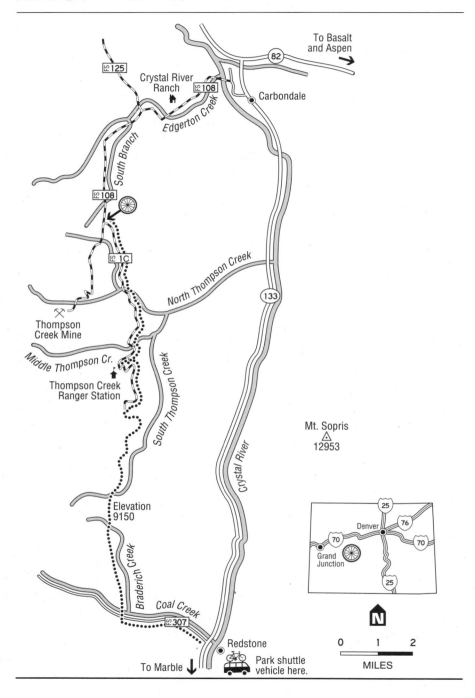

Redstone Castle, two miles south of town, both of which were built in the late 1800s. Both have been elegantly refurbished and offer splendid lodging. Redstone Inn is rumored to have quite a champagne Sunday brunch, while Redstone Castle offers gourmet dinners.

Tall Pines Trail is just one of many rides recommended by Steve (Ride 35, Crystal and Lead King Basin, listed next, is another recommendation). If you enjoy this quietly beautiful area near Aspen, visit him at Life Cycles in Carbondale where he'll have more information, trail suggestions, and maps. Ask about his Sunday rides, too!

General location: The trail begins approximately 6 miles west of Carbondale, which is about 10 miles south of Glenwood Springs. Carbondale is 172 miles from Denver.

Elevation change: The starting elevation is 7,800′; you climb to the highest point of 9,150′ within 11.5 miles. Total intial gain is 1,350′. From there, the trail descends to 7,200′, where the tiny town of Redstone sits, for a loss of 1,950′.

Season: The best times to enjoy this ride are late spring to midautumn, give or take a few light snow days. Riding in July is bound to reward you with patches of wildflowers in bloom. Rifle hunting season typically is early September through late November.

Services: Though water can be found at various creek crossings throughout the trail, it must be treated to be drinkable. Potable water is available at the Thompson Creek Ranger Station, about 5.5 miles from the recommended start-ing point. Food, restaurants, gasoline, phone, and lodging ranging from basic to elegant can be found in both Carbondale and Redstone. Several public camp-grounds—fee and no fee, with and without drinkable water—are located off CO 133, between Carbondale and Redstone. Those campgrounds are Janeway, Avalanche, and Redstone. Also along this stretch of CO 133, on the eastern side of the highway, is the Maroon Bells–Snowmass Wilderness Area, where primi-tive backcountry camping is permitted. The historic and elegant Redstone Inn is worth checking out.

Hazards: Watch out for the typical hazards—low-hanging tree limbs, downed trees across the trail, and seemingly invisible barbed-wire fence gates. If you choose to make this route a loop by riding back to Carbondale on CO 133, you'll have some vehicular traffic with which to share the road. Hunting season commences in early September, ending in late November.

Rescue index: Heaven forbid that an emergency should arise, but if it does, you should plan to return to your car and drive for help, or head into Redstone and call for assistance, whichever is closest. You might find some assistance at the Thompson Creek Ranger Station (about 5.5 miles from the starting point), but that's a big *might*. Tall Pines Trail sees moderate use and you may meet other trail users who can be of help. Shortcuts back into town or to CO 133 are not adequately marked on maps or on the trail.

Land status: Bureau of Land Management. White River National Forest.

Maps: USGS 7.5 minute quads: Carbondale, Cattle Creek, Stony Ridge, Placita, and Redstone, Colorado. Also check with Life Cycles in Carbondale for its own route map on this trail and others in the area.

Finding the trail: Before you head out to the starting point of this ride, you'll need to arrange a vehicle shuttle. Place the end (return) car in the tiny town of Redstone, 18 miles south of Carbondale on CO 133. Park it near the intersection of CO 133 and Forest Service Road 307, which is the trail terminus.

To find the starting point, drive west out of Carbondale on Main Street and follow the road around, eventually taking FS 108 across the Crystal River. By now, the road has become a very passable dirt road. Stay on FS 108 as it takes you past the Crystal River Ranch and, about 3.5 miles from town, past the intersection of another dirt road, FS 125. Stay on FS 108 as it continues to climb and curve towards the southwest. Five miles from town, the road turns due south, parallel to South Branch Edgerton Creek (an intermittent stream which may or may not be obvious, depending on the time of year). Almost 7 miles from Carbondale, look for a jeep road leading off towards the east (left) from FS 108. Park off the road here and begin your riding fun by taking the lesser road, which may or may not be marked FS 1C . This jeep road eventually leads across North Thompson Creek. If you reach Thompson Creek Mine, you missed the fork about 3 miles back.

Sources of additional information:

Life Cycles
0902 CO 133
Carbondale, CO 81623
(303) 963-1149
Owned and operated by Steve Wolfe. If you're lucky, you'll find him here, working instead of out riding. Ask about their Sunday rides, a regular event during the sunny riding months.

White River National Forest
Sopris Ranger District
620 Main Street
Box 309
Carbondale, CO 81623
(303) 963-2266

Bureau of Land Management
Glenwood Springs Resource Area
50629 Highways 6 & 24
P.O. Box 1009
Glenwood Springs, CO 81602
(303) 945-2341

Maroon Bells–Snowmass Wilderness
Gunnison/White River National Forests
2250 Highway 50
Delta, CO 81416
(303) 874-7691

Redstone Inn
0082 Redstone Boulevard
Redstone, CO 81623
(303) 963-2526

Redstone Castle—Cleveholm Manor
0058 Redstone Boulevard
Redstone, CO 81623
(303) 963-3463

Glenwood Springs Chamber Resort Association
1102 Grand Avenue
Glenwood Springs, CO 81601
(800) 221-0098

Notes on the trail: The trail is generally adequately marked, though a small section just after the high point at 11.5 miles tends to be a bit confusing (more about that stretch later). Cruise downhill for about 2.5 miles, at which point you cross the North Thompson Creek. Continue on the trail as it climbs a short hill, then descends to a trail junction. Follow the trail going left. Almost 4.5 miles from the starting point, cross Middle Thompson Creek and begin another climb. In less than a mile, you'll pedal past the Thompson Creek Ranger Station. For the next quarter mile, the route twists and turns and crosses an intermittent stream. Continuing on, the next 5.5-mile section climbs gradually with some level stretches in which to catch your breath. There are several gates along the way; remember to leave them as you found them—open or closed. At almost 11.5 miles, you reach the high point of the ride. From here on, the trail is a delightful and welcome downhill cruise.

Here is the slightly confusing stretch mentioned earlier. At this point, as you head downhill, stay close to Braderich Creek, which may be intermittent, depending on the time of year. It should be on your left. As you emerge from a grove of spruce, you quickly enter a small stand of aspen where you may find the trail splitting. Which trail to take? When in doubt, choose the route that leads downhill, into what appears to be a gully. In a short while, almost a mile from the pass, you'll cross the stream again so that it now flows on your right. The route parallels Braderich Creek for about 2 miles, at which point the trail descends a very steep, challenging portion just before ending on paved FS 307. Beginners: this is the short, rugged section mentioned earlier where you may want to dismount and walk.

Once at FS 307, turn left and follow it; cruise on down to CO 133 and Redstone for some well-deserved refreshment and your shuttle vehicle. As for you lean, mean biking machines bent on making this a longer ride, you can either go back the way you came or follow CO 133 north, looping all the way back to Carbondale some 16 miles away.

RIDE 35 *CRYSTAL AND LEAD KING BASIN*

With only one road leading to this tiny town renowned for its namesake quarried here, only one word describes it: remote. The town of Marble is the starting point of this dramatically scenic 17-mile loop situated between two Wilderness Areas—Maroon Bells–Snowmass and Raggeds. The route encircles Sheep Mountain, following the Crystal River and Lost Trail Creek through towering canyons of sheer rock and jagged peaks, its beauty and drama challenged by the abundance of color-drenched wildflowers. Photography enthusiasts will go nuts over this area, guaranteed.

The loop consists entirely of four-wheel-drive jeep roads. The first six miles up to the old mining site of Crystal can be enjoyed by all cyclists with strong stamina, including beginners. After that, a two-mile portion of the Lead King Basin Road, between Crystal and the summit, becomes so rugged and challenging that even expert riders may prefer to dismount and hike. After the summit, it's all downhill back into Marble. Beginners with the right frame of mind and biking companions can still enjoy this loop.

Allow enough time to explore tiny Marble. The marble quarried here was said to have rivaled the best Italian varieties. Fifty-six tons of marble used in the Tomb of the Unknown Soldier were quarried here as well as a significant amount used in the Lincoln Memorial in Washington, D.C. Recently, the quarry resumed operation and now supplies marble to overseas markets, including Italy, of all places!

To reach Marble, you'll undoubtedly drive through Carbondale. Be sure to stop in at Life Cycles for all your biking needs. Steve Wolfe, the owner and operator there, suggested this ride; he can provide you with information on many more riding possibilities.

General location: This gem of a ride begins and ends in the town of Marble, located about 38 miles south of Glenwood Springs. At 200 miles west of Denver, this loop is sandwiched between two wilderness areas: Maroon Bells–Snowmass and Raggeds.

Elevation change: The ride begins in Marble at 8, 000´ and crests at 10,800´ after 9 miles for a total elevation change of 2,800´.

Season: You can enjoy this ride from mid-June through October. July usually

RIDE 35 *CRYSTAL AND LEAD KING BASIN*

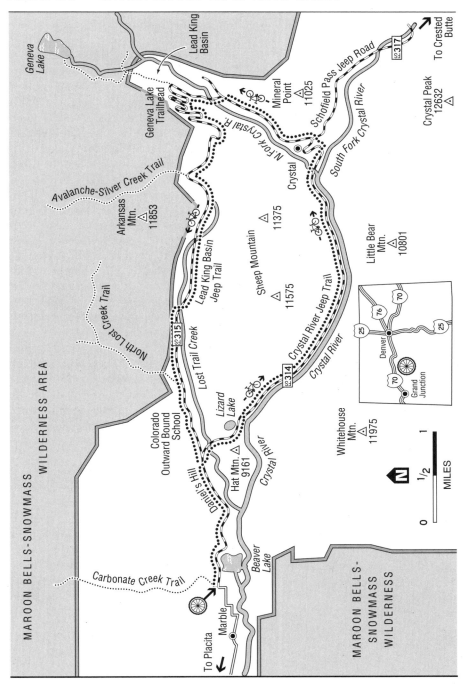

serves up a dazzling display of wildflowers. Afternoon thunderstorms can be scary, particularly from July through August, so plan to complete your ride by early afternoon.

Services: While almost 90% of the route follows the Crystal River and Lost Trail Creek, water is not always easily accessible. Even then, the water from these sources must be treated to be drinkable. It's a wise idea to bring enough water with you rather than depend on finding it en route. There is a small general store in Marble where you can buy snacks and nourishment for your ride. Gasoline is not available in Marble. Magnificent lodging facilities and eateries can be found in nearby Redstone. Bogan Flats Campground is several miles outside of Marble on County Road 3 (also known as Forest Service Road 314 on some maps). McClure Campground is up and over McClure Pass on CO 133. Primitive camping is allowed in the Wilderness Areas.

Hazards: Throughout the loop, watch out for jeep traffic. Portions of the trail are deeply rutted, so be alert, especially when you're flying down Lead King Basin jeep road. A section of the route leading from Crystal to the Lead King Basin jeep trail (FS 315) is extremely rocky and steep, and is a challenge to riders of all abilities. Still, dismounting and hiking your bike is a proven, effective method. Fortunately, it's not terribly long. And last, but not least, keep an eye on the weather, particularly approaching thunderstorms in the afternoon during the summer months. You should plan to be finished with your ride by early afternoon to avoid dangerous lightning situations.

Rescue index: This route is fairly popular with jeep tourists so you may find other trail users who may be of assistance. The loop is entirely accessible by four-wheel-drive vehicles, making motorized evacuation possible in extreme emergency situations. As for the nearest phone, don't expect to find one readily available in Marble; plan on driving back to Redstone (about 14 miles from Marble) to call for help or even driving all the way into Carbondale (about 28 miles from Marble) for medical attention.

Land status: White River National Forest.

Maps: Trails Illustrated® map: #128, Maroon Bells. USGS 7.5 minute quad: Snowmass Mountain and Marble, Colorado. Also check with Life Cycles in Carbondale for its own route map on this trail and others in the area.

Finding the trail: From Glenwood Springs, head south on CO 133, through Carbondale, Redstone, and Placita. About 2 miles past Placita, look for the junction of CR 3 (FS 314), leading left from CO 133. Take CR 3 all the way to Marble, almost 7 miles. Park on the north side of Beaver Lake and begin riding here. To avoid tackling a steep hill on cold leg muscles, drive up Daniel's Hill on CR 3 (FS 314) as far as your two-wheel-drive vehicle will allow and begin pedaling there.

Sources of additional information:

Life Cycles
0902 CO 133
Carbondale, CO 81623
(303) 963-1149
Owned and operated by Steve Wolfe. If you're lucky, you'll find him here, working instead of out riding. Ask about their Sunday rides, a regular event during the sunny riding months.

White River National Forest
Sopris Ranger District
620 Main Street
Box 309
Carbondale, CO 81623
(303) 963-2266

Maroon Bells–Snowmass Wilderness
Gunnison/White River National Forests
2250 Highway 50
Delta, CO 81416
(303) 874-7691

Raggeds Wilderness
Gunnison National Forest
Paonia Ranger District
Box 1030
Paonia, CO 81428
(303) 527-4131

Glenwood Springs Chamber Resort Association
1102 Grand Avenue
Glenwood Springs, CO 81601
(800) 221-0098

Notes on the trail: From Beaver Lake in Marble, pedal east on FS 314 (CR 3), a four-wheel-drive jeep road. The trail quickly begins climbing Daniel's Hill, with Lost Trail Creek gushing below towards town. Nearly 1.5 miles from Beaver Lake, the road forks, with FS 314 continuing to your right to Crystal, an old mining site. To your left is FS 315, also known as the Lead King Basin jeep road—you'll complete the loop by returning on this road.

Make a right turn onto FS 314, the Crystal River jeep trail, and begin your counterclockwise loop. About a half mile from this junction, you come to Lizard Lake with, perhaps, picnickers and folks trying their luck at fishing. Push onward over delightful roller-coaster terrain for a short distance. The trail eventually levels out alongside the Crystal River. From this point on, the road continues almost 3 miles over delightful rolling hills alongside the river. I hope you bring your camera, despite the extra weight, because the scenery is breathtaking. And check out the old mill here, a favorite subject of photographers. This is a good turnaround point for beginners who don't wish to pedal more challenging and steep terrain.

Continuing on, follow FS 314 alongside the North Fork of the Crystal River as the climb increases in steepness and roughness. Persevere! Within a half mile from Crystal, you'll come to the junction of FS 317 (Schofield Pass jeep road) and FS 315 (the Lead King Basin Road). FS 317 leads up and over the pass and down to Crested Butte—another day's ride, to be sure! Stay left on FS 315 and follow the road to the Lead King Basin and Geneva Lake trailhead. Continue climbing alongside the North Fork of the Crystal River on your left. The trail becomes extremely rocky and may require dismounting and hiking. Actually, walking it allows you to savor the dramatic views of sheer canyon walls above and below you.

About 2 miles from Crystal, cross the North Fork and continue climbing past the Geneva Lake trailhead. Don't look now, but here come a couple of switchbacks. The road improves somewhat and the scenery continues to inspire you to push on. About 3 miles from the stream crossing, you reach the summit, sitting at 10,800´. You deserve a break! Enjoy the spectacular scenery—and the millions of dazzling wildflowers in bloom, if your timing is right. From here, you're about 3.5 miles from completing the loop and another mile from your car—just follow Lead King Basin jeep road westward, past several trailheads and the Colorado Outward Bound School. It's all downhill from here. Expect lots of deep ruts in the road. Estimated total mileage: approximately 17 miles.

RIDE 36 SMUGGLER MOUNTAIN/HUNTER CREEK LOOP

For the first-time visitor to this old mining-town-turned-world-class-resort, the Smuggler Mountain/Hunter Creek Loop is a "classic" Aspen-area mountain bike ride. It offers great aerial views of the Roaring Fork valley backdropped by the ski slopes of Aspen Mountain and postcard-perfect Central Colorado.

Climb Smuggler Mountain Road early in the morning when the sun's low-angled, golden rays cast a dramatic light on the waking town and encompassing mountains. Then, drop into the grassy, wildflower-carpeted meadows of Hunter Creek Valley cut by its crystal clear, icy stream. Upstream the valley gives way to the gaping cirques and towering peaks of the Williams Mountains in the Hunter–Fryingpan Wilderness Area.

The basic Smuggler Mountain/Hunter Creek Loop is about an eight-mile, intermediate-level loop, ridden counterclockwise. But, you can spend all day in the area exploring numerous optional loops, out-and-backs, and connecting trails that range from intermediate- to expert-level in difficulty.

The Smuggler Mountain Road begins as an improved two-wheel-drive road, then turns into a four-wheel-drive road at higher elevation. As can be expected, conditions range from smooth, packed dirt to occasional washboards, with loose, pebble- to cobble-sized rocks—and a few ruts tossed in. The descent off Smuggler Mountain into Hunter Creek Valley may be muddy, even though this four-wheel-drive road is usually maintained. The Hunter Creek Trail drops from the valley back towards Aspen, then follows a playful single-track before exiting onto the paved roads of Red Mountain. Here, some of Pitkin County's steepest paved roads offer a smooth but fast descent back to town.

[This route information was provided by John Wilkinson,* Aspen, Colorado.—G. B.]

General location: Immediately northeast of Aspen.
Elevation change: Beginning in Aspen (about 8,000'), the Smuggler Mountain Road rises about 900' to a hang-glider launching platform. Thereafter, the same elevation is lost upon descending back to Aspen.
Season: One of the first Aspen-area rides to open, Smuggler Mountain can be ridden as early as mid- to late April, an enticing diversion from spring skiing. Facing the south, the climb generally dries quickly. But, the descent into Hunter Creek Valley, which faces north, will likely be snowbound (or at least very muddy) until mid-May.
Services: There are no services along this route. Cool water flows in Hunter Creek year-round, but it should be purified before drinking.

Considering the quaint size of this world-class resort town, it is amazing what extensive services are available. Nearly every imaginable food and form of entertainment will be found in Aspen, from simple to extravagant; from enchiladas to chateaubriand (and nearly every cuisine in between); from rustic taverns to a dinner playhouse; from street corner banjo players to a renowned symphony. Likewise, overnight accommodations range from developed Forest Service campgrounds to luxurious, $1,000-per-night hotel suites.

Naturally, Aspen is well served by a number of top-flight bike shops; all are adept in sales and service and offer friendly advice on area bike routes.
Hazards: Weather can change quickly in this mountainous setting. Thus, pack-

---

*John Wilkinson moved to Aspen from Michigan in 1979. He and his wife, Lisa, take advantage of the many trails and dirt roads this Rocky Mountain resort has to offer for cyclists.

Actively involved in Aspen-area cycling, John has organized mountain and road bike races as well as fun rides. Every spring he leads a mountain bike adventure in southeastern Utah's canyon country. As a board member of the Colorado Plateau Mountain Bike Trail Association (COPMOBA), he is currently developing Pitiguf's Trail, which will connect Aspen with Kokopelli's Trail (Ride 45) in Grand Junction.

John is also an avid road cyclist—currently a USCF licensed CAT III rider and past president of the Aspen Velo Cycling Club.

RIDE 36 *SMUGGLER MOUNTAIN / HUNTER CREEK LOOP*

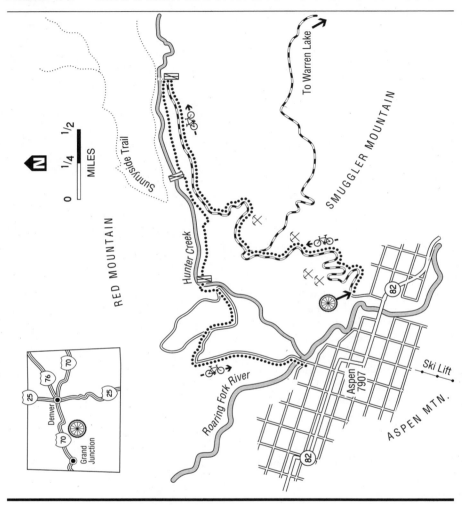

ing along raingear is worth the few extra pounds, especially if you are planning a full day of exploring. Since this route is quite popular, watch for other trail users and yield the right of way with a nod and a friendly smile. Use caution when descending from Red Mountain, for the paved roads are steep and the turns are tight.

Rescue index: Up Smuggler Mountain and down Hunter Creek you are never more than a few miles from a phone and help. Yet, if your travels take you to more remote regions (up Hunter Creek Valley, on the Sunnyside Trail, or

Smuggler Mountain oversees Aspen and Aspen Mountain. Photo: Gregg Bromka.

toward Lenado), the walk out is considerably farther. Bicyclists and hikers frequent the area, so encounters with others are common.

Land status: White River National Forest and private property. Contact the Aspen Ranger District for current trail access status, especially the route's Hunter Creek Valley/Red Mountain trailhead.

Wilderness Areas don't begin until 7 miles up Hunter Creek Valley, so there's plenty of cycling terrain up to the boundary. Remember, no bikes in Wilderness Areas!

Maps: USGS 7.5 minute quadrangle: Aspen, Colorado. Trails Illustrated® map: #127, Independence Pass.

Finding the trail: To get to Smuggler Mountain, ride toward the blue-roofed condominium complex on the east side of Aspen, following CO 82/Cooper Street east out of town. Immediately after crossing the bridge over the Roaring Fork River, turn left onto Park Avenue. Where this road curves left, turn right towards the mountain on Park Circle, then right again onto the Smuggler Mountain Road.

Sources of additional information:

White River National Forest
Aspen Ranger District
806 West Hallam
Aspen, CO 81611
(303) 925-3445

Notes on the trail: Combining a unique blend of old and new, this route follows original mining roads past abandoned shafts, tunnels, and workings of the area's once most productive silver mines—mines that demanded hard labor but often resulted in glorious ore strikes. Later, these strikes turned Aspen into a thriving boom town around the turn of the century. Now, people seek glory not in the mines but in skiing champagne powder and then basking in Aspen's Hollywood-style glamour.

The old, switchbacking jeep road (clearly visible from the valley floor) opens with a short, gentle warm-up, then rises steeply with few "breathers." About 1.5 miles up the Smuggler Mountain Road (where the views are exceptional), a small wooden platform marks the hang-gliding launch pad and an important turn. Take the left fork and continue uphill. This route will wrap around the north side of the mountain, pass by the old Iowa Mine, cross a gate, then descend a series of switchbacks into Hunter Valley. Upon reaching the stream, turn left and follow the path down the valley through the aspens. Soon you will encounter a small wooden bridge spanning Hunter Creek; cross it and continue down on the north side of the creek. After a short distance, the trail exits onto paved roads flanking Red Mountain. Follow Hunter Creek Road and Red Mountain Road down into Aspen at North Mill Street.

RIDE 37 *GOVERNMENT TRAIL*

This route is a single-track lover's delight. Along its length, nearly every challenge imaginable will be encountered: gut-busting climbs, white-knuckle descents and hairpin switchbacks, serpentining trail weaving through eye-poker trees, multiple water crossings, technical terrain that requires supple finesse more than brute strength, some hike-a-biking, plus a generous helping of buffed single-track. Now take these backcountry ingredients, add a pinch of Aspen's high-zoot glitz and a dash of down-to-earth local color, and you have an unmatched recipe for mountain bike bliss in a world-class resort setting.

This ride traverses several watersheds descending from two mountains: Burnt Mountain (Snowmass Ski Resort) and Buttermilk Mountain (Buttermilk/Tiehack Ski Resort). Initially, the route passes through some of Pitkin County's most beautiful, open ranging meadows separating Aspen and Snowmass Village. Good views of 13,000′ Mount Daly are obtained from Owl Creek Divide. The Government Trail then slips across mountain slopes, through immense aspen-clad forests mixed with conifers, and across delicate meadows. During fall, the forested slopes burst into brilliant sun-drenched hues as golden leaves of *Populus tremuloides* quiver in the autumn breezes. This is deer and elk habitat. Also watch for porcupines, foxes, and a wide array of birds.

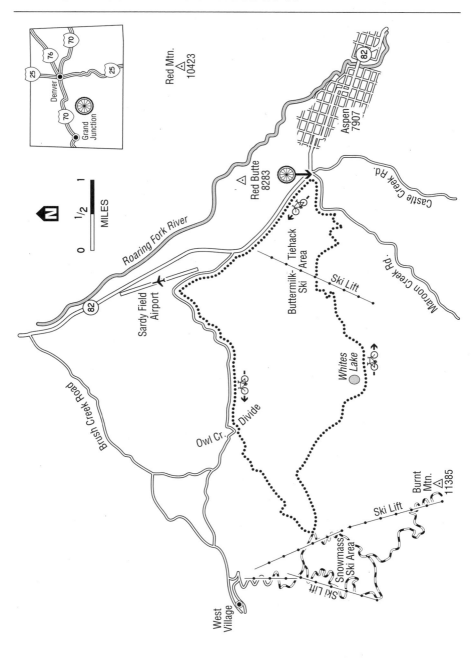

Riding through a grove of aspens along the Government Trail. Photo: Gregg Bromka.

The Government Trail proper is an eight-mile-long point-to-point trail. It is only one part of the 20-mile loop ride described here, beginning with six miles of paved bike path leading from Aspen and followed by a few miles of steady climbing on paved road. Three miles of steeply rising single-track connect with the Government Trail itself. Finally, a few paved miles return to town. Solid, intermediate bike handling skills, moderate fitness, and acute attentiveness are of more advantage here than brute power.

[This description of the Government Trail was provided by John Wilkinson, Aspen, Colorado.—G. B.]

General location: The Government Trail extends from Snowmass Ski Resort (about 10 miles west of Aspen) to the Maroon Creek Road just outside of Aspen.

Elevation change: The ride starts and ends in Aspen at 8,000'. The highest point on the Government Trail Loop (a mile before White's Lake) rises to about 9,400′. Considerable climbing (800′ in less than 3 miles) is encountered on the single-track from Owl Creek Divide up to the Government Trail (led by the "Anaerobic Nightmare" and followed soon thereafter by the "Sequel"). The trail then drops rapidly to the Maroon Creek Road.

Season: Remember, this is high alpine terrain where winter's snow may linger well into late spring and begin again in early autumn. This route can be ridden from late May or early June to early October. Early morning hours are usually dry but cool. During mid- to late summer, rain showers and fierce thunderstorms may occur by midafternoon. Hail storms are not uncommon. Since most of the ride is below treeline, approaching storms are hard to spot until they are directly overhead, yet there is plenty of cover and storms can pass over within a half hour. Weekdays tend to be less crowded than weekends, but it is never so crowded that you do not mind sharing the route with other trail users.

Services: You name it, Aspen has it: burgers and fries to fresh lobster and sushi, local pubs to elegant dining, and country swing to disco. Visitor lodging options are equally extensive, from hostels to exclusive condos. Along the backcountry portion of the route, no services will be found. Water is plentiful in the streams and occasional ponds, but it must be filtered before drinking—remember that cattle ranching is active here.

Hazards: The Government Trail Loop has many inherent hazards, but none are out of the ordinary for this type of challenging single-track. Ride smart and you should not encounter any serious problems. Use extreme caution when descending over loose shale through the series of very tight, steep switchbacks into Maroon Creek. Crossing CO 82 at Owl Creek Road will be your only conflict with motorized vehicles. Of course, when cycling through this alpine setting, changing weather should always be a concern. A warm, clear morning may give way to microburst hail storms and frigid temperatures by midafternoon.

Rescue index: You will be quite a distance from help on this ride. On the middle of the trail, you will be at least an hour by bike and up to 5 miles from the nearest phone. Fortunately, this is a popular route, so other trail users may pass as frequently as every 30 minutes. Naturally, travel well equipped and be self-sufficient, for a mechanical breakdown could be devastating and mean a long walk to either trailhead.

Land status: The Government Trail crosses Pitkin County, White River National Forest, and private property. Although the trail has been designated a right-of-way, private property occurs near White's Lake and on the Buttermilk-Tiehack Resort slopes. To avoid any conflict, stay on the main trail, do not cross any fence lines, avoid descending through the ski resorts, and respect all posted signs. When you ride the Government Trail Loop, plan on riding the *entire* route. Leave all gates as you found them.

Maps: USGS 7.5 minute quadrangles: Aspen and Highland Peak, Colorado. The Government Trail is not correctly located on these maps. Trails

Illustrated® maps: #128, Maroon Bells and #127, Independence Pass. The Government Trail is labeled as Brush Creek Trail on these maps but is not marked in its entirety.

Finding the trail: Start this loop by pedaling out from Aspen on the airport recreation trail, which is next to CO 82.

Sources of additional information:

> White River National Forest
> Aspen Ranger District
> 806 West Hallam
> Aspen, CO 81611
> (303) 925-3445

Notes on the trail: Riding from bustling downtown Aspen to the serenity of high mountain meadows, along a forested trail, then back to town is a joy each time. To negotiate the route, follow the airport recreational trail and bike path to the top of Owl Creek Road Divide (a steady climb that makes for a fun out-and-back ride in itself). Less than one-quarter mile down from the divide, branch left onto an unsigned single-track passing through the meadows. Initially, this path is quite easy, but soon it turns skyward up the "Anaerobic Nightmare." Cross a stream, fork left, and prepare for the even steeper "Sequel." Each is over a mile long; neither needs further defining. Only a few elite cyclists have cleaned both ascents.

You will intersect with the Government Trail, marked by a sign; turn left. (A right turn takes you to the Elk Camp trailhead after a few minutes). Traversing across the long flanks of Burnt Mountain, you will reach "Three Rocky Crossings." These intermittent streams may have water early in the year, but the major obstacle will be their rocky streambeds. Soon after this, you will pass Whites Lake and cross the "Up-Dee-Whoop," a shale ridge uplift.

From here it's just a short distance to the infamous "Rock Garden," a highly technical section notorious for bucking riders into the trees or down the steep fallaway ridge. Do not worry, though. You will be riding slowly, so the only bruise will be to your ego.

Break out onto the West Buttermilk ski slopes and cross, count them, 16 runs. Dodge a few future "Big Macs" complacently chewing their cud, then on to an exhilarating, switchbacking descent through the "Slalom Trees," certainly one of the route's highlights. Cross Tiehack Ski Area, pass through the pedestrian gate, then down another section of tight, steep switchbacks to Maroon Creek. Cross the bridge and climb to the Maroon Creek Road. The sounds of plunking tennis balls will contrast with the natural sounds you have been hearing. Return to Aspen on the bicycle path and reminisce the day's adventure over a cold drink at the historic Hotel Jerome.

Crested Butte

RIDE 38 *PEARL PASS*

First a bit of nostalgia. In the history and development of fat-tire cycling from its infancy, two events may have provided the critical spark that ignited the wildfire of modern-day mountain biking: The Repack Downhill on the slopes of Mount Tamalpias (Mt. Tam for short) in Marin County, California, and the Crested Butte to Aspen Klunker Tour in Colorado, better known as Pearl Pass. Do not assume that the people involved in either of these two events were actively and knowingly pursuing the changes and advancements that would later lead to a bicycle revolution; they just happened to be in the right place and engaged in the right activity when the appropriate forces of nature and time converged. As a result, their names and the events that followed would shape the future of bicycling.

While the Californians were pursuing death-defying speeds down Mount Tam on vintage "clunkers," the locals in Crested Butte ("Crusty Butt" as some call it) were busy entertaining themselves with similar daredevil stunts on their "town bikes." Both groups revamped whatever bikes they could lay their hands on (the classic Schwinn Excelsior, or "newsboy bike," being the one most sought after) and mounted prototype thumb-shifters, drum brakes, reinforced forks, monkey-style handle bars, sometimes multiple gears, and of course the trademark "ballooner" tires as a means to perfect a thrill.

In Crested Butte, when the summer's forest fires had been quenched, it became a common sight to see local firefighters careening down mountain dirt roads at alarming speeds on their town bikes—oftentimes straight down into Main Street. But no one seriously entertained the thought of dragging a near 50-pound bike to the top of 12,705′ Pearl Pass, for any reason. Not until the summer of 1976, that is, when a band of boisterous motorcyclists from Aspen topped Pearl Pass and then descended upon Crested Butte. Trailing a cloud of dust, the bunch parked their sputtering rigs in front of the local watering hole (the Grubstake) and proceeded to raise a whole lot of commotion about their seemingly unsurpassable accomplishment.

These motor-drive upstarts were viewed as a cultural invasion, and the local Crested Butte firefighters (who, under normal circumstances were quite content with the fact that a 13,000′ mountain range separated their isolated community from the Hollywood glitter of their sister town, Aspen) felt the stunt must be

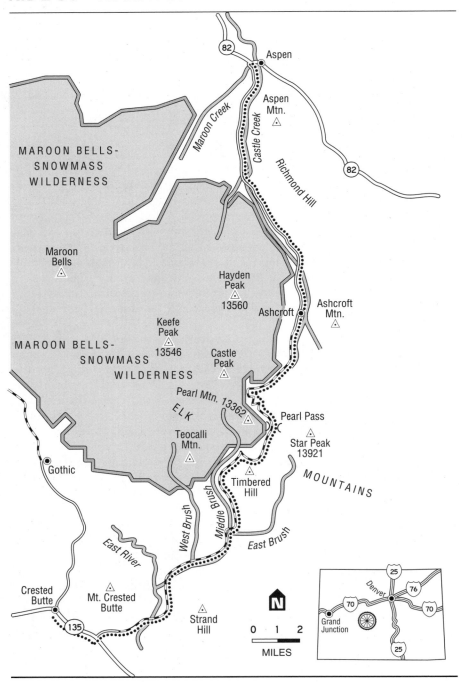

MAROON BELLS-
SNOWMASS
WILDERNESS

Maroon Creek

Castle Creek

82

Aspen

Aspen
Mtn.

Richmond Hill

82

Maroon
Bells

Hayden
Peak
13560

Ashcroft

Ashcroft
Mtn.

Keefe
Peak
13546

MAROON BELLS-
SNOWMASS
WILDERNESS

Castle
Peak

Pearl Mtn. 13362

ELK

Pearl Pass

Star Peak
13921

Teocalli
Mtn.

Gothic

Timbered
Hill

MOUNTAINS

West Brush

Middle Brush

East Brush

East River

Crested
Butte

Mt. Crested
Butte

135

Strand
Hill

N

0   1   2

MILES

Denver

25

76

70

70

Grand
Junction

25

25

Lineup for the 1978 Pearl Pass Tour. Left to right (CA: California, CB: Crested Butte): Wende Cragg (CA), Murdoch (CB), Richard Nielson (CA), Charlie Kelly (CA), Joe Breeze (CA), Jim Cloud (CB), Bob Starr (CB), Richard the Rat Ullery (CB), Gary Fisher (CA), Archie Archuleta (CB), Chris Carroll (CB), Albert Munz (CB). Photo: Dan Peha/Crested Butte Chronicle.

topped in even greater style. And what better way than to ride their town bikes over Pearl Pass and down into Aspen.

About 15 "participants" gathered on a September morning and began riding, pushing, dragging, and hauling their bikes toward Pearl Pass. The two-day event was highlighted by a raucous campout in Cumberland Basin and, according to participants Bob Starr and Rick Verplank, quoted in the *Crested Butte Pilot*, "everyone got drunk and passed out on the pass." The next day, the group continued the ascent on Pearl, and Richard Ullery (hampered by a broken leg, but refusing to be left in town) made history by being the first person to surmount Pearl Pass in a custom-padded bathtub in the back of a support truck. With bike brakes smoking and adrenaline pumping, the band careened down from the mountaintop and piled their clunkers in a heap outside Aspen's Hotel Jerome and had a party. The epic tour was complete.

Of course, word spread quickly and fell upon the ears of the California contingent. Amused by such a maniacal event, a group of five, Charles Kelly, Joe Breeze, Gary Fisher, Mike Castelli, and Wende Cragg, ventured to Crested Butte to see for themselves and partake in the hoopla.

The third annual Pearl Pass Tour went off in a fine style, matching that of previous years. At Cumberland Basin, steaks were cooked, kegs were tapped,

Pearl Pass as viewed from Teocalli Ridge. Photo: Gregg Bromka.

and wild stories recapping the first tour soared like an eagle in the thermals. On the second day, the Coloradans and Californians together crested Pearl Pass, much to the astonishment of a half-dozen motorcyclists approaching from Aspen. The satisfaction of accomplishing such a crazy feat and the bewilderment of their antagonists was overwhelming. A few pictures were taken, tire pressures were checked, a yodeling display echoed through the mountain air, and the crew descended upon Aspen for a night of boasting and partying. Many vowed, "Never again," then quickly drew up plans for next year's tour.

And today? Has the Pearl Pass Tour faded into the mist that often enshrouds the Divide, has it become simply a piece of nostalgia preserved in the minds of those who created it, or has it joined other history-making fat-tire events dangling from the walls of the Mountain Bike Hall of Fame? The Crested Butte to Aspen Klunker Tour has become all of these. While Crested Butte's highly touted trail system and its Fat Tire Bike Week draw national (if not international) attention, Pearl Pass waits quietly for those who wish to relive the mid-1970s adventure. The tour is featured annually during September, but lately it has become less of an organized, sponsored event and reverted to an informal outing as in its original years.

Today, "town bikes" and "clunkers" are replaced by lightweight, high-tech alloy frames; jeans, cutoffs, and t-shirts are replaced with matching Lycra-Spandex shorts and Gore-tex® tops; and locals watch from town as strangers from the far corners of the country struggle up the mountain's slope. Crested

Butte has become the Rockies' self-proclaimed mountain bike mecca, its Fat Tire Bike Week an annual pilgrimage, and the Pearl Pass Tour has become widely accepted as one of *the* original mountain bike rides.

This 39-mile point-to-point route follows mostly hard-packed dirt and four-wheel-drive roads. A short stretch of highway heading out of Crested Butte begins the route, and 14 miles of pavement from Ashcroft to Aspen conclude the route. Although a historic tour, Pearl Pass should not be thought of as tame. This is a highly demanding if not brutal, route, with monstrous vertical gain. The few miles of four-wheel-drive road on both sides of Pearl Pass are quite steep and technical. On a good day, a strong biker might ride 50% of the final three-mile ascent to the Pass; the rest of us will have to succumb to walking nearly all of it.

General location: This ride goes from Crested Butte to Aspen, with the Pass halfway in between.

Elevation change: Crested Butte rests at 8,900′. Pearl Pass rises to a oxygen-deficient elevation of 12,705′, for a total elevation gain of about 3,800′. Aspen lies at 7,900′.

Season: Due to high elevations, Pearl Pass has a very limited season, usually about two months, from late July through mid-September. Snowdrifts will linger on the Aspen side later into the summer than on the Crested Butte side. Weather should be a primary concern, for it will always be chilly on the Pass and snowstorms have been known to occur even during midsummer. Prepare for foul weather by packing along extra clothing and raingear. Since surmounting Pearl Pass is largely a lesson in "dis-mountain" biking, the extra weight won't really matter.

Services: There are no services along this route and all surface waters should be purified before drinking. Crested Butte and Aspen, the route's trailhead and endpoint, respectively, offer all visitor-related services. Carry plenty of high-energy food and water.

Hazards: Again, weather should not be taken lightly. Sparkling morning skies can turn to vicious thunderheads by afternoon. Rain on Pearl Pass may be accompanied by bitter cold, if not hail or snow. Packing along extra clothing and raingear is recommended.

Both sides of Pearl Pass are marked by very rough four-wheel-drive roads. The ascent to Pearl is largely a push. The descent off Pearl can be highly technical, for the route is laden with loose gravel, cobbles, and boulders. Carry a well-equipped repair kit. Plan on getting your feet wet for there are a few stream crossings, and spring runoff may be channeled down the road near the Pass.

Rescue index: The actual summit of Pearl Pass is remote, and rescue from it would be difficult. A telephone might be found at ranches in Brush Creek Valley (Crested Butte side) or perhaps in Ashcroft (Aspen side), but emergency assistance will have to come from the route's endpoint towns. Avoid mechanical emergencies by making sure your bike is working properly and by carrying a well-equipped repair kit.

Land status: Gunnison National Forest. White River National Forest.

Maps: USGS 7.5 minute quadrangles: Aspen, Crested Butte, Gothic, Hayden Peak, and Pearl Pass, Colorado.

Finding the trail: The route traditionally begins straight out of Crested Butte by following CO 135 south 2 miles and then turning left on Brush Creek Road. Pearl Pass is atop the Middle Brush Creek jeep road.

Sources of additional information:

Gunnison National Forest and Bureau of Land Management
Taylor River Ranger District
216 North Colorado Street
Gunnison, CO 81230
(303) 641-0471

White River National Forest
Aspen Ranger District
806 West Hallam
Aspen, CO 81611
(303) 925-3445

Paradise Bikes and Skis
P.O. Box 1460
232 Elk Avenue
Crested Butte, CO 81224
(303) 349-6324

Fat Tire Bike Week
P.O. Box 782
Crested Butte, CO 81224
(303) 349-6817

Richard's Mountain Bike Book, by Charles Kelly and Nick Crane. New York: Ballantine Books, 1988.
Consult pages 37 to 47 for a titillating version of the Pearl Pass Tour and a historic account of the development of the sport now called "mountain biking." As someone who lived the dream, Kelly offers a captivating chronicle of simultaneous events in Marin County, California, and Crested Butte, Colorado, that later became legendary in the annals of mountain biking.

"The First Pearl Pass Klunker Tour" in the *Crested Butte Pilot*, September 17, 1976. (Courtesy of Carole Bauer and the Mountain Bike Hall of Fame and Museum.)

Mountain Bike Hall of Fame and Museum
P.O. Box 845
Crested Butte, CO 81224
(303) 349-7382
Contact or stop into the Mountain Bike Hall of Fame and Museum in Crested Butte, Colorado. Bicycles, photos, magazines, articles, and memorabilia representative of the era are displayed along with contributions made by the sport's pioneers. The Hall of Fame is nonprofit, and the whole shebang is mobile, too.

Notes on the trail: Saddle up and head out of Crested Butte, pedaling south on CO 135. About 2 miles down the highway, turn left on Brush Creek Road toward Skyland Ranch. Pavement turns to hard-packed dirt as the road wraps around the southern flank of Mount Crested Butte and northward up the East River Valley. Pass the trailhead for Farris Creek at mile 6, then cross Brush Creek and pass through private property that straddles the road.

Brush Creek Road splits. The road to the left (north) goes to West Brush Creek and the approach to Teocalli Ridge. Stay right for Middle Brush Creek and Pearl Pass. Shortly after this fork cross West Brush Creek itself. The stream crossing is followed by another split in the road. Follow Middle Brush Creek Road.

At mile 11.5, the road crosses Middle Brush Creek. Immediately thereafter, stay left on Middle Brush Creek Road where East Brush Creek Road enters from the right. Now the route begins to climb more steeply up the glacial trough valley between Teocalli Ridge and Timbered Hill. Pearl Pass is still hidden from sight.

Around mile 14 pass by the trail leading up to Twin Lakes and cross over Middle Brush Creek once, then again, less than a mile farther. Wolf down an energy bar and load up on the carbo fuel, for this is where the fun (?) begins. It is just 3 more miles to Pearl Pass, but 2,000′ of vertical stand in the way.

After the last crossing of Middle Brush Creek, the road bends southward as it begins scaling the lower flank of Pearl Mountain and then wraps northward and up through a series of glacial cirques. Beyond these high, alpine bowls, Pearl Pass is gained. Reward for your struggle is a view of the top of the world. The scene transcends description in words, but it is a splendid display of the Central Rockies.

From Pearl Pass, it is downhill to Aspen. Do not be over-zealous, for the descent from the Pass can be a technical endeavor due to very rough four-wheel-drive conditions. Dirt turns to pavement near Ashcroft followed by 14 miles of cruising down to Aspen. Traditionally, the Jerome Bar in the Hotel Jerome is the post-ride watering hole.

RIDE 39 *TRAIL 401 LOOP*

Trail 401 is one of the area's finest single-tracks. Like skiing a shot of untouched, bottomless virgin powder, riding 401 is one of those exhilarating experiences destined to occupy a space in your memory banks. Even if Trail 401 were a gentle, smooth road, its scenic majesty would certainly place it near the top of any mountain biker's "must do" list. In short, 401 is loaded with big views and big fun.

This is a tough ride! It requires polished mountain bike skills plus good endurance. To begin with, the climb past Emerald Lake to Schofield Pass is a steep, granny-gear climb followed by 20 minutes of hike-a-biking right from the trailhead. Farther along 401 you'll encounter demanding climbs, fast technical descents, exposure to steep side slopes, stream crossings, portages, and nearly every other natural single-track obstacle imaginable. Combining these challenges with both the beautiful approach and a giant panorama from the trail's summit makes 401 a Colorado classic.

Trail 401 proper is about a nine-mile point-to-point ride from Schofield Pass to Gothic. Described here as a loop originating in Gothic, the route is closer to 16 miles. Many choose to head out straight from Crested Butte with a long warm-up through Gothic and then head up to Schofield Pass. This extended loop is closer to 32 miles.

[This trail description was submitted by Steve Cook,* Crested Butte, Colorado.—G. B.]

General location: Trail 401 proper begins at Schofield Pass at the summit of Gothic Road (about 15 miles north of Crested Butte), then winds south and exits near the old townsite of Gothic.

Elevation change: The townsite of Gothic (the route's suggested beginning) rests amidst the East River Valley at 9,500′. Schofield Pass (401 trailhead) rises to 10,700′. From here, the trail climbs an additional 600′ to 11,300′ on the flanks of Bellview Mountain and then descends back to Gothic. If one is originating the ride from Crested Butte, it is an 1,800′ climb to Schofield Pass over 15 miles.

Season: Trail 401 Loop takes a while to melt out. Don't expect to ride it until late June to early July or much after mid-September. At this high elevation,

---

*Steve Cook is known by some as a hot mountain bike racer of the mid-1980s, to others as one of the first inductees to the Mountain Bike Hall of Fame in Crested Butte, and to still others as the arrogant know-it-all with the big ego. He is owner and operator of Paradise Bikes and Skis, in business since 1981. But mostly, Steve is just an old hippie who loves to ride bicycles.

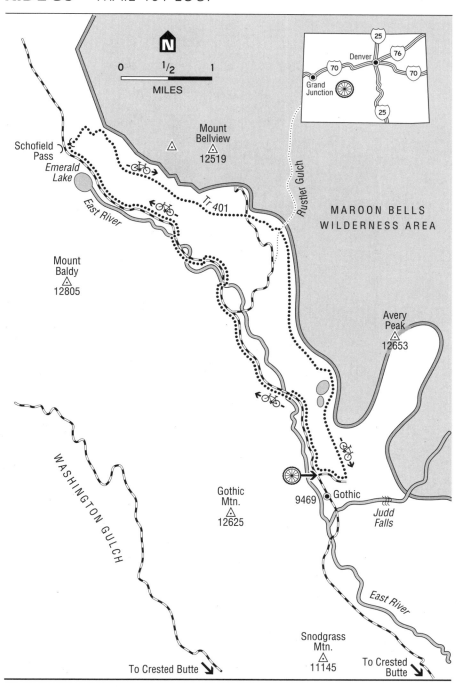

A long view down the East River Valley. Mount Crested Butte (left), Snodgrass Mountain (right). Photo: Gregg Bromka.

midsummer alpine mornings are typically clear but may give way to rain, hail, and (by no means unheard of) snowstorms by afternoon.

Although this may sound foreboding, realize that when lower trails have lost their wildflowers by midsummer, Schofield Pass and 401 are just reaching their vivid peak. Fireweed, mule ear, and asters paint the hillsides with vibrant colors backdropped by grassy mountain slopes and melting snowfields.

Services: Outside of Crested Butte, which has all visitor needs, services are limited. Water, a variety of snacks, and even ice cream bars can be found at the general store in Gothic, which is usually open during the day throughout the summer. Along the route to Schofield Pass, primitive and developed Forest Service camping exists (a few locations offer tables and toilets, but none offer water). Once you commit to 401's single-track, you must be self-sufficient.

Hazards: The upper section of Trail 401, after the initial portage, is exposed to fallaway slopes along the flanks of Mount Bellview, so control and keen handling skills are necessary. Aside from an array of technical challenges, the lower section (past Rustler Gulch) may contain deadfall in early summer before the folks from the Pathfinders have had a chance to clear the trail. When pedaling along the Gothic Road, be alert to vehicular traffic and be prepared to share the road.

Rescue index: When traveling up Gothic Road to Schofield Pass, motorists are numerous and campers abound. Emergency contacts can be made in Gothic, but Crested Butte is where medical attention will be found. Along the 401 Trail you may encounter other bikers, hikers, and equestrians. Also, you will commonly find people at Schofield Pass, Rustler Gulch, and Judd Falls, each popular access points to nearby Wilderness Areas.

Land status: Gunnison National Forest. This route borders designated Wilderness Areas where mountain biking is strictly prohibited. Of course, be considerate of other trail users, especially equestrians, where the trail is narrow and exposed.

Maps: USGS 7.5 minute quadrangles: Gothic, Oh-Be-Joyful, and Snowmass Mountain, Colorado. USGS 1:50,000 scale county map: Gunnison County #2, Colorado. *The Pathfinders Trail Map,* revised. Available from Paradise Bikes and Skis in Crested Butte, Colorado. This large fold-out map shows all of Crested Butte's mountain bike rides.

Finding the trail: If you start near Gothic, a good spot to leave vehicles is the parking lot for the Judd Falls trailhead, which is a short distance east of Gothic; just follow the signs. Before parking in or around the townsite of Gothic, obtain permission, for most of this land is private. If you pedal straight from Crested Butte (a fantastic all-day affair), tack on 8 miles to Gothic first.

Sources of additional information:

Gunnison National Forest
Taylor River Ranger District
216 North Colorado Street
Gunnison, CO 81230
(303) 641-0471

Paradise Bikes and Skis
P.O. Box 1460
232 Elk Avenue
Crested Butte, CO 81224
(303) 349-6324

Paradise Bikes is known locally as "The Shop that Finds and Maintains the Trails" around Crested Butte. Not only does this shop take pride in its high quality service, sales, and rentals, it also strives to put something back into the sport and protect the environment. Along with the Pathfinders, owner Steve Cook has installed signs and maintained trails to make mountain biking around Crested Butte safer, more enjoyable, and respected by other trail users and land owners. In short, Paradise Bikes and Skis is owned and staffed by folks who truly love bikes: selling and servicing them, talking about them, and especially riding them.

Notes on the trail: From the old townsite of Gothic, pedal up the Gothic Road as it winds up the East River Valley. Pass Emerald Lake and continue up to Schofield Pass. Look for the single-track trail heading east and uphill. The trail usually has a sign—unless porcupines or bears have made a meal of it.

The trail starts out as a strenuous portage for 20 to 30 minutes, climbing to near timberline. As you leave the forest, follow trail markers and rock cairns across the meadow to the east, but not too far. Trail 401 branches south towards Gothic. (A hiking trail that joins from the north goes to the Maroon Bells–Snowmass Wilderness Area.) This is where the big views and big fun begin. The trail traverses and descends the steep southern flank of Mount Bellview hundreds of feet above the East River Valley. For the next 3 miles or so the trail swoops, dips, and clings to the mountain's side. At times the trail-side foliage grows taller than your handlebars. The single-track dives into Rustler Gulch. You can bail out here by taking the dirt road down to the Gothic Road.

To continue the lower portion of Trail 401, cross Rustler Gulch Creek to more technical single-track. This lower portion of Trail 401, from Rustler Gulch to Gothic, is not exposed to steep slopes but is a technical potpourri of roots, logs, bogs, stream crossings, and rock-filled ravines, plus a few nice, steep ups and downs thrown in for good measure. Along the single-track, a dirt road branching to the right offers a direct descent to the Gothic Road, but climb left and back up to more single-track for some faster, smoother descending, ending at the parking lot just north of Gothic.

Cruising through the old mining supply town of Gothic conjures up visions of the rollicking gold and silver boom days of yesteryear. Today, the townsite is home to the Rocky Mountain Biological Lab, which performs environmental studies on plants, animals, and ecosystems. The staff resides in many of the original turn-of-the-century buildings.

The ride up Gothic Road is always a very beautiful approach to 401, which explains the frequent abundance of sightseers and campers visiting the valley. The East River Valley is a long, broad, glacial trough. Its ancient river of ice has been replaced with a gently flowing stream meandering through luxuriant grassy meadows pocketed with stands of conifers and aspens. Wildflowers explode with color and steal your attention away from majestic mountains— Snodgrass and Gothic, mounts Baldy and Bellview, and Avery Peak—which govern the terrain.

Prior to descending across the flank of Mount Bellview, take time to study this marvelous alpine vista. The Maroon Bells–Snowmass Wilderness Area is to the northeast; just the very tops of its purple-tainted jags poke above the ridgeline. To the north, the Crystal River drops dramatically towards the towns of Marble and Crystal; to the south, the East River Valley stretches past Gothic to the base of Mount Crested Butte—an unmistakable, volcanic castle reigning the lower valley.

RIDE 40 *FARRIS CREEK*

Farris Creek is a fine introduction to Crested Butte–area mountain biking. Both intermediate and expert cyclists will find this trail loaded with fat-tire fun, coupled with plenty of eye-popping views.

From the route's very beginning, you will become captivated by the remarkable scenery that sets Crested Butte apart from other cycling destinations. Broad, grassy floodplains straddle the tranquil East River as it loops through gooseneck meanders. By late afternoon, the pastoral valley is smothered by shadows cast from the jagged shoulder of Mount Crested Butte. Farris Creek itself weaves through a smaller but equally beautiful valley full of long meadows outlined with aspen groves.

These scenes are no doubt inspiring, but you will stop in your tracks upon reaching the trail's high point, where fantastic views of Teocalli Mountain await. Teocalli Ridge, which obscures all but the 13,000′ apex of Teocalli Mountain, hosts yet another of the area's world-class single-tracks.

Farris Creek is a moderately difficult, ten-mile loop well suited for intermediate mountain bikers. It combines smooth four-wheel-drive roads with exciting, moderately technical single-track. Aggressive novice cyclists will find the route challenging and may have to walk a few of the rougher portions, especially the single-track descent off Strand Hill. But the preceding tour through Farris Creek Valley and the rolling single-track that follows are well worth a few dismounts.

[Route information was submitted by Steve Cook, Crested Butte, Colorado.—G. B.]

General location: Farris Creek is located about 5.5 miles east of Crested Butte on Brush Creek Road.

Elevation change: The Farris Creek loop starts at 9,000′ and begins with a brisk, 300′ climb over about a half mile, followed by fast-paced, undulating terrain. Circling the east side of Strand Hill, the route rises gently to 9,800′ and then loses most of the cumulative elevation gain over the ensuing mile-long, technical descent. Rolling single-track returns you to the trail's beginning. If you pedal to the trailhead from town, the ride out is relatively flat (a good beginner ride in itself as an out-and-back).

Season: This trail gets plenty of sun and is low in the valley, so it is usually one

RIDE 40 *FARRIS CREEK*

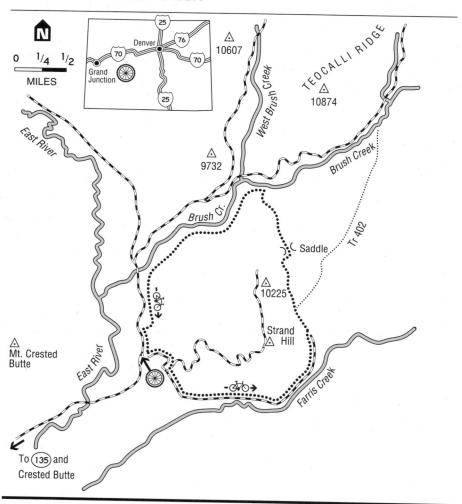

of the first rides to clear of snow, and is rideable from late May to late October. Early in the season, nearly 90% of the trail can be dry, with only a few lingering snow patches on the protected downhill portion.

Services: No services will be found along this route. Water from Brush and Farris creeks should be purified before drinking, since cattle ranching is heavy in this area.

Unlike its glamorous sister town to the east, Aspen, Crested Butte is embellished with a more rustic glow, with a simpler, laid-back atmosphere. You may

The rugged Elk Mountains engulf Crested Butte. Photo: Gregg Bromka.

not find pricey fur coats and limousines, but Crested Butte boasts a full range of visitor services and accommodations from the modest to the extravagant. And, since Crested Butte and mountain biking are synonymous, there is plenty of friendly service and advice to supplement your mountain bike adventure.

Hazards: Use caution when descending the single-track off Strand Hill. Loose rocks, tree roots, a few tight turns, and steep slopes will challenge most riders.

After the descent flattens you must make a route choice. The trail heading straight (north) soon crosses Middle Brush Creek before exiting onto Middle Brush Creek Road. This stream can be deep, swift flowing, and icy-cold, making for a dangerous ford. The trail branching sharply left (west) continues the Farris Creek loop and eventually crosses a slow-flowing, but knee-deep, irrigation canal. Riding through the canal would be difficult, so be prepared to soak your feet and carry your bike across.

Rescue index: This route is quite popular, so other trail users may be encountered. But from the farthest point on the trail, you are about 4 to 5 miles from Brush Creek Road (where passing motorists are frequent), then another 5.5 miles from Crested Butte.

Land status: Gunnison National Forest.

Maps: USGS 7.5 minute quadrangles: Cement Mountain, Crested Butte, Gothic, and Pearl Pass, Colorado. USGS 1:50,000 scale county map: Gunnison County #3, Colorado. *The Pathfinders Trail Map,* revised. Available from

Paradise Bikes and Skis, Crested Butte, Colorado. This large, fold-out map shows all of Crested Butte's mountain bike rides.

Finding the trail: Go about 1.5 miles south of Crested Butte on CO 135. Turn east onto Brush Creek Road, passing Skyland Resort and the airport. The Farris Creek trailhead is less than a mile past the quaint little ranch sprawled out on the East River valley floor, about 4 miles down Brush Creek Road from CO 135. A wire gate on the right side of the road (usually closed) marks the route's beginning.

Sources of additional information:

> Gunnison National Forest and Bureau of Land Management
> Taylor River Ranger District
> 216 North Colorado Street
> Gunnison, CO 81230
> (303) 641-0471

> Paradise Bikes and Skis
> P.O. Box 1460
> 232 Elk Avenue
> Crested Butte, CO 81224
> (303) 349-6324

Notes on the trail: The loop begins with a short, stiff, but smooth climb. A forewarning of what lies ahead? No, just a little anaerobic interval training. Gradual descents and gentle inclines follow as the double-track circles around the southern flank of Strand Hill. The grass-filled, aspen-rimmed valley through which Farris Creek flows is a beautiful sight.

As the route bends northward on Strand Hill's eastern side, it begins to climb, gently at first, then more steeply, to a saddle. (Trail 402 branches to the right about halfway up.) Views of Teocalli Ridge and Teocalli Mountain are inspiring. The single-track descending from the saddle to the north is steep and technical. If you are not confident in your bike handling skills, simply take your bike for a brief walk.

There is a junction in the sage flats at the bottom of the descent, sometimes marked with a post. Turn sharply left to continue on single-track. Rounding out the ride is a great rolling trail contouring the base of Strand Hill. Be ready for intermittent rocky patches, some overgrown brush draping the trail, and of course a knee-deep splash as you portage through the irrigation canal. A number of fencelines cross the route. Be sure to close all gates behind you.

For advanced mountain bikers, Farris Creek is a jump-off point to other enticing options, including the hill climb to the summit of Strand Hill and Trail 402.

RIDE 41   *UPPER LOOP*

Everyone enjoys the Upper Loop, perhaps for different reasons: novice and intermediate cyclists can develop and hone their single-track skills, whereas seasoned cyclists can venture onto more technical side trails. The route is short, quick, and close to town; hop on your bike and before you know it you've logged ten miles. Dense aspen groves set among fields of delicate wildflowers invoke a feeling of remoteness. The Upper Loop is the local, springtime hot spot for those itching to don bike shorts and get in some trail time, for it melts out early. And, the Upper Loop is one of the few area rides that offer good views of Crested Butte nestled among the guardian Rockies.

The official Upper Loop trail is less than three miles long. When incorporated into a clockwise loop originating from town, it makes a ride about ten miles long, more than half of which is on paved roads. This route hovers somewhere between easy and moderately difficult. Moderately strong legs and lungs will aid in tackling the initial three-mile, paved-road climb from town to the base of Mount Crested Butte Ski Area. Thereafter, the single-track trail is generally smooth, declining gradually. Yet, dispersed throughout the ride are a number of short, moderately technical downhills where ruts and scattered rocks are common. These sections offer excellent opportunities for learning or improving your single-track skills. An optional mile and a half near the route's end is much more technical.

[This trail information was submitted by Steve Cook, Crested Butte, Colorado.—G. B.]

General location: Directly east of the town of Crested Butte on the lower, western flanks of Mount Crested Butte Ski Area.

Elevation change: The town of Crested Butte rests at 8,900′. Over the first 3 miles, the paved road to Mount Crested Butte rises 350′ to nearly 9,250′. This elevation is gradually lost over the course of the single-track and the return paved roads.

Season: The Upper Loop is the first ride to melt out and the last to become snowbound, for it is low in the valley and traverses southwest-facing slopes. Although seasonal snowfall will determine the route's accessibility, it will be rideable typically from mid-April to late October or mid-November.

Services: All visitor services are available in the town of Crested Butte, and most are offered near the trail's beginning at Mount Crested Butte Ski Area. But you will find no water along the route. Of course, you can always drop by the nineteenth hole at Skyland Resort for one of your favorite "après-ride" beverages.

RIDE 41 *UPPER LOOP*

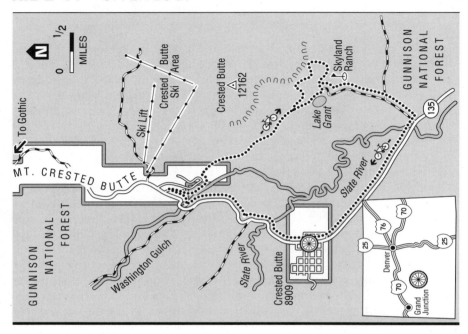

Hazards: The high volume of bike traffic tends to keep the single-track smooth, fast, and fun, but occasionally creates a few ruts on the steeper downhills. First-time cyclists should proceed cautiously and dismount when confronted by more technical sections.

A couple of easy stream crossings and three fences will be encountered. All fences have stairs, or stiles, over them, thanks to the Pathfinders at Paradise Bikes. After the single-track's third fence crossing, the trail passes shortly through an archery range. The archers are aware that cyclists frequent this trail, but use caution just the same and make a little extra noise so your presence is known. Do not reenact Custer's last stand!

Half of the time is spent on paved roads, so ride with due respect for motorists.

Rescue index: You are never more than a mile or so from a telephone: Mount Crested Butte Ski Area is located at the single-track's beginning, Skyland Ranch marks the end of the off-road section, and the town of Crested Butte is only a few miles away. Motorists are numerous on the paved roads.

Land status: This trail crosses private property, although access has been granted. Consequently, it is imperative that all bikers practice acceptable mountain bike etiquette to insure the continued privilege of riding this trail.

A tangle of aspens encloses Upper Loop. Photo: Gregg Bromka.

Maps: USGS 7.5 minute quadrangles: Crested Butte and Gothic, Colorado. USGS 1:50,000 scale county map: Gunnison County #2, Colorado. *The Pathfinders Trail Map,* revised. Available from Paradise Bikes and Skis, Crested Butte, Colorado. This large, fold-out map shows all of Crested Butte's mountain bike rides.

Finding the trail: From Crested Butte, pedal 3 miles north and east on the paved Gothic Road to the margins of Mount Crested Butte Ski Area. Turn right on Hunter Hill Road, climb to the switchback, and spot the obvious but unsigned trail heading up and into the sagebrush.

Steve Cook of Paradise Bikes and Skis—the old shop.

Sources of additional information:

Paradise Bikes and Skis
P.O. Box 1460
232 Elk Avenue
Crested Butte, CO 81224
(303) 349-6324

Notes on the trail: From the Hunter Hill Road trailhead, the route angles up through the sage, heading generally southeast. For the next few miles, it dips and climbs beneath the craggy slopes of Mount Crested Butte. After the third fence crossing, you will enter into the archery range. If you stay to the right, the trail will drop out of the woods and onto a dirt road to Lake Grant. The dirt road continues past Skyland Ranch and connects with the highway leading back into town.

To extend this route and delve into technical tree riding, fork left instead of taking the right fork to Lake Grant to pursue the "upper" section of the Upper Loop. ("Tree riding" is riding through tightly spaced trees.) This is a 2-mile slalom course circling through tight aspens. Upon entering the trail network, a series of right turns will quickly bring you to the lake. Left turns will lead you deep into aspens where exacting skills and good stamina are required. Since the risk of getting lost is quite low, it is worthwhile to chase this challenging option branching from the main route.

From the trail's end near Lake Grant, the valley scene is unsurpassed. Crested Butte, a spirited one-horse town, sits contently amidst coalescing glacial valleys and beneath towering peaks and ridgelines. Over your shoulder, the jagged cliffs of Mount Crested Butte bear down with an unnerving presence.

Early morning, when the sun's first, warm rays break the cool stillness, and again in the evening, as the last fiery hues bounce off the surrounding peaks, are both rewarding times to pedal the Upper Loop.

Gunnison

RIDE 42 *THE RAGE IN THE SAGE*

If you are looking for a ride with variety, look no further than the Hartmans Rocks Loop, also known as "The Rage in the Sage." This Gunnison-area favorite follows the course of the annual spring mountain bike race and overflows with fat-tire excitement: gut-busting climbs, screaming descents, smooth jeep road cruises, and swooping, off-camber turns along luge-type single-track.

But there is more to life than killer single-track, so ease up on the throttle and study the local scenery. This domed highland is a medley of lithified fins, ribs, and knobs that reach 100′ in height and shadow the area with surrealism. You can see why "The Rocks" is a popular technical rock climbing and bouldering area. From high points along the route, you are treated to fine vistas of the surrounding mountain ranges: the rugged San Juans to the south and west, the West Elk Mountains to the north (with Crested Butte beyond), and Fossil Ridge to the east. Midway through the route, in Beaver Creek, the route passes Aberdeen Quarry. Granite extracted from this quarry was used in the construction of the Colorado State Capitol building in 1890.

The Gunnison area is a low-alpine desert vegetated mainly with sage and scrub brush, and dotted with occasional pinyon and juniper. But groves of aspen, cottonwood, and willows flourish in some of the draws. Cacti abound off the beaten path and burst into colorful blooms during early spring. Despite its apparently desolate nature, the area hosts abundant wildlife, including deer, porcupine, coyote, fox, a variety of birds of prey, and even eagles.

Geared for strong intermediate to expert riders who have fine-tuned their bike handling skills, this 18-mile counterclockwise loop combines very easy sections of smooth jeep roads with technically demanding single-track (about 75% of the ride). But, with a good map and local advice, less-aggressive riders can shortcut the more difficult segments or explore less demanding side loops that crisscross the area. As the race's name implies, much of the trail weaves through low alpine sage. Expect sandy conditions during prolonged dry periods, and sticky mud when it's wet. Still, for the most part, the hard-packed trail is a "ragers" delight.

By the way, Gunnison, Colorado, has hosted one of the state's largest mountain bike teams since 1986, the Tuneup Team. Sponsored by the Tuneup Bike Shop in Gunnison, the team has produced a number of world-class riders, including Dave Weins and Keith Austin.

THE RAGE IN THE SAGE

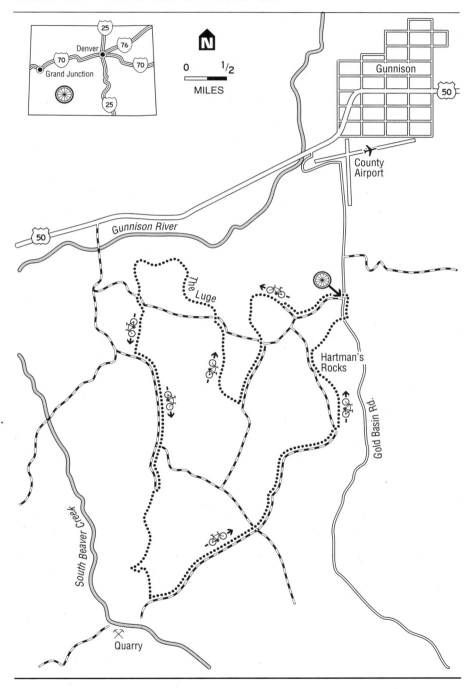

[The Rage in the Sage route information was provided by Gregg Morin,* Gunnison, Colorado.—G. B.]

General location: This ride begins near Hartmans Rocks, about 2 miles south of Gunnison.

Elevation change: The Rage in the Sage begins at 7,700′ and rises to only 8,300′ midroute. However, the loop's many climbs and descents add up to nearly 2,000′ of vertical gain.

Season: The best season to ride is from May through October. But since it is possible to ride during large portions of the winter months, this route makes for great off-season cycling, especially when nearby Crested Butte is still snow-bound. Be prepared for afternoon rain during summer months and cold temperatures during the winter.

Services: You will find no services or potable water along this route, but Gunnison is only minutes away and offers all visitor services, including bike shops.

Hazards: Avoid venturing off the beaten path, for cacti thrive (enough said), and unfortunately broken glass may appear in a few spots. The technical nature of this route demands total concentration, but keep one eye on the trail and one eye ahead of you, for barbed wire gates may be closed across the path. Four-wheel-drive traffic is common on the numerous dirt roads, but should not pose a problem (the same is true for cattle in the area, which, of course, should never be harassed).

Rescue index: Depending on what part of the course you are on, access by jeep roads may be easy to nearly impossible. Fortunately, a jeep road is never more than a short, 30-minute walk away, and Gunnison is about 2 miles from the route's beginning.

Land status: Bureau of Land Management.

Maps: USGS 7.5 minute quadrangles: Gunnison and Iris NW, Colorado. USGS 1:50,000 scale county map: Gunnison, Colorado. *Gunnison Area Mountain Bike Map.* Available through Gunnison Country Chamber of Commerce, or The Tuneup Ski and Bike Shop.

Finding the trail: Drive, or ride, west out of Gunnison on US 50, then turn left (south) onto Gold Basin Road, which follows along the airport landing strip. About 1 mile south of crossing Tomichi Creek turn right (west) onto a dirt road with a sign for Hartmans Rock. Park here.

---

*Gregg Morin plays a dual role as both operator of the Tuneup Shop and member of the Tuneup Team, one of Colorado's largest mountain bike teams. Besides being an avid racer, Gregg also enjoys backcountry pedaling in and around the Gunnison area. Dedicated to preserving and promoting mountain biking, he marks and maintains the "Rage in the Sage" trail as well as other local routes.

Sources of additional information:

Gunnison National Forest and Bureau of Land Management
Gunnison Resource Area
216 North Colorado
Gunnison, CO 81230
(303) 641-0471

The Tuneup Ski and Bike Shop
222 North Main
Gunnison, CO 81230
(303) 641-0285
The Tuneup Bike Shop can assist you with all your mountain and road bicycling needs, for everyone from the recreational cyclist to the discriminating racer. The Tuneup Bike Shop has produced a trail map of the Gunnison area; an accompanying guidebook is forthcoming.

Gunnison County Chamber of Commerce
P.O. Box 36
Gunnison, CO 81230
(303) 641-1501

Notes on the trail: The main Rage in the Sage course has been rerouted in the past and will invariably be altered in the future. Contact the Tuneup Bike Shop for updated information. The route is marked with brown poles, and perhaps with orange flagging tape as well. When you come to a junction, turn in the direction of the pole. This wavering route is difficult to describe, but here is a short summary.

The route begins on the Hartmans Rocks Road, heading west. If you round a fence and are faced with a brutal-looking climb, you are on the right track—pick a granny gear for this one; it is one of the toughest.

Atop the first hill, the road splits. Turn right and onto a technical single-track descending northward and through a meadow. Wrap south while climbing steeply along double-track onto a ridge. At a 4-way junction of dirt roads, continue due south on a smooth dirt road and then turn back north again for a fast, single-track descent down "The Luge." This section, aptly named, contains numerous banked, velodromelike turns. Use extreme caution, for many turns are blind and "booby-trapped" with rocks. Now, at the very northwest corner of the loop, turn southward and climb alongside a fence line. Pass through a couple of gates and cross a jeep road. A very steep downhill precedes the junction with McCabe Lane; stay left, then continue southward on intermittent double- and single-track. At the loop's southwest corner, turn left and up a gully, and then through a gate. Cross the power line road while pursuing more single-track punctuated with intermittent slickrock to the loop's southernmost extent. Double-track and single-track recross the power line road and angle northward for gentle climbing and descending. Pass the entrance into the "Upper Luge." Over the next mile, the jeep road heads north past several side trails that descend over the slope's edge. Double-track turns back to single-track to finish the loop with serpentining trail, a smattering of slickrock, ledges, and gullies, back to the front of Hartmans Rocks and the parking area.

Grand Junction

COLORADO PLATEAU MOUNTAIN-BIKE TRAIL ASSOCIATION

Imagine mountain biking 130 miles through the remote desert backcountry, over sun-drenched redrock formations and slickrock expanses, across deep river canyons, and past forested mountain slopes. Dream of a premier mountain biking trail that connects two states but recognizes no border between them. Picture volunteers and private businesses banning together—without a budget, without bylaws, and without bickering. Think of federal land agencies lending feverish support, cutting through often beleaguering red tape to approve the 10 miles of hand-built single-track. And, envision the Hopi Indians performing a sacred dance to bless the route.

In as little as 6 months all of these "would-be" dreams came true for coordinator Timms Fowler and a dedicated group of bicycling enthusiasts under the guidance of the newly organized Colorado Plateau Mountain-Bike Trail Association (COPMOBA). With the assistance of the Bureau of Land Management, U. S. Forest Service, private businesses, and dozens of volunteers, Kokopelli's Trail—a visionary trail linking Grand Junction, Colorado, with Moab, Utah—was created and built.

Kokopelli's Trail is the first leg in a multiple trail system crossing the Colorado Plateau, connecting other cycling destinations and towns in both Colorado and Utah. Fueled by undying motivation and ceaseless determination, COPMOBA has created a trail system that will become an inspirational model to future trail builders.

"Mountain biking is a vehicle to promote low impact outdoor recreation, natural history education, bike safety, and land use ethics on the Colorado Plateau. We believe mountain biking is not a fad, it is the future, because it combines fun, fitness, and fantastic scenery—always with an eye on protecting the land we love."

For a detailed brochure about Kokopelli's Trail, current and future projects, and becoming a COPMOBA member, contact The Colorado Plateau Mountain Bike Trail Association (COPMOBA), P.O. Box 4602, Grand Junction, CO 81502-4602, (303) 241-9561.

RIDE 43 *ROUGH CANYON*

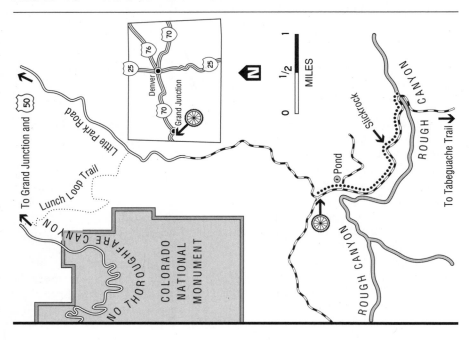

RIDE 43 *ROUGH CANYON*

The quick trip into Rough Canyon is a good introduction to Grand Junction–area mountain biking and is a great way to start the morning or end the day. Whether you approach the trail by car or by pedaling directly from Grand Junction, you'll find inspiring views of the Colorado National Monument rising to the west—a monocline of glowing redrock cliffs and deep canyon amphitheaters striped with desert varnish and freckled with juniper and pinyon. To the east, Grand Mesa oversees the floodplain confluence of the Gunnison and Colorado rivers, which junction gives rise to this city's name.

The canyon bottom is a picturesque setting complete with potholes and a small waterfall that flows during the spring and after rains. There are good, short hikes back up the creek bed. Ute Indians once inhabited the wash, as evidenced by steps cut into the far sandstone wall, well-concealed rock art, and campfire remnants detected from carbon in the sand.

There is a good dose of slickrock along the Rough Canyon trail. Photo: Gregg Bromka.

Rough Canyon is a five-mile "down-and-back-up" route that follows both smooth and rough four-wheel-drive roads punctuated with sand patches. And although Grand Junction is miles from Moab, Utah, the route offers a small sampling of free-style slickrock. Dropping into the canyon is fast and fun, with moderate technical difficulty. The climb back out is steep, but short. Do not hesitate to venture from the dirt-and-sand road to explore the nearby slickrock inclines; the traction alone is worth it.

[This trail description was submitted by Rick Corbin,* Clifton, Colorado.— G. B.]

General location: Nine miles southwest of Grand Junction, Colorado.
Elevation change: Near the route's beginning overlooking Rough Canyon is

---

*After years of trying to improve his ten kilometer times, Rick Corbin began to develop back problems. While evaluating the choice between having surgery or finding an alternative to running, he journeyed to Crested Butte during the summer of 1983 and bought his first mountain bike. Since then, mountain biking has taken hold in his life more than any other sport.

Rick Corbin moved to Grand Junction in 1984 and has been active in the mountain biking community ever since. Now a board member of the Colorado Plateau Mountain-the ride's highest point at 6,180′. In only a few miles, the trail loses about 800′, descending to 5,400′ in the canyon bottom.

Season: This route can be pedaled nearly year-round, but spring and fall are the most enjoyable seasons. During midsummer, the route is hot and dry. In winter, between snowstorms when sunny days prevail, the route dries and proves to be quite pleasant. Even when the ground is frozen in the dead of winter, bicycling through Rough Canyon can be great fun. (Just be sure the temperatures remain below freezing; otherwise the thawing ground will engulf you in a sea of viscous mud.) Prepare for changing temperatures, unpredictable weather patterns, and lack of water during any season.

Services: Grand Junction yields all visitor services, including several bike shops. No water will be found along the trail except for small amounts trapped in a pothole or two after rain, but these dry up quickly. Purify any water found on the trail before drinking.

Hazards: Cliffs, stay away from the cliffs! There are only one or two places where the trail skirts the edge of 50′ to 100′ cliffs. A high speed descent on the smooth slickrock on unfamiliar terrain could result in a new sport, "para-mountain biking." Be on the lookout for cacti, also. The upper road above Rough Canyon can turn from soft silt to deep mud when wet.

Rescue index: This ride is within the response area of the Grand Junction Fire Department, and the closest phone would be at one of the houses 3 miles back down Little Park Road. Rough Canyon is an area growing in popularity and, as part of COPMOBA's Tabeguache Trail, it will certainly draw more recreational users. Even so, traffic is variable. You may experience complete solitude on the weekends or, at other times, have to share the route with a multitude of bikers, hikers, equestrians, and off-road vehicle users.

Land status: Bureau of Land Management.

Maps: USGS 7.5 minute quadrangles: Grand Junction and Island Mesa, Colorado. USGS 1:50,000 scale county maps: Mesa County #2, Colorado.

Finding the trail: From Interstate 70, take Exit 31/Airport–Horizon Drive and drive southwest into Grand Junction. (Most of the access route is marked with brown Colorado National Monument signs.) Cross Twelfth Street and turn left on Seventh Street and into the heart of the city. Turn right onto Grand Avenue, then cross the bridge over the Colorado River. Turn left onto Monument Road, left again on Rosevale Road (this is where you leave the access route to Colorado National Monument), and fork right onto Little Park Road.

From this turn, the pavement ends after 3.5 miles. Two miles farther is a turnout on the road's crest where parking is available (next to a bullet-ridden sign, "NO SHOOTING!"). If you cross a cattle guard, you have gone too far.

(continued from page 217)

Bike Trail Association, Rick is working with other members and land management agencies to improve off-road bicycling throughout the area.

A BLM sign marks the trailhead and the route is periodically signed with brown carsonite posts.

Sources of additional information:

Bureau of Land Management
Grand Junction Resource Area
2815 H Road
Grand Junction, CO 81506
(303) 244-3050

Colorado Plateau Mountain-Bike Trail Association (COPMOBA)
P.O. Box 4602
Grand Junction, CO 81502
(303) 241-9561

Notes on the trail: Characteristic of multiple-use areas, there are multiple roads, all of which lead the same way. From the parking area proceed downhill to the south. In less than half a mile, you will come to an earthen dam and a stock pond. Cross the dam and immediately find a cattle guard and a junction. Continue straight ahead and up a short incline where once again you will discover multiple roads. When in doubt, bear right. Within half a mile the climb will level and you should sight the slickrock portion of the ride. From here, head southeast following the four-wheel-drive roads. Once again bear right and save the sightseeing (and there is plenty to see) for the ride back up. Descend as far as desired toward (or all the way into) the bottom of Rough Canyon. Return via the same route.

Even where trail markers are visible you will swear you are lost. Just keep in mind that the route is pinned between the cliffs to the west and the hills to the east. Finding your own route is part of the fun.

Across Rough Canyon the four-wheel-drive road continues as an unforgiving, 3-mile climb. This begins the Tabeguache Trail (tab'-a-watch), a multi-use trail system extending Kokopelli's Trail (see Rides 44, 45) over the Uncompahgre Plateau and to Montrose, Colorado. It is the second leg of the Colorado Plateau Mountain-Bike Trail Association (COPMOBA) trail.

Although pedaling into Rough Canyon after a recent rainfall is ill-advised, the sight of glistening sandstone cliffs is a rare delight. Exploring the dry canyon reveals potholes and pour-over cliffs that may hold water several days after a rain. Up the canyon, a narrow side drainage is cool and hosts a surprising display of lush vegetation and even a solitary Douglas fir, an anomaly in this parched region.

RIDE 44 *MARY'S LOOP*

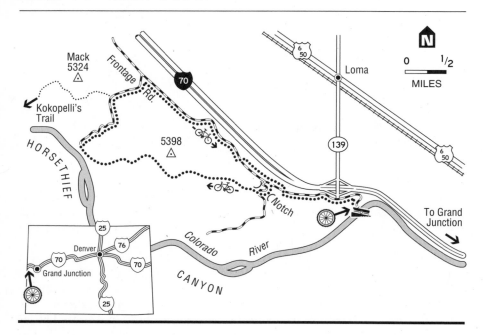

RIDE 44 *MARY'S LOOP*

Mary's Loop is a good 13-mile introduction to Kokopelli's Trail, especially if the logistics of riding that 130-mile, multi-day bike tour seem overwhelming. Approximately 1.5 miles of this route is single-track that makes for exciting riding. The single-track winds along the pink and white sandstone cliffs high above the Colorado River. Exposure to these dramatic fallaways is what makes this route so dynamic.

Mary's Loop was named in honor of Mary Nelson, who passed away during the fall of 1989. Mary was a natural leader, but humble, known and admired by all in the Grand Junction community. Her resume included years of dedication as a social worker and Director of the United Way. An environmentalist, she held great respect for the physical, spiritual, and cultural ingredients that comprise the intermountain West. And, Mary was an avid bicyclist, both on- and off-road. Like many others who envisioned an interstate bike system, she volunteered many hours to the development and construction of Kokopelli's

Trail. An unobtrusive marble plaque, located two miles from the Loma trailhead, memorializes her efforts and contributions.

This high desert area is characterized by pinyon and juniper trees intermixed with cactus, fragrant sage, and tufts of prairie grasses. The desert canyon scenery is most spectacular where the trail traces the edge of the cliffs carved long ago by the Colorado River.

Although only 13 miles in length, Mary's Loop is moderate to difficult. This route combines improved dirt roads, primitive four-wheel-drive roads, and single-track. Riders will encounter rough, loose conditions, and some steep sections may require walking, especially where the trail crosses a boulder-filled talus slope.

[Route information was submitted by Peggy Utesch,* Glenwood Springs, Colorado.—G. B.]

General location: Mary's Loop begins at the Loma Boat Launch, located 15 miles west of Grand Junction.

Elevation change: Elevation change is slight. The Loma Boat Launch, the loop's beginning, lies at 4,460′. The route's high point rises to 5,080′, for an elevation change of only 620′.

Season: Mary's Loop and much of Kokopelli's Trail can be ridden nearly year-round, depending on snowfall. Like Moab, Utah, this region is arid and hot during midsummer, so spring (as early as mid-March) and fall (as late as mid-November) are the most enjoyable seasons to pedal this route.

Services: Full visitor services are available in Grand Junction, located approximately 15 miles east of the trailhead. The smaller towns of Mack and Loma are closer; however, they offer limited services.

Hazards: Much of the trail, including four-wheel-drive roads, is rough and loose, but should not pose a problem for the attentive rider. Riders should plan to carry all of their water. There are several water crossings and springs along the way (many of which are seasonal); however, due to the presence of cattle and the toxic dissolved mineral salts, the water should be purified before drinking. Riders should also carry ample food. And do not forget sunscreen, for this is a high desert area with little shade.

Rescue index: Phones are available in the towns of Mack and Loma, which are

---

*A native of Colorado, Peggy Utesch grew up in the Rockies. Colorado instilled in her a deep love for the outdoors from an early age, while hiking and adventuring in the pristine wilderness around Rabbit Ears Pass near Steamboat Springs. And, when Peggy was not in the mountains, she lived on her bicycle. (Her parents were baffled when she spent $600 on a bike, and that was when Volkswagens were $1995.)

The advent of the mountain bike has allowed Peggy to combine the two activities she loves most, bicycling and enjoying the backcountry; subsequently she has logged hundreds of miles in the mountains and deserts of Colorado and Utah.

Peggy Utesch.

only a few miles from the trailhead. Call services in Grand Junction for medical help. A Port of Entry station is near the trailhead as well. In addition, the return part of the loop parallels Interstate 70.

Land status: This section of trail travels across Bureau of Land Management (BLM) land. Be sure to leave all gates as you found them, for the surrounding land is open range.

Maps: USGS 7.5 minute quadrangle: Mack, Colorado. USGS 1:100,000 metric topographic series: Grand Junction SW/4, Colorado.

(continued from page 223)

Currently living in Glenwood Springs, Colorado, Peggy splits her time between grant-writing for the local mental health center and free-lance writing. Her first book, *The Colorado-Utah Mountain-Biking Trail System, Route 1, Moab to Loma—Kokopelli's Trail,* is published by Canyon Country Publications. (See "Sources of additional information.")

Finding the trail: Mary's Loop (Kokopelli's Trail) begins at the parking lot for the Loma Boat Launch, located 15 miles west of Grand Junction. From I-70 take Exit 15/Loma, cross over the interstate to the south and head east (left, away from the Port of Entry) one-third mile down the gravel road. Park in the area provided for the Loma Boat Launch. The trailhead is marked with a BLM sign designating Kokopelli's Trail. The trail follows a gravel road along the south side of the interstate.

Sources of additional information:

Bureau of Land Management
Grand Junction Resources Area
2815 H Road
Grand Junction, CO 81506
(303) 244-3050

Colorado Plateau Mountain-Bike Trail Association (COPMOBA)
P.O. Box 4602
Grand Junction, CO 81502
(303) 241-9561

The Colorado-Utah Mountain Biking Trail System, Route 1, Moab to Loma—Kokopelli's Trail, by Peggy Utesch. Moab, Utah: Canyon Country Publications, 1990.
This is a detailed guide to the 130-mile mountain bike trail system that stretches across the Colorado Plateau from Moab, Utah, to Grand Junction, Colorado. For ordering information contact Canyon Country Publications, P.O. Box 963, Moab, UT 84532, (801) 259-6700.

Notes on the trail: Begin riding west at the Loma Boat Launch parking lot. Travel back uphill to the I-70 access intersection and pedal west on a dirt road. Turn left at 1.2 miles. (This begins the "loop." Later, you will return on the road forking to the right.) Climb through a notch in the ridge where Horsethief Canyon, as well as some sandstone tower formations, can be seen. Within half a mile turn off to the right on a more primitive track, which is marked with Kokopelli's Trail emblems. This is where the first section of single-track begins. Wind along the tops of 5 canyons and pass through a fence. Continue on more single-track (rated as difficult). At mile 5.1, the single-track ends and joins an off-road vehicle trail. At mile 6.1, what appears to be a cow path turns left just below a stock watering pond.

The "cow" path to the left is the continuation of Kokopelli's Trail to Rabbit Valley. Moab is 100 miles away. But to ride Mary's Loop, stay on the gravel road and climb a steep hill. At the top of the hill, pass through a fence, then ride downhill and turn right on a frontage road parallel to I-70. Ride east over the low, roller-coaster hills back to the trail's beginning.

The entire Kokopelli's Trail is marked with brown, fiberglass posts having directional arrows. Watch for them every mile or so, as well as at intersections. In addition, Mary's Loop has special decals posted in her honor.

This section of Kokopelli's Trail travels, at times, across the purple shale bluffs of the Morrison Formation, high above the Colorado River. The Morrison Formation is a shale and sandstone deposit rich with dinosaur remains. Less than a mile from Kokopelli's Trail, in Rabbit Valley, is one of Colorado's largest dinosaur quarries.

RIDE 45   *KOKOPELLI'S TRAIL*

This epic trail, linking Colorado with Utah, was named after Kokopelli, a mystical being recognized by the Native American groups who inhabited the Colorado Plateau. Kokopelli is the humpbacked flute player associated with the Flute Clan of the Hopi Indians. According to legend, he traveled from village to village with a bag of songs on his back and was able to drive back winter with his flute playing. Usually depicted in petroglyphs with a phallus, Kokopelli is a symbol of fertility whose presence was welcomed in the lives of the agriculturally based Native American nations of this region.

The terrain along this trail encompasses elevations from 4,000′ to 8,000′, including the pinyon-sage zone as well as the ponderosa pine–quaking aspen forests of the La Sal Mountains. Spring is particularly lovely in this area, for a variety of cacti and wildflowers decorate the red soils of the region. An abundance of wildlife is equally varied. The colorful collared lizard can often be seen basking in the sun, as can a variety of other desert creatures. Deer are prevalent as are coyote and (ugh) cattle. Mountain lions are present but rarely seen, except for tracks left in sandy sediments. Because people have lived along the Colorado River for centuries, everything from petrogylphs and arrowheads to homesteads and old grave markers can be found along the route.

Kokopelli's Trail is 130 miles of what is perhaps the most beautiful desert mountain biking that Colorado and Utah have to offer. This magical route links Grand Junction (Colorado's largest western-slope city) with Moab (gateway to southern Utah's canyon country) and may be ridden in either direction. It is a multi-day adventure that combines a variety of riding challenges, from hard-packed dirt roads to rugged four-wheel-drive roads to single-track, all within the natural beauty of the Colorado Plateau. When tackled for several days as a camping trip, the trail is expert-level. With vehicle support, Kokopelli's is still an arduous route but can be enjoyed by a variety of ability levels. There is always the option of exploring shorter segments as single day trips that are as difficult as the rider cares to make them.

RIDE 45 *KOKOPELLI'S TRAIL*

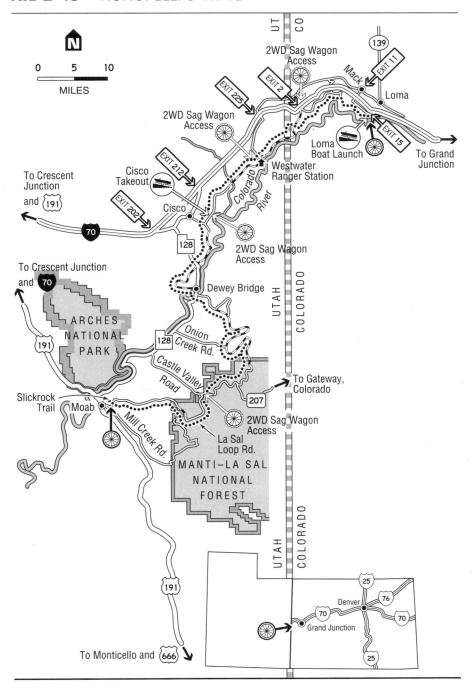

Along Kokopelli's Trail. Photo: Pat Weiler

[Information on Kokopelli's Trail was provided by Peggy Utesch, Glenwood Springs, Colorado.—G. B.]

General location: Kokopelli's Trail begins in Loma, Colorado (about 15 miles west of Grand Junction), and ends in Moab, Utah.

Elevation change: The elevation at the Loma trailhead is 4,460′. The trail's high point is approximately 8,400′, reached between Beaver and Fisher mesas. The elevation of the Slickrock Bike Trail in Moab (route's official western trail-head) is 4,600′. In between, the route gains and loses hundreds of feet in elevation as it climbs through canyons, onto mesas, back into canyons, through the foothills of the La Sal Mountains, and finally down again to the desert floor.

Season: Kokopelli's is best when ridden in spring (before June) or late summer to fall (mid-August to late October). In addition to intense heat, insects can make summer riding unpleasant.

Contacting the BLM in advance of a springtime ride is advised, for heavy snowfall can close parts of the trail and create heavy runoff as it melts.

Services: All services are available in Grand Junction, Colorado, and Moab, Utah. In between, there are no towns or services and all surface waters should be purified. (The trail does go by the small town of Cisco where a telephone might be found, but Cisco offers no other services—not even gasoline or food.) Riders should be prepared for *all* human and bike emergencies.

Camping is available along most of the route, with the exception of the single-track section on the Grand Junction end, which is not accessible by vehicle. Some BLM campsites have been built, but no water taps are available. There are numerous primitive sites along the route as well. Please remember to use "desert ethics" when using primitive sites.

Hazards: Because of the remote nature of this trail, riders are encouraged to be prepared for all human and mechanical emergencies. The most serious hazard is heat exhaustion. Be aware that the combination of warm temperatures, strenuous exercise, and dry climate can have serious consequences. Drink plenty of water (1 gallon a day), carry high-energy foods, and rest often in the shade. Conversely, hypothermia can be a problem, both at high elevations and at night. The possibility of being caught out at night means smart riders carry clothing that would seem unnecessary in daytime desert temperatures. As always, keep an eye on the sky for approaching storms, for flash floods are a possibility in small canyons that cross the trail. Other than some difficult trail sections—rough surfaces, precipitous single-track, and water crossings—cacti, biting insects, "no-see-ums," and cow pies are the worst of the rider's worries.

Contact the BLM for an update on current trail conditions.

Rescue index: Emergency phone calls might be made from Cisco, at the Westwater Range Station (seasonally), and perhaps from a radio phone at an occasional ranch. However, most of Kokopelli's Trail travels through remote deserts where assistance is simply not available. Grand Junction and Moab have medical facilities.

Land status: Bureau of Land Management: Grand Junction Resources Area, Colorado; Grand Resource Area, Utah. Manti–La Sal National Forest: Moab District.

Maps: USGS 7.5 minute quadrangles: Agate, Big Triangle, Bitter Creek, Blue Chief Mesa, Cisco, Dewey, Fisher Valley, Fisher Towers, Moab, and Westwater, Utah; Ruby Canyon and Mack, Colorado. USGS 1:100,000 metric topographic series: Moab, and Westwater, Utah; Grand Junction, Colorado.

Finding the trail: *Eastern trailhead (Loma)*: Travel 15 miles west out of Grand Junction on Interstate 70 and take Exit 15/Loma. At an intersection south of the interstate, turn east (away from the Port of Entry). Travel down a short hill of broken pavement to the Loma Boat Launch. Parking is provided.

Western trailhead (Moab): The official trailhead is the Slickrock Bike Trail. From Moab, travel east on 100 North, turn right on 400 East, then left on Mill Creek Road. At the Y intersection, fork left on Sand Flats Road. Slickrock Bike

Trail is located prior to where Sand Flats Road turns from pavement to improved sand-gravel.

For midroute access points, consult the sources listed below.

Sources of additional information:

> Bureau of Land Management
> Grand Junction Resource Area
> 2815 H Road
> Grand Junction, CO 81506
> (303) 244-3050

> Bureau of Land Management
> Grand Resource Area
> Sand Flats Road
> P.O. Box M
> Moab, UT 84532
> (801) 259-8193

> *The Utah-Colorado Mountain Bike Trail System, Route 1, Moab to Loma—Kokopelli's Trail,* by Peggy Utesch. Moab, Utah: Canyon Country Publications, 1990. Contact Canyon Country Publications, P.O. Box 963, Moab, UT 84532, (801) 259-6700.

> Colorado Plateau Mountain Bike Trail Association (COPMOBA)
> P.O. Box 4602
> Grand Junction, CO 81502
> (303) 241-9561

Notes on the trail: Much of the trail on the Grand Junction end is single-track that clings to the cliffs high above the Colorado River before plummeting into the Salt Creek drainage. (In the past, crossing Salt Creek meant a waist-deep ford, but now the BLM has built a small bridge suitable for vehicles.) Moving across the Colorado border into Utah, the route travels on both improved dirt roads as well as rough, four-wheel-drive roads. It passes beautiful Arrowhead Arch and crosses the Colorado River on the historic Dewey Bridge. The route then lifts riders away from the river, climbing through Lower and Upper Cottonwood canyons into Fisher Valley on a variety of surfaces ranging from easy to difficult.

Climbing continues as the trail reaches North Beaver Mesa and Fisher Mesa at the base of the La Sal Mountains, where ponderosa pines have smoothed the trail with their long needles. Views from the mesas into the Colorado River basin reveal the extraordinary rock formations of the Fisher Towers and Castle Rock Tower. Fisher Mesa is the highest point on Kokopelli's Trail. Heading into Moab, riders will encounter a stretch of pavement on Castleton/Gateway Road before tackling the rough and rutted section of oak brush corridor that leads to the rim of Porcupine Draw and spectacular views into Castle Valley. Finally, the trail joins Sand Flats Road and descends through handsome sandstone formations to the famous Slickrock Bike Trail just above Moab.

Although the trail is punctuated with many difficult and challenging sections that only expert riders will appreciate, most of these demanding portions have alternate routes, making the trail system accessible and enjoyable for most riders. Because of the trail's length, it can be ridden in many different configurations. Day rides are a viable option. Riding several or all sections with the help of a support vehicle is another popular approach, as is signing on for a guided tour. There are several Colorado- and Utah-based guide groups that bike Kokopelli's (usually in 4 to 5 days) skirting some of the most difficult parts. This is a good choice for less experienced riders.

Montrose

RIDE 46   ROUBIDEAU TRAIL

The Roubideau Trail offers an intimate look at western Colorado's Uncompahgre Plateau. Positioned in the region between the biking "hot spots" of the Colorado Rockies and Utah's canyon country, the plateau's diverse environment is characteristic of both. Cool, wet, rolling hills stem eastward from its crest as long, parallel, fingerlike mesas. The uplift's western flank descends abruptly to a maze of ravine-notched mesas and hot, dry lowlands.

"Roubideau" is a misspelled version of Robidoux. Antoine Robidoux was a fur trapper who worked the streams and rivers of western Colorado in the early nineteenth century. The Roubideau Trail is part of an extensive stock driveway system that has been used since the 1880s. Today, the Roubideau is part of the newly created Tabeguache Trail that connects Grand Junction and Montrose, Colorado. This 130-mile trail system is the second leg of the Colorado Plateau Mountain Bike Trail System (the first leg being Kokopelli's Trail, which connects Moab, Utah, with Loma, Colorado).

The Roubideau Trail is a 20-mile point-to-point ride, although a number of loop trips are feasible due to many intersecting side roads. Most of the trail follows four-wheel-drive roads composed of flat stretches mixed with steep grades, moderately technical canyon traverses, plus 15 perennial creek crossings. The trail surface ranges from packed clay and organic soils to rocky, sandy areas. Two and one-half miles of single-track offer a little variety.

[The Roubideau Trail description was submitted by Bill Harris,* Montrose, Colorado.—G. B.]

---

*Bill Harris is a resident of Montrose, Colorado. An avid outdoorsman who enjoys backpacking, fishing, cross-country skiing, and mountain biking, he also pursues interests in photography, archaeology, and the environment.

Bill purchased his first mountain bike in 1985 and became an immediate enthusiast. The following summer, his infatuation with fat-tire cycling spurred him to write *Bicycling the Uncompahgre Plateau* (see "Sources of additional information). He was involved with the creation of the Tabeguache Trail, which connects Kokopelli's Trail (Grand Junction) with the Uncompaghre Plateau (Montrose). He also serves on the board of directors of the Colorado Plateau Mountain-Bike Trail Association (COPMOBA).

RIDE 46   ROUBIDEAU TRAIL

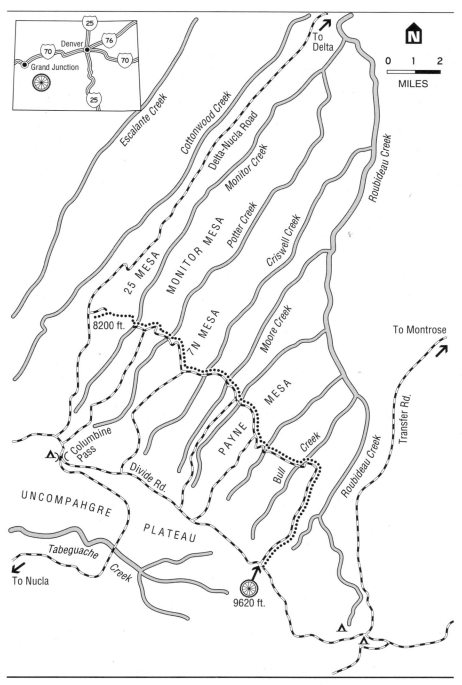

Along the Roubideau Trail. Photo: Bill Harris.

General location: The Roubideau Trail is located 35 miles west of Montrose, on the Uncompahgre Plateau.

Elevation change: The route's eastern trailhead (off the Divide Road) is the highest point, at 9,600′. The portage through Potter Creek near its northwestern end drops to 7,900′. Although the net elevation loss is 1,700′, the regular loss and gain of altitude from crossing the many creeks and divides brings the total elevation gain to over 2,500′.

Season: The trail is accessible from early June to early October. Riding after early October is possible, but hunting season makes backcountry biking risky and a bit unnerving. June and September are the most comfortable months to ride the trail; July and August can be rewarding but also very hot.

Services: Delta and Montrose are the nearest towns offering all visitor services and bike shops, but no services are available along the route or near the trailheads. Antone Spring and Iron Spring campgrounds, located 5 to 6 miles east of the Divide Road trailhead, offer tables, toilets, and drinking water. The Columbine Campground is on the Delta-Nucla road 5 miles south of the western trailhead.

Hazards: Intermittent rocky, steep sections are the most apparent hazards. At least 6 portages are necessary to complete the entire route. Monitor, Potter, and Criswell canyons offer the greatest challenges. Late afternoon thunderstorms are common during July and August. Midsummer days are usually hot, so carry extra water. All stream water should be treated before drinking. Think twice before riding this trail during big-game hunting season, which starts in early October.

Rescue index: Emergency medical facilities are available in Montrose and Delta, 1 hour's drive from either main access point. Due to the remote, rugged nature of the surrounding countryside, rescue operations would be difficult and time-consuming. You may encounter trail users periodically, but don't count on it. Bow hunters are common during late summer and early fall, and are usually cordial. Campers are frequent near the eastern trailhead.

Land status: Uncompahgre National Forest. The short, single-track section near the western trailhead was constructed to circumvent private land.

Maps: USGS 7.5 minute quadrangles: Ute, Antone Springs, Davis Point, and Moore Mesa, Colorado. USGS 1:50,000 scale county series: Montrose County #1, Colorado. *Uncompahgre National Forest Travel Map.* This route is labeled as trails 544, 546, and 547.

Finding the trail: The trail's most used access point is along the Divide Road where it intersects the East Bull Road (eastern access point). The Divide Road can be reached by driving west of Montrose on CO 90. This road turns to gravel and then intersects the Divide Road 23 miles southwest of Montrose. Bear right and follow the Divide Road another 7.5 miles to the access point (5.5 miles past Antone Spring Campground).

The route's western trailhead is along the Delta-Nucla Road (25 Mesa Road), 30 miles south of Delta. Take County Road 348 from Delta until it intersects with the Delta-Nucla Road. Follow this road to the intersection with Cottonwood Road. Take the left fork and continue another 1.25 miles. Look for a brown carsonite marker labeled with a Tabeguache Trail decal just beyond a cattle guard. Park vehicles just north of the cattleguard. The trail begins as a single-track bearing east. (Alternatively, reach the western trailhead by continuing on the Divide Road to Columbine Pass and then to the Columbine Campground. Turn right on the Delta-Nucla Road (25 Mesa Road) and travel about 5 miles to the Cottonwood Road.)

Sources of additional information:

Uncompahgre National Forest
Supervisor's Office
2250 US 50
Delta, CO 81416
(303) 874-7691

Uncompahgre National Forest
Ouray Ranger District
2505 South Townsend
Montrose, CO 81401
(303) 249-3711

Colorado Plateau Mountain-Bike Trail Association (COPMOBA)
P.O. Box 4602
Grand Junction, CO 81502
(303) 241-9561

Bicycling the Uncompahgre Plateau, by Bill Harris. Ouray, Colorado: Wayfinder Press, 1988.
This guidebook details the plateau's physical, environmental, and historical setting, and describes 20 biking trails. Available from Wayfinder Press, P.O. Box 1877, Ouray, CO 81427.

Tabeguache Trail Tips and Loops and Mountain Bike Trails near Montrose, Colorado. Available from Cascade Bicycles, 25 North Cascade Street, Montrose, CO 81401.

Notes on the trail: The most popular trail access point is from the east, where the Divide Road intersects with East Bull Road. From here, the first 4.5 miles descend gradually and then intersect with the Coalbank Trail. The trail makes a sharp left-hand turn and continues west, climbing in and out of 15 drainages before reaching 25 Mesa. On 25 Mesa, just before a gate, turn left onto the 2-mile section of single-track. Follow the trail to the south and west to reach the Delta-Nucla Road. Although the numerous intersecting jeep roads could make navigation a nightmare, the Roubideau Trail is clearly marked with brown carsonite posts labeled with a Tabeguache Trail decal.

Several jeep roads intersect with the Roubideau Trail, creating numerous feasible loops. The Payne Mesa, 7N Mesa, and Long Creek roads are those most often used to link up with the Divide Road to close loops.

In and out of the many drainages along the trail, a rich mosaic of plant life can be found—shaded aspen groves filled with wildflowers, majestic ponderosa pines surrounded by thickets of scrub oak, and lush riparian areas. The trail hovers near the 8,000′ mark. Since the transition between the pine-oak and aspen-fir zones occurs at about this elevation, both plant communities are found in close proximity and accompany you throughout the entire route. An exceptionally scenic time to ride the trail is mid- to late September, when golden hues of aspen appear in grand profusion.

Telluride

RIDE 47 *SNEFFELS RANGE LOOP*

Circling the Sneffels Range unveils the grandeur and glory of the San Juan Mountains. From lofty perches, a chaotic sea of Mount Fuji–type peaks, vertical walls of stone, and deep glacial valleys compose the scene. Within a single day, and often within an hour's time, the route ventures from barren ridgelines beneath deep blue, open skies to the serene confines of dense forests. Trickling creeks that cascade from lingering snow fields thread alpine meadows, then coalesce into roaring streams that rip down gullies before meandering through low, broad valleys.

Not only is this a scenic route, passing through one of Colorado's most pristine and rugged mountain assemblages, it is a historic route that connects the old mining districts of Telluride, Ouray, and Ridgway.

The entire route is a grandiose, 70-mile loop that follows mostly good four-wheel-drive roads. On the north side of the Sneffels Range, the route follows sections of double- and single-track of varying technical difficulty. A few streams must be crossed on this section, but none flow dangerously swift or deep even during high runoff.

The loop can be completed by expert riders in a single day—a very long, tiring day. But, to fully experience the pristine Sneffels Range and San Juan Mountains, make this a multi-day ride with overnight stays in Ouray and Ridgway. Even then, the route is still moderate to difficult. Although overall technical difficulty is low to moderate, good cardiovascular ability and acclimation to high altitude are prerequisites. In a nutshell, if you are novice-level in technical ability you are more likely to find segments of this trail enjoyable than if you are novice-level in cardiovascular terms.

[The Sneffels Range Loop description was submitted by Joe Ryan and Mike Turrin,* Telluride, Colorado.—G. B.]

---

*Joe Ryan and Mike Turrin operate the San Juan Huts System near Telluride, Colorado. To Joe and Mike, smiling faces and thrilling stories from those who have completed a trip are the lasting memories that make a mountain bike–hut journey rewarding. For more information about the San Juan Huts System, see "Sources of additional information."

RIDE 47   *SNEFFELS RANGE LOOP*

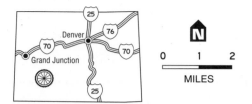

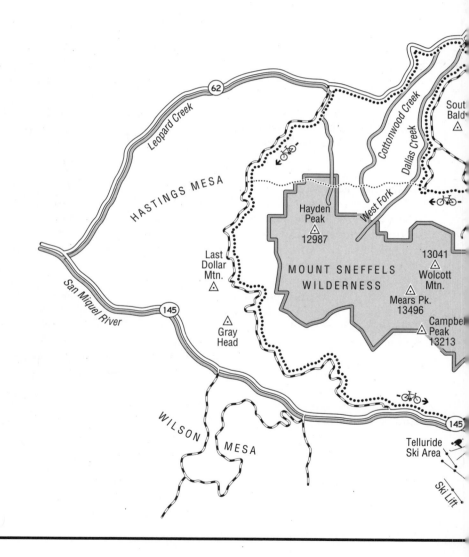

To Montrose ↑

550

62

Ridgway

Beaver Creek

Uncompahgre

Dallas Trail

Corbett Creek

River

Ouray

Mt. Sneffels
14158

Potosi
Mtn.
13786

llas
ak

Sneffels Creek

Sneffels Creek

Camp Bird

uride

United States
Mtn.

Upper Camp
Bird

Imogene
Pass
13114

Telluride
Peak

To Silverton
and Durango ↓

550

Pedaling the Last Dollar Road, backdropped by the Wilson Mountains. Photo: San Juan Huts System.

General location: The Sneffels Range is the unmistakable massif directly north of Telluride. This route circumnavigates the entire range, connecting the towns of Telluride, Ouray, and Ridgway, Colorado.

Elevation change: Telluride sits at a whopping 8,744′, where the air is thin. The ride begins with a leg-burning, lung-searing ascent to Imogene Pass (13,114′), a 4,500-foot climb in less than 8 miles. The big payoff is an unbelievable, 12-mile descent through Camp Bird to Ouray (7,700′). Then it's back up again. A long, steep climb out of the Uncompahgre River Valley rises up to, then traverses through, Blaine Basin, which reaches over 10,800′. The route then connects with the Dallas Divide Trail, which hovers near 9,600′. Descending the West Fork of Dallas Creek, the trail dips below 8,000′ near Ridgway. Still more climbing awaits with a long-winded pull to Last Dollar Divide (10,660′). Finally, a 2,000′ descent returns to Telluride, closing the loop.

Total vertical gain exceeds 11,000′; total elevation change exceeds 22,000′. Whew!

Season: Riding the Sneffels Range Loop is limited by a short cycling season. Winter's snow lingers well into May and June and commences again by mid-October. This leaves 3 months of practical cycling. Remember, you will be topping mountain passes between 10,000′ and 13,000′, so even midsummer afternoon temperatures are relatively cool and very often cold. Dress accordingly.

Services: Telluride, Ouray, and Ridgway offer full visitor services. Water is plentiful along the route in the many alpine streams; however, purifying all surface waters before drinking is strongly recommended since ranching is common here.

Hazards: Perhaps the greatest hazard associated with this ride is lack of preparedness. In this rugged, alpine setting, weather can range from glorious to unforgiving, from gleaming, sunny mornings to afternoon skies choked with hellish thunderclouds. At the ride's highest elevations well above treeline, shelter is minimal to nonexistent. Carry adequate clothing (including raingear), food, and water, plus emergency supplies and a first-aid kit.

Technical difficulty is generally low on dirt roads and moderate along double- and single-track segments (Dallas Divide Trail). Those visiting from lower elevations should allow a few days to acclimate to the oxygen-deficient air prior to embarking.

Although the route is quite evident when following dirt roads, sections of the Dallas Divide Trail are inaccurately marked on maps. Carrying the appropriate topographic maps and possessing the knowledge to interpret them is strongly recommended.

Rescue index: Emergency help is at most 15 miles away, which means several hours by bike. Motor vehicles are common on the dirt roads and emergency vehicles can reach most points along the route, but it may take them time to get there. A number of dirt roads provide access to sections of the Dallas Divide Trail, the most remote portion of the ride. Telluride and Ouray each have medical clinics, but Ridgway does not.

Land status: Uncompahgre National Forest. All roads outside of the national forest boundary are public access.

Maps: USGS 7.5 minute quadrangles: Gray Head, Ironton, Mount Sneffels, Ouray, Sams, and Telluride, Colorado. *Uncompahgre National Forest Travel Map.*

Finding the trail: The Sneffels Range Loop begins in Telluride. Follow Oak Street to Tomboy Road. This is the way to Imogene Pass. The Sneffels Range Loop can be started from Ouray and Ridgway as well.

Sources of additional information:

Uncompahgre National Forest
Ouray Ranger District
2505 South Townsend
Montrose, CO 81401
(303) 249-3711

San Juan Huts System
P.O. Box 1663
Telluride, CO 81435
(303) 728-6935

What was initially a hut-to-hut system developed for backcountry ski touring in the Sneffels Range has been expanded to a 215-mile system of huts and mountain bike trails linking Telluride with Moab, Utah, during the summer. The route offers the incredible diversity of both Telluride's alpine terrain and Moab's slickrock, canyon country. The system allows bikers the luxury of a week-long mountain bike tour with the comfort of huts at night, while traveling with minimal gear during the day.

The hut-to-hut idea has been an established means of exploring the backcountry by ski touring, but an extended route like this one is new and exciting for mountain bikes. The San Juan Hut System attempts to provide simplicity and comfort in the backcountry without diminishing the beauty and uniqueness of open spaces.

Notes on the trail: The route is quite evident, with the appropriate maps. The only portion that is not signed and often inaccurately located on maps is the Dallas Divide Trail, which wraps around the north slope of the Sneffels Range. Heading north out of Ouray on the paved highway, look for a trail breaking through the red cliffs and entering Corbett Creek Canyon. This route will turn north and climb steeply over the mountain's flank, then turn west and pass through Moonshine Park en route to the Dallas Divide Trail.

If you are not inclined to bite off the entire loop, consider 2 single-day variations. *Option One:* To obtain the breathtaking views of the Sneffels Range and the San Juan Mountains without the grueling assault on Imogene Pass, pedal the Last Dollar Road, located northwest of Telluride, to Last Dollar Mountain. The maintained dirt road offers moderate climbs with little technical difficulty and spectacular angles of mountains and valleys. If you car-top your bikes to the pass, then saddle up and coast downhill back to Telluride, you'll get an excellent overview of the region; this alternate route is well-suited for novice cyclists. Or, shuttle a support vehicle to Dallas Divide on CO 62 east of Ridgway for a memorable trip across Hastings Mesa backdropped by the Sneffels Range and the Wilson Mountains.

Option Two: For outstanding mountain biking along jeep roads, double-track, and single-track that weave through mixed aspen and pine forests and lush meadows, head for the Dallas Divide Trail on the north side of the Range. Several dirt roads lead south and up to the trail from CO 62. Consider a long loop incorporating the West Fork of Dallas Creek and Miller Mesa Road with the option of bailing out down the East Fork of Dallas Creek midway along the trail.

A *final note:* If your legs quiver and head throbs just at the thought of tackling Imogene Pass, here is a bit of motivation—a carrot in front of the horse, if you will. What goes up must come down. And when you descend into Ouray, you will find numerous private, natural hot springs in which to soak your weary muscles and revitalize your soul.

RIDE 48 *ILLIUM VALLEY AND THE LOCAL'S LOOP*

Experienced single-track riders with a short amount of time on their hands will enjoy this 6.5-mile total out-and-back route starting near the town of Telluride. Depending on your skill level, it can be ridden within 45 minutes or 2 hours. The mostly level, narrow trail weaves through boulders and lush, densely forested areas and offers splendid views of Mount Wilson toward the south. If you have more time, this lively ride can be extended to include "The Local's Loop," a 19-mile route that requires moderate stamina and basic technical skills. It's briefly described as an option at the end of this chapter.

Joëlle and I found this short ride to be truly exhilarating. Traversing a mountainside on a narrow path, skirting extremely steep and rocky drop-offs for 50 yards or so was thrilling and demanded our complete attention. Several spots were downright scary, so I dismounted and carried my bike for a few yards. Cyclists who are not yet comfortable on single-track trails should build up their confidence on easier narrow trails before trying this one. Still, a novice biker with the right attitude can develop better bike handling skills and feel a sense of accomplishment after this ride.

General location: This route is basically 3 miles west of Telluride, which is 327 miles southwest of Denver.
Elevation change: This route starts in Telluride at approximately 8,744′, the highest point of the ride. It then descends to the lowest elevation, 8,138′, at the turnaround point. Total elevation loss is about 600′.
Season: Enjoy this ride between May and October, depending on the last and first snowfall, respectively. The period from mid- to late September offers a dazzling display of golden aspens shimmering in the late afternoon autumn light.
Services: Telluride is a popular, well-known community that's trying to decide how popular and well known it wants to be. Though it's not glitzy and star-

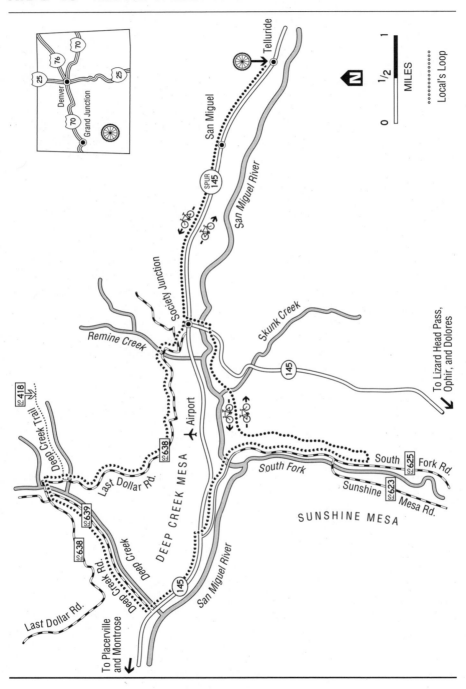

Check out this single-track and you'll be smiling too.

studded like Aspen, its annual international film festival is said to be on par with the Cannes Festival in southern France. Recent years have seen practically unbridled residental and commerical developments, to the point that locals who have enjoyed the small, quiet, mountain town lifestyle are clamoring to put the brakes on growth. In any case, all services can be found in Telluride. You'll find food stores and restaurants, bike stores, quaint little shops, and lodging ranging from modest to extravagant. In fact, accommodations can be arranged by contacting the Telluride Central Reservations at (800) 525-3455 (outside of Colorado) or (303) 728-4431 (in state). At the eastern edge of town, Telluride offers Town Park Campground, complete with drinking water, shower, and toilet facilities—all for a small fee. During the summer months, all the sites are usually taken early on a first-come, first-served basis. Outside of town, Uncompahgre National Forest offers several managed campgrounds, including Sunshine Campground with its splendid view of Mount Wilson. A fee is charged and water is available. Primitive campsites—that is, without water— are nearby and do not require a fee.

Hazards: Though most experienced riders wouldn't consider this trail hazardous, be forewarned that portions of it are simultaneously narrow, severely steep and sloping, and bordering deep drop-offs. Boulders and rocks along the trail are so plentiful and closely positioned that catching a pedal and subsequently being thrown off balance is a frequent possibility.

Another hazard worth mentioning, regardless of skill level, is sudden encounters with other trail users. This trail is often extremely narrow and, in some stretches, the plant cover is dense. This makes for limited visibility, particularly where the trail curves. Because this is a popular trail with bikers and hikers, you'll need to control your speed well enough to avoid collisions. Though it may be effective to scream out a blood-curdling warning such as "Bikers on the trail!", this is not the preferred warning method for safety. This sort of action disrupts the enjoyment of other trail users, particularly hikers. Hikers have right of way.

Rescue index: Emergency evacuation along the single-track portion of this route must be on foot. Fortunately, none of the single-track trail is more than several miles from a vehicle access point. So, the injured rider who can still pedal or walk can speed emergency help by getting to one of several dirt roads along the route and waiting there for medical assistance to arrive. The nearest phone is generally back in Telluride, although several homes and businesses along CO 145 may offer use of a phone or assistance.

Land status: Uncompahgre National Forest.

Maps: Trails Illustrated® map: #141, Silverton, Ouray, Telluride, Lake City. USGS 7.5 minute quads: Telluride and Gray Head, Colorado. Olympic Sports Trail Map: *Hiking Trails, Mountain Biking, Jeep Trails*. To order, write to Telluride Sports, Box 1140, Telluride, CO 81435, or call (800) 828-7547 (in Telluride, call 728-4477).

Finding the trail: This ride starts on Colorado Avenue, the main street in the town of Telluride. Note, some folks and maps refer to this avenue as CO 145, and it is in fact, a spur of CO 145. So when you get 3 miles into this ride, reaching a 3-way intersection on the western side of Telluride near Society Junction, don't be confused that all roads are labeled CO 145.

Sources of additional information:

Uncompahgre National Forest
Norwood Ranger District
1760 East Grand Avenue
P.O. Box 388
Norwood, CO 81423
(303) 327-4261

Telluride Mountain Biking and Hiking Trail Map
Telluride Visitor's Center and Chamber Resort Association
666 West Colorado Avenue
Box 653
Telluride, CO 81435
(303) 728-3041

Telluride Sports
150 West Colorado Avenue
Box 1140
Telluride, CO 81435
(303) 728-4477

Notes on the trail: Pedal west out of town on Colorado Avenue for 3 miles to the junction of CO 145. At this point, also known as Society Junction, CO 145 runs in 2 directions: south towards Ophir, Cortez, and Durango, and west towards the airport and Placerville. Turn left onto southbound CO 145 and immediately look for the unmarked trailhead in a dirt clearing on your right (west).

Follow the single-track trail as it leads west and downhill, through mounds of gravel. After a short distance, the trail begins taking you on a roller-coaster ride alongside the rushing sound of the San Miguel River, through dense undergrowth and groves of pine and aspen. The trail becomes narrow and soon leads you across a stream, which, depending on your skill level, may require you to dismount.

Eventually, the trail levels out and weaves itself through boulders and stands of aspen and pine trees. As you look southward, the peak straight ahead is Mount Wilson, sitting at 14,246'. On your right (west) is Sunshine Mesa. Eyes back on the trail, you soon traverse a mountainside accented with extremely steep and deep drop-offs.

After nearly 3.5 miles, the single-track trail ends at South Fork Road (Forest Service Road 625), a two-wheel-drive, wide dirt road. At this point, you can either reverse your direction and return to town for a total mileage of 6.5 miles, or continue onto the Local's Loop, as described below.

Local's Loop option: Instead of turning around, continue right onto the dirt road. Follow it towards CO 145 and the San Miguel River, passing the Church Camp and a gravel company on the way. By now, the road has become pavement. After almost 2 miles, turn right onto a dirt road, located immediately before a highway department maintenance building, and pedal a short distance to CO 145. Turn left onto the paved CO 145, being careful as you cross the highway, heading west. Pedal for 2 miles to the junction of Deep Creek Road, FS 639, a four-wheel-drive dirt road. Turn right onto Deep Creek Road. Follow it and the creek as it climbs for about 2 miles to a bridge crossing on your right. Go right, taking the bridge across the creek and onto Last Dollar Road (FS 638), another dirt jeep road that leads basically south. Stay on this road as it traverses Deep Creek Mesa for almost 2.5 miles, passing the airport sitting far below the jeep road. The views of Mount Whipple (11,922'), Wilson Mesa, and Telluride in the valley below are stunning. Eventually, Last Dollar Road ends at the airport road, at which point you turn left and pedal it for 2 miles to CO 145, terminating near Society Turn. Go left (east) onto CO 145 and ride the shoulder of the pavement for 3 miles back into Telluride. Total mileage of the Local's Loop, including the Illium Valley Trail, is approximately 19 miles. For a slightly easier loop, consider reversing the direction of this loop—that is, pedal it counterclockwise.

RIDE 49 *BEAR CREEK*

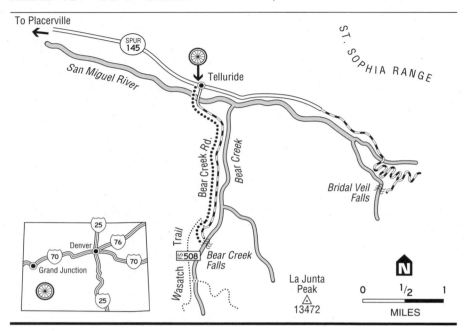

RIDE 49 *BEAR CREEK*

Looking for a quick ride that you can pick up right from town? Here's a lovely, short, 4.5-mile out-and-back route that virtually anyone with strong stamina and mastery of basic technical skills can enjoy. There is nothing really technical about this ride, except that because this route is one of the busiest, if not *the* busiest, trail in Telluride, you need to have complete speed control on the downhill run. Fortunately, the trail is wide, and hikers, runners, and bikers share the road comfortably.

The popularity of Bear Creek Trail is due to its soothingly scenic views and accessibility from town. Accompanied by rushing Bear Creek, the road climbs gradually for almost 2.5 miles through lush, dense forests of aspen and fir to the bottom of a magnificent waterfall. It's a marvelous picnic spot, and the views of the Saint Sophia Range towards the north are quietly inspiring and representative of the splendid surroundings of Telluride's own backyard. Speedsters with topnotch bike control will love this added perk: it's all downhill back into town.

Joëlle is propelled uphill by the idea of flying downhill non-stop on the return.

General location: The route is on the south edge of Telluride. The starting point of the ride itself is in town. Telluride is approximtely 327 miles southwest of Denver.

Elevation change: The ride begins at 8,744′ and climbs to the highest point at 9,780′. Total elevation gain is 1,035′ in 2.3 miles.

Season: The route can be ridden between midspring and midfall, depending on snow conditions. When Joëlle, my biking pal, and I rode in late June, we encountered lots of snow runoff on the trail. In fact, when we reached the waterfalls, there were massive patches of snow left by an intense and enduring winter. Mid- to late September offers breathtaking views of the landscape painted with groves of gold and green vegetation, especially brilliant in the late afternoon.

Services: All services are available in Telluride.

Hazards: As mentioned earlier, Bear Creek Trail is one of the busiest routes in

Telluride. And since the ride back into town is all downhill, bikers need to be in total control of their speed to avoid collisions with other trail users. Heaviest use is in the summer.

Rescue index: For extreme emergency situations, rest assured that this route is four-wheel-drive accessible. Otherwise, medical assistance can be found in Telluride. You are likely to find other trail users who may be of help.

Land status: Uncompahgre National Forest.

Maps: Trails Illustrated® map: #141, Silverton, Ouray, Telluride, Lake City. USGS 7.5 minute quad: Telluride, Colorado. Olympic Sports Trail Map: *Hiking Trails, Mountain Biking, Jeep Trails.* To order, write to Telluride Sports, Box 1140, Telluride, CO 81435, or call (800) 828-7547 (in Telluride, call 728-4477).

Finding the trail: The trail begins at the south end of Pine Street in Telluride. Generally, most riders bike from wherever they're lodging in town. Otherwise, street parking is available on Pine Street and neighboring streets.

Sources of additional information:

Uncompahgre National Forest
Norwood Ranger District
1760 East Grand Avenue
P.O. Box 388
Norwood, CO 81423
(303) 327-4261

Telluride Mountain Biking and Hiking Trail Map
Telluride Visitor's Center and Chamber Resort Association
666 West Colorado Avenue
Box 653
Telluride, CO 81435
(303) 728-3041

Telluride Sports
150 West Colorado Avenue
Box 1140
Telluride, CO 81435
(303) 728-4477

Notes on the trail: Once you've come to the south end of Pine Street, continue pedaling over the bridge and onto Bear Creek Road, a wide jeep road. Begin to climb—persevere! This initial half mile is the steepest segment of this route. Follow the road due east, as it rises above town. The road soon curves south, away from Telluride, and continues to climb alongside Bear Creek. After approximately 2 miles of climbing, you come to the junction of Wasatch Trail (FS 508), a single-track trail. Technically accomplished riders can tackle this trail to the top of the waterfall. A few yards farther, the Bear Creek Road ends near a huge, single boulder that may be swarming with rock climbers practicing their skill. Dismount here and hike the remaining short distance to the falls.

As you hike into the lush foliage, be prepared for a shower, as the mist from the falls is heavy. La Junta Peak (13,472′) sits in the southeast and the Saint Sophia Range majestically lines the northern horizon. The return is a fast and slightly technical downhill run all the way into town. Depending on the prevailing weather, consider putting on a jacket. Just remember to watch out for other trail users and, perhaps, fallen logs on the road. Total mileage is about 4.5 miles from the south end of Pine Street.

RIDE 50 *MILL CREEK TO JUD WIEBE LOOP*

For a fun little loop that can be ridden in under two hours, consider this 6.5-mile route. It starts and ends in Telluride and includes 1.5 miles on paved road, about 1.5 miles on jeep road, and almost 4 miles on richly wooded, rolling single-track trails. Joëlle, my biking buddy, and I enjoyed this moderately challenging loop in mid-June, late in the afternoon, when the golden sunlight delicately illuminated portions of lush green Mill Creek Canyon. Several segments of the loop skirted the northern edge of the Telluride valley, giving us a splendid overall view of the town's magnificent mountain surroundings. If you enjoy riding through densely forested canyons of aspen and fir, accompanied by the sound of a rushing creek and combined with some technical and stamina challenges, then you'll be pleased with this loop.

General location: This loop starts in Telluride and traverses the northwest side of the valley. Telluride is approximately 327 miles southwest of Denver.
Elevation change: The ride begins at 8,744′ and climbs to the highest point at 9,740′. Total elevation gain is 995′.
Season: The route can be ridden between midspring and midfall, depending on snow conditions. Midspring offers views of snow-capped Mount Wilson and surrounding ranges. Aspen groves are brilliantly golden and spectacular in the fall, especially in the late afternoon sun.
Services: All services are available in Telluride.
Hazards: Like any other mountain biking trail, one biker's hazard is another's thrill. This route encompasses a steep uphill on a two-wheel-drive road, narrow, roller-coaster single-tracks that weave through boulders and dense forests, and several water crossings. The more experienced you are, the more you'll enjoy these sorts of features.

There are, however, 2 hazards that bear mention here. First, visibility in some spots is limited on the single-track as it threads through the dense forest.

RIDE 50 *MILL CREEK TO JUD WIEBE LOOP*

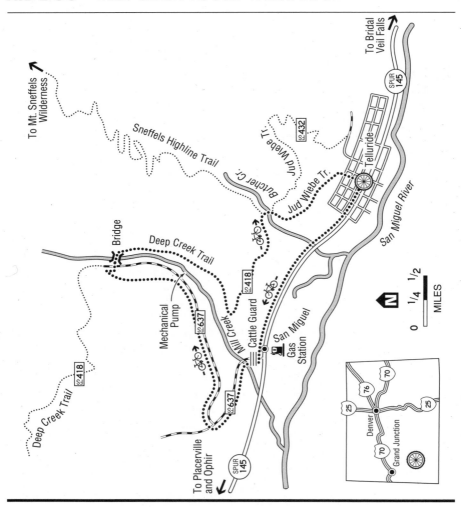

Complete alertness is required to avoid collisions. Secondly, the Jud Wiebe Trail portion of the loop, which drops back into Telluride, is an extremely steep, single-track trail, punctuated with water bars, hairpin turns, and loose dirt and gravel. What makes this section so treacherous is that it is a popular hiking trail and so, while you're maneuvering through the obstacles, controlling your speed and maintaining traction as you brake are critical. You really need fairly accomplished technical skill here.

Rescue index: The bulk of this loop is on single-track, so medical assistance or

Pedaling through a rich concert of quaking aspens.

evacuation is likely to be on foot and thus require some time. Chances are good that you'll meet other trail users who may be of help. A phone can be found at the gas station on CO 145 near the beginning of the loop's dirt road or in Telluride. Medical assistance can be found in town.

Land status: Uncompahgre National Forest.

Maps: Trails Illustrated® map: #141, Silverton, Ouray, Telluride, Lake City. USGS 7.5 minute quad: Telluride, Colorado. Olympic Sports Trail Map: *Hiking Trails, Mountain Biking, Jeep Trails.* To order, write to Telluride Sports, Box 1140, Telluride, CO 81435, or call (800) 828-7547 (in Telluride, call 728-4477).

Finding the trail: Begin the ride in Telluride by pedaling west on Colorado Avenue towards the gas station at San Miguel.

Sources of additional information:

Uncompahgre National Forest
Norwood Ranger District
1760 East Grand Avenue
P.O. Box 388
Norwood, CO 81423
(303) 327-4261

Telluride Mountain Biking and Hiking Trail Map
Telluride Visitor's Center and Chamber Resort Association
666 West Colorado Avenue
Box 653
Telluride, CO 81435
(303) 728-3041

Telluride Sports
150 West Colorado Avenue
Box 1140
Telluride, CO 81435
(303) 728-4477

Notes on the trail: Begin the loop by pedaling west out of Telluride on Colorado Avenue, the paved spur of CO 145. Look for a gas station on your left, on the south side of the CO 145 spur, about 1.5 miles from town. Just beyond it, on your right (north side of the road), look for a dirt road with a cattle guard across it. Here is your turnoff onto Forest Service Road 637.

Go right (north) through the cattle guard, and follow the road uphill as it switches back to the east. Stay right on the jeep road at any junction you meet. As you continue climbing, your view toward the south becomes more spectacular, with Telluride lying far below in the valley and Mount Wilson's peak looming at 14,017´. Less than a mile from the cattle guard, the jeep road levels out as it continues to traverse the mountainside above Telluride.

After a few yards, the road curves up a densely forested canyon, obscuring all views of the town. As you pedal up this canyon with Mill Creek roaring on your right, look for a single-track trail on your left, marked by a green road sign for Deep Creek Trail across from some sort of mechanical water pump unit in the creek. Take this gorgeous little single-track as it climbs and weaves through a lovely grove of aspen for almost a half mile. At that point, you reach the junction of the Deep Creek and Mill Creek trails. Bear right, staying on Mill Creek Trail. (The Deep Creek Trail to the left offers another loop possibility that involves several miles of extremely technical terrain. If you're looking for a real challenge, ask any local rider or the bike folks at Olympic Sports in Telluride to tell you about it.) Several yards after the Deep Creek junction, continue following the single-track across a well-made wooden bridge over Mill Creek.

After the bridge, the direction of the trail is basically back down the canyon with Mill Creek on your right. It's peaceful here, and if you're riding in the late afternoon as we were, you'll see lovely rays of sunlight shimmering in and out of the tree leaves. In about a tenth of a mile, the single-track trail leads you over another creek, only this time you must dismount and carry your bike over a primitive bridge made of fallen logs.

Pick up the single-track trail again on the other side of the creek and enjoy a gentle roller coaster of hills for the next 2 miles. Soon, you'll be rewarded with glimpses of Wilson Peak and Sunshine Mountain. This portion of the trail requires quick manuevering around tree stumps and boulders. Stay alert for other bikers coming towards you, as the trail is quite narrow and visibility is limited. Eventually, you emerge from the densely forested canyon and begin traversing a mountainside above Telluride.

Two miles from the creek crossing that required the dismount, you reach the junction of the Sneffels Highline Trail. (This trail leads to a Wilderness Area where bikes are not allowed.) Bear right to a marked intersection indicating direction to 3 trails: Jud Wiebe, Deep Creek, and Sneffels Highline. Turn right through a switchback, following the direction to the Jud Wiebe Trail. After several yards, cross Butcher Creek and reach the actual intersection of the Jud Wiebe Trail. Turn right onto it and follow it down through steep hairpin turns, over water bars, and on loose, powdery dirt and gravel. Be alert for other trail users as this is a popular path. After cruising downhill for less than a mile, the trail ends at the north end of Aspen Street. Total loop mileage, from Colorado Avenue in the middle of Telluride to Aspen Street, is approximately 6.5 miles.

Silverton

RIDE 51 *ALPINE LOOP*

Can you imagine yourself zooming down an unrelenting, 16-mile stretch of jeep road with some of the country's most spectacular and majestic scenery as your backdrop? This is only one of the many payoffs to this grueling, 50-mile loop that includes cycling over Cinnamon Pass (12,620′) and Engineer Pass (12,800′) with the highest point of the route sitting at 13,040′. The lowest point is Lake City, resting at 8,672′, making a total elevation gain of 4,368′. As part of The National Scenic Byway System—a program that highlights the country's most scenic *paved* roads—the Bureau of Land Management (BLM) successfully urged the inclusion of backcountry dirt and gravel jeep roads *(unpaved)* and thereby established the Back Country Byway Program. The Alpine Loop was one of the BLM's first Back Country Byways to be recognized.

For mountain bikers, incredible stamina and enough endurance for the long haul, especially in the higher elevations, is required on this loop. Other than a short, extremely loose, rocky section near Engineer Pass, the route is easy in terms of technical skills needed. The entire loop is composed of wide, easy jeep roads. Although it's not recommended, daring motorists in two-wheel-drive passenger vehicles have driven up to the passes successfully. If you're a serious, hard-core cyclist, you could do this loop in one day, probably within 8 to 12 hours.

On the other hand, why deny yourself the opportunity of truly enjoying this bountiful region? It has plenty to offer. Consider riding this loop with an overnight stay in Lake City, either with your own camping gear or in any of the town's lodging establishments. Lake City thrives on the summer tourist season so you can count on decent restaurants and, occasionally, local entertainment in the evening. Or how about breaking up the loop's 50 miles with several camping nights so that, by day, you and your bike can explore other trails. Enjoy fishing? Many creeks and lakes are stocked with all kinds of trout. Maybe you're a mining history buff? If you are, this area was once loaded with deposits of gold, silver, copper, lead, and zinc, and attracted mining operations that produced over millions of dollars' worth of minerals in the the late 1800s. Remnants of old mines are scattered throughout this region. Though access inside the mines and adjacent structures is prohibited, there is still much to see and explore around the outside of these buildings.

RIDE 51   *ALPINE LOOP*

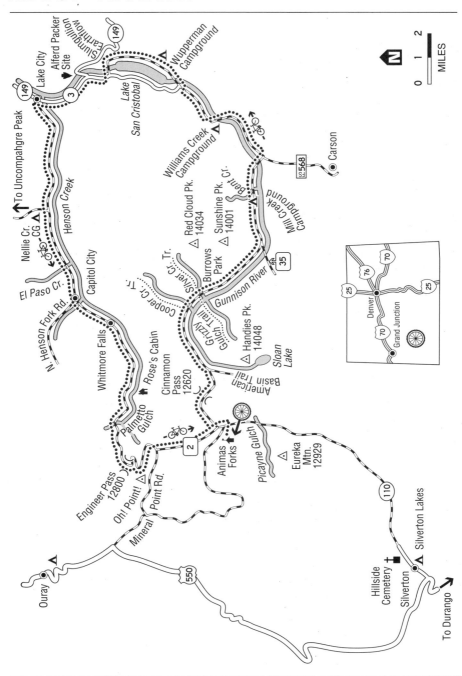

No matter how cold and windy it was atop Cinnamon Pass, Linda and Joëlle were just happy to be there. From the Pass, it was literally all downhill for the next 16 miles into Lake City.

My riding companion, Joëlle, and I rode this loop as a two-day trip in late June. We started at Animas Fork, reached via Silverton. After loading camp gear onto our bikes, we hit the road in a counterclockwise direction, preferring to tackle Cinnamon Pass within our first 2.5 miles. Massive, deep fields of snow covered the Pass. Road crews typically clear the road up to and over the Pass by early June. With weighted bicycles and steep terrain, we finally reached Cinnamon Pass after walking and pushing our bikes in several spots. Bundled in our cold-weather clothing, we sat at the top, soaking in the expansive views of snow-covered mountains, with several peaks over 14,000´, and quickly forgetting about our torturous climb just moments before. We were just happy to be there, quietly marveling at Mother Nature's artistry and our good fortune to be able to enjoy it. The sky was brilliantly blue and its puffy wisps of clouds seemed so low that we could almost reach up and touch them as they floated by. We climbed back on our bikes and began flying downhill almost 16 miles to Lake City, where we spent the night. Though the thrill of speed was addicting, we couldn't help interrupting our descent to check out the scenery, as we moved from snowfield to alpine and subalpine flora regions, to below treeline and finally through a sheer rock canyon carved open by the Gunnison River. No wonder *Outside* magazine listed this route as one of the ten best rides in the United States.

The following day, after a hearty breakfast in town, we completed the loop back to our car by riding 18 miles up to Engineer Pass and then a half mile farther to the highest point beyond. Though the landscape throughout this stretch was just as spectacular as the first half of the loop, those were the longest 18 miles we've ever ridden. The climbing, though gentle, was constant, and the level spots never seemed frequent or long enough for our lungs or legs. Having our bikes weighted with camping gear only added to our workout, as did an uninvited mild headwind, which accompanied us throughout most of this uphill section. Still, after some walking, and fueled by much determination, we finally reached the top of Engineer Pass after almost five hours in the saddle. We had reached the high point of our journey—or so we thought. Our hearts sank when we realized that our road continued uphill, traversing around the west side of Engineer Mountain. Fortunately, the unexpected climb was short— three-quarters of a mile. It hardly registered on our topo maps. We finally reached the highest point of the loop and I found myself fantasizing about never-ending bowls of chips and salsa at Romeros, a Mexican restaurant in Silverton. Maybe my dream was due to thin air, or exhaustion, or the anticipation of meeting our goal—who cares? All I know is that we deserved it. From that point on, it was a gradual cruise down into the valley to where our car was parked. We did it!

General location: The loop itself is over 300 miles southwest of Denver in the San Juan Mountain range. You can get to the route from several towns: Silverton, Ouray, and Lake City. For our torturous challenge, Joëlle and I began the ride at the Silverton access point, which is approximately 11 miles northeast of town.

Elevation change: We begin this ride at the Animas Fork access point, which sits at 11,200′. Cinnamon Pass rises above timberline at 12,620′ and Engineer Pass is higher still at 12,800′. The loop's lowest point is in Lake City, at 8,672′, while the highest point sits at 13,040′, just west of Engineer Pass. Whichever direction—clockwise or counterclockwise—or access point—Silverton, Lake City, or Ouray—you take, total elevation change is 4,368′.

Season: The usual season is between June and October, when the roads are open, depending on snow conditions from the preceding winter. Call the local BLM office at (303) 247-4082 to check road conditions as heavy snows or late winters may make the passes inaccessible. When Joëlle and I tackled this loop in late June, we found muddy spots on the road as well as massive fields of snow at both passes. Road crews had cut through snow drifts to keep the road passable. Some sections of the cuts were well over 10′ deep! Wildflowers typically reach their peak of dazzling color, from mid-July through early August, while autumn colors paint the landscape for miles in mid-September.

Services: Though water is plentiful throughout the ride, it must be treated before drinking. Giardia is present in the water, as is contamination from old mining operations. I highly recommend carrying some sort of water purification system since you need to consume lots of water on a ride of this length and altitude. It's a pain to carry cumbersome quarts of water on as strenuous a ride as this. My compact backpacker water-pump system answered the need for lightweight, reliable purification. Immediately drinkable water is available only at designated campgrounds and in Lake City. Those campgrounds are Mill Creek, Williams Creek, and Wupperman, all of which are on the southern half of the loop. There are no immediately drinkable water sources on the northern half of the loop.

Pit toilets are inconspicuously located close to the route and are marked throughout the Alpine Loop.

Of the 3 nearby towns, only Lake City is right on the loop. Silverton and Ouray are 11 and 8 miles, respectively, off the Alpine Loop, down in the valley. Though limited, all services are available in each town, including lodging, restaurants, food stores, gas, phones, and private campgrounds with showers. Ouray and Lake City both have bike shops, too. Consider rewarding yourself with a long soak in any of Ouray's hot springs pools after your journey. If you're uncomfortable with leaving your bike unlocked outside on the street while you check out a shop or restaurant, consider bringing a lock with you.

Camping in undeveloped areas, whether adjacent to the road or farther in, is permitted on public land throughout the loop, except where posted. The 10-mile stretch between Lake City and Capitol City, on the north side of the loop, is closed to camping except at Nellie Creek meadow. This closure helps prevent contamination of Lake City's municipal water supply. The developed public campgrounds of Mill Creek, Williams Creek, and Wupperman require a small fee. Private campgrounds can be found in Silverton, Ouray, and Lake City. Silverton Lakes Campground in Silverton, a privately owned and operated site on the eastern edge of town, is clean, comfortable, and convenient, and can be contacted at (303) 387-5721. Joëlle and I camped there and found hot showers, a public phone, and a convenient food and sundry store, as well as friendly owners.

For more information regarding lodging and other available services, contact the chambers of commerce of the various towns, as well as local tourist offices. Addresses are listed below.

Hazards: The Alpine Loop is extremely popular with jeep tourists, so be forewarned that you'll be eating dust and exhaust occasionally, especially on the uphill climb. Fortunately, most drivers are courteous and cautious, especially when it comes to passing bikers. In fact, drivers almost always slow down enough to shout out encouraging remarks and marvel at your courage and fitness. Admittedly, Joëlle and I wanted to deck a couple of sedentary tourists who took delight in snickering at us, "It's an awfully tough, long ways up, girls. Sure you wanna be doing this?" Talk about incentive! The downhill run is fast and exhilarating, and the temptation is great to "push the envelope," so to speak. Just expect oncoming traffic when you round a curve.

Since this route has you spending a lot of time over 10,000′, you should always be prepared for inclement weather by wearing proper clothing, which you can peel off and stash in a pannier. The passes are likely to be cold and windy, and snow showers are not unusual, even in the middle of July. More frequent, though, are thunder and lightning storms, typically in mid-summer, and these are extremely dangerous in the higher, expansively exposed elevations. Trust me, you don't want to be above 10,500′ when the light show starts. There is not much shelter to be found at these naked elevations.

Rescue index: Should you need emergency attention that you or your companions cannot supply on the road, medical services are available in Ouray, Silverton, and Lake City. If anyone is unable to pedal and needs immediate attention, most motorists can probably help by offering a lift back into town. There are no public phones available throughout the Alpine Loop, although private residents close to Lake City may be helpful. Otherwise plan to descend to Ouray, Silverton, or Lake City, whichever is closest, and call or find medical help.

Land status: Bureau of Land Management.

This route is designated as one of BLM's Back Country Byways, part of the National Scenic Byway System. Gunnison National Forest.

Maps: Trails Illustrated® map: #141, Silverton, Ouray, Telluride, Lake City. USGS 7.5 minute quads: Ouray, Wetterhorn Peak, Uncompahgre Peak, Lake City, Ironton, Handies Peak, Redcloud Peak, Lake San Cristobal, Silverton, Howardsville, and Snowden Peak, Colorado.

Finding the trail: *From Silverton:* Follow CO 110 due east, through town and past the Hillside Cemetery. This paved road soon becomes Forest Service Road 586, a two-wheel-drive dirt road. As it begins to climb due northeast, you begin to see signs directing you to the ghost town of Animas Fork as well as the Alpine Loop National Back Country Byway, which is identified by a blue columbine logo. The drive up this road, from Silverton to Animas Fork, is approximately 12 miles. Park off the road, on any barren, previously used spot you can find near Animas Fork. Begin pedaling up the jeep road for almost a mile, at which point you will come to a sign designating Cinnamon Pass to the right and Engineer Pass to the left. This is it: you are on the Alpine Loop, and here is where you decide which way to ride the loop, clockwise or counterclockwise.

From Lake City: Park your car in town and find the loop road from the south end of town. If you've elected to ride the loop in a counterclockwise direction, look for a green sign that directs you to Engineer Pass, due west. This road is part of the loop and starts off as pavement; it soon becomes a smooth, wide, two-wheel-drive dirt road with Henson Creek on the south side. If you chose to ride in a clockwise direction, then pedal south on CO 149 to CO 3, toward Lake San Cristobal.

From Ouray: Drive south on US 550 for just over 3 miles. Watch for Mineral Point Road, a jeep road leading off on your left (the east side of US 550) marked by an Alpine Loop Back Country Byway sign with a blue columbine logo. Follow it for about 7 miles, due northeast, and you eventually connect to the Alpine Loop. There are pit toilets near the junction with the Alpine Loop. Park off the road, on any barren, previously used spot that you can find. Pedal up the jeep road and after a short distance you reach the Alpine Loop, at which point you can elect to ride it clockwise toward Engineer Pass or counterclockwise toward Cinnamon Pass.

Sources of additional information:

Gunnison National Forest and Bureau of Land Management
Gunnison Resource Area
216 North Colorado
Gunnison, CO 81230
(303) 641-0471

Bureau of Land Management
San Juan Resource Area
701 Camino del Rio, Room 203
Durango, CO 81301
(303) 247-4082
In addition to your request for specific information, be sure to ask for the general though excellent and very useful publication, *The Alpine Explorer: Recreation Guide to the Alpine Triangle*, published and distributed by the Bureau of Land Management (BLM), a division of the U.S. Department of the Interior, with the help of the Southwest Natural and Cultural Heritage Association and the Western Colorado Interpretive Association. Also ask about another BLM publication, *BLM Colorado Mountain Biking Adventures*. A fee is charged for both materials.

Uncompahgre National Forest
2505 South Townsend
Montrose, CO 81401
(303) 249-3711

San Juan National Forest
701 Camino del Rio
Durango, CO 81301
(303) 247-4874
Ask about the pamphlet, *Bicycle Routes on Public Lands of Southwest Colorado*, second edition. A fee is charged for this publication.

Ouray Chamber of Commerce and Visitor's Center
P.O. Box 145
Ouray, CO 81427
(303) 325-4746
You can find this office in the north end of town, by the pool.

Lake City Chamber of Commerce and Visitor's Center
P.O. Box 430
Lake City, CO 81235
(800) 569-1874 or (303) 944-2527
You can find this office in the center of town on Silver Street.

Silverton Chamber of Commerce and Visitor's Center
P.O. Box 565
Silverton, CO 81433
(800) 752-4494 or (303) 387-5654
You can find this office on the south end of Greene Street at the Y intersection.

The Colorado Guide, by Bruce Caughey and Dean Winstanley. Golden, Colorado: Fulcrum Publishing, 1991. To order, write Fulcrum Publishing, 350 Indiana Street, Suite 350, Golden, CO 80401.

Notes on the trail: The following description reflects the way in which Joëlle and I rode this fabulous loop, that is, from Animas Fork above Silverton and in a counterclockwise direction, over a 2-day period, with the overnight stay in Lake City.

From your car near Animas Fork ghost town, begin pedaling up the jeep road that's signed for Engineer and Cinnamon passes and the Alpine Loop. The starting elevation here is about 11,200′, basically at timberline. After almost a mile of steady climbing, you reach the actual Alpine Loop dirt road and, at that point, you can go either left to Engineer Pass or right to Cinnamon Pass. Turn right toward Cinnamon Pass and continue pedaling—or walking and pushing your bike—on the rocky and steep road. The view looking down into the Picayne Gulch valley and across to Eureka Mountain are stunning—it's a welcome distraction as you try to suck more air into your lungs. Within 2 miles, you may encounter snowdrifts that have been plowed through by road crews, leaving puddles and mud. By now, you are clearly above timberline. The wind gets chillier and the climb gets steeper.

Finally, after almost 2.5 miles, you reach Cinnamon Pass at 12,620′. Chances are, you and your riding companions won't be the only ones there enjoying the spectacular, panoramic views of the San Juans. This is a destination for most jeep tourists. Looking east and southeast, you can see several peaks: Handies (14,048′), Redcloud (14,034′), and Sunshine (14,001′).

And now, as promised, here's the part of the loop that makes all that huffing and puffing worth it: a 16-mile, 3,948′, fast descent into Lake City. Before hopping back on your bike, though, now would be a good time to put on warmer clothing. That way, you won't have to interrupt the thrill of your downhill flight. The road is not overly steep, but it continues to be slightly rocky, with enough loose gravel to keep it interesting and make stopping on a dime impossible. With that in mind, watch out for all sorts of vehicles—passenger cars, trucks, jeeps, off-highway vehicles, and motorcycles.

After several whizzing miles, the loop cruises back under timberline and pine trees begin to line the road. Approximately 4.75 miles from the top, another jeep road connects to the Alpine Loop and leads to the American Basin Trail, reported to travel one of the most gorgeous valleys in the San Juans, with brilliant displays of wildflowers in midsummer. The trail also leads to Handies Peak and Sloan Lake (take note, all you fishermen and women, it's stocked with cutthroat trout). If you decide to explore this area, check for possible trail closure to mountain bikes.

Incidentally, there are pockets of private property within these public lands and you come to one of them soon after the American Basin Trail turnoff. The Alpine Loop travels alongside and through them. Please respect those properties by staying on the road. Continue your downhill cruise on the Alpine Loop, following the Gunnison River. After several miles, the majestic, rust-colored peak of Sunshine Mountain rises straight ahead, above lush evergreen trees. The road crosses Cooper Creek and, within the next half mile, you reach Burrows Park and the 2 trailheads of Grizzly Gulch and Silver Creek trails. At Burrows Park, you'll find several old wooden structures that were built in the late 1800s and probably were part of a town that served the mining district. Grizzly Gulch Trail leads to Handies Peak while Silver Creek Trail leads to Redcloud and Sunshine peaks. There is a rest room available at the Silver Creek trailhead.

After checking out Burrows Park, continue to follow the Alpine Loop downhill. About 5 miles from the trailheads, you reach the junction of Hinsdale County Road 35. At this point, you are a little beyond 12 miles from your car and about 14 miles from Lake City. The Alpine Loop road becomes wider and smoother, basically a two-wheel-drive road at this point. Stay on the Alpine Loop and after several more descending miles, Mill Creek Campground appears on your right, on the other side of the Gunnison River. Drinkable water is available here as are toilet facilities. If you like to camp and sleep to the sound of a rushing creek, this spot will please you. Twenty-two campsites are offered and a small fee is required. About a half mile down the road, at Bent Creek Trail, additional rest rooms are available. Another half mile farther on the Loop road puts you at the junction of Wagner Gulch Road, FS 568. Ghost town enthusiasts might want to consider checking out this steep jeep road as it leads to the old townsite of Carson, a well-preserved historic mining town.

As you continue on, you realize that it had to happen, sooner or later—you reenter civilization. Ranch homes can be seen in the distance and speed limit signs are posted. Adjacent to the road, tucked between the evergreen trees, is a bed-and-breakfast lodge called the Old Carson Inn. A short distance from that is Castle Lakes Campground, a privately owned and operated site. Almost 2 miles farther on the road, in the Gunnison National Forest, is the public campground of Williams Creek, with 23 campsites, drinking water, and toilet facilities. Overnight stays require a fee.

In the next several miles, still following the Alpine Loop, the dirt road begins to level out and leads you through a narrow but towering rock canyon, carved out by the Gunnison River on your right. Nearly 3 miles from Williams Creek Campground, you reach the southern tip of Lake San Cristobal, Colorado's second largest natural lake and a popular recreation area. The lake was created by the Slumgullion Earthflow landslides that occured hundreds of years ago. An oozing stew of mud and rock crept 4 miles downslope and blocked the Lake Fork of the Gunnison River, which created the lake. If you're a student of geology, this area is sure to interest you.

When you reach the southern tip of the lake, you have the option of riding the paved road skirting the west side of the lake or the dirt road on the east side. Both roads reconnect at the northern end of the lake. I highly recommend the dirt road because it avoids some of the fast traffic on the paved road. To reach this dirt road, which is a slight, 2.5-mile deviation from the Alpine Loop, continue on the dirt road, turning right, and following the road over a bridge across the Gunnison River. Stay on the road as it skirts the east side of the lake. The dirt road takes you on a short roller-coaster ride and leads you past lovely homes that overlook the lake, with a view of towering rims of mountain peaks. Please stay on the road as it travels past private property.

In the early summer months the peaks are snow-capped, while in the autumn the area around the lake is golden with aspen trees. Lake San Cristobal is popular for boating and fishing. Rainbow and brown trout are the usual catch, although rumor has it that 20-pounders are occasionally hooked. You can extend your enjoyment of this area, if you want, thanks to the Wupperman Public Campground, which maintains 40 sites between this dirt road and the water's edge. Drinking water and toilet facilities are available and a fee is required for overnight stays.

As you approach the northern end of the lake, the dirt road takes you through the private property of the Lake View Equestrian Center. (For a different kind of mountain traveling experience, consider joining these folks on one of their horseback outings.) As you pedal farther, leaving the equestrian center, the dirt road rejoins the Alpine Loop, which, at this point, is paved CO 3. Turn right onto CO 3, onto the shoulder, and watch out for traffic whizzing past you. Follow CO 3 for about a mile to the T intersection of CO 149, another paved road. (If you're interested in a notorious bit of history, look for a marker to the right of this intersection, just before the Lake Fork Bridge leading up toward Slumgullion Pass. This is the site of Alferd B. Packer's infamous, cannibalistic repast in the winter of 1874.) At this T intersection, make a left turn onto CO 149 and continue pedaling north into Lake City. Caution! This is a heavily traveled road and the shoulder is barely adequate. Fortunately, this segment of the Alpine Loop is only 2 miles long and takes you into Lake City.

Lake City is a delightful little old town that's worth taking the time to explore. The discovery of a rich gold vein above Lake San Cristobal in 1874 gave birth to the Golden Fleece Mine and transformed the tiny mining camp of Lake City into a boomtown. There's lots of history and stories about colorful characters and events of the past here. If you're hungry for more local information—of the past and the present—the best place to visit is the Chamber of Commerce on Silver Street in the center of town. From Silverton, Lake City is just beyond the halfway point on the Alpine Loop and, at 8,672´, it is the lowest point.

Now, after checking out the town, you can't put off the inevitable: it's time to tackle the 18-mile climb to Engineer Pass and, ultimately, back to your car. Find the Alpine Loop again by heading to the south edge of town on CO 149. Look for a green sign that points the way to Engineer Pass. If you cross Henson Creek, you've gone too far. Once you find the Alpine Loop road, follow it west, as it gradually climbs along the north side of Henson Creek. The pavement eventually becomes a wide, two-wheel-drive dirt road.

The terrain is a dramatic combination of towering, rugged ridges of rock on the right and miles of lively, roaring Henson Creek on your left, with spruce trees lining the road and dotting the ridges. Try to focus more on the scenery than the climbing. If you're thinking of camping, keep in mind that it's prohibited along the 9-mile stretch between Lake City and Capitol City, except at the meadow at Nellie Creek. Located nearly 5.5 miles from Lake City, the meadow is reached via FS 877, a jeep road that skirts Nellie Creek on its way to the Uncompahgre Peak trailhead and the Big Blue Wilderness, on the north side of the Alpine Loop.

Continuing on, nearly 8 miles from Lake City, cross El Paso Creek amidst gorgeous stands of aspen trees. At approximately 9.5 miles, you come to a clearing and the intersection of North Henson Fork Road, an alternate route to Uncompaghre Peak. The sign here states that Engineer Pass is 9 miles ahead. Stay left on the Alpine Loop and you reach Capitol City after crossing North Fork Creek, a tributary of Henson Creek. (Incidentally, I found a slight discrepancy from the Trails Illustrated® map here. I found Capitol City to be on the southwest side of North Henson Fork Road, not on the northeast side as the map indicates.) The city was founded in 1877 by George Lee, a successful smelter and mill owner. Inspired by the surrounding beauty, he had high hopes of Capitol City becoming the capitol of the state. A rest room is located about a quarter mile farther up the Alpine Loop from this historical site.

By now, the road has gotten slightly steeper and bumpier, becoming a four-wheel-drive road. Nearly 2 miles from Capitol City, take another breather and check out Whitmore Falls. It's not visible from the road but there is a path leading to an overlook, just yards from the road.

Pedal on and you soon come to a fork in the road. The right fork leads to Engineer Pass while the left takes you to Rose's Cabin, another historical site that you can visit. Built by Corydon Rose, the cabin housed a bar, an eatery, and

22 tiny rooms. It was the one and only popular entertainment and socializing spot for miners in this area, being more accessible than Lake City.

Onward! You're about 2.5 miles from Engineer Pass and about another half mile from the highest point of the Alpine Loop. Keep pedaling—or walking—and your view becomes more expansive and spectacular. The terrain is alpine tundra, covered with vegetation typically found in the Arctic. Look for an educational sign posted a mile from the Pass that tells about this fragile tundra. Cross Palmetto Gulch and you begin to rise above timberline. The road becomes steeper and rockier. Within a mile, you reach Engineer Pass, sitting at 12,800′. Enjoy your accomplishment but don't let go of your perseverance just yet. The highest point of the route—at 13,040′—is still a half mile up from the Pass.

When you come to a lookout site called Oh! Point!—a long, narrow plateau jutting west—you have surmounted the highest spot. The road remains extremely rugged and strewn with loose rocks. Follow the road as it leads you through a roller coaster of hills, all the while traversing the west side of Engineer Mountain. There are other jeep roads and trails that lead off from the Alpine Loop. Many of them are unmarked and can be confusing. Stay on what appears to be the main road. After almost 1.5 miles, look for a road sign for San Juan County Road 2, immediately before a hairpin turn with another jeep road leading off from the top of that turn. Make a right turn here, descending the steep hairpin turn leading into the valley. The terrain becomes very technical, and there are several more steep, hairpin turns to come.

After riding for about a half mile, you come to a T intersection and a sign designating the direction to Engineer Pass and Animas Fork. The unmarked jeep road on your right leads west and down to Ouray. This is Mineral Point Road, though it is not marked on the trail at this intersection. Continue straight, taking the road towards Animas Fork. The road descends over extremely loose, rocky terrain. Within 2 miles from the T intersection, the road leads you under old cables that connect to an abandoned mine. You're on the right track. Pedal a half mile more and when you come to the sign that indicates Engineer Pass to the left and Cinnamon Pass to the right, you've completed the loop. From this point, pay your last respects and a fond farewell to the Alpine Loop, and retrace your path back to your car below. Congratulations!

[Editor's Note]: For an even longer tour, let me suggest an extension of Linda's route. Begin in Telluride, head west and then south on CO 145 to Ophir, then begin your jeep-road climb to Ophir Pass. Zoom down the other side to US 550 and head south to Silverton. Spend your first night at The Teller House. It's located halfway up Main Street (and on your next day's route), on the second floor, above the French Bakery Restaurant. What could be better?

Next, pedal Cinnamon Pass to Lake City (second night); from there, ride over Engineer Pass to Ouray (third night); and finally, go up and over Imogene Pass back to Telluride. There's not a better 100-mile taste of the San Juan

Mountains, nor one that's tougher. And speaking of taste . . . there's a great deal of history in these parts. Lake City, for example, is the town in which Alferd B. Packer was tried and convicted for killing and eating four of his companions while trapped by a snowstorm in the nearby mountains. As Gregg and Linda have warned, listen to a weather report before you hit the trail.

This route is highlighted on a map you can obtain free by writing to the Silverton Chamber of Commerce (address listed earlier, in "Sources of additional information"). Ask for *Jeep Roads & Ghost Towns of the San Juans*.

Cortez

ANASAZI INDIAN RUINS IN SOUTHWEST COLORADO

Mountain biking in this region is unlike that of any other area in Colorado. Unlike nearby Durango or Crested Butte, you are not likely to find bike festivals and races south and west of Cortez. Instead, the focus here is Indian cultures and archaeology. Undeniably, there is a tremendous wealth of Native American history, right here in Montezuma County. Though much study, research, excavation, and exploration have been done to learn about the life and culture of the various groups of people who lived here over a thousand years ago, what is known is a combination of empirical data and speculation by archaeologists, at best. At the risk of oversimplifying the historical and cultural timeline of this region, here is a summary of the important events in Anasazi history. Perhaps it will inspire you to learn more about this area through other, more detailed sources of information and, thus, turn enjoyable bike rides into something much more memorable and significant.

In the time before Christ, nomadic hunters and gatherers roamed this region of Colorado. Not much is known of them, for they left little behind (the forerunners of low-impact camping, perhaps?). Archaeologists concluded that at the time of Christ, communities of people, now called the Anasazi Indians, began to settle here by building structures, farming the mesas for beans, corn, and squash, and creating domestic wares such as woven baskets and, later, pottery. Between A.D. 1 and A.D. 1300, these communities grew economically, politically, culturally, and spiritually, as evidenced by excavated artifacts and the remains of sophisticated architectural structures designed for everyday living and for religious practices. A network of trails connected the various thriving communities. Then, about A.D. 1300, these communities began to desert this region; to this day, the reasons are unconfirmed. The mysterious departure of these incredibly accomplished groups of people has inspired many sociological, scientific, spiritual, religious, and magical theories. Two hundred years later, the Navajo and Ute Indians roamed and inhabited the area and subsequently discovered the ruins of this previous civilization. They were awed by what they found and, out of respect, named the culture the Anasazi, meaning the "Ancient Ones."

Today, the Ute tribe and government agencies preserve and manage numerous archaeological ruins in this region. Hundreds of other sites, large and small, well-defined and obscure, are unmarked and unfenced, accessible by mountain bike. Here are a few of the many areas worth checking out by bike, as well as museums and other historical sites worth visiting:

Mesa Verde National Park is the site of an incredible, awe-inspiring, huge cliff-dwelling complex of the Anasazi Indians. The entrance is located about eight miles east of Cortez on US 160, and bikes are allowed only on paved and designated roads. Contact Mesa Verde National Park, CO 81330, (303) 529-4465 or (303) 529-4475.

Ute Mountain Tribal Park is home to hundreds of Anasazi surface ruins and cliff dwellings, as well as Ute wall paintings and petroglyphs. The park covers about 125,000 acres, surrounding a 25-mile stretch of the Mancos River, and is located about 10 miles south of Mancos along the southeastern edge of Mesa Verde National Park. Access to the park is restricted in that visits require reservations, a fee, and accompaniment by a Ute Mountain Tribal Park guide. Mountain bike tours reportedly can be arranged for one- to four-day trips, and are said to be a combination of moderately challenging riding and hiking. If you're interested in riding this region, I highly recommend that you call at least a couple of weeks in advance for all the park logistics and then make your reservations accordingly. My riding companion, Joëlle, and I were unsuccessful in arranging a tour in mid-June, 1993, given our limited time. We called the phone number listed in numerous visitor's and biking guides but didn't receive an answer until after the fourth attempt later that day. And even then, the Ute Mountain Tribal Park employee who answered was unfamiliar with mountain bike tours. I eventually spoke with the Tribal Park Director, who also did not have much information about the bike tours, but assured me that the Park had plans to become more accessible for bikers. Who knows? It was late June and maybe we were too early for their tourist season. If archaeological ruins appeal to you, my suggestion is to persevere. I'm sure the adventure will be worth the effort. Write Ute Mountain Tribal Park, Towoac, CO 81334; phone (303) 565-3751, ext. 282, (303) 565-8548, or (800) 847-5485 from out of state. You might have better luck going through Mountain Bike Specialists (a bike shop) P.O. Box 1389T, Durango, CO 81301, (303) 247-4066.

Hovenweep National Monument is considered to be one of the most incredible Anasazi ruins in this region. It straddles the Colorado-Utah border about 43 miles west of Cortez on unpaved roads. Contained within this plot of land are six well-preserved ruins: Square Tower and Cajon are in Utah while Holly, Hackberry Canyon, Cutthroat Castle, and Goodman Point are in Colorado. The best preserved site is Square Tower, also the easiest to reach by car. A public campground is maintained there. All other sites are more isolated and without convenient water or toilets. Cutthroat Castle Ruins is accessible on Ride 52, described later in this chapter. To reach the monument headquarters, campground, and Square Tower Ruins, drive southwest out of Cortez on US 666 for 3 miles. Turn right (west) onto McElmo Canyon Road and follow the signs to Hovenweep National Monument for 39 miles, crossing into Utah.

Lowry Pueblo Ruins, named for homesteader George Lowry, is located about 28 miles northwest of Cortez. This significant, well-preserved site, containing 8 kivas and 40 rooms, may be visited on a self-guided tour. To reach these ruins, drive north out of Cortez on US 666 for 20 miles to Pleasant View. Turn left (west) onto County Road CC and drive the remaining 9 miles to the site. Better yet, if you can't take sitting in a car any longer, park your car at this intersection, hop on your bike, and pedal to the ruins.

You probably already know this, but it's worth repeating: Respect for our cultural heritage means not removing, marring, or disturbing structures, rock art, and other archaeological pieces and finds at any site; it's against federal and state laws and, who knows, perhaps spiritual laws, too.

Sources of additional information:

Crow Canyon Archaeological Center and School
23390 County Road K
Cortez, CO 81321
(800) 422-8975
(303) 565-8975
This is a nationally known archaeological center that offers exploration, excavation, and cultural programs to the public throughout the year.

Anasazi Heritage Center
Bureau of Land Management
27501 CO 184
Dolores, CO 81323
(303) 882-4811
Adjacent to the Dominguez and Escalante ruins, this world-class museum contains over two million records, samples, and artifacts from the Dolores Archaeological Program. Because of its extensive displays, this modern, high-tech museum is a must-visit for all Anasazi archaeology enthusiasts.

Cortez Center—University of Colorado Museum
25 North Market Street
P.O. Box 1326
Cortez, CO 81321
(303) 565-1151
In addition to excellent exhibits, guest lectures, and programs on Native American culture, the museum offers educational materials and presentations on NASA space exploration and aerospace research.

The Mesa Verde—Cortez Visitors Information Bureau
P.O. Drawer HH
Cortez, CO 81321
(800) 253-1616

Cortez Welcome Center
P.O. Box 968
928 East Main Street
Cortez, CO 81321
(303) 565-3414

Bureau of Land Management
San Juan Office
701 Camino del Rio, Room 203
Durango, CO 81301
(303) 247-4082

San Juan National Forest:

Mancos District
41595 East US 160
Mancos, CO 81328
(303) 533-7716

Dolores District
100 North Sixth
Dolores, CO 81323
(303) 882-7296

RIDE 52 *CUTTHROAT CASTLE RUINS AND NEGRO CANYON LOOP*

The problems I had with this adequately marked 19-mile loop were two: I had great difficulty keeping my eyes on the trail, and there wasn't enough time in the day to enjoy this outing. The route itself is not overly difficult or long. In fact, it's rated as intermediate in both technical skills and stamina level. Since the area is part of the Hovenweep National Monument, there were numerous unmarked ruins along the route that required a sharp eye. I wanted to stop and explore each site, no matter how small. While pedaling along, I found myself trying to visually scour the landscape for abandoned stone structures, instead of watching the road. Due to a late start, my riding buddy, Joëlle, and I reluctantly curtailed our exploring urges. We completed the loop in almost six hours.

Perhaps you'll satisfy your curiosity about Indian ruins with a short hike to Cutthroat Castle Ruins, which is reached within the first two miles of the ride. "The Castle," built by the Anasazi Indians over a thousand years ago, offers a splendid view of Hovenweep Canyon. My suggestion is to start early, just in case you get bitten by the exploring bug.

RIDE 52 *CUTTHROAT CASTLE RUINS AND NEGRO CANYON LOOP*

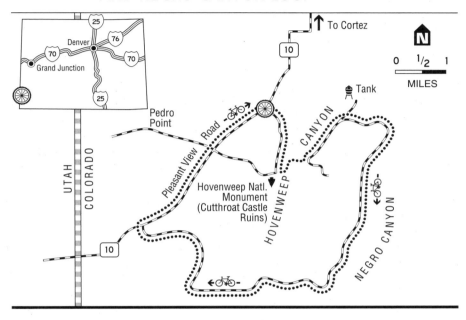

General location: The loop within the Hovenweep National Monument is located approximately 37 miles northwest of Cortez.

Elevation change: The terrain lies between 5,360′ and 6,100′, with a total elevation change of 740′.

Season: This area can be enjoyed between early spring and late autumn and sometimes through the dry winter season. The best times for this outing are midspring and midautumn, when the temperatures are warm but not blazingly hot. Portions of the loop include fine, soft, red clay roads that can become dreaded traps of thick, deep mud holes during prolonged rains. In fact, it's a good idea to check road conditions ahead, since all roads in Hovenweep National Monument are rough, dirt roads and can be impassable after a storm.

Services: No services are offered at the starting point or throughout the loop. Before leaving town, pack enough water and food. Don't count on finding water on the route as creeks are likely to be dry most of the year. Though a public campground is maintained near Cutthroat Castle (at the monument headquarters at Square Tower Ruins), water and phone are not available. All services—water, phone, toilets, lodging, private campgrounds, food and restaurants, and gas are offered in Cortez.

Hazards: There are few potential hazards worth noting on this ride. Bring

Joëlle begins her descent into dry and arid Negro Canyon, home to numerous Indian ruins.

enough water with you since it is generally unavailable on the loop. Rattlesnakes live at this altitude, so be careful where you ride and step, especially when exploring off the trail. There are a variety of road conditions here but none are particularly hazardous—unless you're preoccupied with looking for ruins up on the cliffsides when you should be watching the road.

Rescue index: The nearest medical facility is in Cortez, approximately 38 miles away from the ride's starting point. Most of the loop is four-wheel-drive accessible, though some portions are more difficult due to narrowness and sandy road conditions, especially during and after storms. Negro Canyon is the most remote stretch of the loop and you are not likely to see anyone else for assistance. So, your best bet is to pedal yourself or your injured riding partner back to your vehicle and drive back into Cortez for medical attention.

Land status: Bureau of Land Management. Hovenweep National Monument.

Maps: USGS 7.5 minute quads: Negro Canyon and Ruin Canyon. Bureau of Land Management: Cortez, 1:100,000 scale.

Bicycling: Mountain and Road Bike Routes. Produced by the Mesa Verde County Tourism and Convention Bureau. Provides general route maps and descriptions of other rides in the vicinity. Address listed below.

Bicycle Routes on Public Lands of Southwest Colorado. Second edition. Produced and distributed by U.S. Forest Service—San Juan National Forest division and the Bureau of Land Management, as well as numerous merchants and friends in the southwest region of Colorado. Sold by local merchants.

Finding the trail: To reach the starting point of the loop, drive northwest out of Cortez on US 666 for 19 miles. Turn left (west) onto County Road BB, a dirt road, marked by a sign to Hovenweep National Monument. Follow this road for just over 6 miles, to the intersection of CR 10, where another Hovenweep National Monument sign is posted. Make a left (south) at Pleasant View Road (CR 10) and follow it for a little over 11 miles. At this point, look for another Hovenweep sign and a dirt road leading off to your left (east). Park your car on the side of the road at this intersection and begin pedaling from here.

Sources of additional information:

Bureau of Land Management
San Juan Resource Area
701 Camino del Rio, Room 203
Durango, CO 81301
(303) 247-4082

Hovenweep National Monument
c/o Mesa Verde National Park, CO 81330
(303) 529-4465
Inquiries about the monument are handled by the park office.

BLM Colorado Mountain Biking Adventures
Produced by the Department of the Interior, Bureau of Land Management. Contact the BLM San Juan Office listed above.

Bicycling: Mountain and Road Bike Routes
Mesa Verde Country Tourism and Convention Bureau
928 East Main
Cortez, CO 81321
(800) 346-6528 (from outside Colorado)
(303) 565-3414 (from within Colorado)
Ask for the complete visitor's package of information as well as this pamphlet.

The Colorado Guide, by Bruce Caughey and Dean Winstanley. Golden, Colorado: Fulcrum Publishing, 1991. To order, write Fulcrum Publishing, 350 Indiana Street, Suite 350, Golden, CO 80401.

Notes on the trail: One look at the arid surroundings and you'll automatically know to bring lots of water with you. If you're into photographing Indian ruins, don't forget your camera. The loop begins on the rugged four-wheel-drive dirt road leading southeast. Follow this fairly level and slightly rocky road for a little over 1.5 miles. At that point, you'll see a sign off to the right for the hiking trail to Cutthroat Castle Ruins.

After exploring the ruins, return to this spot and continue pedaling on the dirt road, bearing left and following it down into Hovenweep Canyon. Trail conditions generally become more rocky as you descend into the canyon. Once you reach the bottom, you'll find large areas of deep sandtraps that like to zap your momentum, forcing you to dismount and walk for a few yards. Actually, as you push your bike along, this is a great opportunity to check out the canyon walls on both sides of you. At some point along this stretch in the canyon floor, Joëlle and I stopped on the trail to adjust a pack or clothing. I happened to look up towards the cliffs and spotted a tiny abandoned stone structure that may have been an Indian food cache or other shelter. From that point on, my eyes were glued to the cliffs, hoping to discover more ruins.

Continue pedaling on this rolling road, crossing streams (most likely dry) and, in about 2 miles, you begin a short, steep climb out of Hovenweep Canyon. Pass through a fence and almost immediately you should spot a large metal containment tank a short distance away, straight ahead. Watch for bicycle emblem markers, particularly before the tank facility at the junction of another jeep road leading off to your right. Take this right turn, following the bicycle signpost to Negro Canyon. At this point, you've pedaled nearly 5.5 miles from your car.

The next 4 miles through Negro Canyon lead you through gates and fences, cross several dry creeks, and include some short descents and ascents. The road is moderately rocky but without sandtraps. Rock formations on both sides of the road are apt to make you wonder if any ruins are hidden there.

By the time you've pedaled 9 miles, the road begins to lead you on a steep but short climb out of Negro Canyon. The 360-degree view of the rolling landscape is quietly splendid and you'd think you could see forever. Pass through the first of a series of gates and begin a set of long ascents and descents for approximately 3.5 miles. When Joëlle and I rode this loop in mid-June, the ground here was so bone-dry, it had become scarred with huge, gaping cracks, creating an interesting obstacle course.

At about 12.5 miles, you pass through the last gate. When the road leads you past a modern, wooden corral, you've pedaled just over 15 miles. Continue following the jeep road for several yards farther, to the junction of Pleasant View Road (CR 10), a two-wheel-drive gravel road. Turn right (northeast) here and complete the loop by pedaling the remaining 3.5 miles back to your car. Total mileage of the loop is nearly 19 miles.

RIDE 53   *CANNONBALL MESA*

Let's face it, there's more to mountain biking than mastering difficult technical skills. Simple, basic skills can provide you with endless miles of mountain biking enjoyment.

A case in point is this easy, ten-mile out-and-back ride. There is nothing really technical about this five-mile trail. And the elevation gain is a mere 500′, to a high point of 5,600′, with lots of mesa-top riding and 360-degree views of the surrounding semiarid canyon.

Sound like a yawner? Hardly. Joëlle and I explored this short ride for one reason: to check out remote archaeological ruins abandoned by the Anasazi Indians in approximately A.D. 1300. We were richly rewarded. Our weather in mid-June was hot, accompanied by a gentle, dry breeze. As we explored and silently sat among the ruins, overlooking the canyon and creek, we tried to envision the site alive with a community of families and the air smelling of campfires, cooking the day's meal. Joëlle and I agreed that this is definitely a place of transcending spirits. And for these reasons, you should allow enough time to explore the ruins and to let your mind wonder about the people who lived here hundreds of years ago.

General location: The access point of this ride is about 22 miles west of Cortez and approximately 30 miles west of Mesa Verde National Park. Cortez is located in the Four Corners region where the Arizona, New Mexico, Utah, and Colorado state lines converge, about 377 miles southwest of Denver.

Elevation change: The ride begins at 5,100′ and rises to the highest point of 5,600′, for a total elevation gain of 500′ in about 2 miles.

Season: This outing can be enjoyed from early spring to late autumn, and even during dry winter months. Keep in mind that summer months are likely to be scorchers and that shade from the sun is almost nonexistent.

Services: There are no services at the trailhead nor throughout the route. Your best plan is to take care of your needs in Cortez before heading out to this ride. In Cortez, you'll find drinking water, food and restaurants, toilet facilities, public phone, gas, a bicycle store, and lodging establishments.

Hazards: Bring plenty of water because this region is typically hot and dry, spring through autumn. Don't depend on finding water on the route. If you are dying of thirst and do find water, you need to treat it for Giardia before consuming it. Bring sunscreen or extra clothing to protect your skin from the blazing sun. Watch out for rattlesnakes on and off the road.

Rescue index: For emergency medical situations, rest assured that this route is four-wheel-drive vehicle accessible. It is not unusual to meet other trail users on

RIDE 53 *CANNONBALL MESA*

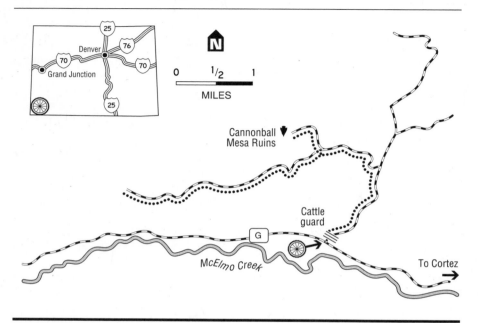

this route, who may be able to give assistance. The nearest medical facility is in Cortez, about 22 miles away, over mostly gravel road.

Land status: Bureau of Land Management. San Juan National Forest. Hovenweep National Monument.

Maps: USGS 7.5 minute quad: Bowdish Canyon, Colorado. Bureau of Land Management: Cortez, 1:100,000 scale. *Bicycling: Mountain and Road Bike Routes.* Produced by the Mesa Verde County Tourism and Convention Bureau. Provides general route maps and descriptions of other rides in the vicinity. Address listed below.

Finding the trail: To reach the starting point, drive 2 miles south out of Cortez on US 666/CO 160, also known as McElmo Canyon Road. Watch for the M & M Truckstop and Cafe at the junction of this road and County Road G. At this intersection, turn right (west) onto CR G and stay on it for approximately 15 miles to where the pavement is replaced by a gravel road. Continue on the gravel road for about 5 miles more to an unmarked dirt road with a cattle guard across it. Park off the road, anywhere except adjacent to the cattle guard. Begin your ride here.

Riding by these huge boulders, we couldn't help wondering if they housed hidden, ancient Indian shelters or food caches.

Sources of additional information:

San Juan National Forest
701 Camino del Rio, Room 301
Durango, CO 81301
(303) 247-4874

Bureau of Land Management
San Juan Resource Area
701 Camino del Rio, Room 203
Durango, CO 81301
(303) 247-4082

Hovenweep National Monument
c/o Mesa Verde National Park, CO 81330
(303) 529-4465
Inquiries about the monument are handled by the park office.

Bicycle Routes on Public Lands of Southwest Colorado. Second edition. Produced and distributed by U.S. Forest Service—San Juan National Forest division and the Bureau of Land Management, as well as by numerous merchants and friends in the southwest region of Colorado. Sold by local merchants.

BLM Colorado Mountain Biking Adventures. Produced by the Department of the Interior, Bureau of Land Management. Contact the BLM San Juan Office listed above.

Mesa Verde Country Tourism and Convention Bureau
928 East Main
Cortez, CO 81321
(800) 346-6528 (from outside Colorado)
(303) 565-3414 (from within Colorado)
Ask for the complete visitor's package of information, as well as their biking trails pamphlet.

The Colorado Guide, by Bruce Caughey and Dean Winstanley. Golden, Colorado: Fulcrum Publishing, 1991. To order, write Fulcrum Publishing, 350 Indiana Street, Suite 350, Golden, CO 80401.

Notes on the trail: Though the roads are not all marked, this route uses obvious jeep roads. Start your adventure by pedaling across the cattle guard onto the road marked "Private—Stay on road." The jeep road immediately climbs, though not steeply, for approximately a quarter of a mile due north, through rolling, dry terrain, dotted with scrub. Eventually, the road leads you through dramatic rock formations.

About 1.5 miles from the cattle guard, you reach a fork in the road marked by a BLM sign. Take the left turn here, basically due west, following the jeep road as it curves and climbs steeply for about a half mile to the top of Cannonball Mesa. From this point on, the road is a fun combination of slickrock and rust-colored dirt, threading through scattered pinyon-juniper bushes. The route remains fairly level, punctuated with a few short, roller-coaster hills and a constant, 360-degree view of the semiarid landscape.

Approximately 3.5 miles from the beginning of the ride, the main road is joined by an unmarked fork to the right. Postpone exploring this direction of the main road (due west) for the return trip. Take the right fork, a four-wheel-drive, double-track, rugged road, and follow it due northwest as it travels downhill, levels out, curves, and crosses massive slickrock. The road ends at the archaeological ruins.

After exploring the ruins, return to the main jeep road, turn right, and resume following the road due west. After 1.5 miles of cruising on top of Cannonball Mesa, the road begins a gradual, half-mile descent. The road ends at a barbed-wire fence that stretches across the narrow mesa and offers a splendid view of a fertile, green valley off to your left (south). This road was named Wood Road when it was used as a wagon route to Bluff, Utah.

Return the way you came.

RIDE 54 *DOLORES RIVER CANYON*

On a hot summer's day, there may be no better place to pedal than along the banks of the Dolores River. Locked within a 2,000´-deep canyon, the Dolores flows briskly beneath terraced, redrock palisades streaked with desert varnish and stained with yellow-green lichens. Stretch out on stream-side micro-meadows, or roost on a boulder mid–river channel to bask in the midday sun. Pack along a pair of wading shoes and a fly rod, for swimming holes, swirling eddies, and fishing opportunities abound.

The depths of the Dolores River Canyon give rise to an environment quite different from that of the sage-covered plateaus above. Juniper-pinyon forests dot the terraced canyon walls and thick oak brush lines riverbank meadows. Scattered stands of ponderosa pine and even patches of aspen huddle in the canyon's cool, protected recesses. Perhaps you will flush wild turkeys from the brush or send jackrabbits scampering. And when you stop to cool off, an array of birdcalls ricocheting off the lofty canyon walls contend with the sounds of the churning river.

This 26-mile, one-way trip (52 miles total, out-and-back) is moderately difficult. The first 11 miles are fairly easy, for the jeep road heads downstream, hugging the river's bank. Beyond the Pyramid rock formation the grade is still gentle, but conditions become more rough as the road crosses several rocky side drainages. After the river ford (mile 15), the route is notably more difficult, as it rises sharply to shortcut one of the river's giant meander loops, then exits the sandy river corridor via a rigorous, one-mile, 10% grade. The remaining five-mile dirt road is fairly smooth and easy. Technical difficulty is moderate overall.

General location: Forty miles north of Cortez, Colorado (or 5.5 miles east of Dove Creek, Colorado).

Elevation change: Along the banks of the Dolores, the river road declines unnoticeably. The route's starting point at the pump station near Mountain Sheep Point is about 6,100´. Heading downriver for over 15 miles, the trail drops to near 5,600´. That is only a 500´ vertical drop! In-between the trailhead and trail end, a multitude of "strainers" add vertical gain quickly, but all are short and rideable.

Season: Temperatures in this portion of southwest Colorado are generally quite warm during midsummer, but the Dolores River Canyon harbors much cooler climes than the surrounding plateaus. Even if you are traveling on a hot day, the river is wonderful. Although winter brings minimal snowfall, it is very cold inside the gorge. All in all, the Dolores River Canyon maintains a long riding season, from late March through November.

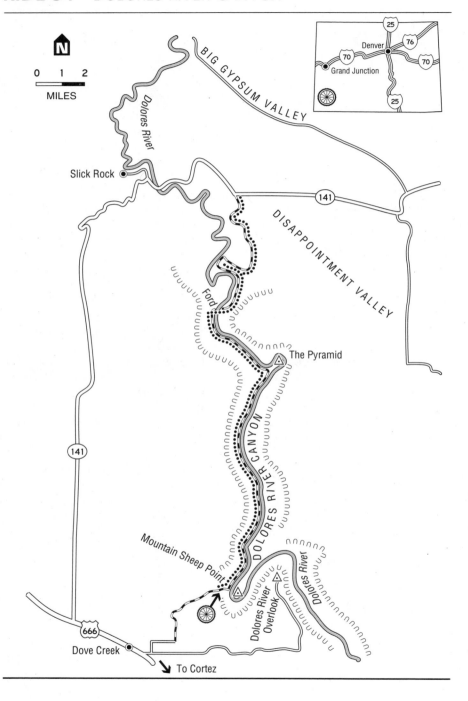

A calm back eddy reflects cliffs lining Dolores Canyon.
Photo: Gregg Bromka.

Services: All visitor services can be found in Cortez, Colorado, located about 40 miles south of the trailhead. Near the trail's beginning, the small farming town of Dove Creek ("The Pinto Bean Capitol of the World") yields limited services—namely, gas, a small grocery store, a liquor store, and a convenience store; what more could you want? Camping and RV hookups are also available. Primitive, backcountry camping is available at the trailhead (but, beware of a shameful amount of broken glass).

Nearly 20 of the route's 26 miles are spent right next to or near the river's channel, so water is always close at hand. A small water bottle and a lightweight water purifier may substitute for several oversized bottles.

Hazards: Since you will spend much of the time craning your neck to view the canyon's enclosing redrock walls, you may be startled by the frequently rocky trail.

Afternoon rains are not uncommon; the region is surrounded by several mountain ranges that collect thunderclouds. Consider carrying a lightweight poncho, for you will not see a storm brewing until it is directly overhead, and shelter is limited. Dirt access roads (especially the steep descent to the canyon's bottom) may be impassable when wet.

One very important note: You will have to ford the Dolores River about 15 miles into the ride (4 miles past the Pyramid). This should not be attempted during high water, usually mid-April through May, especially if the flow is greater than 200 cubic feet per second. Call the Dolores River Hot Line for flow information: (303) 882-7600.

Rescue index: Inside the canyon you are a long way from medical attention (up to 10 miles and several hours from either trailhead, and then over 40 miles from Cortez), so plan accordingly. Carry ample water supplies or means of purification, sufficient food, extra clothing in the event of changing weather, and appropriate first aid. Remember, the first 15 miles or so is the easy part.

Land status: Bureau of Land Management. Portions of the route skirt private property near its end.

Maps: USGS 7.5 minute quadrangles: Hamm Canyon, Horse Range Mesa, Joe Davis Hill, and Secret Canyon, Colorado. USGS 1:50,000 scale county maps: Dolores #1 and San Miguel #1, Colorado.

Finding the trail: From Cortez, drive north on US 666 about 34 miles. Immediately southeast of Dove Creek, turn right at a large brown sign: "Public Access, Dolores River Canyon and Overlook." Follow signs for the Dolores River Canyon access on a zigzag course of (usually) good dirt roads. In less than 3 miles you will begin a very steep descent into the Dolores River Canyon. Upon reaching the river, turn left at the pump house and park next to the huge ponderosa. Please register.

To get to the trail's other end and parking area (for leaving a car shuttle), drive west past Dove Creek on US 666, north on CO 141, then 4 miles past Slick Rock and the Dolores River Bridge. Watch for the Nichols Wash sign. One-half mile past the wash, turn right on CR 13R and park.

Sources of additional information:

> Bureau of Land Management
> San Juan Resource Area
> 701 Camino del Rio, Room 203
> Durango, CO 81301
> (303) 247-4082

> The Mesa Verde Country Tourism and Convention Bureau
> 928 East Main
> Cortez, CO 81421
> (303) 565-3414 (in state)
> (800) 346-6528

Bicycling Guide in the Cortez, Dolores, and Mancos, Colorado Area, by the Mesa Verde County Tourism and Convention Bureau (see address and phone, above).

Notes on the trail: For the first 11 miles you cannot get lost: just follow the four-wheel-drive road north and downriver. About 10 miles into the ride, the road rises above the river and passes through a saddle near the Pyramid rock formation. Here the Dolores bends sharply west around the Pyramid. (If you do not have the advantage of a car shuttle, this is a good point to turn around, resulting in a moderately difficult, 22-mile out-and-back tour.) Continue straight and downhill to rejoin the river's edge (not left and uphill—a dead end).

Four miles past the Pyramid, the route drops off the embankment where you must ford the river. Less than 3 miles past the crossing, bear right up and over a hill, and descend again to the river. Cross a second small hill, then turn right (southeast) as the road begins a steep, 1.5-mile climb out of the canyon. (If you continue straight along the river, you cross private property.) Stay on the main road and turn left at an old junked car. A bit more than a mile farther, turn left on CR 13R, then cross Disappointment Creek Bridge and follow CO 141, which leads to the parking area.

Durango

RIDE 55 *HERMOSA CREEK*

Replete with all the dynamic ingredients that comprise the Colorado Rockies, the San Juan Mountains are a glorious sight. Volcanic domes, wind-swept Matterhorns, and jagged arêtes form white caps above a turbulent mountain-scape. Gray, sullen rock faces streaked with yellow, orange-brown, and purple aprons delineate mineral-rich motherlodes feverishly pursued over a century of mining. Melting snowfields, wind, and water chisel rock walls into cuspate cirques that embrace steel-blue tarns, while braided rivulets coalesce into cascading creeks and thundering flumes which slice the forested land into narrow gorges and broad, connecting valleys.

The Hermosa Creek Trail does not surmount improbable mountain passes from which dizzying views of the surrounding highlands are gained. Instead, it dives into the heart of the San Juan National Forest—a fertile world of changing ecosystems, where mighty forests rise from luxurious streamside vegetation, where a glittering creek nourishes a glorious canyon and the multitude of life it harbors. In Spanish, *hermosa* means "beautiful," and Hermosa Creek is a beautiful ride.

Even though this 20-mile point-to-point route is largely a downhill trip, it still requires good conditioning and endurance. Numerous short, midroute climbs demand quick bursts of energy, while two more lengthy hills call for sustained pedaling and possibly some walking. Much of the route follows single-track that has its fair share of technical challenges. Thus, good bike handling skills are advantageous. But, all things considered, the Hermosa Creek Trail is within grasp of aggressive novice cyclists; advanced bikers will relish in a day full of mountain bike ecstasy.

General location: The northern trailhead is located about 8 miles west of Purgatory Ski Area off of the Hermosa Park Road (Forest Service Road 578). Its southern trailhead joins with FS 576 (County Road 201) northwest of Hermosa. Hermosa is about 10 miles north of Durango, and Purgatory is about 28 miles north of Durango—both on US 550.

Elevation change: Beginning at 8,840′, the trail drops a total of only 1,000′ over 20 miles to the junction with FS 576. Thereafter, the dirt road quickly drops an additional 1,100′ in 3.5 miles to its junction with US 550, at 6,650′.

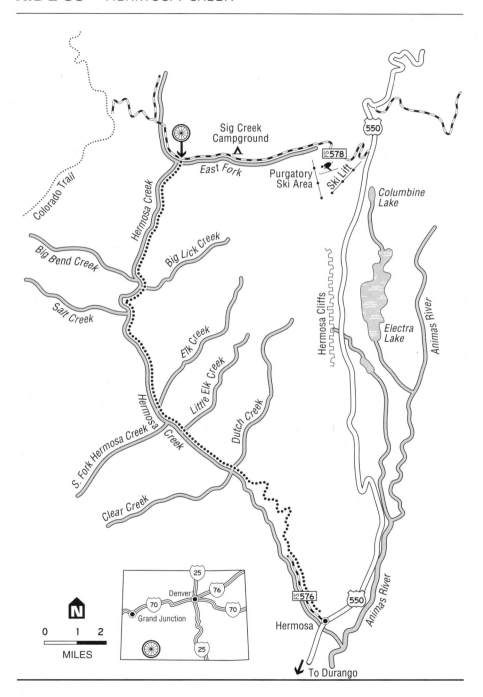

Sig Creek
Campground

East Fork

Colorado Trail

Hermosa Creek

Big Bend Creek

Salt Creek

Big Lick Creek

Elk Creek

Little Elk Creek

S. Fork Hermosa Creek

Hermosa Creek

Clear Creek

Dutch Creek

FS 578

Purgatory
Ski Area

Ski Lift

550

Columbine
Lake

Hermosa Cliffs

Electra
Lake

Animas River

N

0   1   2
MILES

25

Denver

70

Grand Junction

76

70

70

25

FS 576

Hermosa

550

Animas River

To Durango

A fading view of the rugged San Juan Mountains prior to embarking on the Hermosa Creek Trail. Photo: Gregg Bromka.

Thus, from top to bottom just over 2,000′ net elevation is lost. Keep in mind, however, that total mid-route climbs and descents exceed 1,500′.

Season: June through October, depending on lingering snow. After rainfall, clayey portions of the trail may turn to a muddy paste.

Services: Overnight accommodations, dining, plus a bike rental shop can be found at Purgatory Ski Area. A small cafe and telephone can be found at Hermosa. Otherwise, Durango (10 miles south of Hermosa) offers all services. There is plenty of water along this route since it parallels the creek for nearly 15 miles, but surface waters should be purified.

Hazards: Once inside the canyon, it may be difficult to see threatening weather approaching. There is plenty of cover to wait out a storm, but portions of the trail become greasy when wet. Pay close attention to the trail's many obstacles, especially when it contours steep side slopes. The Hermosa Creek Trail is a multi-use Forest Service trail open to hikers, bicyclists, equestrians, and motorcycles. Be considerate of these other trail users.

Rescue index: This is a remote backcountry route that requires careful preparation. Pack appropriate repair and emergency equipment plus ample water and food, for there are *no* passing motorists to flag down and walking out may be a day-long prospect. Once you are committed, there are no shortcuts. Telephones are available at Purgatory Ski Area and at Hermosa.

Land status: San Juan National Forest.

Maps: USGS 7.5 minute quadrangles: Elk Creek, Hermosa, Hermosa Peak, and Monument Hill, Colorado. USGS 1:50,000 scale county maps: La Plata #1 and La Plata #3, Colorado. San Juan National Forest Recreation Map.

Finding the trail: This point-to-point ride requires a vehicle shuttle. Leave one vehicle at Hermosa (located about 10 miles north of Durango on US 550). Car-top your bikes 18 miles north to Purgatory Ski Area, then follow FS 578 (Hermosa Park Road) about 2 miles past Sig Creek Campground. A parking area is provided across the creek to the left. The trail begins at a cattle gate, then leaves the meadows and follows the creek south. (Note: Close this and subsequent gates after passing through.)

Those who cringe at driving their vehicles on dirt/gravel roads can reach the trail by either pedaling the Forest Service road or taking advantage of Purgatory's mountain bike trail system. First, piggyback your bike up the chairlift, then drop off the resort's northern side via Brush Rake Road and onto the Hermosa Park Road above Sig Creek Campground. Purgatory Ski Area has hand-out maps for its trail system, and additional route information can be found at the base-area bike shop.

Sources of additional information:

San Juan National Forest
701 Camino del Rio, Room 301
Durango, CO 81301
(303) 247-4874

Animas Ranger District
110 West Eleventh Street
Durango, CO 81301
(303) 385-1283

Bicycle Routes on the San Juan National Forest. Produced by the U.S. Forest Service.
Available from the San Juan National Forest Association, a nonprofit organization that helps the U.S. Forest Service promote public education, conservation, and interpretation of natural and cultural resources. The booklet's revised edition includes descriptions and maps for 37 rides (including on road and off-road), from easy to expert, located on public lands in southwest Colorado. Contact the San Juan National Forest Association at P.O. Box 2261, Durango, CO 81301, or call (303) 385-1210.

Notes on the trail: Initially, the route follows an old four-wheel-drive road paralleling Hermosa Creek. Imbedded rocks are numerous, creating a jarring ride at times, but the trail's gentle decline makes the pedaling easy. After 5 miles, the route crosses Hermosa Creek once near Big Bend, and a second time a mile farther just before Salt Creek. In the past, these 2 streams required portaging through swift-moving, knee-deep waters, but they are now covered by footbridges. (There is a third, unbridged water crossing, but only your toes may get wet.) Hereafter, the route grades to single-track, which first hugs the stream's bank and then gradually rises up the creek's eastern slopes. After 2 lengthy climbs (the first near Little Elk Creek, the second and more strenuous past Dutch Creek), the remaining trail contours the hillsides and then exits at the southern trailhead onto County Road 201 (FS 576), a maintained dirt road. The ensuing descent to Hermosa is fast and furious. Beware of washboards, loose gravel, and vehicular traffic.

RIDE 56 *LIME CREEK*

This is a great family mountain bike ride—it is a bit unusual to find ten miles of relatively flat road in this part of the Rocky Mountains. This route follows the original highway from Durango up to Silverton, used by cars and buses for over 30 years. Abandoned in 1959, when the state highway department paved the road over Coal Bank Pass, this route still can take you to either side of the pass without the steep climb.

The Lime Creek Road winds through smooth-patterned aspen stands, then spruce and fir forests with many openings and vistas, including spectacular views of the Needle Mountains just outside the Weminuche Wilderness Area (largest in Colorado). Near the route's end, the road enters the old Lime Creek Burn, where once-charred lodgepole pines contrast with healthy Engelmann spruce on the mountainsides. Culturally-minded riders may want to study the remnants of the "China Wall," a hand-built rock guardrail located about four miles from the route's beginning. Stop at the interpretive sign along the highway going up the north side of Coal Bank Pass for a bit of history.

The average rider will find this 11-mile route an easy one-way trip, although the rocky dirt road will make riding more difficult for inexperienced cyclists. The one-way route can be completed in under two hours.

The high altitude usually offers the greatest difficulty for those visiting from lower elevations. Only intermediate or stronger riders should attempt the loop option, because half of the loop follows the paved Durango-Silverton Highway, which climbs steeply over Coal Bank Pass (10,661′).

RIDE 56 *LIME CREEK*

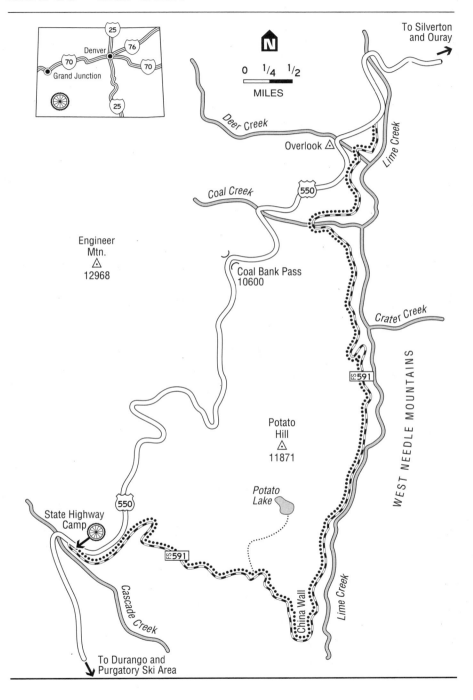

To Silverton and Ouray

Deer Creek

Overlook ⚠

Lime Creek

550

Coal Creek

Engineer Mtn.
⚠
12968

Coal Bank Pass
10600

Crater Creek

591

Potato Hill
⚠
11871

WEST NEEDLE MOUNTAINS

Potato Lake

State Highway Camp

550

591

Cascade Creek

China Wall

Lime Creek

To Durango and Purgatory Ski Area

Denver

Grand Junction

25

76

70

70

25

N

0 1/4 1/2

MILES

Just around the corner from Lime Creek are miles of trails at Purgatory Ski Resort. Photo: Marona Photography/Purgatory Ski Resort.

[Ride information was submitted by Don Hoffheins,* Kremmling, Colorado.—G. B.]

General location: Lime Creek is between Durango and Silverton, just north of Purgatory Ski Area and south of Molas Pass, off US 550.

Elevation change: Elevations range from 8,800´ to 9,800´, with a total elevation gain of about 1,400´ from south to north.

Season: This route is rideable from snow-thaw to snowfall—generally late

---

*Don Hoffheins, employed by the U.S. Forest Service in Colorado, served as editor for the booklet *Bicycle Routes on the San Juan National Forest*. Except for using bikes for commuting to school or work, Don had not ridden much before 1985. Then, while recovering from a leg injury that prevented his normal weekly runs, he began riding. A

June to early October. The ideal time is early September to mid-October, when summer rains have decreased and autumn colors are at their peak.

Services: There are no services along this route. Purgatory, Cascade Village (a few miles south), and the town of Silverton (11 miles to the north) offer most visitor services.

Hazards: This route is also used by motor vehicles, all-terrain vehicles, and motorcycles, so watch out for other traffic as you ride. Granted, the surrounding mountainscape begs for your attention, but the rocky road surface can always cause a spill if you are not careful. The altitude and rapidly changing weather and temperature may pose hazards for the unprepared.

Rescue index: Due to the high amount of use the Lime Creek Road receives, you can seldom travel the route without seeing someone. Emergency help, on the other hand, may take a long time to arrive. For emergencies, the State Highway Camp is just across the road from the parking area at the route's beginning; Cascade Village is a mile or so to the south.

Land status: San Juan National Forest.

Maps: USGS 7.5 minute quadrangles: Engineer Mountain and Snowden Peak, Colorado. USGS 1:50,000 scale county maps: La Plata #1 and San Juan #1, Colorado. *San Juan National Forest Recreation Map.*

Finding the trail: The southern end of the Lime Creek route is located about 30 miles north of Durango on US 550. A large parking area is on the south side of the road, with signs for Lime Creek Road (Forest Service Road 591). Look for the large sweeping highway bend a mile past Cascade Village and just north of Purgatory Ski Area. If you are traveling from the north on US 550 out of Silverton, cross over Molas Pass. Just as the highway begins to climb towards Coal Banks Pass, the northern end of Lime Creek Road turns off to the south.

Sources of additional information:

San Juan National Forest
701 Camino del Rio, Room 301
Durango, CO 81301
(303) 247-4874

Animas Ranger District
110 West Eleventh Street
Durango, CO 81301
(303) 385-1283

(continued from page 292)

year later, he joined some friends on his first mountain bike ride on the Hermosa Creek Trail. The air was cool, the sun was warm, peace and quiet filled the valley, and he spied a coyote standing in a meadow—Don was hooked. Now he bikes several times weekly and competes in numerous cycling races each year.

Bicycle Routes on the San Juan National Forest. Produced by the U.S. Forest Service. Available from the San Juan National Forest Association, P.O. Box 2261, Durango, CO 81301, or call (303) 385-1210.

Notes on the trail: The ride can begin at either end of Lime Creek Road but, described here, the route is one-way, beginning at the south end near Purgatory. Leaving the parking area, the Lime Creek Road (FS 591) heads generally east for about 4 miles. The road rolls over small ridges and through subdued drainages with short climbs. It turns north to traverse well above Lime Creek and then drops down next to the stream.

A great side trip is a visit to Potato Lake, reached via a 1-mile trail. This natural, subalpine lake offers a peaceful setting surrounded by the rocky landscape. If you do not have time for this side trip, at least stop along the lily-covered ponds near the Potato Lake trailhead.

Here is a tip for the "roadies." The Durango-Silverton Highway is the route for the Iron Horse Bicycle Classic held annually over Memorial Day weekend since 1972. This tour de force road trek originated as a challenge between Durango cyclists and personnel of the Denver and Rio Grande/Silverton Narrow Gauge Railroad. At the sound of the train whistle in Durango, cyclists raced the train 50 miles to Silverton, surmounting 2 tough mountain passes en route (each over 10,500′ in elevation).

Today, hundreds of cyclists make the trek, most at a more casual pace. Serious riders still match their strength and stamina in the race between man and machine, hoping to better the record time of 2 hours and 6 minutes. Professional and amateur class mountain bike races have since been added to the multi-day Iron Horse event.

RIDE 57 *KENNEBEC PASS*

The La Plata Mountains are characteristic of the "rugged Rockies," and few other area rides venture through such a complete transition of vegetative zones and geologic formations. High, craggy peaks of mostly barren rock surround La Plata Canyon. Sculpted by ice, water, and wind, these light-colored volcanics have intruded brilliant sedimentary rocks, which lap against the mountains' flanks and fill lower valleys. Sparse grasses and fields of wildflowers struggle to grow on the peaks and in the high mountain meadows. The lower valleys and ridges are blanketed with dense stands of spruce, fir, and aspen, whereas the foothills support pine and oak brush.

The La Plata Range has a strong history of hard-rock mining, with some gold and silver mines still in operation. The Gold King Mine millsite attracts both amateur and professional photographers. History buffs and those wishing to

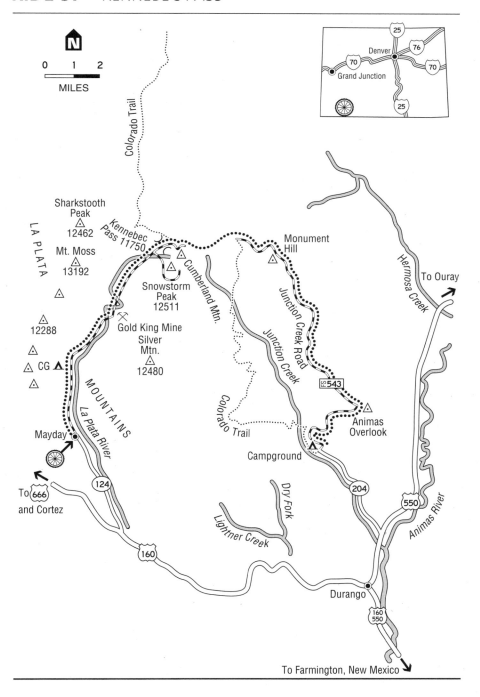

try their hand at panning for gold will find many pleasure-filled hours in La Plata Canyon. Along the Junction Creek descent, the Animas Overlook offers scenic views of the regional setting plus interpretive signs explaining the area's history and management.

This point-to-point ride is 28 miles long. Although most of the route is on well-maintained gravel roads, it is considered an expert route for riders in good condition. There are many miles of steady, uphill climbing, with the steepest parts above 10,000'. Near Kennebec Pass, four-wheel-drive roads are typically narrow, with ruts and rocks that may make bike handling difficult. From Kennebec Pass the route drops across an unstable talus section where walking is recommended, then through a series of tight switchbacks, before resuming on good dirt roads down to Junction Creek.

[This ride description was submitted by Don Hoffheins, Kremmling, Colorado.—G. B.]

General location: The La Plata Mountains are located just west of Durango.
Elevation change: From Mayday (elevation 8,735') to Kennebec Pass (11,600') the route climbs 2,865' over 10 miles. From Kennebec Pass on, most of the route is downhill, although there are a couple of climbs, totaling almost 400'. The ride ends (below Junction Creek Campground) at 7,000'. Thus, total climb for the one-way route is about 3,200'.
Season: Use of this route is limited by the yearly snowfall; it is typically open for a 3-month period from July through September. Although wildflowers reach their peak in August, afternoon thunderstorms with lightning are common and may limit riding times. Late September to early October is a good time to ride and enjoy the fall colors.
Services: Durango has all visitor services, including several bicycle shops. Hesperus, at the intersection of US 160 and County Road 124 south of Mayday, has a small gas station and store, cafe, and phone. Water is available at the Kroeger Campground above Mayday, but no other commercial services or water are available along the route.
Hazards: The most hazardous section of the route is the Sliderock Trail east of Kennebec Pass. Here, the trail crosses talus slopes of loose, angular rocks—walking is recommended. Watch for vehicular traffic on both the La Plata Canyon Road and Junction Creek Road, and be especially cautious when rounding curves that have washboards. Sudden weather changes and summer lightning storms near Kennebec Pass can be potentially hazardous. An overnight stay on the mountain is not unheard of if problems arise, so be prepared for cold, wet weather at all times.
Rescue index: This route is relatively close to Durango, but it would take at least an hour for emergency vehicles to reach Kennebec Pass from either road. Be sure to ride with others and leave word of your travel plans.
Land status: San Juan National Forest.
Maps: USGS 7.5 minute quadrangles: Durango West, Hesperus, La Plata

Canyon, and Monument Hill, Colorado. USGS 1:50,000 scale county maps: La Plata #2 and La Plata #3, Colorado. Unfortunately, these slightly out-of-date topographic quadrangles may not show the trail or even the upper Junction Creek Road. *The San Juan National Forest Recreation Map* shows both roads and the Colorado Trail/Sliderock Trail section.

Finding the trail: From Durango, travel west on US 160 about 11 miles to Hesperus. Turn north on CR 124 and go another 4 miles to Mayday, where pavement ends and the ride begins. To get to the east trailhead in Junction Creek, travel west out of Durango on Twenty-fifth Street and CR 204 about 4 miles. Pavement ends at the national forest boundary.

Sources of additional information:

San Juan National Forest
701 Camino Del Rio, Room 301
Durango, CO 81301
(303) 247-4874

Animas Ranger District
110 West Eleventh Street
Durango, CO 81301
(303) 385-1283

Mancos Ranger District
41595 East US 160
P.O. Box 330
Mancos, CO 81328
(303) 533-7716

Bicycle Routes on the San Juan National Forest. Produced by the U.S. Forest Service. Available from the San Juan National Forest Association, P.O. Box 2261, Durango, CO 81301, or call (303) 385-1210.

Notes on the trail: Most of the route—the long, grinding ascent up La Plata Canyon and even longer descent along Junction Creek Road—is quite evident. But a few words are needed to guide you along the route's summit.

About 9 miles above Mayday at the panoramic summit (after climbing up through Cumberland Basin), turn right through the parking area and follow signs for the Colorado Trail. Immediately thereafter turn left. Be sure not to take the main jeep road branching to the right up to "the Notch" between Cumberland Mountain and Snowden Peak, unless of course you are only taking a side trip for the views. After riding east over a couple of rolling ridges to Kennebec Pass, you will begin the rough, talus descent on the Sliderock Trail. Continue down a steep trail that bears left and leads through a couple of tight switchbacks to the Champion Ventures Road. Go left here and in a mile you will connect with the main Junction Creek Road. Turn right onto 8 miles of undulating road followed by another 8 miles of downhill to the Junction Creek

Campground. One mile past the campground, pavement begins on CR 204 at the national forest boundary.

For cyclists seeking an even *greater* challenge, this route can be ridden as a loop beginning and ending in Durango. This variation will approach 50 miles in length with over 5,400′ of elevation gain and is recommended for experienced, well-conditioned riders (to say the least).

RIDE 58 *DRY FORK LOOP*

Dedicated in 1988, the 470-mile Colorado Trail succeeded in connecting Denver with Durango. Created more recently, the Dry Fork Loop segment provides area cyclists with a backcountry route close to Durango. Some people ride only as far as the new Junction Creek footbridge and enjoy a day of good stream fishing.

You will ride past ridges and mesas resulting from the La Plata Mountains' uplift. From Gudy's Rest (named in honor of Gudy Gaskill, the Colorado Trail's principal coordinator), enjoy the scenic panorama of the forested La Plata foothills bordering Durango. Occasional views of the La Plata Mountains are quite pleasing, especially throughout early summer and again in late fall when peaks are snowcapped.

Most of the ride passes through pine-timbered stands, but scattered oak brush, aspen, and cottonwood add variety, especially during fall, when leaves turn to beautiful shades of yellow, gold, and crimson. It is not unusual to spot deer and elk foraging amidst the trailside foliage.

This loop ride contains six miles of single-track, three miles of dirt road, and nine miles of paved road. It is excellent for intermediate riders wanting to perfect their bike handling skills, a challenge for novice cyclists, and pure delight for advanced bikers. Climbs and descents are moderately difficult. The most technical portion is in the Junction Creek area, where narrow, single-track sections are routed along steep canyon sides. A series of tight switchbacks scaling the west slope of Junction Creek will challenge any rider.

[This ride description was submitted by Don Hoffheins, Kremmling, Colorado.—G. B.]

General location: This route begins and ends in Durango and loops counterclockwise (west) into the foothills of the La Plata Mountains.

Elevation change: Total climbing is 1,480′. Durango lies at 6,520′. The Colorado Trail starts at 7,000′ at Junction Creek; Gudy's Rest is at 8,000′; and the end of the Dry Fork Trail is at 7,400′.

Season: From June through late fall. The Dry Fork Road is very slick when wet, so it should be avoided after snowmelt and rainfall. Weather changes

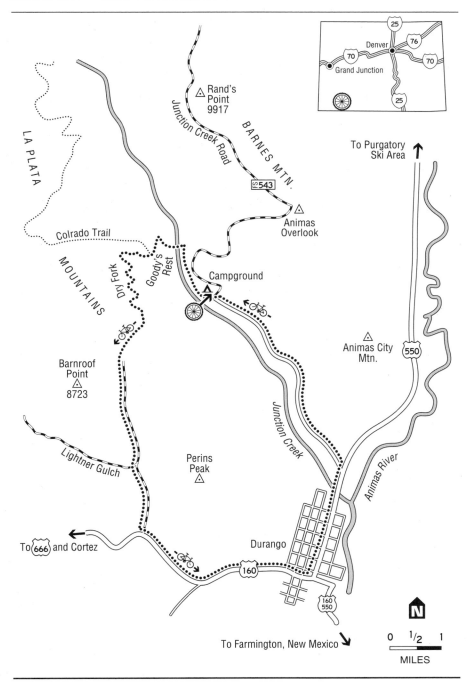

An endless view from Gudy's Rest. Photo: Don Hoffheins.

rapidly, even at these lower elevations, so be prepared for unseasonably cold or wet conditions. Since the lowest portions of the area are big-game wildlife winter range, early season use is discouraged.

Services: No services are available along the route, but Durango is a short distance away and offers all visitor services. With this convenience, grab a bite to eat before or after the ride and travel light, carrying only a small snack and water.

Hazards: The single-track portion along Junction Creek, a tantalizing challenge for many, can be hazardous for the unexperienced or careless rider. The Forest Service–maintained trail may contain a number of obstacles, including imbedded rocks, tree roots, log water bars, and patches of thick, coarse sand. Use caution when pedaling the narrow, paved county roads as their graveled shoulders are often uneven. Changing weather conditions can always create problems, but at this intermediate elevation they are more an inconvenience than a hazard.

Rescue index: The route stays relatively close to Durango and there are private residences along the paved roads.

Land status: San Juan National Forest. The loop follows county and state roads to and from the Colorado and Dry Fork trails, respectively, which are located in the national forest. Remember to stay on the roads in the Dry Fork area because here the adjacent Division of Wildlife lands are closed to mountain bikes.

Maps: USGS 7.5 minute quadrangle: Durango West, Colorado. USGS 1:50,000 scale county maps: La Plata #2 and San Juan #3, Colorado. *San Juan National Forest Recreation Map.* These maps will help orient you to the area in general, but neither the Colorado Trail nor Dry Fork Loop is shown.

Finding the trail: The Colorado Trail's Junction Creek trailhead is 3 miles west from the center of Durango (25th Street) on County Road 204. The Dry Fork trailhead (trail end) is found 4.5 miles west of Durango on US 160, then 4 miles north on CR 207 (Forest Service Road 572).

Sources of additional information:

> San Juan National Forest
> 701 Camino del Rio, Room 301
> Durango, CO 81301
> (303) 247-4874
>
> Animas Ranger District
> 110 West Eleventh Street
> Durango, CO 81301
> (303) 385-1283
>
> *Bicycle Routes on the San Juan National Forest.* Produced by the U.S. Forest Service. Available from the San Juan National Forest Association, P.O. Box 2261, Durango, CO 81301, or call (303) 385-1210.

Notes on the trail: This section of the Colorado Trail begins as single-track following the valley bottom of Junction Creek. After crossing 1 small side stream, the trail gradually climbs the canyon's side (where portions are exposed to steep slopes), then crosses the footbridge spanning Junction Creek.

Now the single-track trail ascends the west side of the canyon through a set of challenging, but rideable, switchbacks at about an 8% grade to the high point at Gudy's Rest. One-quarter mile farther, the Dry Fork Trail single-track intersects from the left (south); turn onto it. This section descends gradually, crosses a small drainage, climbs a minor ridge, then continues to descend to the national forest boundary. An effortless coast down CR 207 (FS 572) concludes the off-road portion of the loop.

The Colorado Trail in its entirety is a multi-use trail system. This portion of the Durango section is very popular with a variety of recreationists who are seeking a rewarding backcountry experience. Always abide by the principles of mountain bike etiquette and never let your quest for fun be at the expense of other trail users or the environment.

Alamosa

There's more to south central Colorado than the Great Sand Dunes National Monument. Admittedly, the monument is quite a startling attraction, seemingly out of place at the base of the snow-peaked Sangre de Cristo Mountains. Most people in search of mountain biking adventures don't consider biking in south central Colorado. The fact is that even though National Off-Road Bicycle Association (NORBA)–sanctioned races are held in this region, organizations in other areas, particularly near larger towns and resorts, do a better job of promoting and publicizing bike routes in their backyards. South central Colorado doesn't hold a candle to them in terms of getting the word out. Ironically, this section has more rideable months out of the year than other parts of the state.

The truth of the matter is that there are lots of relatively unknown but fabulous mountain bike trails here. Problem is that though trails and jeep roads exist, they are not always marked. Complete, detailed, and up-to-date maps do not exist. On the maps that do exist, the roads and trails shown are generally accurate but not complete. In the summer of 1993, with the help of Eric Burt of Kristi Mountain Sports in Alamosa and Steve Luxemberg, a volunteer national forest worker out of the Saguache Ranger District office, I discovered that the National Forest Service and the Bureau of Land Management have hopes and plans to publicize mountain biking on these lands. Much preparatory work, which includes scouting, signing, enhancing, and reinforcing the trail and roads, needs to be done. With the perennial small budget and a handful of dedicated volunteers, the Forest Service, BLM, and local bike clubs are slowly but surely establishing the routes and getting the word out.

So what are these unknown trails like? At least moderate technical skills are required, although experienced novices with the right attitude can manage quite well. On the other hand, for all riders, above-average physical fitness combined with the right frame of mind is a necessity. Bikers who want a backcountry adventure that tests their map- and terrain-reading skills and are comfortable with varying degrees of uncertainty will have a terrific time in this area. Since uncertainty can make for a long day's ride, long-term endurance is important. Novice riders with limited experience in the backcountry and time on the saddle will probably not enjoy these rides as much and may even make others in the riding group uncomfortable. Still, for those who want to test their backcountry leadership skills, having a novice in the group could be interesting, to say the least. So, if you're truly adventurous and want to get away from the hordes of mountain biking maniacs, check out this undiscovered region of Colorado. And if you haven't visited the Great Sand Dunes National Monument, it's worth a side trip.

Sources of additional information:

Kristi Mountain Sports
San Luis Valley Cycling Club
7565 West US 160
Alamosa, CO 81101
(719) 589-8319 or (719) 589-9759
Ask for Eric Burt, the owner. He is instrumental in promoting mountain biking here.

Creede Bike Club
Box 434
Creede, CO 81130
(719) 658-2351
Ask for Robert Sullivan. Like Eric of Kristi Mountain Sports, he is a great source for ride suggestions and activities in this area.

Bureau of Land Management offices in the south central region:

San Luis Resource Area
1921 State Street
Alamosa, CO 81101
(719) 589-4975

Gunnison Resource Area
216 North Colorado
Gunnison, CO 81230
(303) 641-0471

Rio Grande National Forest Headquarters
1803 West US 160
Monte Vista, CO 81144
(719) 852-5941

U.S. Forest Service district offices in this region:

Creede Ranger District
Third and Creede Avenue
Box 270
Creede, CO 81130
(719) 658-2556

Del Norte Ranger District
13308 West US 160
Box 40
Del Norte, CO 81132
(719) 657-3321

Saguache Ranger District
46525 CO 114
P.O. Box 67
Saguache, CO 81149
(719) 655-2547

In 1993, this office had a small, mostly volunteer staff that scouted and marked mountain bike routes. The ride descriptions of their routes have been compiled and are available to the public.

San Juan National Forest
Pagosa Ranger District
P.O. Box 310
Pagosa Springs, CO 81147
(303) 264-2268

Mancos Ranger District
41595 East US 160
Box 330
Mancos, CO 81328
(303) 533-7716

Great Sand Dunes National Monument
11500 CO 150
Mosca, CO 81146
(719) 378-2312

Chambers of Commerce:

Alamosa Chamber of Commerce
Cole Park
Alamosa, CO 81101
(719) 589-3681

Del Norte Chamber of Commerce
P.O. Box 148
1160 Grand Aveune
Del Norte, CO 81132
(719) 657-2845

Monte Vista Chamber of Commerce
1125 Park Avenue
Monte Vista, CO 81144
(719) 852-2731

Sangre de Cristo Chamber of Commerce / Economic Development Council
P.O. Box 9
San Luis, CO 81152
(719) 672-3355

The Colorado Guide, by Bruce Caughey and Dean Winstanley. Golden, Colorado: Fulcrum Publishing, 1991. To order, write Fulcrum Publishing, 350 Indiana Street, Suite 350, Golden, CO 80401.

RIDE 59 *LIMEKILN–GOPHER GULCH LOOP*

When you're riding in these parts, one thing for certain is that you won't bump into anyone else! In fact, this 13.5-mile loop was completely scouted and marked in mid-1993 by Eric Burt and his biking buddies of the San Luis Valley Cycling Club. Eventually, part of this loop was included in a NORBA-sanctioned race held later that year. Eric and his cohort Steve volunteered to show the route to Joëlle and me earlier that summer. At that time, we wound up still scouting and marking the route with cairns and taking more trail notes.

On behalf of my riding buddies, we're proud to include this 13.5-mile, moderately challenging loop in this book. In addition to being a fun, enjoyable ride, its terrain is not like that of most other rides in the state. It is more desert-like in vegetation and landscape, and the elevation is lower, which makes for a longer riding season compared to regions farther north. Riders ranging from intermediate-to-expert will enjoy the technical sections on the loop. Less skilled riders can still join in the fun of this route because the technical sections are not long or overly difficult. Climbs are short and the trail is mostly double-track. Several sites of deteriorating limekilns, found near the beginning of the loop, offer a hint of the area's history.

General location: This loop is about 10 miles west of Monte Vista, which is approximately 230 miles southwest of Denver.
Elevation change: The loop begins at approximately 8,100′ and reaches its highest point, 9,000′, in about 7 miles. Total elevation gain is roughly 900′.
Season: This loop can be ridden between early April and mid-September. During the summer, this region can be a scorcher; spring and early fall are the most enjoyable times. Though the route is rideable for most of the fall, I don't recommend it after mid-September, as hunting is popular here.

RIDE 59   *LIMEKILN–GOPHER GULCH LOOP*

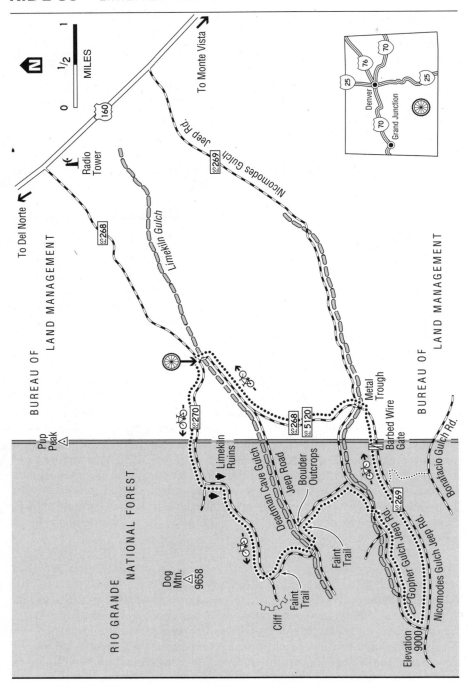

Eric, Joëlle, and Steve were willing to share the road but the herd of sheep decided they wanted nothing to do with them, prefering the other side of the gulch.

Services: No services are available at the loop access point or throughout the route. Streams and creeks are intermittent, so you should bring enough water at the outset. Amenities such as drinkable water, food, toilets, public phones, as well as restaurants and a few lodging establishments can be found in Monte Vista. The nearest public campgrounds are Rock Creek and Comstock in the Rio Grande National Forest, about 2 miles south of Monte Vista, reached via jeep road, approximately 14 miles from CO 15. Note that drinkable water is not available at these two sites. No fee is charged but reservations are recommended (call (800) 283-2267). Dozens of other public camping sites are also found within the national forest boundary, though farther away. For more information on these fee and no-fee sites, contact the Rio Grande National Forest as listed below. There are lots of private campgrounds in the vicinity as well, and the chambers of commerce of the San Luis Valley Tourism Council are a great source for this sort of information (see addresses below).

Hazards: Other than the usual loose rocks and bumpy terrain, there are a few hazards that require mention here. Watch out for strands of barbed wire used as gates across the road. They're hard to spot, especially when you're cruising at a fast speed. Another condition to be aware of is the spiny, needlelike cacti that are found alongside the roads throughout the loop. The other hazard that demands caution is rattlesnakes. These sunbathing beauties can sometimes be found snoozing in the middle of a jeep road. Look at it this way: they'll help you perfect your quick-hopping reflexes.

Rescue index: Should you or any of your riding companions need serious medical attention, rest assured that virtually every inch of the loop is four-wheel-drive vehicle accessible for emergency evacuation. However, it's a long way to medical help, as the nearest phones are back in Del Norte and Monte Vista, about 12 and 11 miles, respectively, from the starting point of the ride.

Land status: Bureau of Land Management. Rio Grande National Forest.

Maps: USGS 7.5 minute quads: Monte Vista and Dog Mountain, Colorado.

Finding the trail: Drive out of Monte Vista on US 160, due northwest, for about 9.5 miles and, at this point, watch for a radio tower adjacent to the road. Nearby is the intersection of Forest Service Road 268, a two-wheel-drive dirt road. Turn left (southwest) onto FS 268 and follow it for nearly 3.5 miles alongside a stretch of rock cliffs, and eventually you'll come to an intersection in a clearing. Here, FS 270 branches off to the right (west) and FS 268 continues to the left (southwest). Park your car here and begin the loop from this intersection.

Sources of additional information:

Rio Grande National Forest
Forest Headquarters
1803 West US 160
Monte Vista, CO 81144
(719) 852-5941

Kristi Mountain Sports
San Luis Valley Cycling Club
7565 West US 160
Alamosa, CO 81101
(719) 589-8319 or (719) 589-9759
Ask for Eric Burt, the store owner. He is instrumental in promoting mountain biking here and can suggest other rides.

Bureau of Land Management
San Luis Resource Area
1921 State Street
Alamosa, CO 81101
(719) 589-4975

Sangre de Cristo Chamber of Commerce / Economic Development Council
P.O. Box 9
San Luis, CO 81152
(719) 672-3355

San Luis Valley Tourism Council
P.O. Box 609
Monte Vista, CO 81144
(800) 835-7254

The Colorado Guide, by Bruce Caughey and Dean Winstanley. Golden, Colorado: Fulcrum Publishing, 1991. To order, write Fulcrum Publishing, 350 Indiana Street, Suite 350, Golden, CO 80401.

Alamosa Chamber of Commerce
Cole Park
Alamosa, CO 81101
(719) 589-3681

Del Norte Chamber of Commerce
P.O. Box 148
1160 Grand Aveune
Del Norte, CO 81132
(719) 657-2845

Monte Vista Chamber of Commerce
1125 Park Avenue
Monte Vista, CO 81144
(719) 852-2731

Rio Grande County Museum and Cultural Center
580 Oak Street
P.O. Box 430
Del Norte, CO 81132
(719) 657-2847

Notes on the trail: Begin the loop by heading west on FS 270, in a counter-clockwise direction. After approximately 1.5 miles, keep your eyes peeled for another jeep road leading off on your left. Make a left turn onto this dirt road (not marked by a Forest Service sign) and head south. Straight ahead, immediately after taking the turn and slightly uphill on your right (west), is the first of two limekiln ruins on this route.

This abandoned kiln is unfenced and easily accessible. If you stop to inspect it, help protect it from further deterioration by staying out of the actual kiln. Between the early 1870s and 1940s, lime was mined from the vicinity and slaked (combined with water) in kilns such as this one to produce mortar, plaster, whitewash, and disinfectants. Rich deposits of lime, and the abundance of pinyon pine trees needed to fuel the kilns, made this process economically important to this region. Demand rose for the slaked lime from as far away as Kansas.

Several yards farther, after climbing a steep and loose rock segment, you'll find more kiln ruins on your left. The jeep road is narrow and faint in spots, but don't worry: it becomes obvious within a few yards. When you've reached the top of this little climb, enjoy the 360-degree view of lonely landscape and then get set to zip down a short but technical portion of the jeep road. Take care to control your speed down the loose rock and boulder segments, for if you crash and burn, you may find yourself plagued with millions of tiny, annoying cactus needles. To be sure, clusters of cacti hide behind shrubs and boulders.

After that fast downhill, climb again and, at the top of the next hill, the view becomes more expansive. Make sure you look back, towards the northeast and, if it's not hazy, you can see the white landscape of the Great Sand Dunes National Monument with Blanca Peak (14,345´) immediately to the southeast of it. At this point, you've pedaled just over 2 miles from your car—how much more fun can you have in such a short distance?

Hang on to your helmet. There's more thrilling, roller-coaster cruising to come, punctuated by short, technical segments. Continue on the rugged jeep road, climbing to another 360-degree view. If you're quiet and lucky, you may spot a deer or two in the distance. Just as soon as you reach the top, it's time to descend, this time into a basin where several trails meet. At the time of our ride, this junction was unmarked. The right fork, due southeast, leads you to a dead end, stopping at the edge of a cliff. Take the left fork, a jeep trail, as it continues down due east and, in less than a half mile, you connect with Deadman Cave Gulch jeep trail. Getting to this connection point, however, is slightly tricky in that the trails and junctions are not completely marked; at least they weren't when we rode this loop. (Eric tells me that better markers have since replaced the cairns we built along the way.) A few yards farther, keep an eye out for a marker or cairn that indicates a faint, double-track jeep trail leading off to the right. This portion is steep and rocky—a technical wiz's delight. After several yards, as the trail snakes its way through a small valley, the double-track becomes even more faint with overgrown vegetation. Pedal a few more yards and bingo! You've come to the junction of Deadman Cave Gulch Road.

Take the left turn onto Deadman Cave Gulch Road, as if you're heading back down to town and your car. Follow the double-track and continue cruising up and down in a wide, open, narrow valley. Almost a half mile from the left turn onto Deadman, you reach a ridgetop and begin a gradual downhill run, still on the double-track. About a half mile from the ridge, look for a marker or cairn that signifies the continuation of Deadman, bearing left. The faint trail on your right leads to Gopher Gulch jeep road. This is a good point to check your time and the weather, for if you need to shorten the loop, you can do that by continuing on Deadman Cave Gulch Road, returning to your starting point in approximately 3 miles.

Assuming you have your heart set on riding the complete loop, connect to Gopher Gulch jeep road by taking the faint trail to your right, riding through low boulder outcroppings. If you're unsure of the trail, consider this landmark: Look for a stand of aspen trees, which are uncharacteristic to the desertlike terrain. Turn your back to the aspen trees and you should be facing the faint trail threading through a pile of boulder outcroppings. As soon as you pedal through the outcroppings, the trail immediately flattens out and begins to appear more defined. In less than a quarter mile, you reach the junction of Gopher Gulch Road, which is indicated by a marker or cairn. (This is another opportunity to shorten the loop. Taking the left turn (east) and following Gopher Gulch Road down will return you to your car in approximately 2.5 miles.)

To complete the loop as originally planned, turn right (west) onto Gopher Gulch Road. At this point, you have pedaled just over 5.5 miles from the starting point. Go into and across Gopher Gulch, riding up the other side of the creek bed, which, more than likely, is dry. Stay on the faint trail as it skirts the creek bed for almost a half mile. At that half-mile point, the trail plunges into the dry creek bed and climbs out on the other side to another trail leading uphill. Don't follow that trail. Instead of following the trail out of the creek bed, ride up the creek for several yards; you'll see the trail reemerging from the creek on your left. Continue on the trail with the creek now on your right for nearly a mile, at which point the path crosses the creek bed again and emerges on the other side. This is your last dry creek crossing. With the creek now on your left, follow the jeep trail up and away from the creek.

The trail gradually widens into a jeep trail and, after a half-mile climb from the last creek crossing, you reach the junction of Gopher Gulch and the top of Nicomodes Gulch jeep road. The 360-degree view of the surrounding mountain range is lovely and makes a peaceful backdrop to a camping spot, as a campfire ring confirms.

From this spot, it's a 6-mile downhill cruise back to the starting point and the completion of the loop. Turn onto Nicomodes Gulch jeep road, FS 269, which may still be unmarked. Follow the jeep road due northeast as it becomes more well defined as a four-wheel-drive, smooth, dirt road.

The downhill cruise is gradual and delightful and your bike will be yearning to fly. Go ahead, let it go. Have fun dodging around and over the occasional loose rocks and boulders on the road. Just make sure you have enough air in your tires or you'll wind up like Eric—a pinch flat with a tiny gash in his tire to show for it. We all chuckled and watched our resourceful buddy repair the gash temporarily by lining the inside of the tire with a PowerBar wrapper. (See, there's a logical reason why those wrappers are so tough to rip open.) Our chuckles became louder when, in the amidst of his repair, we realized that a herd of sheep was headed our way. If you've ever ridden in a sea of whining sheep, you also know of the interesting road hazards that accompany it. Needless to say, our continued descent on Nicomodes Gulch Road was *different*. Maybe you'll get lucky, too, when you cruise down this portion of the loop.

As you continue your journey, you'll notice groves of aspen and long-needle pine trees growing among the boulders and scrub. About 2 miles after your turn onto Nicomodes Gulch Road, a jeep road leading to Bonafacio Gulch Road connects to it. Bypass this turnoff, continuing on Nicomodes Gulch Road, past huge red boulders on the now clearly defined four-wheel-drive dirt road. About a half mile farther, watch out for a barbed-wire fence across the road. This is the boundary line between the Rio Grande National Forest and BLM land. Remember to leave the gate as you found it—open or closed. Pedal another half mile and you come to a clearing that seems like a major intersection of dirt roads. There is a weathered metal trough here, and, if you look to your left (west), you see a faint double-track trail. That's the lower end of Gopher Gulch Road. At this point, you've reconnected with what appears to be FS 268 on the map. But it's identified by a marker as FS 5120.

Follow FS 5120 and, after nearly a mile, bypass the lower end of Deadman Cave Gulch Road. Continue to follow the main road for about 2 miles more, over flat terrain, back to the starting point and your car. Approximate total mileage of the loop is 13.5 miles.

RIDE 60 *UTE PASS LOOP*

You aren't likely to see anyone else on this 17-mile loop. That's because it hasn't been publicized as a mountain bike route, at least not before 1993. In the summer of that year, Joëlle and I hooked up with Steve Luxemberg, a summer volunteer worker for the Saguache Ranger District of the Rio Grande National Forest. His assignment was to help scout existing jeep roads, mark them with mountain bicycle signposts, and compile ride descriptions for free public distribution. Not a bad summer job for a New Jersey resident! Steve showed us this loop, which he had just marked a couple of weeks before. Other than his ranger office publication, and this book, you won't find this ride described anywhere else.

Rated intermediate in both stamina and technical skill requirements, the loop uses both two- and four-wheel-drive dirt roads, and contains two hill climbs. The ride begins with the first unrelenting, moderately steep climb to Ute Pass, gaining 1,224′ in just under four miles. After that, the road becomes a fast downhill blast, losing 1,304′ in about 3.5 miles. Next comes the second climb; though not as steep, it gains 1,260′ in approximately 5.25 miles. Once you've topped this final summit, it's a screaming, fast, and technical two-mile downhill back to your car. Combine all that with a splendid mixture of expansive rolling meadows, desertlike terrain and vegetation, contrasted by lush forests of pine and aspen, distant views of the Sangre de Cristo mountain range, and sweet, singing creeks. What you get is one satisfying mountain bike ride.

General location: The access point of the the loop is about 3 miles northwest of Saguache, which is about 240 miles southwest of Denver.
Elevation change: The loop begins at 8,680′ and climbs 1,264′ in almost 4

RIDE 60 *UTE PASS LOOP*

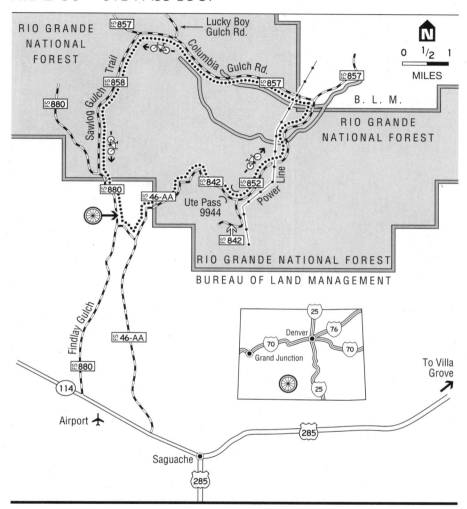

miles to Ute Pass, elevation 9,944´. For the next 3.5 miles, you lose all that you gained and then some, reaching the lowest point of the loop at 8,640´ just after the halfway point of the loop. After that, the route climbs again, gaining 1,260´ in about 5.25 miles. Total elevation gain is 1,304´.

Season: Since the highest point is under 10,000´, chances are good that the trail will remain snow-free for most of the year, probably from mid-April to mid-November. Check with the Colorado Division of Wildlife for hunting season

Joëlle and Steve ascending Columbia Gulch Road, a gentle uphill section.

dates and specific locations (303) 297-1192. In the past, hunting season began in mid-October and was limited to private land only.

Services: The only service available at the route access point is a small area for parking your car. You need to bring your own water and food before leaving town. Creeks designated on maps should be considered intermittent year-round. A few restaurants, lodging, and public phones can be found in Saguache, just 3 miles southeast from the loop's starting point. The nearest public campground is Buffalo Pass in the Rio Grande National Forest, about 24 miles west of Saguache. A few private campgrounds in and around Saguache are closer to the loop. Joëlle and I found a very clean, private campground, complete with shower and laundry facilities, in Villa Grove, nearly 20 miles northeast of Saguache on US 285. Call the San Luis Valley Campground, (719) 655-2220.

Hazards: Watch out for rattlesnakes near the beginning of the route, where the elevation is lower and the ground is drier. Be aware of any approaching thunder and lightning clouds, especially since the first 6 miles are somewhat exposed, at least enough to be scary during a storm. The last 3.5 miles back to the car are fast, technical descents, covering extremely rocky terrain. Believe me, if you don't have shock absorbers on your bike, you'll wish you did.

Rescue index: Most of the route is made up of two- and four-wheel drive, smooth, dirt roads, so motorized rescue is easy. In fact, after 8.5 miles, you'll find several ranch homes on private property along the loop. The only section that is not easily accessible by vehicles is Sawlog Gulch. Even so, in an extreme emergency, a jeep could be driven on it. Be prepared to administer first aid to yourself or companions while on the trail and to pedal out on your own power. This is not a well-known route, so you shouldn't depend on finding other trail users who may be of help.

Land status: Rio Grande National Forest. Bureau of Land Management. Private property.

Maps: USGS 7.5 minute quads: Saguache, Klondike Mine, and Graveyard Gulch, Colorado. *The Best Trails of Colorado's San Luis Valley.* Produced by the San Luis Valley Economic Development Council, Alamosa, CO 81101. Copyright 1990.

Finding the trail: From the tiny town of Saguache, follow CO 114 west. After about a mile, watch for Forest Service Road 46-AA, a dirt road on your right, just before the municipal airport on your left. Go past this road and continue on CO 114 for approximately 1.5 miles, where you will find another dirt road on your right, marked FS 880, Findlay Gulch. Take a right turn onto this road and follow it for almost 3.5 miles to the junction of FS 858 (Sawlog Gulch Trail). Park at the designated site. Begin your pedaling by backtracking down FS 880 to the first left turn.

Sources of additional information:

Rio Grande National Forest
Saguache District Ranger Office
46525 CO 114
Saguache, CO 81149
(719) 655-2547
Contact them for a copy of their latest mountain bike route descriptions.

Bureau of Land Management
San Luis Resource Area
1921 State Street
Alamosa, CO 81101
(719) 589-4975

Notes on the trail: This is such an easy and obvious route that you probably will refer to your map only a couple times over the course of the ride. The first time may be at the very beginning, within the first 2 miles from your car.

From your parked vehicle, hop on your bike and cruise back down FS 880 for almost 1.5 miles, at which point you turn left (east) onto another dirt road. The terrain throughout this sweet little downhill warm-up is open and dry with desert-type vegetation. After you make the left turn, follow it for a very short distance to the junction of FS 46-AA, another dirt road. Here is your first bicycle sign, an unobtrusive, brown post with a brown and white bicycle symbol sign nailed to it.

Go left onto FS 46-AA. At this point, you have pedaled about 2.25 miles. Now is the time to psyche yourself up to attack the moderately steep, 4-mile climb up to Ute Pass. The beginning of this section takes you through wide open terrain. If you timed it just right, your uphill push will be encouraged by the sight of delightfully colored wildflowers. When you cross the cattle guard into the Rio Grande National Forest, you have pedaled just over 3 miles. The closer you come to Ute Pass at 9,944', the better your view of the San Luis Valley towards the south and the San Juan mountain range towards the southwest. You might have to gear down because the steepness increases during the last 1.5 miles from the top. Road conditions remain fairly smooth and wide with few rocky spots.

Almost 6 miles from the start, you reach the top of Ute Pass. Now comes your reward: an exhilarating downhill flight that's nearly 3.5 miles long. At the top here, there are 2 other jeep roads that lead down from Ute Pass, in addition to the road you just rode up. The road you want—FS 852—follows the overhead power lines downhill, sort of due northeast. This jeep road leads you down the back side of Ute Pass through groves of aspen, offering you occasional glimpses of the Sangre de Cristo mountain range, which may still be snow-covered, depending on the time of year. Be alert—delicate bunches of deeply colored columbines and other wildflowers will try to distract your eye from the rugged, slightly rocky road under your wheels. Slow your descent so that you can comfortably handle the few blind curves in the road. The power lines gradually deviate from your road and soon disappear over a forested ridge on your left (west). Stay on FS 852, the main, more obvious, road, especially when other roads or trails connect to it.

Eventually, the road becomes smoother, turning into a two-wheel-drive, wide, dirt road, and takes you out of the Rio Grande National Forest, into BLM land and then onto private property. Passage through private property is allowed, so long as you stay on the road, as posted signs demand. The road levels out and takes you across a cattle guard, amidst several residental homes. Before you know it, you've come to the junction of FS 852 and FS 857, also known as Columbia Gulch Road.

Are you ready for the second and final major climb of this loop? It gains 1,260' in 5.25 miles, over a gradual, generally smooth, dirt road. Here it comes. Turn left onto FS 857, heading west. In less than a half mile, you pedal through a gate; at this point, you leave BLM land and reenter the Rio Grande National Forest. Follow the road as it climbs gradually, edged by pine trees on the right and dry Kerber Creek on the left. When we rode this loop in mid-June, the creek was trickling with water about 2.5 miles from the gate, creating marshy conditions on the left side of the road. Eventually, the road gives you a break from climbing, as it frequently levels out, offering you a chance to catch your breath before resuming your climb through lush groves of aspen filled with birds singing to each other.

Continue on Columbia Gulch Road (FS 857) as it skirts the marsh and the singing Kerber Creek on your left. In a small, open area near the end of the marshy area, Sawlog Gulch Road (FS 858, a jeep road) crosses the creek and connects to Columbia Gulch Road from your left. At this point, you've pedaled about 4 miles from the Rio Grande National Forest reentry gate. Turn left onto Sawlog Gulch Road, crossing the creek and following it up a steep grade for about a quarter of a mile over rugged terrain. Persevere, as this is the last push to the final high point of the loop!

The top of the climb is 9,900' and rests on the edge of a grassy meadow, surrounded by a thick forest of aspen. This is a good place to take a break, catch your breath, and prepare yourself mentally for a fast and fairly technical descent. The final 2-mile stretch back to your car is wide, punctuated with potholes and tufts of grass, with loose rocks scattered throughout. As you pick your way down, there are fewer stands of aspen and more pine trees. A short section towards the end of this stretch becomes extremely rocky—moderately skilled riders may want to slow way down or dismount. This is the sort of trail that makes shock absorbers worth every penny. Eventually, the road becomes smooth, the evergreen trees disappear, and the terrain changes to desertlike conditions overgrown with shrubs. The final half-mile stretch is a fun, roller-coaster ride back to your car.

Buena Vista

Did you know that Chaffee County, home of the upper Arkansas River valley, is fast becoming a world-class mountain biking region? Thanks to the communities of Buena Vista, Salida, and Poncha Springs, and efforts by the local Banana Belt Fat Tracks Mountain Biking Club, there are over 12 documented and marked biking trails within this 30-by-20-mile stretch of churning whitewater and towering mountain peaks. Plus, there are lots of lesser known, shorter trails, spurs, and routing possibilities to consider. And those peaks aren't just any old mountain toppers—all 15 of them rise over 14,000′. No other region in Colorado can boast of such a high concentration of summits. With the towering Continental Divide and the Sawatch Range on the west, and the Arkansas River with its numerous little tributaries cutting through the landscape on the east, can you imagine the beauty of this region?

Did you also know that, unlike at other biking meccas in Colorado, here you can ride most of the trails almost year-round? That's right. In the winter, it's possible to alpine ski at Monarch Ski Resort in the morning and then ride the snow-free trails in the afternoon. During the summer, when other areas in the state are frying, temperatures here range from 60 to 85 degrees. Pretty impressive. No wonder this region is called the Banana Belt.

You could spend a week riding here and still not have covered all the trails. And the routes range from leisurely, flat, dirt road jaunts to major, all-day expeditions that require great technical skill and lots of huffing and puffing due to elevation. In August, Chaffee County hosts the nationally sanctioned Monarch Mountain Challenge; it is, so far, the highest mountain bike race in the nation. In September, when the aspens are spinning gold, the Banana Belt Loop circuit race is held for riders of all levels. Sponsored and supported locally each year by the host towns, Banana Belt Fat Tracks, and private citizens, the loop race is a huge community welcome mat for riders.

So where is Chaffee County? Located about 120 miles southwest of Denver, just south of Leadville, it encompasses the towns of Buena Vista, Salida, and Poncha Springs, conceived as mining settlements in the mid- to late 1800s. The region still reflects its historical upbringing. There's a wealth of railroad history here that literally laid the groundwork for some of the area's favorite mountain bike trails.

The discovery of gold and silver in the upper Arkansas River region in the 1860s attracted miners and, eventually, settlers. Farming and ranching took hold. The population grew and the rip-roaring towns of Leadville, Buena Vista, and later, Salida, were born, full of promises of prosperity. The fever was on. In 1880, the Denver & Rio Grande Railroad company extended tracks north through the valley to Leadville and southwest over Marshall Pass to the Gunnison region. At the same time, the Denver South Park & Pacific Railroad company constructed the Alpine Tunnel, cutting through the Continental Divide, in an effort to reach the Gunnison area first. It lost the race and, in 1910, after about 28 years of sporadic operation, it shut down; the Denver & Rio line continued its southwestern route. Meanwhile, in the late 1880s, the Colorado Midland Railroad company had extended its tracks into the upper river valley where the Denver & Rio Grande line was already in operation. Competition ensued. In 1918, falling into financial trouble, the Midland company chugged its last train through the valley. To this day, the Denver & Rio Grande Western railroad (as it is now called), continues to run through the upper Arkansas River valley to Leadville and beyond.

In 1990, the U.S. Forest Service, with the aid of the Bureau of Land Management, the towns of Buena Vista and Salida, and the Banana Belt Fat Tracks club, converted some of the abandoned railroad beds into bike, hiking, and recreational vehicle trails. The region's trail system continues to grow and improve for bikers looking for more terrain to explore.

For more information about the Rails-to-Trails program in Colorado and throughout the country, contact Colorado State Parks, Rails-to-Trails, 1313 Sherman Street, Room 618, Denver, CO 80203. Phone: (303) 866-3203, ext. 336.

RIDE 61 *LENHARDY–MIDLAND RAILROAD GRADE TRAIL*

This is a set of trails that offers lots of routing possibilities, limited only by your endurance, time, and the number of vehicles among your riding buddies. You can ride these trails as either a loop, an out-and-back, or a point-to-point. (Take a look at the map and you'll realize the possibilities. Variations are described briefly at the end of this chapter.)

Here's a popular version: A 17-mile point-to-point route that requires a vehicle shuttle. Place the bottom vehicle in the town of Buena Vista and take the top car about eight miles northwest out of town to the trailhead. Other than a few steep, short ascents, particularly in the first two-and-a-half miles, the ride is mostly downhill, with an elevation loss of about 1,500′. As the trail weaves through pinyon and juniper trees, with aspen and spruce on the higher terrain, you'll be treated with spectacular views of the Collegiate Peaks, rising above 14,000′.

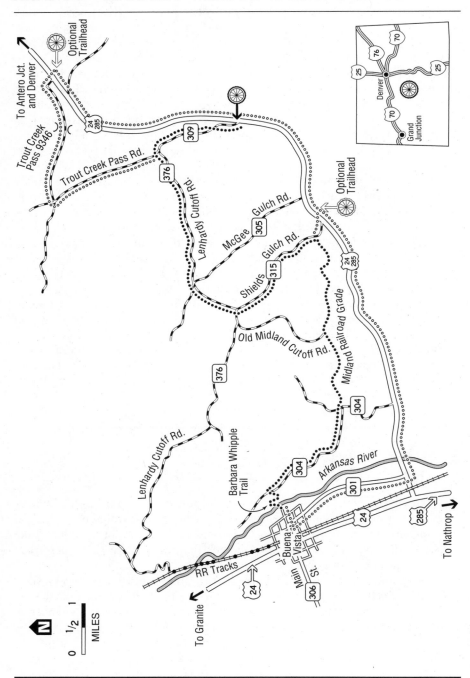

On the Midland Trail, evidence of the past remains: old railroad ties, weathered telegraph poles, and partially grown-over hillside cuts. The route travels mostly over two- and four-wheel-drive gravel roads and old railroad beds, with a 5.5-mile section of slightly technical single-track. Rated as a moderate ride overall due to the distance, beginners who seek a challenge and hope to improve their skills will enjoy this ride. Knowing when to dismount and walk your bike is part of the sport. For all you hard-core riders, if you want to skip the shuttle and make a loop, be my guest. Read further for options.

General location: The trailhead is about 8 miles northwest of the town of Buena Vista. The town is approximately 120 miles southwest of Denver.

Elevation change: Starting at 9,010′, the trail climbs to 9,750′ within 3 miles and finishes at 7,955′. Total elevation loss is about 1,795′. (If you begin at the optional Trout Creek Pass/Chubb Park starting point, the trail begins at 9,480′ and climbs to the same high point of 9,750′.

Season: Generally, these trails are rideable between April and October. Depending on the severity of snowstorms and snowmelt, it's possible to ride during the winter. The lower trails are almost snow-free year-round. Ask local bikers about prevailing conditions in the winter.

Services: All trailheads have information and map displays but no water, toilet, or other services. However, all services are available in Buena Vista and Johnson Village.

Hazards: The initial climbing section on the Lenhardy Cutoff contains a few rocky spots. Then, as you're making a fast descent on Shields Gulch Trail, watch out for sandy patches that'll want to swallow your tires. On the Midland Trail, portions of the single-track section that cross several ravines are short and steep, ascending and descending, and strewn with loose rocks, so controlling your speed is critical here. When you approach the end of the ride, expect a steep descent on the Barbara Whipple Trail.

Rescue index: There are no phones at the trailheads. These trails do not see lots of use, so if you're injured near the beginning of the ride, your best move is to go back to your car and drive for help. Depending on where you are on the trail, it may be faster to ride down McGee Gulch or Shields Gulch to US 24/285 and flag down a passing motorist. Or, follow the highway back down into Johnson Village and call for help. If you're near the end of the ride, you'd be better off following the rest of the route to the end in Buena Vista. The Buena Vista–Salida area has 911 emergency phone service.

Land status: San Isabel National Forest. Bureau of Land Management.

Maps: Trails Illustrated® maps: #129, Collegiate Peaks. This map shows a detailed rendering of most of the route. USGS 7.5 minute quads: Buena Vista East, Marmot Peak, and Antero Reservoir. *Banana Belt Fat Trackers 14ers Region Mountain Bike Trail Guide.* Compiled by the Banana Belt Fat Tracks biking club and Arkansas Valley Publishing Company. For a map and club information, contact any of the local groups and bike shops listed below.

Finding the trail: Park the bottom shuttle car at the end of East Main Street in Buena Vista. Take the top shuttle to the trailhead by following US 24 south out of Buena Vista. Turn left (east) at Johnson Village onto US 24/285 and drive just over 8 miles to County Road 309, the turnoff to Trout Creek Pass. There's a parking area on the east side of the highway, across from the intersection. Start your ride by pedaling up CR 309.

An optional starting point is Trout Creek Pass, 4.5 miles beyond CR 309 on US 24/285. This option adds about 5 miles to the ride at the outset, but the gentle terrain gives your legs a chance to warm up before tackling the uphill portion of the Lenhardy Cutoff Trail. Park at Trout Creek Pass and begin your ride on CR 311, a two-wheel-drive road.

Sources of additional information:

Bureau of Land Management
Royal Gorge Resource Area
3170 Main Street
P.O. Box 2200
Cañon City, CO 81215
(719) 275-0631

San Isabel National Forest
Salida Ranger District
325 West Rainbow Boulevard
Salida, CO 81201
(719) 539-3591

The Trailhead
707 US 24 North
P.O. Box 2023
Buena Vista, CO 81211
(719) 395-8001

Banana Belt Fat Tracks/Otero Cyclery
108 F Street
Salida, CO 81201
(719) 539-6704

Arkansas Valley Publishing Company
125 East Second Street
Salida, CO 81201
(719) 539-6691

Arkansas Valley Publishing, in conjunction with the Banana Belt Fat Tracks, has produced the very useful *Banana Belt Fat Tracks 14ers Region Mountain Bike Trail Guide* for the past several years. It describes 15 rides and shows twice as many other trails on the map.

Colorado State Parks
1313 Sherman St., Room 618
Denver, CO 80203
(303) 866-3437
For more information about the rail trail program in Colorado.

Heart of the Rockies Chamber of Commerce
406 West Rainbow Boulevard
Salida, CO 81201
(719) 539-2068

Buena Vista Chamber of Commerce
343 South US 24
P.O. Box P
Buena Vista, CO 81211
(719) 395-6612

Notes on the trail: Begin your ride by pedaling almost 2 miles northwest on CR 309, Trout Creek Road, a two-wheel-drive dirt road. Then turn left onto CR 376.2, the Lenhardy Cutoff, a four-wheel-drive dirt road.

Trout Creek Pass/Chubb Park trailhead option: Starting at Trout Creek Pass, pedal on CR 311 as it leads north and then immediately west. Continue on this trail for almost 3 miles as it crosses Trout Creek and eventually intersects CR 309, leading to Chubb Park. At this junction, turn left, south, onto CR 309. Follow it for 3 more miles until it meets the Lenhardy Cutoff Trail, leading off on your right. Take this right turn. Here is where this optional route rejoins the basic route, described below.

Let the fun begin! For the next 2.5 miles, put yourself in a lower gear and begin your 670′ climb. Expect a few rocky, tricky sections. As you huff and puff your way up, rest assured that this is the most difficult part of the entire ride. Soon, you reach the ridge top at 9,750′ and enjoy a spectacular panorama of the Collegiate Peaks in the Sawatch Range towards the west.

Get ready to enjoy a sweet descent. Pedal just over a mile to the intersection of McGee Gulch, which is CR 305. Don't turn here. Instead, continue on CR 376.2 for another mile to the next intersection, marked Shields Gulch (CR 315), a two-wheel-drive dirt road. Turn left onto CR 315 and begin your descent to the Midland Trail, a little more than 2 miles down. There are sandy patches here that would love to see you do a face-plant, so be alert and control your speed.

Soon you reach the intersection of the Midland Trail. Hang a right onto the single-track and pedal 100 yards or so to the the railroad bed. For the next 4 to 5 miles, follow the single-track trail due west. The trail takes you to the north side of several ravines where you see remnants of the original wooden and steel trestles. Here is the tough section I spoke about: short, steep, loose rock ravines with deep sand in the bottoms. Rideable, but there's nothing wrong with walking.

Shortly after crossing the last ravine, the Midland Trail intersects CR 304, a single-lane dirt road. At this junction, bear right, due west. Cruise down CR 304 for 2.5 miles and keep your eyes peeled for the Barbara Whipple Trail off to your left.

Follow the Barbara Whipple Trail, a single-track, as it descends a steep and technical section to the Arkansas River footbridge. Consider walking your bike over this short segment. Cross the bridge over to the east end of Main Street, where you've left your shuttle car. Approximate total distance: 17 miles.

There are several ways to make this an out-and-back, loop, or point-to-point shuttle ride. Study the map and you'll begin to create your own routes. Here are a few suggestions.

Option One—The Out-and-Back: Return the same way you came. The scenery will assuredly look different and just as spectacular. And you guessed it . . . it's mostly uphill!

Option Two—The Loop: Take the paved roads back to the start, traffic and all. It's still a climb, but a much easier one on pavement. To do this route, continue down Main Street for a few yards and then turn left (south) onto CR 301, a paved road through the east side of town. Follow CR 301 for almost 3 miles as it intermittently follows the Arkansas River on your left. When you intersect US 24/285, turn left (east) onto it, and pedal up the gradual grade for almost 8.5 miles to the Trout Creek Pass turnoff and to where you've parked your car. Total distance is approximately 27.5 miles.

Option Three—Point-To-Point (A different one!): Place your bottom shuttle car at the junction of Shields Gulch Road and the Midland Trail. Then, in the other shuttle car, drive to one of the following start points to begin pedaling: the junction of CR 309 and US 24/285, or the junction of CR 311 and US 24/285. This is a good option to keep in mind, for it offers a bail-out path to escape inclement weather near the beginning of the ride. Another option is to ride into Buena Vista as initially described. Then, return to this shuttle car by riding US 24/285.

Option Four—Yet another Point-to-Point or Loop route: Start your ride at the junction of Shields Gulch Road and the Midland Trail. Ride only the Midland Trail into Buena Vista, skipping the Lenhardy Cutoff and Shields Gulch portions entirely. This point-to-point ride on just the Midland Trail and CR 304 ends in Buena Vista; total mileage is approximately 8 miles. For a loop ride, continue through Buena Vista and return to your car via US 24/285, for a total distance of approximately 16 miles.

To explore other options, get your hands on the *Banana Belt Fat Tracks 14ers Region Mountain Bike Trail Guide.*

RIDE 62   *COLORADO TRAIL TO MOUNT PRINCETON HOT SPRINGS*

How does this sound to you: grunting up 1,280′ in 3 scenic miles, then enjoying 5.5 miles of sweet, moderately challenging single-track, followed by a soothing soak in hot springs? What are we waiting for? Let's go!

This is a trail that's sure to make everyone happy, because the routing options can accommodate every skill level in your group. You can do an out-and-back, with or without the technical loop option (about 17 miles total plus almost 4.5 miles for the techncial segment). Or consider a point-to-point route with a shuttle car at the start and another at the terminus where the hot springs are located (approximately 8.5 miles one-way). A loop that includes cruising on pavement and lots of miles is a possibility too (roughly 21.5 miles round-trip).

Most of this ride encompasses two- and four-wheel-drive dirt roads up Bald Mountain, and a portion of the Colorado Trail, a single-track trail that meanders through a forest of aspen and spruce. Though it's rated advanced on skill requirements, an experienced beginner with good stamina and a can-do attitude is sure to enjoy this ride. The gonzo rider looking for more technical challenges can tackle an optional loop on the return run of the Colorado Trail.

General location: The trailhead is located about 4.5 miles west of Buena Vista. The town is approximately 120 miles southwest of Denver, just south of Leadville.

Elevation change: The ride starts at 8,400′ and climbs to 9,680′ in just over 3 miles, for a gain of 1,280′. From there, the Colorado Trail ascends to an elevation of approximately 10,160′ to Mount Princeton Hot Springs, a gain of about 480′. This is the highest point of your ride. Returning the way you came is mostly downhill. If you do the big loop using paved roads, your lowest point is 7,955′, near the junction of County Road 321 and CR 306.

Season: The best time to ride this route is May through October, give or take a few snow days. Depending on the severity of the winter snowstorms, this trail is rideable almost year-round.

Services: No services are available at the starting point. All services are available in Buena Vista, about 4.5 miles east. At Mount Princeton Hot Springs Resort, you'll find a convenience store, pay phone, restaurant, lodging, hot springs, and, yes, convention facilities too. Open year-round. There are plenty of public and private campgrounds in and around the San Isabel National Forest. Reservations at most national forest campgrounds can be made at least 10 days in advance by calling MISTIX at (800) 283-CAMP.

Hazards: Be aware that the first 3 miles up Bald Mountain are quite exposed— not a good place to be during the dreaded afternoon thunder and lightning storms. To add variety to an already splendid trail, there is a section on the

RIDE 62 *COLORADO TRAIL TO*
MOUNT PRINCETON HOT SPRINGS

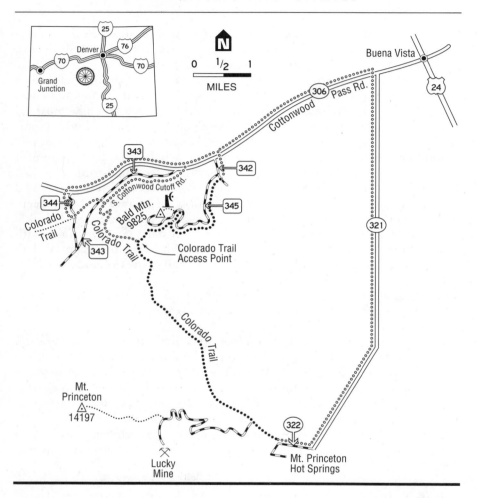

Colorado Trail that has some wooden steps that you and your bike can bounce down. Also, watch out for occasional traffic on this portion. If you decide to take the pavement back to the starting point, expect a fair amount of traffic. Deer and elk hunting are popular here, beginning in August with bow-hunting season. September through November is the season for rifle hunting.

Rescue index: During the summer months, the Colorado Trail is quite popular with hikers and bikers who may be of help in case of emergency. There are no shortcut or bail-out paths. For help, you must either go up to Mount Princeton

At 14,197′, it's not unusual to see Mt. Princeton with its head in the clouds.

Hot Springs or back down to your car and drive into town for help.

Land status: San Isabel National Forest. Maxwell Park, State of Colorado.

Maps: Trails Illustrated® maps: #129, Collegiate Peaks, and #130, Shavano Peak. The Colorado Trail map: #3. USGS 15 minute quad: Buena Vista, Colorado. USGS 7.5 minute quads: Mount Antero, Buena Vista West, and Mount Yale, Colorado. *Banana Belt Fat Tracks 14ers Region Mountain Bike Trail Guide.* Compiled by the Banana Belt Fat Tracks biking club and Arkansas Valley Publishing Company. For a map and club information, contact any of the local groups and bike shops listed below.

Finding the trail: From Buena Vista, drive southwest out of town on County Road 306 (Cottonwood Pass Road). After about 5.5 miles, turn left (south) onto CR 342, a two-wheel-drive dirt road. Continue on this road for a few yards and then turn right onto CR 345, another dirt road. Though you may find a shady spot a bit farther up, this is a good spot to park and begin your ride. The road here is fairly level for the next half mile or so and will give your muscles a chance to warm up before you begin your climb up Bald Mountain. Or, you can continue on CR 345 all the way up to the Colorado Trail access point. By doing this, you avoid most of the climbing. During good, dry weather, this road is passable by most two-wheel-drive vehicles with sufficient clearance.

Sources of additional information:

San Isabel National Forest
Salida Ranger District
325 West Rainbow Boulevard
Salida, CO 81201
(719) 539-3591

The Trailhead
707 US 24 North
P.O. Box 2023
Buena Vista, CO 81211
(719) 395-8001

Banana Belt Fat Tracks/Otero Cyclery
108 F Street
Salida, CO 81201
(719) 539-6704

Arkansas Valley Publishing Company
125 East Second Street
Salida, CO 81201
(719) 539-6691

Arkansas Valley Publishing, in conjunction with the Banana Belt Fat Tracks, has produced the very useful *Banana Belt Fat Tracks 14ers Region Mountain Bike Trail Guide* for the past several years. It describes 15 rides and shows twice as many other trails on the map.

Mount Princeton Hot Springs Resort
15870 County Road 162
Nathrop, CO 81236
(719) 395-2447

Notes on the trail: This ride is described as an out-and-back, with total mileage of about 17 miles. Optional routings are mentioned at the end of this section.

Once you've parked your car near the intersection of CR 342 and CR 345, start your ride by heading up CR 345 (west) on the south side of Bald Mountain. The first half mile or so is fairly level, a good stretch of road to warm up your climbing legs. For the next 3 miles, this dirt road requires little technical skill since it is mostly smooth, with a few potholes, rocks, and spots of loose gravel. The only really big challenge on this segment is the sustained climbing. Fortunately, there are a few short, level stretches in which to catch your breath. On a sunny day, the view of the upper Arkansas River valley becomes more expansive and exhilarating, while the sky toward the north seems more blue than ever. The road traverses east and then back to the west, offering a splendid view of Mount Princeton (14,197′), which, depending on the time of year, may be majestically snow-covered. There is at least one less-traveled road leading off to the right (north). Stay on the main road. When you pass the radio towers, sitting high up on your right on exposed terrain, you're within a half mile of the Colorado Trail access point and 3 miles from the start.

After the radio towers, notice that CR 345 leads you into a shady, forest area. Look for small, wooden Colorado Trail directional signs stuck to trees, directly across from where the road makes a major turn to the right. Follow the Colorado Trail signs through the trees for about a quarter of a mile, sort of due west, away from the road and up a couple of short, steep segments. When you reach the Colorado Trail (it's a marked, single-track trail), turn left (south).

For the next 5.5 miles, the Colorado Trail travels along the east side of Mount Princeton, cruising between 9,600′ and 10,160′. It leads you through a peaceful forest of spruce, aspen, and pine, and up and down small drainages. This single-track trail is generally smooth, with few tree roots and boulders, and accented with several sharp turns to keep you challenged. Keep in mind that hikers enjoy this peaceful trail too, so control your speed, dismount, and let them pass. Yelling "Bikers on the trail!" disrupts the serenity for everyone, including the wildlife. After about 5.5 miles, the Colorado Trail joins CR 322, a dirt road. When you reach CR 321, a paved road, turn right and coast down to Mount Princeton Hot Springs Resort. From this point, you have several options for your return route.

But, wait! Want to bag a fourteener while you're up here? The peak of Mount Princeton (14,197′) is nearly 4 miles from this point. Hike or ride up an extremely steep, four-wheel-drive dirt road for about 2 miles, then hoof it the rest of the way up.

Option One: Return exactly the way you came. Distance covered is about 8.5 miles one way, approximately 17 miles total.

Option Two: Use a shuttle plan by leaving your end car at Mount Princeton Hot Springs. Then, in your other shuttle car, drive to the original starting point near the intersection of CR 342 and CR 345. That way, all you do is pedal up and drive down. To reach the resort, drive almost a mile west out of Buena Vista on CR 306, then south on CR 321, a paved road, for about 7.5 miles. Pedaling distance is about 8.5 miles.

Option Three: Return the way you came, but include the lower portion of the Colorado Trail, an extremely technical segment. As you coast back down the single-track, continue on the Colorado Trail past your original access point to CR 345. This part of the trail becomes very difficult as it is a descent on mostly loose and rocky terrain for the next 2 miles. The Colorado Trail soon intersects CR 343, also known as the South Cottonwood Creek Cutoff Road, a four-wheel-drive dirt road. At this point, you can either take the Cutoff Road or stay on the Colorado Trail.

If you choose the Cutoff Road, follow it heading east and running parallel with the creek and CR 306 (the paved road). After about 2 miles, this road ends on CR 306. Head right (east) on CR 306 for almost a mile, then turn right onto CR 342 and pedal back to your car. Total mileage is approximately 21.5 miles.

If you didn't get enough of this technical section, stay on the Colorado Trail through the Cutoff Road intersection, and continue on for a very short distance to the junction with CR 344, a dirt road. Turn right (north) onto this road and you almost immediately reach CR 306. Take a right (east) onto this paved road and enjoy a gradual cruise down nearly 3 miles to CR 342. Hang a right here, onto the dirt road and pedal back to your car. Total mileage is almost 22 miles.

Option Four: Make a huge loop by returning to the start via 10.5 miles of pavement. At the point where the single-track trail ends at CR 322, near the hot springs resort, turn left (east) onto this dirt road. Follow it around and after a mile, you arrive at the junction of CR 321, a paved road. Turn left (north) onto CR 321 and coast down to Buena Vista. After about 7 miles, turn left onto CR 306, which is the paved road that returns you to the start of the ride. Pedal up CR 306 for almost 4 miles to CR 342. Make a left turn here and pedal back to your car. Total mileage is approximately 21.5 miles.

RIDE 63 *MONARCH CREST AND RAINBOW TRAILS*

Though this ride requires a shuttle vehicle arrangement, it's worth the effort to set it up. One car takes you up to Monarch Pass, where the ride begins, and another is left in Poncha Springs, the ride terminus. Total pedaling distance of this ride is a whopping 34 miles, give or take a mile—making it a major under-taking, requiring six to ten hours. There are a few variations that can shorten or lengthen the time and mileage, though finishing at the same place.

In terms of stamina, this is an intermediate to difficult ride due to moderate climbs (mostly at the beginning of the ride), high elevation, and length. While not technically challenging, there are moderately difficult but enjoyable descents and a couple of short sections where you might want to dismount and walk. The trail is mostly single-track, though you can combine any number of dirt roads to create your desired mileage and challenge. The ride uses segments of the Colorado Trail, the Continental Divide Trail, the Rainbow Trail, old rail-road-graded dirt roads, and US 285.

As the trail leads you from atop Monarch Pass to Marshall Pass along the Continental Divide, the westward views into the valley below are expansive and absolutely exhilarating. Eastward descents off the Divide take you through open meadows and groves of evergreens and aspens woven with quietly singing creeks. Keeping your eyes peeled and your riding quiet, you will most likely see deer and elk. And for Mother Nature's sake, especially through the woods and around tight curves, stay alert so that you don't *run into* a deer or elk, literally, like my riding buddy Bill almost did.

General location: The start of this ride is located just 17 miles west of the town of Ponchas Springs. The town is about 135 miles southwest of Denver.

Elevation change: Beginning at Monarch Pass, 11,312′, the trail quickly climbs approximately 833′ within the first 4 miles. Thereafter, the route leads up and down until you reach Marshall Pass (10,842′), at which point you will have lost 1,143′. The next mile leads you right back up to 11,280′, a climb of 438′. Once you've made it this far (about 12 miles), it's virtually all downhill from here. The ride finishes in Poncha Springs, at 7,500′. Total elevation loss is 3,812′.

Season: The best time to enjoy this trail is from late spring to early fall. If you ride at the beginning of the season, you're sure to be rewarded with meadows of wildflowers. Bill and I rode this trail in late August. A few days prior to our outing, the area got hit with a freak (but mild) snowstorm, and we encountered a few patches of snow on the higher elevations. Although it was sunny throughout the day, the coolness forced us to keep our jackets and leggings on throughout most of the ride.

Services: Water, phone, and toilet facilities are available near the Monarch Pass summit at the Aerial Tramway station, generally open from May to October. Don't count on finding water on the trail until you reach Silver Creek after 12 miles. Even then, the water from the creek must be treated to be drinkable. I would suggest bringing at least three bottles of water and plenty of food to keep you going. An alternative to carrying all that water is to bring along a back-packer purification water filter pump.

There are numerous public and private campgrounds nearby. Heading west on US 50, between Poncha Springs and Monarch Pass, you'll find 4 camp-grounds containing at least 77 sites: Angel of Shavano, North Fork Reservoir, Garfield, and Monarch Park campgrounds. At this writing, North Fork Campground is free, and the others charge a fee. Located near the end of this ride is O'Haver Lake Campground, with 30 sites. For fee information and possible reservation requirements, contact the Salida Ranger District Office, (719) 539-3591. Complete services (restaurants, lodging, gas, etc.) are also available in the nearby communities of Poncha Springs, Salida, and Buena Vista. Contact the local chambers of commerce for more information (addresses and phone numbers listed below).

Hazards: Because the ride leads you above timberline, and hence, onto widely exposed terrain, lightning is a great hazard, particularly during the summer months. Fortunately, the most exposed sections are early in the ride, within the first 8 to 9 miles. If you ride during the lightning months, allow enough time for everyone in your group to clear this section before the light show starts. The entire route is generally smooth with few rocky but easily managed stretches. Between miles 17 and 18, watch out for fallen aspen trees across the trail: a sure sign of busy-little-beaver country. Also within this section, just before the Kismuth Mine, the trail travels over a field of extremely loose rocks. Even Bill, my accomplished riding buddy, cautiously half-biked this section—that is, one

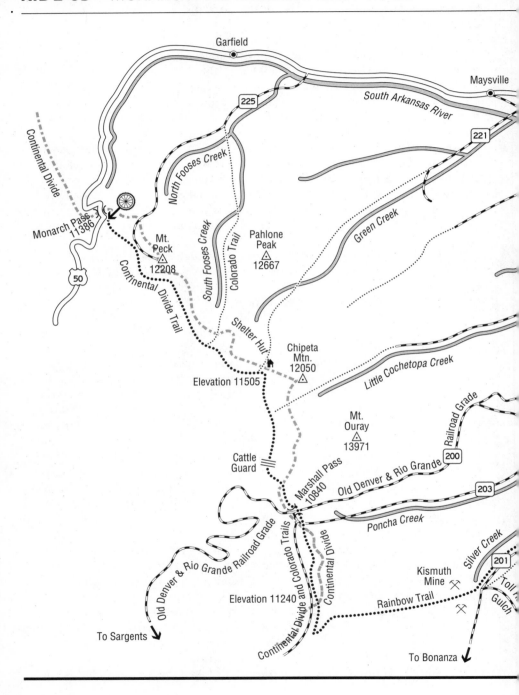

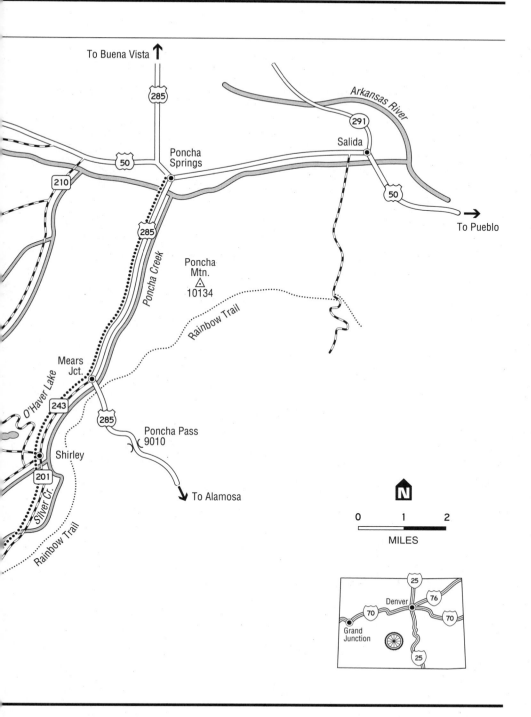

Bill was just delighted to be here on top of the world, despite the patches of snow that dotted the mountainsides on this mid-August outing.

foot in a pedal, the other foot on the rocks. Other hazards include sudden encounters with vehicles on the dirt roads. It can really make your day to smash into a jeep while taking a curve on a fast and exhilarating descent.

Rescue index: It's a long, long way back into town and to a pay phone. Marshall Pass is accessible by two-wheel-drive vehicles and you may find some-one there who can help in an emergency. O'Haver Lake Campground does not have a pay phone, but in cases of extreme emergency, nearby residences may be able to provide assistance. The Colorado Trail and the Rainbow Trail are single-track and not easily accessible by motor vehicles.

Land status: San Isabel National Forest.

Maps: The Colorado Trail maps: #15, #16, and #17. USGS 7.5 minute quads: Bonanza, Garfield, Poncha Springs, Pahlone Peak, Maysville, and Mount Ouray, Colorado. (Check for updated versions, as the current maps do not show the Colorado Trail or the Rainbow Trail in their entirety.) *Banana Belt Fat Tracks 14ers Region Mountain Bike Trail Guide.* Compiled by the Banana Belt Fat Tracks biking club and Arkansas Valley Publishing Company. For a map and club information, contact any of the local groups and bike shops listed below.

Finding the trail: The start of your adventure requires that you arrange a vehi-cle shuttle: one that takes you up to the trailhead at Monarch Pass and another at the end in Poncha Springs. Monarch Pass is approximately 17 miles from

Poncha Springs. Depending on the number of riders in your group and your car space, the shuttle could take up to 45 minutes to set up. To pick up the trail-head, drive west from Poncha Springs on US 50. Continue past Monarch ski area to Monarch Pass, where you'll find the Aerial Tramway and Monarch Crest parking lot on your left. Park here.

Sources of additional information:

San Isabel National Forest
Salida Ranger District
325 West Rainbow Boulevard
Salida, CO 81201
(719) 539-3591

The Trailhead
707 US 24 North
P.O. Box 2023
Buena Vista, CO 81211
(719) 395-8001

Banana Belt Fat Tracks/Otero Cyclery
108 F Street
Salida, CO 81201
(719) 539-6704

Arkansas Valley Publishing Company
125 East Second Street
Salida, CO 81201
(719) 539-6691
Arkansas Valley Publishing, in conjunction with the Banana Belt Fat Tracks, has produced the very useful *Banana Belt Fat Tracks 14ers Region Mountain Bike Trail Guide* for the past several years. It describes 15 rides and shows twice as many other trails on the map.

Buena Vista Chamber of Commerce
343 South US 24
P.O. Box P
Buena Vista, CO 81211
(719) 395-6612

Heart of the Rockies Chamber of Commerce
406 West Rainbow Boulevard
Salida, CO 81201
(719) 539-2068

Notes on the trail: Begin your ride by pedaling up the jeep road behind the tram building. Watch for a Crest Trail mileage sign with the Continental Divide symbol, off to your right, just a few yards from the start. Take this turnoff onto the narrow, gently climbing, smooth, single-track trail that leads you through a forest of spruce and pine. After about a mile you reach a jeep road and sign inscribed "North Fooses Trail/South Arkansas River—7 miles," pointing towards a small trail. (If you're looking for a shorter ride, this is an alternate route back down to US 50. Other routes exist farther up the trail.) Stay right (south) on the jeep road towards Marshall Pass and pedal another half mile or so. There's another Continental Divide Trail sign: "Marshall Pass—9 miles." Follow the direction to the summit, a right turn onto a single-track path.

The next 2 miles lead you around Mount Peck and up the ridge to the highest point, 12,145′. Now, after all this climbing, take a breather to enjoy the westward view of the valley below. Don't be surprised if you can faintly hear the traffic from US 50. The ridge you've reached is above timberline and the 180-degree view is spectacular. Keep an eye on the weather, though—it's not a safe place to be during a lightning storm.

Onward! Back on the Continental Divide Trail. The next sign you see marks the South Fooses Creek Trail linkup and tells you that the South Arkansas River is 8 miles down it. In fact, this is the point where the Continental Divide Trail and the Colorado Trail (South Fooses Creek Trail) become one and the same trail, leading over Marshall Pass to the Rainbow Trail. (South Fooses Creek Trail is another alternate route back to US 50.) Go right onto the Colorado/Continental Divide Trail and follow the signs to Marshall Pass. The trail is generally a smooth single-track with a few rocky and gravel spots. Watch out for the bigger rocks on the trail—they're just waiting to catch your pedal. The views to the north, east, and south are breathtaking, especially after snow has dusted the peaks of Pahlone Peak (12,667′), Chipeta Mountain (12,850′), and Mount Ouray (13,971′). Believe it or not, Bill and I found snow on the ground here in late August. A snowball fight between the two of us ensued and I won.

Continue on and the trail begins a gradual descent back into the woods. When you bike pass a little shelter hut, you're about 6.5 miles into the journey. Pedal another half mile and there is a sign indicating the Green Creek Trail linkup on the left. (This trail is another alternate route eastward back to US 50.) Stay on the Colorado Trail for about a mile and find another sign identifying the junctions of Little Cochetopa Trail to the left. (Here is yet one more alternate way back to US 50.) Slightly farther up the Colorado Trail is the junction with the Agate Creek Trail, which leads westward down to the town of Sargents.

Stay straight on the Colorado Trail and let the fun, gradual downhill begin. The next 3.5 miles into Marshall Pass are pure exhilaration. The trail is generally smooth, with enough rocks for your dodging pleasure. Stay alert, though, because about a mile into the descent, you may encounter a loose rocky section, as we did the day we rode this segment. Pedal another 1.5 miles and you find the remains of an old mine. Check out whatever might be on the ground that's catching the sunlight. At first glance, we thought we saw pieces of broken glass. At closer look, Bill and I guessed these to be bits of layered quartz. Interesting, fragile stuff. Hop back on the saddle again and continue with the descent into Marshall Pass. As you're blasting down the hill and the trail is becoming a jeep road, be aware there is a cattle guard crossing about a mile after the mine.

At the end of your downhill flight, your trail intersects a two-wheel-drive dirt road, CR 200, which is the Marshall Pass Road, also known as the Old Denver & Rio Grande Railroad Grade. (For a very easy cruise back down to US 285 that shortens the route by 8 or 9 miles, follow this gravel road all the way.) Go right onto Marshall Pass Road. Just ahead is a curve, and once you've rounded it, you find yourself at Marshall Pass, 10,842′.

Facing south, you now have 3 routes from which to choose. You can take Poncha Creek Trail, another two-wheel-drive gravel road, back down to US 285. Or, you can take the high road, continuing on the Colorado Trail (still a single-track) to the Rainbow Trail. Or, you can take the lower jeep road (Forest Service Road 486), which rejoins the Colorado Trail after a couple of miles. Our suggestion is stay on the Colorado Trail because it's much prettier and climbs just as much as the jeep road. Taking our advice, continue riding through the woods. Stay quiet and alert and you may spot a deer or two. The Colorado Trail and the lower jeep road (FS 486) reconnect at a sign reading "Silver Creek/Rainbow Trail, 1 mile."

Stay on the Colorado/Continental Divide Trail until you reach the junction of the Rainbow Trail. (At this point you are about 14.5 miles into the ride.) Turn left (east) onto the Rainbow Trail, a double-track that quickly becomes a single-track. Get ready for another exhilarating, quick descent, with tight switchbacks and traverses over meadows and through groves of aspen and pine. Watch for wildlife as you fly down the Silver Creek drainage.

After pedaling the Rainbow Trail for about a mile, you'll find the trail levels out slightly and remains a smooth, narrow single-track, following Silver Creek on your right. As you cruise through the lush aspen groves, expect fallen trees across the trail, a sign that you're in beaver country.

Shortly thereafter, you arrive at a section that may have been a massive rock-slide from long ago. Consider dismounting in order to cross this sloping, short, loose, rocky segment. Though the drop-off to the creek on your right is not steep or deep, it can be unnerving. The next landmark you see is the Kismuth Mine, on the other side of the creek. At this point, you've ridden just over 18 miles from the starting point. Slightly farther down the Rainbow Trail, portage your bike over logs lying across the creek.

The single-track Rainbow Trail gradually turns into a four-wheel-drive road. At this point, the Rainbow Trail and the Silver Creek Road become one and the same path. When you come to a fork in the road marked Toll Road Gulch, FS 869, stay to the left and continue down the jeep road.

Pedal a bit farther, to almost 20 miles, and locate a sign that marks the separation of the Silver Creek Road and the continuation of the Rainbow Trail #1336. From this point, you can either continue down the Silver Creek Road (a jeep road, CR 201), or branch off to the right and follow the Rainbow Trail, a single-track on your right (due northeast). Both are virtually 9 miles in length and will take you to almost the same spot on US 285, though CR 201 is faster. By this time, you've been in the saddle for about 5 or 6 hours and might be aching for a smooth and fast downhill run. Bill and I certainly were. Our solution: Take the Silver Creek jeep road, staying left and heading northeast. Let the many dips in the road shoot you airborne for a cheap thrill. But watch for vehicles.

Almost 5 miles from the Silver Creek Road and Rainbow Trail fork, you reach an area named Shirley at the junction of CR 200, CR 201, CR 203 and CR 243. CR 200 leads to O'Haver Lake, while CR 203 is the end of the Poncha Creek Trail that we bypassed earlier. Continue northeast on CR 243, following the creek down about 2.5 miles to US 285. Watching out for traffic, make a left (north) onto the wide shoulder of US 285 and cruise on down to Poncha Springs to where you left a vehicle.

Cañon City

RIDE 64 *SHELF ROAD*

The Shelf Road is one of Colorado's best off-road tours, and is definitely not to be missed. From the plains and foothills surrounding Cañon City, the Shelf Road winds through spectacular Helena Canyon to the historic mining district of Cripple Creek–Victor, then returns past ghostly granite formations hiding in Phantom Canyon.

The Shelf Road itself was built in 1892 as a freight toll road to the Cripple Creek mining district. The route's other half, Phantom Canyon, served as a freight and stage road before being converted in 1894 to a narrow gauge railroad. Along the rail, gold was hauled from the mines down to millsites in Florence.

Along this route, there are many places of historic, prehistoric, and geologic interest, including a small dinosaur excavation, a turn-of-the-century adobe schoolhouse, and several old wooden trestles and train tunnels remnant from the days when the narrow gauge rail operated in Phantom Canyon. Scenically impressive Helena Canyon doubles as an outdoor classroom for several universities' summer geology camps. The Cripple Creek District is famous for the gold mined there in the late 1800s and has many attractions, including its large burro population.

The entire 65-mile loop is considered advanced-level, if tackled in one day— one very long day. With vehicle support, or if you stay overnight in Cripple Creek or Victor, the Shelf Road makes for a lengthy but pleasant intermediate-level tour. Novice cyclists will enjoy shortened out-and-back tours. Overall, it is a gentle uphill pull to Cripple Creek–Victor, except for about five miles of fairly steep climbing. The return portion of all rides is mostly coasting. The route travels on good dirt roads with segments of pavement at the beginning, middle, and end.

RIDE 64 *SHELF ROAD*

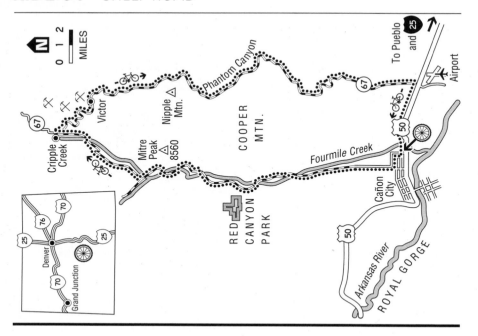

[Route information was submitted by Carol Boody,* Cañon City, Colorado.—G. B.]

General location: The Shelf Road begins 12 miles north of Cañon City on County Road 9 and heads north to the towns of Cripple Creek and Victor.

Elevation change: Cañon City, the tour's origin, sits at 5,300′. Cripple Creek (the ride's midpoint and highest point) rises to 9,700′. Most of the elevation gain is gradual except for a 5-mile stretch through the "Hole-in-the-Wall" Canyon. This section gains 2,000′ and will leave you wishing for lower gears.

Season: Cañon City is in Colorado's "Banana Belt." It is not uncommon for temperatures to reach 100 degrees during midsummer, so plan to start your ride early. Brief summer rainstorms with hail may be expected in the afternoons.

---

*Author of *A Mountain Bike Tour Guide for Cañon City, Colorado,* Carol Boody has been riding in the Cañon City area since 1984, when her family bought her a Rockhopper for Mother's Day. Now, husband Dale, son Jeff, and daughter Andrea all have mountain bikes and enjoy riding in the area (occasionally accompanied by their dog, Rebound).

For more information about *A Mountain Bike Tour Guide for Cañon City, Colorado,* see "Sources of additional information."

The Shelf Road. Photo: Carol Boody.

The very scenic Shelf Road has very little vehicular traffic, but Phantom Canyon road can be very busy, especially on weekends and holidays. Fall and spring, when tourist traffic is light and days are cooler, are excellent times to tour this area. The basin from Cañon City to Cripple Creek and Victor is a southern slope and, except for a few days after an occasional winter snowstorm, this route can be traveled nearly year-round.

Services: Two large-capacity water bottles should just get you to Cripple Creek if the weather is cool, but carry extra if conditions are warm. Do not plan on treating the creek water since it is polluted by mine drainage. Cañon City has all visitor services, including one bike shop. Cripple Creek and Victor also provide all visitor services.

Hazards: Traffic on the uphill portion of this tour is generally quite light, but traffic on Phantom Canyon Road is usually heavy during the summer, especially on weekends and holidays. During prolonged dry spells, the Phantom Canyon Road can become very dusty, so a bandanna might come in handy. Phantom Canyon Road is mostly 2 lanes, but beware of wavering traffic just the same.

Rescue index: Although these roads are not patrolled frequently, it should be possible to get help from passing motorists. Emergency contacts can be made from Cripple Creek and Victor; medical assistance has to come from Cañon City.

Land status: Bureau of Land Management and private property—it is difficult to tell which is which. This route follows county and state roadways.

Carol Boody and family. Photo: George W. Young.

Maps: USGS 7.5 minute quadrangles: Big Bull Mountain, Cañon City, Cooper Mountain, Cripple Creek South, Florence North, and Phantom Canyon, Colorado. USGS 1:100,000 metric topographic series: Cañon City and Pikes Peak, Colorado.

Finding the trail: At the east end of Cañon City, turn north at the first traffic light onto Dozier Avenue. Park in one of the government office lots (inquire first), unload, and pedal north uphill. At the top of the hill, Dozier turns west and becomes Central. Follow Central about a mile to Field Avenue; turn right (north) and continue on CR 9, which leads towards Cripple Creek and Victor.

Sources of additional information:

A Mountain Bike Tour Guide for Cañon City, Colorado, by Carol J. Boody. Cañon City, Colorado: Mountain Bike Tour Guides, 1989.

This book is the result of many Boody family outings and trips with the local Cañon City Cycling Club. It highlights over 30 local mountain bike tours throughout Cañon City and surrounding mountains. Currently, Carol is scouting out trails for a second guide centered around the towns of Westcliffe and Salida, Colorado, and in the Sangre de Cristo Mountains. For ordering information, contact Mountain Bike Tour Guides, 1248 North Raynolds, Cañon City, CO 81212.

Notes on the trail: The first 8 miles on CR 9 are paved. The next 5 miles are graveled county roads with some washboards. At about 13 miles, where the Shelf Road actually begins, the county road becomes a single-lane dirt road with some wider turnouts all the way to Cripple Creek. If you are going on to Victor and the Phantom Canyon Road, there are 3.5 miles of pavement before maintained dirt and gravel roads resume in Phantom Canyon.

For shorter 8- or 30-mile out-and-back tours, car-top your bikes 13.5 miles north of the traffic light to the fork in the Banks-Shelf Road, unload, and pedal up the right fork (Shelf Road). For the 8-mile tour, turn around just past the creek crossing or another mile farther, before the hard climb. This rolling climb gains about 450′. For the 30-mile tour, continue on to the fork in the road about 14 miles into your ride. The left fork goes to Cripple Creek. Elevation for this option amounts to about 3,100′. Be sure to take note where you come onto the pavement so you can find your way back for the return trip. If you are taking the 65-mile loop, turn right here to take a shortcut to Victor. At Victor, rest, eat, etc. To find Phantom Canyon from Victor, go one block left at the main business district, then turn right on the dirt road. Stay on the right fork at the Goldfield intersection and to the right at the Skagaway intersection. (Follow signs for Phantom Canyon and CO 67.) Enjoy your 3-hour coast back to Cañon City. Look for CR 123 just after you leave the canyon and turn right to complete your loop.

Between mile markers 2 and 3 on CR 9, there is a monument that commemorates the site of an 1877 dinosaur dig by professors Marsh and Cope. The dinosaurs found here are shown in relief on the tablet. About 2 miles past this, there is an old adobe schoolhouse, which was built by local ranchers about 1900 when the log school burned down. Red Canyon Park to the west of this road is a mini–Garden of the Gods, featuring redrock sandstone monoliths, cliffs, and unusual rock formations like those near Colorado Springs. The "Banks," located at the Shelf Road fork on CR 9, are limestone cliffs known internationally for technical climbing.

Wildlife is nearly as abundant as the scenery is beautiful: ouzels, kingfishers, blue herons, and cliff swallows nest along the creek's side; wild turkeys, deer, and coyotes may be seen in the hay fields and ranching areas; and bighorn sheep, hawks, eagles, and cougars hide in the granite canyons. The juniper, pinyon, and cactus that flourish in Cañon City's dry climate yield to aspen, fir, spruce, and bristlecone pine at higher elevations.

Colorado Springs

RIDE 65   CAPTAIN JACK'S FRONT SIDE

Here's a ride that's guaranteed to test your map-reading skills, as well as your bike handling technique. The route itself is not overly challenging in terms of stamina and skill—it's only four miles long—and experienced novices with the right attitude may find it enjoyable. Judging from several maps and other biking information I found, many trail options exist that enable you to lengthen the route and vary the technical challenge. A word of advice, though, if you are not a local (Stacie and I were not): take a fairly detailed map and be mentally prepared to patiently reconcile your map to the actual trail, which can be frustratingly confusing. The trails were not particularly well marked when we rode this loop in 1992. Not that you will get lost, mind you. In fact, the day we rode, we found lots of local mountain bikers flying down the various trails, after stopping a moment to give us directions. Still, if you have a sense of adventure and enough time to check out where a trail leads, this popular area of Colorado Springs is for you.

Stacie and I rode this four-mile loop late in the year, thinking we wouldn't find snow on the trail because of its lower elevation. If you've lived in Colorado long enough, you know that anything can happen, at any time and at any place. It did snow a few days before we rode in mid-November. Nevertheless, we found the trail completely snow-free, under sunny skies, and the temperature in the mid-60s. As we grunted and groaned our way up the narrow single-track, we could see our breath in the crisp, cold air. Once we reached the top of the climb, out of breath, we were rewarded with a brilliantly blue sky and a panoramic view. What exhilaration!

General location: The access point of this route is several miles west of Colorado Springs, up Cheyenne Canyon Road. Colorado Springs is 70 miles south of Denver.

Elevation change: This loop begins in the parking lot at 7,490′, climbs to 8,280′, and levels out before making a final climb to 8,380′, all within the first 2 miles. From that high point, the route is downhill all the way back to your car. Total elevation change is 890′.

Season: Depending on the amount of snowfall and the temperature afterwards, you can enjoy this ride almost all year.

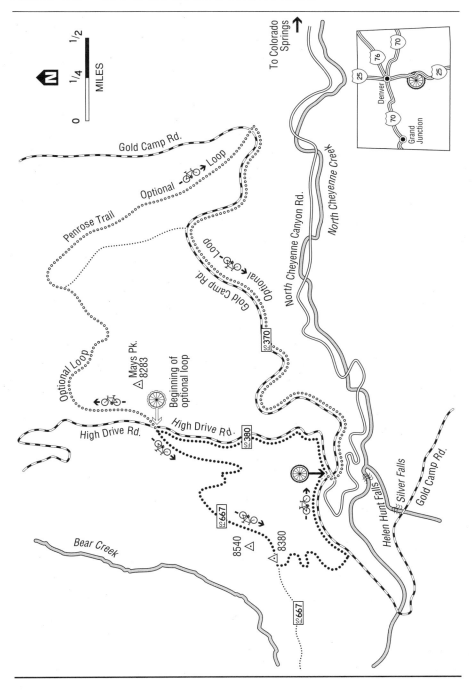

Services: Though no services are available at the beginning of this loop, parking is abundant. Don't count on the Visitor Center that you pass on Cheyenne Canyon Road to have water or toilet facilities, as its hours of operation vary throughout the year. Your best bet is to take care of all your needs in town before driving up the canyon. Colorado Springs offers a variety of restaurants and food stores, and lodging ranging from economy motels to luxurious bed-and-breakfast inns and world-class hotels. Many public and private campgrounds are nearby. In fact, the Colorado Springs Chamber of Commerce can send you lots of information on all services available (address listed below).

Hazards: Being so close to town, this area attracts lots of bikers, hikers, and motor bikers. Because of that, be prepared to dismount and let other trail users pass. Keep your speed under control, especially on the extremely narrow, soft dirt, steep, downhill segments of this short loop. Several areas of the route are accented by steep dropoffs, which can be a hazard or thrill, depending on your skill level. You may encounter motor vehicles during the last mile back to your car on High Drive Road.

Rescue index: Fortunately, this loop is short, so if you or anyone in your group needs medical attention, help is not far away in terms of distance and time. Since this is a popular area, particularly in the summer, you can probably find help from other trail users. The nearest phone is back down Cheyenne Canyon Road, inside the Starsmore Discovery Center, not necessarily open year-round. Your best bet for calling for help is back in town.

Land status: Pike National Forest.

Maps: USGS 7.5 minute quad: Pikes Peak, Colorado. *Mountain Biking Map—Pikes Peak Area.* Available from Vision Cartographics, Inc., 1925 Old Ranch Road, Colorado Springs, CO 80908.

Finding the trail: From the center of Colorado Springs, drive south on Twenty-first Street, towards the Broadmoor Hotel. After almost 2 miles, Twenty-first Street becomes Cresta Road. Travel on Cresta Road for about a half mile, at which point it intersects Cheyenne Canyon Road (also known as Cheyenne Boulevard). Go right (southwest) onto Cheyenne Canyon Road and follow it for about a mile as it winds through North Cheyenne Canyon Park, passing Helen Hunt Falls and the Starsmore Discovery Center. The pavement ends at a gate that closes High Drive Road to autos and trucks. Park in the lot near the gate and begin the ride by pedaling up (north) High Drive Road.

Even though the distance from town is short, I don't recommend cycling up to this point. Because many hiking trails are accessible from Cheyenne Canyon Road, it is subject to heavy traffic. Breathing exhaust fumes while pedaling uphill for several unrelenting miles is no fun, no matter how strong you are. So, for those reasons, I highly recommend that you drive up Cheyenne Canyon Road and park in the lot provided.

Sources of additional information:

Pike National Forest
Pikes Peak Ranger District
601 South Weber Street
Colorado Springs, CO 80903
(719) 636-1602

Colorado Springs Chamber of Commerce
P.O. Drawer B
Colorado Springs, CO 80901
(719) 635-1551

Colorado Springs Convention and Visitors Bureau
104 South Cascade Avenue, Suite 104
Colorado Springs, CO 80903
(800) 88-VISIT

Pikes Peak Area Trails Coalition
P.O. Box 34
Colorado Springs, CO 80901
(719) 596-5640

Notes on the trail: If you're the type of rider who needs a warm-up, I suggest you ride around the parking lot a few hundred times. Stacie and I wished we had. This loop begins with a fairly steep climb of about a mile on High Drive Road, a smooth, wide, two-wheel-drive dirt road. When Stacie and I tackled this ride, High Drive Road was closed to automobiles, so we were able to huff and puff our way up without eating dust and smelling exhaust. And never mind that the autumn morning was chilly, we soon had to shed a layer of protective clothing. That was our warm-up.

After pedaling just over a mile, you reach a car parking area on your right. At this point, the single-track trail you want for this counterclockwise loop begins on the left side of the road, across from the parking lot. (Note that another single-track trail leads off into the trees directly from the north end of the parking area. This route is the other part of Captain Jack's Trail (the back side) and is mostly downhill, punctuated with several steep but short climbs. You can add miles to your loop by including this portion. See the optional loop described at the end of this chapter.)

Cross High Drive Road to the single-track trail leading south through the woods. Here begins a grueling climb up a steep, narrow, soft dirt trail. Several portions of the trail skirt steep dropoffs, guaranteed to keep you awake. Almost a mile through this technical section, the path rounds a curve and emerges on top of a rocky clearing, offering an exhilarating panoramic view. What a great place to catch your breath.

Back in the saddle again, continue on the single-track as it takes you on a gentle roller-coaster ride over some gravel and possibly muddy spots. In less than a half mile, you've reached the highest point on the loop, 8,380′, and a trail junction, marked by a pile of deliberately placed dead tree limbs. This trail that leads off to the left is not as obvious as the main trail you have been following. Make a left turn onto this smaller single-track. This is the begining of Lower Captain Jack's Trail. (Continuing straight on the main trail is yet another way to add mileage and distance to this loop. Refer to a detailed map for routing options, keeping in mind that these trails may not be adequately marked.)

Lower Captain Jack's Trail is virtually all downhill from here. You'll cruise through a sparse forest of lodgepole pine, making tight hairpin turns, and picking your way over tree roots and tricky segments of boulders and rocks in your path. After about a half mile, the single-track connects you to a two-wheel-drive dirt road—is it Gold Camp Road or High Drive Road? Who knows? It's not clearly marked. No matter. Turn left (east) onto this dirt road and pedal up an easy hill for almost a half mile to your parked car. Total mileage of this loop is 4 miles.

Optional Loop: You can create an alternate 9-mile loop from the second parking lot to which you have just ridden. This is a moderately strenuous route and requires advanced technical skills. To ride this option, pick up the single-track trail on the north side of the second parking lot. Follow the path as it cruises delightfully up and down and around Mays Peak, through sparse groves of pine. Approximately 1.5 miles from the beginning of this optional trail, you reach the high point, 7,920′. After that, for the next several miles, the trail heads south, traveling up and down along a ridge and offering expansive views of Colorado Springs. When the trail joins Gold Camp Road, turn right (west) and continue pedaling for approximately 2 miles farther, to return to your car. Total distance of this loop is approximately 9 miles.

If you're really ambitious and aching for a more grueling ride, combine the first described loop with this option, riding a figure-8 route, for a total loop ride of approximately 11 miles.

Denver

RIDE 66 CASTLEWOOD CANYON STATE PARK

The Castlewood Canyon Loop provides unparalleled views of the Rocky Mountain Front Range, from Pikes Peak near Colorado Springs to Longs Peak rising above Boulder, a distance of about 100 miles. Each of these pinnacles, along with Mount Evans in between, scrapes the sky at over 14,000´.

In contrast to the distant mountaintops, which harbor numerous high-altitude cycling opportunities, this route passes through Colorado's high plains—an expansive sea of coalescing alluvial fans emanating from the base of the Front Range. Short prairie grasses and abundant juniper coat the plains. Pine and cottonwood thrive in the canyons and gulches, wherever water is present.

The counterclockwise loop through Castlewood Canyon State Park is 25 miles long. Due to very good dirt-road surfaces and the fact that the entire ride takes place below 7,000´, this route is suitable for strong novice cyclists. The ride's length warrants modest physical conditioning, and two moderately difficult hills are encountered, but each is less than a half-mile long and rises little more than 200 vertical feet. Shorter but steeper hills will require quick bursts of energy.

As you ride through Castlewood Canyon State Park, picture yourself as an early settler crossing the Great Plains, only to be awestruck by the seemingly impenetrable Rockies rising abruptly from the grassy flatlands.

[This route description was submittted by Stuart Black, Denver, Colorado.— G. B.]

General location: This loop begins and ends in Castle Rock, which is located about 30 miles south of Denver.

Elevation change: This ride begins at 6,200´ (in Castle Rock), then rises to its high point of about 7,000´ after 6 miles. The route then descends to 6,100´ near Franktown. Returning to Castle Rock on CO 86, the road climbs to about 6,600´ atop Wolfenberger Hill.

Season: This ride can be done nearly any time of the year. During winter (November through February), many clear, sunny days will allow for good cycling conditions. During spring (March through May), be prepared for fast moving, heavy snowstorms.

Summer offers the best views of native Colorado wildflowers, and early morning rides may offer rewarding sightings of coyotes, hawks, owls, and deer.

Fall rides offer glorious colors from an assemblage of sumac, oak, willow, and cottonwood, plus a rich harvest of juicy raspberries and chokecherries to satisfy your munchies.

Services: All visitor services are available in Castle Rock, including several restaurants, but services are limited in Franktown. Water is not available in Castlewood Canyon State Park, but may be found in Franktown and Castle Rock.

Hazards: Be prepared for very warm summer temperatures and carry extra water. Although you are not in the mountains, unpredictable weather is common, especially during the summer. If exploring the numerous side roads or trails, use caution, for snakes are common in this area. Use caution pedaling CO 86, for the shoulder is narrow and traffic can be heavy.

Rescue index: Aside from a few houses scattered along the route, help can be summoned from Castle Rock and Franktown, and perhaps from the park's northern entrance station during the summer. Motor traffic is variable along the dirt-road portion of this ride but is more frequent along the paved highway.

Land status: Castlewood Canyon State Park is run by the Colorado State Division of Parks and Outdoor Recreation. All dirt county roads are public access roads. Lands adjacent to the route are privately owned, so obtain permission from landowners before venturing from the main route.

Maps: USGS 7.5 minute quadrangles: Castle Rock North and Castle Rock South, Colorado. USGS 1:50,000 scale county map: Douglas County #2, Colorado.

Finding the trail: From Denver, travel 30 miles south on Interstate 25 to Exit 181/Castle Rock. Park with discretion.

Sources of additional information:

Colorado State Parks
1313 Sherman
Denver, CO 80203
(303) 866-3437

Castlewood Canyon State Park
P.O. Box 504
Franktown, CO 80116
(303) 688-5242

Notes on the trail: Begin near I-25 in Castle Rock by pedaling east through town on Plum Creek Road, then south on Gilbert Street. About 9 miles into the ride, turn left onto Castlewood Canyon Road (County Road 51), then descend gradually into Cherry Creek Canyon and through Castlewood Canyon State Park. This segment of nonmaintained dirt road can be quite rutted but is suitable for passenger cars under most conditions. Upon reaching Franktown, head west on CO 86. The climb to Wolfenberger Hill is followed by a fast descent into Castle Rock. Turn left at Wilcox Avenue to return to your vehicle.

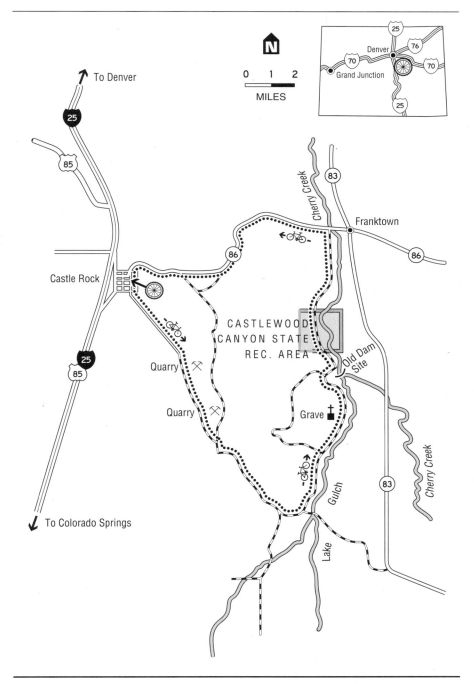

N

0   1   2
MILES

25
Denver
70   76
Grand Junction   70
70
25

To Denver

25

85

Cherry Creek

83

Franktown

86

86

Castle Rock

CASTLEWOOD
CANYON STATE
REC. AREA

Old Dam
Site

25
85

Quarry

Quarry

Grave

83

Cherry Creek

Gulch

To Colorado Springs

Lake

Castlewood Canyon itself is the result of the erosive action of Cherry Creek—the only river in the Denver area that does not have its headwaters in the mountains. Side trails climbing the canyon's walls offer excellent overviews of the canyon floor but are extremely steep and difficult for mountain bike travel. The most easily accessible route is the Eastern Rim Trail, which starts near the old dam ruins at the south end of the canyon. Inquire locally for current trail status.

Just before reaching the mouth of Castlewood Canyon, watch for the grave marker of Charles Mosell, a pioneer who was killed by Indians in 1864. The grave marker is on the west side of the road about 2 miles from the old dam ruins. An inscription is carved in the sandstone walls above the grave.

At the park's southern entrance, the ruins of an old dam can be seen in the canyon. The dam was originally built for irrigation in 1890. On August 3, 1933, the dam collapsed, claiming two lives and causing $1 million in flood-related damages. Scars from this flood can still be seen throughout the canyon.

Appendix I

CYCLING EVENTS FOR EVERYONE

Whether you're an amateur or professional, recreational or hard-core, social or family-oriented cyclist, there are special bicycling events in Colorado sure to appeal to you. The state has a growing number of events throughout the spring, summer, and fall. It's great fun participating in mountain bike festivals, rides, and races, making new friends and enjoying a sense of camaraderie with other enthusiasts. Many rides can be enjoyed on mountain, road, hybrid, or recumbent bikes; on tricycles and tandems; on bikes with trailers hauling a child or dog; and on just about anything else that's self-propelled. And it's a scream to see the outrageous attire and bike adornments lots of riders bring to the event. If you haven't been to these kinds of events, round up your friends and family and head for the mountains for a sun-filled weekend of great riding and entertainment. Here's a sample listing of mountain and road biking events, by month, from around the state. For more information, contact the local bike shops or chambers of commerce.

May:
Iron Horse Bicycle Classic, Durango
Kokopelli's Classic™, Grand Junction
Tour of the Moon, Grand Junction
Tour of the Alpine Banks, Glenwood Springs
Avon's Big Wheel Rally (for children ages 5 and under), Avon, near Vail

June:
Ride for Your Life, Vail
Women on Wheels, Breckenridge
Telluride Bicycle Classic, Telluride
Ride the Rockies (covers many regions of the state); phone: (303) 820-1338
Fourth Annual Fat Tire Poker Ride, Breckenridge
Vail Village Criterium, Vail
Pedal the Peaks, Durango
Telluride Fat Tire Festival, Telluride

July:
Mountain Bike Round-Up, Frisco
Purgatory Cup, Purgatory-Durango Ski Resort, Durango
Wildflower Festival, Crested Butte
Fat Tire Week, Crested Butte
Annual Day of the Bicycle, Breckenridge

August:
Mountain Bike Festival, Winter Park
Women on Wheels, Breckenridge
Kauneeche Klassic Mountain Bike Race, Grand Lake
Steamboat Road & Mountain Bike Challenge, Steamboat Springs
Tour of the Valley, Grand Junction
Durango Century Classic, Durango
Tour of Aspen Bicycle Race, Aspen

September:
Annual Breckenridge Fall Classic, Breckenridge
Frisco's Citizen's Criterium, Frisco
Pearl Pass Bike Tour, Crested Butte
Bicycle Tour of the San Juans, Durango, and Telluride
Ophir Pass Hill Climb, Telluride

For information on these and other events, contact any local bicycle shops or these chambers of commerce or visitor's bureaus:

Durango Area Chamber of Commerce
(800) 525-8855 or (303) 247-0312

Telluride Chamber Resort Association
(303) 728-3041

Crested Butte/Mount Crested Butte Chamber of Commerce
(800) 545-4505 or (303) 349-6438

Grand Junction Visitors and Convention Bureau
(800) 962-2547 or (303) 244-1480

Vail Resort Association
(800)525-3875
Vail and Beaver Creek Reservations
(800) 525-2257

Breckenridge Resort Chamber
(303) 453-6018

Summit County Chamber of Commerce
(303) 668-5800

Winter Park Fat Tire Society
(800) 521-BIKE or (800) 247-2636

Steamboat Springs Parks and Recreation Department
(303) 879-4300

Steamboat Springs Resort Chamber
(800) 922-2722

Glenwood Springs Chamber Resort Association
(800) 221-0098

Aspen Chamber Resort Association
(800) 262-7736

Snowmass Village Resort Association
(800) SNOWMASS

Aspen Bicycle Club
(303) 925-7978

Appendix II

Local bicycling organizations:

Banana Belt Fat Tracks
108 F Street
Salida, CO 81201
(719) 539-6704

Bicycle Colorado
P.O. Box 3877
Littleton, CO 80161
(303) 756-2535

Breckenridge Fat Tire Society
P.O. Box 2845
Breckenridge, CO 80424
(303) 453-5548

Cañon City Cycling Club
1248 North Reynolds
Cañon City, CO 81212
(719) 275-1963

Colorado Bicycle Program
4201 East Arkansas Avenue,
Room 225
Denver, CO 80222
(303) 757-9982

The Colorado Guide, revised edition,
by Bruce Caughey and
Dean Winstanley
Fulcrum Publishing
350 Indiana Street, Suite 350
Golden, CO 80401
Sold in area stores (including the
major supermarkets) throughout
the state.

Colorado Heart Cycle
P.O. Box 100743
Denver, CO 80210

Colorado Plateau Mountain-Bike
Trail Association (COPMOBA)
P.O. Box 4602
Grand Junction, CO 81502
(303) 241-9561

Colorado Springs Cycling Club
P.O. Box 49602
Colorado Springs, CO 80919
(719) 594-6354

Crested Butte Mountain Bike
Association
P.O. Box 1133
Crested Butte, CO 81224
(303) 349-5409

Denver Bicycle Touring Club
P.O. Box 101301
Denver, CO 80250-1301
(303) 756-7240

Fat Tire Week
P.O. Box 782
Crested Butte, CO 81224
(303) 349-6817

International Mountain Bike
Association (IMBA)
P.O. Box 412043
Los Angeles, CA 90041
(818) 792-8830

Mountain & Road Biking
Association of Rocky Flats
13533 West 21st Avenue
Golden, CO 80401
(303) 966-5135

National Off-Road Bicycling
Association (NORBA)
1750 East Boulder Street
Colorado Springs, CO 80909
(719) 578-4717

Rails-to-Trails Conservancy
National Office
1400 Sixteenth Street, N.W.
Suite 300
Department 292
Washington, DC 20036
(202) 797-5400

In Colorado:

Colorado State Parks
1313 Sherman Street, Room 618
Denver, CO 80203
(303) 866-3437

San Luis Valley Cycling Club/Kristi
Mountain Sports
7565 West US 160
Alamosa, CO 81101
(719) 589-8319 or (719) 589-9759

Summit County Government
Attention: Planning Department
P.O. Box 68
Breckenridge, CO 80424
(303) 453-2561

Related clubs and organizations:

Boulder County Parks and Open
Space Department
2045 Thirteenth Street
P.O. Box 471
Boulder, CO 80306
(303) 441-3950

Bureau of Land Management
U.S. Department of the Interior
Colorado State Office
2850 Youngfield Street
Lakewood, CO 80225
(303) 239-3600

Colorado Association of
Campgrounds, Cabins, and Lodges
5101 Pennsylvania Avenue
Boulder, CO 80303
(303) 499-9343

Colorado Association of Ski Towns
Box 1414
Vail, CO 81658

Colorado Division of Wildlife
Department of Natural Resources
6060 Broadway
Denver, CO 80216
(303) 297-1192
For hunting information.

Colorado State Parks
1313 Sherman Street, Room 618
Denver, CO 80203
(303) 866-3437

Colorado Tourism Board
1625 Broadway, Suite 1700
Denver, CO 80202
(303) 592-5410

The Colorado Trail Foundation
548 Pine Song Trail
Golden, CO 80401
(303) 526-0809

Jefferson County Open Space
700 Jefferson County Parkway
Suite 100
Golden, CO 80401
(303) 271-5925

Maps Unlimited
899 Broadway
Denver, CO 80202
(303) 623-4299

MISTEX (for campground
reservations)
(800) 283-CAMP (2267)

North Fork Trails Network
1508 Black Canyon Road
Crawford, CO 81415

Pikes Peak Area Trails Coalition
P.O. Box 34
Colorado Springs, CO 80901
(719) 596-5640

Recreational Equipment, Inc. (REI)
In Denver area:
4100 East Mexico Avenue
Building B
Denver, CO 80222
(303) 756-3100
and:
8991-B Harlan Street
Westminster, CO 80030
(303) 429-1800

San Juan National Forest Association
P.O. Box 2261
Durango, CO 81302
(303) 385-1210

Sierra Club—Rocky Mountain
Chapter
777 Grant Street, Suite 606
Denver, CO 80203
(303) 861-8819

Tenth Mountain Trail Association
1280 Ute Avenue
Aspen, CO 81611
(303) 925-5775

Trail Mates™ of Colorado, Inc.
10597 North Routt Lane
Westminster, CO 80021
(303) 465-1033
A useful resource guide for all
trail users.

U.S. Forest Service
Regional Office
P.O. Box 25127
Lakewood, CO 80225
(303) 275-5370

United States Geological Survey
(USGS)
Map Sales
By mail and over the counter:
Box 25286
Federal Center, Building 810
Lakewood, CO 80225
(303) 236-7477

Volunteers for Outdoor Colorado
1410 Grant Street, Suite B-105
Denver, CO 80203
(303) 830-7792

Afterword

A few years ago I wrote a long piece on this issue for *Sierra* magazine that entailed calling literally dozens of government land managers, game wardens, mountain bikers, and local officials to get a feeling for how riders were being welcomed on the trails. All that I've seen personally since, and heard from my authors, indicates there hasn't been much change. We're still considered the new kid on the block. We have less of a right to the trails than horses and hikers, and we're excluded from many areas, including:

a) wilderness areas
b) national parks (except on roads, and those paths specifically marked "bike path")
c) national monuments (except on roads open to the public)
d) most state parks and monuments (except on roads, and those paths specifically marked "bike path")
e) an increasing number of urban and county parks, especially in California (except on roads, and those paths specifically marked "bike path")

Frankly, I have little difficulty with these exclusions and would, in fact, restrict our presence from some trails I've ridden (one time) due to the environmental damage and chance of blind-siding the many walkers and hikers I met up with along the way. But these are my personal views. The authors of this volume and mountain bikers as a group may hold different opinions.

You can do your part in keeping us from being excluded from even more trails by riding responsibly. Many local and national off-road bicycle organizations have been formed with exactly this in mind, and one of the largest—the National Off-Road Bicycle Association (NORBA)—offers the following code of behavior for mountain bikers:

1. I will yield the right of way to other non-motorized recreationists. I realize that people judge all cyclists by my actions.

2. I will slow down and use caution when approaching or overtaking another cyclist and will make my presence known well in advance.

3. I will maintain control of my speed at all times and will approach turns in anticipation of someone around the bend.

4. I will stay on designated trails to avoid trampling native vegetation and minimize potential erosion to trails by not using muddy trails or short-cutting switchbacks.

5. I will not disturb wildlife or livestock.

6. I will not litter. I will pack out what I pack in, and pack out more than my share whenever possible.

7. I will respect public and private property, including trail use signs and no trespassing signs, and I will leave gates as I have found them.

8. I will always be self-sufficient and my destination and travel speed will be determined by my ability, my equipment, the terrain, and the present and potential weather conditions.

9. I will not travel solo when bikepacking in remote areas. I will leave word of my destination and when I plan to return.

10. I will observe the practice of minimum impact bicycling by "taking only pictures and memories and leaving only waffle prints."

11. I will always wear a helmet whenever I ride.

Now, I have a problem with some of these—number nine, for instance. The most enjoyable mountain biking I've ever done has been solo. And as for leaving word of destination and time of return, I've enjoyed living in such a way as to say, "I'm off to pedal Colorado. See you in the fall." Of course it's senseless to take needless risks, and I plan a ride and pack my gear with this in mind. But for me number nine smacks too much of the "never-out-of-touch" mentality. And getting away from civilization, deep into the wilds, is, for many people, what mountain biking's all about.

All in all, however, NORBA's is a good list, and surely we mountain bikers would be liked more, and excluded less, if we followed the suggestions. But let me offer a "code of ethics" I much prefer, one given to cyclists by Utah's Wasatch-Cache National Forest office.

Study a Forest Map Before You Ride
Currently, bicycles are permitted on roads and developed trails within the Wasatch-Cache National Forest except in designated Wilderness. If your route crosses private land, it is your responsibility to obtain right of way permission from the landowner.

Keep Groups Small
Riding in large groups degrades the outdoor experience for others, can disturb wildlife, and usually leads to greater resource damage.

Avoid Riding on Wet Trails
Bicycle tires leave ruts in wet trails. These ruts concentrate runoff and accelerate erosion. Postponing a ride when the trails are wet will preserve the trails for future use.

Stay on Roads and Trails
Riding cross-country destroys vegetation and damages the soil.

Always Yield to Others
Trails are shared by hikers, horses, and bicycles. Move off the trail to allow horses to pass and stop to allow hikers adequate room to share the trail. Simply yelling "Bicycle!" is not acceptable.

Control Your Speed
Excessive speed endangers yourself and other forest users.

Avoid Wheel Lock-up and Spin-out
Steep terrain is especially vulnerable to trail wear. Locking brakes on steep descents or when stopping needlessly damages trails. If a slope is steep enough to require locking wheels and skidding, dismount and walk your bicycle. Likewise, if an ascent is so steep your rear wheel slips and spins, dismount and walk your bicycle.

Protect Water bars and Switchbacks
Water bars, the rock and log drains built to direct water off trails, protect trails from erosion. When you encounter a water bar, ride directly over the top or dismount and walk your bicycle. Riding around the ends of water bars destroys them and speeds erosion. Skidding around switchback corners shortens trail life. Slow down for switchback corners and keep your wheels rolling.

If You Abuse It, You Lose It
Mountain bikers are relative newcomers to the forest and must prove themselves responsible trail users. By following the guidelines above, and by participating in trail maintenance service projects, bicyclists can help avoid closures which would prevent them from using trails.

I've never seen a better trail-etiquette list for mountain bikers. So have fun. Be careful. And don't screw up things for the next rider.

Dennis Coello
Series Editor

Glossary

This short list of terms does not contain all the words used by mountain bike enthusiasts when discussing their sport. But it should serve as an introduction to the lingo you'll hear on the trails.

ATB all-terrain bike; this, like "fat-tire bike," is another name for a mountain bike

ATV all-terrain vehicle; this usually refers to the loud, fume-spewing three- or four-wheeled motorized vehicles you will not enjoy meeting on the trail—except, of course, if you crash and have to hitch a ride out on one

bladed refers to a dirt road which has been smoothed out by the use of a wide blade on earth-moving equipment; "blading" gets rid of the teeth-chattering, much-cursed washboards found on so many dirt roads after heavy vehicle use

blaze a mark on a tree made by chipping away a piece of the bark, usually done to designate a trail; such trails are sometimes described as "blazed"

BLM Bureau of Land Management, an agency of the federal government

buffed used to describe a very smooth trail

catching air taking a jump in such a way that both wheels of the bike are off the ground at the same time

clean while this may describe what you and your bike *won't* be after following many trials, the term is most often used as a verb to denote the action of pedaling a tough section of trail successfully

combination This type of route may combine two or more configurations. For example, a point-to-point route may integrate a scenic loop or out-and-back spur midway through the ride. Likewise, an out-and-back may have a loop at its farthest point. (This configuration looks like a cherry with stem attached; the stem is the out-and-back, the fruit is the terminus loop.) Or a loop route may have multiple out-and-back spurs and/or loops to the side. Mileage for a combination route is for the total distance to complete the ride

deadfall	a tangled mass of fallen trees or branches
diversion ditch	a usually narrow, shallow ditch dug across or around a trail; funneling the water in this manner keeps it from destroying the trail
double-track	the dual tracks made by a jeep or other vehicle, with grass or weeds or rocks between; mountain bikers can ride in either of the tracks, but you will of course find that whichever one you choose, and no matter how many times you change back and forth, the other track will appear to offer smoother travel
dugway	a steep, unpaved, switchbacked descent
feathering	using a light touch on the brake lever; hitting it lightly many times rather than very hard or locking the brake
four-wheel-drive	this refers to any vehicle with drive-wheel capability on all four wheels (a jeep, for instance, has four-wheel drive as compared with a two-wheel-drive passenger car), or to a rough road or trail that requires four-wheel-drive capability (or a *one*-wheel-drive mountain bike!) to negotiate it
game trail	the usually narrow trail made by deer, elk, or other game
gated	everyone knows what a gate is, and how many variations exist upon this theme; well, if a trail is described as "gated" it simply has a gate across it; don't forget that the rule is if you find a gate closed, close it behind you; if you find one open, leave it that way
Giardia	shorthand for *Giardia lamblia*, and known as the "backpacker's bane" until we mountain bikers expropriated it; this is a waterborne parasite that begins its life cycle when swallowed, and one to four weeks later has its host (you) bloated, vomiting, shivering with chills, and living in the bathroom; the disease can be avoided by "treating" (purifying) the water you acquire along the trail (see "Hitting the Trail" in the Introduction)
gnarly	a term thankfully used less and less these days, it refers to tough trails
hammer	to ride very hard
hardpack	a trail in which the dirt surface is packed down hard; such trails make for good and fast riding, and very painful landings; bikers most often use "hard-pack" and "hard-

packed" as an adjective, and "hardpacked" as an adjective only (the grammar lesson will help you when diagramming sentences in camp)

jeep road, jeep trail a rough road or trail passable only with four-wheel-drive capability (or a horse or mountain bike)

kamikaze while this once referred primarily to those Japanese fliers who quaffed a glass of saké, then flew off as human bombs in suicide missions against U.S. naval vessels, it has more recently been applied to the idiot mountain bikers who, far less honorably, scream down hiking trails, endangering the physical and mental safety of the walking, biking, and equestrian traffic they meet; deck guns were necessary to stop the Japanese kamikaze pilots, but a bike pump or walking staff in the spokes is sufficient for the current-day kamikazes who threaten to get us all kicked off the trails

loop This route configuration is characterized by riding from the designated trailhead to a distant point, then returning to the trailhead via a different route (or simply continuing on the same in a circle route) without doubling back. You always move forward across new terrain, but return to the starting point when finished. Mileage is for the entire loop from the trailhead back to trailhead

multi-purpose a BLM designation of land which is open to many uses; mountain biking is allowed

out-and-back a ride where you will return on the same trail you pedaled out; while this might sound far more boring than a loop route, many trails look very different when pedaled in the opposite direction

point-to-point A vehicle shuttle (or similar assistance) is required for this type of route, which is ridden from the designated trailhead to a distant location, or endpoint, where the route ends. Total mileage is for the one-way trip from trailhead to endpoint

portage to carry your bike on your person

quads bikers use this term to refer both to the extensor muscle in the front of the thigh (which is separated into four parts) and to USGS maps; the expression "Nice quads!" refers always to the former, however, except in those instances when the speaker is an engineer

runoff	rainwater or snowmelt
signed	a "signed" trail has signs in place of blazes
single-track	a single, narrow path through grass or brush or over rocky terrain, often created by deer, elk, or backpackers; single-track riding is some of the best fun around
slickrock	the rock-hard, compacted sandstone that is *great* to ride and even prettier to look at; you'll appreciate it even more if you think of it as a petrified sand dune or seabed, and if the rider before you hasn't left tire marks (from unnecessary skidding) or granola bar wrappers behind
snowmelt	runoff produced by the melting of snow
snowpack	unmelted snow accumulated over weeks or months of winter—or over years in high-mountain terrain
*spur*a	road or trail that intersects the main trail you're following
technical	terrain that is difficult to ride due not to its grade (steepness) but to its obstacles—rocks, logs, ledges, loose soil. . .
topo	short for topographical map, the kind that shows both linear distance *and* elevation gain and loss; "topo" is pronounced with both vowels long
*trashed*a	trail that has been destroyed (same term used no matter what has destroyed it . . . cattle, horses, or even mountain bikers riding when the ground was too wet)
two-wheel-drive	this refers to any vehicle with drive-wheel capability on only two wheels (a passenger car, for instance, has two-wheel-drive); a two-wheel-drive road is a road or trail easily traveled by an ordinary car
water bar	an earth, rock, or wooden structure that funnels water off trails to reduce erosion
washboarded	a road that is surfaced with many ridges spaced closely together, like the ripples on a washboard; these make for very rough riding, and even worse driving in a car or jeep
wilderness area	land that is officially set aside by the federal government to remain *natural*—pure, pristine, and untrammeled by any vehicle, including mountain bikes; though mountain bikes had not been born in 1964 (when the United States Congress passed the Wilderness Act, establishing the National Wilderness Preservation system), they are consid-

ered a "form of mechanical transport" and are thereby excluded; in short, stay out

wind chill   a reference to the wind's cooling effect upon exposed flesh; for example, if the temperature is 10 degrees Fahrenheit and the wind is blowing at 20 miles per hour, the wind-chill (that is, the actual temperature to which your skin reacts) is *minus* 32 degrees; if you are riding in wet conditions things are even worse, for the wind-chill would then be *minus 74 degrees!*

windfall   anything (trees, limbs, brush, or fellow bikers) blown down by the wind

Linda Gong

Gregg Bromka

Linda Gong was bitten by the bicycling bug in the early sixties, when she discovered how to "pop wheelies" with her brothers on her little pink Stingray bike, sans training wheels. Fast forward to 1988, where she became an avid recreational road cyclist and an award-winning graphic designer at Catalyst Communication, a marketing firm specializing in the bicycle industry in Boulder, Colorado. In 1992, she finally found a mountain bike that accommodated her 5'0" height, and she has been hitting the high country trails ever since. Today, after 12 years in Colorado, she now lives in Pacific Grove, California, where she continues her design career, with an occasional assignment as a tour leader assistant in France for Europeds, a California-based bicycle touring company.

A native of upstate New York, Gregg Bromka ventured west in 1983 to pursue graduate studies in geology at the University of Utah in Salt Lake City. What Gregg found was a wealth of recreational opportunities in Utah's diverse environment, of which hiking and skiing were his favorites.

Although initially hesitant about mountain bikes in the mid-1980s, Gregg was persuaded to reluctantly venture on his first off-road ride, on Moab's famous Slickrock Trail. By day's end he was hooked. The thrill and exhilaration of fat-tire cycling led to the immediate purchase of his own ATB—scotching any thoughts of moving back East.

The mountain bike has become the preeminent means of backcountry travel by which Gregg explores the far reaches of Utah and the intermountain West. What began merely as a hobby—searching out new and enticing terrain—first resulted in the guidebooks, *Mountain Biking Utah's Wasatch and Uinta Mountains* and *Mountain Biking Utah's Canyon and Plateau Country*, and now *The Mountain Biker's Guide to Colorado*. Gregg is also the author of another book in this series—*The Mountain Biker's Guide to Utah*.